THE SINGULAR PILGRIM

THE
SINGULAR
PILGRIM

TRAVELS ON
SACRED GROUND

ROSEMARY
MAHONEY

HOUGHTON MIFFLIN COMPANY
BOSTON   NEW YORK
2003

For information about permission to reproduce selections
from this book, write to Permissions, Houghton Mifflin Company,
215 Park Avenue South, New York, New York 10003.

Visit our Web site: www.houghtonmifflinbooks.com.

*Library of Congress Cataloging-in-Publication
data is available.*
ISBN 0-618-02262-7

Printed in the United States of America

Book design by Victoria Hartman

QUM 10 9 8 7 6 5 4 3 2 1

AUTHOR'S NOTE: To protect the privacy
of individuals, I have changed the names of many
and slightly altered identifying details of some.

TO THE MEMORY OF
MARGARITA BAKI

ΕΙΣ ΤΗΝ ΜΝΗΜΗ ΤΗΣ
ΜΑΡΓΑΡΙΤΑΣ ΜΠΑΚΗΣ

1963–2001

CONTENTS

A whole popedom of forms one pulsation of virtue
can uplift and vivify.

— Ralph Waldo Emerson
address to divinity students, July 15, 1838

INTRODUCTION

A few years ago a friend of mine, whom I know to be an intelligent and compassionate woman, listened carefully as I told her about a Greek Orthodox pilgrimage I had witnessed on the tiny Cycladic island of Tinos in the Aegean Sea. Each year on August 15, the Feast of the Assumption, which marks the spiritual and bodily assumption of the Virgin Mary into heaven, the Greek Orthodox faithful travel great distances to Tinos to venerate an icon of the Virgin housed in a church atop a small hill at the end of an avenue of marble paving stones. The icon, which was discovered in the early nineteenth century amid the rubble left by an earthquake, is said to have worked miraculous cures and to have granted many pilgrims their individual wishes. The pilgrims arrive by ferry. The moment the gangplank touches the dock, they rush forward, fall to the ground, and begin making their way to the church on hands and knees. Some slither the half-mile on their bellies, poling themselves forward with their elbows in the manner of besieged soldiers creeping through underbrush. Some lie across the street and, like horizontal dervishes, roll themselves slowly up the gradual incline across stones baked torrid by the August sun. As they proceed they pray for miracles and for mercy. Some weep, others call out the name of the Virgin. Many carry on their backs offerings of wax candles the length of their bodies. In the terrible heat the candles droop and sweat. Elderly white-haired widows in black dresses inch their way silently up the hill, humbling themselves in hope of the Virgin's attention, their frail backs forming saddles for the punishing sun. (Many women in need of divine intervention in some grave family matter — an illness, a wayward or disobedient child, a financial bind, an unfaithful husband — vow to return to Tinos every year if the Virgin will grant the desired outcome.) By the time they reach the church after several hours of crawling, their hands and knees are galled into raw and bloody emblems of their belief. Once before the icon they prostrate themselves in a rapture of spiritual desire.

My friend, who had listened patiently to my story, suddenly shook her head and said with disdain, "How pathetic!"

Her remark struck me with a disorienting slap of surprise. It was uncharacteristically dismissive, and it was far enough from my own response to the Tinos pilgrims that I suffered a moment of self-doubt. Had I been wrong in my view of them? Were they in fact pathetic? It was true that standing at the edge of that Tinos street I had been astonished by what I saw, had even looked with skepticism upon some of the more ostentatious displays of piety, and when a military parade of admirals and ensigns came quick-marching up the street in honor of the Virgin I had found the procession pompous and incongruous. But at the end of that day (the flow of pilgrims ran long into the night), after watching untold numbers of elderly women crawling gravely, silently toward their goal, making their souls vulnerable by extending an invitation to one they deemed infinitely superior, something in me was impressed. Belief, whether blind or examined, divinely guided or superstitiously misguided, had made those pilgrims singular and bold, strange and determined. I am attached to reason and am not easily awed by the miraculous powers of the Virgin Mary, but I was awed by her pilgrims. It wasn't their religion that interested me so much as their faith, that palpable surge of the soul. Were they pathetic? I didn't think so.

NOT LONG after my visit to Tinos I found in a trunk in my basement an old college notebook in which, nearly twenty years before, I had written: "I'm too forgetful to pray and I fool with religion as though it's some kind of game to be resumed when I have the urge." The words surprised and unsettled me. I was thirty-eight, and that was *still* an accurate description of my relationship to spiritual concerns — a curious but evasive flirtation, one that burgeoned when it was convenient and died when it wasn't. For years I had been aware of something faintly glowing at the back of my own soul, and for years I had effectively ignored it. To thoroughly examine one's spirituality, to question with care the source and the essence of creation was a maddening, sometimes nauseating struggle. I had simply found it easier to fend off those questions with the false promise that I would deal with them later.

Spurred by the Tinos pilgrims and the words of my younger self, I fished out of the same basement trunk my college Bible, the only one I owned at that time, and began rereading the New Testament. In the Gospel according to Matthew, I found several passages that I had long ago marked with a dull pencil. One stood out: "Take no gold, nor silver, nor copper in your belts, no bag for your journey, nor two tunics, nor sandals, nor a staff; for the laborer deserves his food. And whatever town you enter, find out who is worthy in it, and stay with him until you depart." I had drawn a mushy graphite box around the words. Unlike most of my other underlinings and bracketings, this was not a pithy aphorism or a wise piece of advice that I thought applicable to myself. It was a command from Jesus to his disciples to trust, travel humbly, and spread his word. As soon as I read the passage I knew why I had marked it. It had seemed — as it seemed now — entirely unrealistic. No money? No provisions? No change of clothing? Live off the generosity of those you encounter along the way? Find out who is worthy? It was a command to wander and spread the word, and in the age I lived in, that proposition was not only preposterous, it was dangerous. (Within six months of my noting those words in Matthew, Ronald Reagan and the pope had both been shot at, and John Lennon had been shot dead.)

I put down the musty Bible, called my mother, and asked her how she would react if I gave away all of my material possessions, my extra clothing, and whatever tiny wealth I had accumulated, and went walking across the country with no cash on my person, nothing but one pair of sandals and a tunic, and no plan but to seek God and spread the word of Jesus Christ. Would she think I had lost my mind? Would she worry? Would she be horrified by the direction my life had taken, as parents often are when a child under the influence of a religious cult radically alters the course of his life? My mother, a devout Catholic, answered with certitude, "Not at all. I would think that finally one of my children had got it right." (For my mother the redeeming factor in this hypothetical journey was its particular focus on Jesus. Had I proposed the same scenario of material divestment and extended travel with, say, Buddha as my inspiration and spiritual focus, or Krishna and Shiva, or Allah and Muhammad, or the Hebrew God, or Mother Earth, or Elvis Presley, I am certain that her answer would have been markedly different.)

Although the possibilities and meaning inherent in the human search for spirituality had always inspired curiosity in me, and though from time to time I had been nagged by uncertainty over the lack of spiritual focus in my life, my rare attempts at spiritual enlightenment had been halfhearted, conventional, and thwarted by a wavering faith. Upon reading the New Testament I may have mused about embarking on a spiritual peregrination, but there had never been a time in my life when it was even remotely likely that I would take to the road with nothing but a pair of sandals on my feet, looking for God. My experiences with shrines and holy places, as at Tinos, had been strictly touristic — glancing and accidental observations of the devotions of true pilgrims, whose realm I stood apart from. I had never been a participant.

When I lived in China in the late 1980s, I watched with fascination the scores of Chinese peasants who walked hundreds of miles in flimsy cloth slippers from their farms to the city to pay homage at Buddhist temples in hopes of a prosperous planting season. I had seen Irish Catholic pilgrims climbing the mountain Croagh Patrick on their knees in order to save their souls. In New Mexico I had seen crutches and canes hanging from nails driven into the wall of the Santuario de Chimayo, where the soil of the chapel floor is said to have curative properties. In Coptic Cairo I had seen evangelical Korean Christians singing hymns, eyes closed in devotion, near the purported hiding place of Jesus and Mary.

Though my interest in such pilgrimage exercises was passive, it was never difficult for me to sense the spiritual weight of these holy places and the weight of feeling the pilgrims carried with them, believing wholeheartedly and seeking unabashedly as they do. Their pilgrimages triggered in me a small degree of envy. If it is true that the largest human gatherings in the world are those of religious pilgrims to Rome and Jerusalem during Holy Week or Mecca during Ramadan or the banks of the Ganges at the Kumb Mela festival, what inspires that phenomenon, and why hadn't it managed to reach me? Why wasn't I drawn to participate in such activities?

I read Jennifer Westwood's comprehensive guide, Sacred Journeys, and learned that across the ages the forms of pilgrimage have been as varied as its goals and results. Some pilgrims see the very difficulty of their physical journey as the ultimate source of redemption and renewal. Medieval Christians, for example, felt that mortification of the flesh was the most direct route to salvation: for each arduous journey to a European shrine of note, centuries were believed to be subtracted from the stay in purgatory. Hindus also believe that mortification of the flesh leads to higher spirituality and virtue as well as the expiation of sins. Other pilgrims see physical contact with or proximity to the relics of saints or prophets as salubrious. Still others focus on geological wonders that are thought to be invested with a divine force. Many pilgrims, seeing their journey as a transaction, set off with specific temporal rewards in mind: a cure, a change of fortune, a better job, high marks on an examination. (Westwood writes of a shrine in Mexico where drug traffickers annually pay homage to a dead bandit — lighting votive candles, wearing scapulars, seeking the bandit's intervention for a healthy harvest for the cocaine and marijuana farmers, as well as blessings for the safe passage of drugs into the United States. "Their hit men reputedly ask him to bless their bullets.") Whatever its purpose, pilgrimage seemed both a preparation for death and a hedge against it.

Drawn by the subject of pilgrimage, I began reading Chaucer's *Canterbury Tales* and found myself asking new questions. With the modern corrosion of organized religion and the emergence of quick spiritual fixes and alluring self-help seminars now available in exchange for little more than money, why was the religious pilgrimage — a practice that reached its height in medieval times — not only still thriving at the end of the twentieth century but enjoying a marked resurgence? How had the ease and swiftness of modern travel altered the traditional pilgrimage? What stories lay behind contemporary spiritual searches, who undertook them, what exactly constituted a pilgrimage, and why, at any point in history, have human beings felt the need to leave the place they know and travel great distances to envision or experience God at a previously ordained site? Why do certain places on earth seem to possess a greater holiness than others? Why would God be likely to show his face in one place and not another? The self can certainly be transformed by a physical journey, but in what way would it be changed by a physical journey with a spiritual intent?

What most appealed to me in Chaucer's tales was their revelations about the nature of medieval secular life precisely as it intertwined with the religious devotion of his pilgrims. Their stories create an entire world in which the physical body is contrasted with the spirit, and the basest impulses of human nature coincide with the highest. The concerns of the Canterbury pilgrims run the gamut from proper social mores, chivalry, piety, and honor to blasphemy, lechery, lasciviousness, and buffoonery. The pursuit of God in the face of mundane pressures and demands, the force of true belief, and the lengths to which people are willing to go to transcend their humanity and find spiritual solace are elemental and have remained fundamentally unaltered through the ages.

IN 1999 I was inspired to explore several religious pilgrimages that interested me and to write about my experiences, the people I met, and the meaning of these journeys undertaken in the name of an unknowable, unseeable God. I visited the shrine at Lourdes, walked the medieval pilgrimage trail to Santiago de Compostela, participated in the penitential Irish pilgrimage at St. Patrick's Purgatory on Station Island, spent two weeks in the Hindu holy city of Varanasi, attended the Anglican pilgrimage to the Marian shrine at Walsingham, England, and visited several pilgrimage sites in the Holy Land. While the resulting six chapters are discrete, each with its own particular cosmos and religious references, they are all parts of one longer journey.

At its core the pilgrimage search concerns the relationship of the individual self to God, beyond the standard rituals of a religious institution; it is an attempt to achieve a direct personal connection with the divine. As a result, this is less a book about religion than a book about belief. In the two years that I spent on the road I met a variety of pilgrims from diverse religious backgrounds; the one constant among them was belief. If I was struck by anything, it was the shared human struggle to find reason, to confront our natural fears of uncertainty and obscurity.

Concluding the second chapter of *The Way of Perfection,* written for the Discalced Nuns of Our Lady of Carmel of the First Rule, Theresa of Ávila wrote: "I do not remember what I had begun to say, for I have strayed from my subject. But I think this must have been the Lord's will, for I never intended to write what I have said here." Starting out on these pilgrimage journeys I felt uneasy — religion as a topic as well as my own uncertainty about God made me uneasy. I used my curiosity and my intentions as a writer as an excuse, an apology, an explanation to myself. I told myself it was merely my job, an intellectual pursuit, that I was writing about the religious aspirations of real pilgrims, which had little to do with me. But I am approximately as strange, conventional, fearful, susceptible, and pathetic as the next person. I don't look forward to death, and whether I want to admit it or not I share in the human struggle to find reason. What I carried with me on the road was myself, with a history, a disposition, an opinion, and a sensibility through which my experiences were filtered and which, in turn, my experiences altered. I set out to discover one thing and discovered something else. Looking back now, I realize that, like Theresa of Ávila, I never intended to write what I have written in this book.

· 1 ·

WALSINGHAM

On a Saturday morning at the end of May 1999 I left the town of Fakenham in Norfolk, England, and set off on the five-mile walk to the village of Walsingham. I walked along a small country road beneath great oak trees, between dense hedgerows, through wind-tossed fields of scarlet poppies and long, undulating grass that looked as soft as hair. The sky was overcast with a high film of pearl-gray clouds, but the day was unseasonably warm. In the bushes blackbirds sang with noisy vigor and clarity, like happy mechanics whistling over their work. There were few cars on the road, and yet its grassy shoulders were littered with a surprising number of rabbits and game birds struck dead by passing vehicles. The few times I left the road and walked through the fields, startled pheasants regularly flapped up out of the grass, their grating cries in turn startling me. I was little more than a hundred miles north of London, yet the place felt as rural as northern Scotland. There were sprawling farms here and cottages so quaint their roofs looked thatched, though they weren't.

I was on my way to attend the Anglican National Pilgrimage at Walsingham's shrine to the Virgin Mary. The shrine was famous, but until an English friend of mine urged me to visit it I had never heard of it — the only English place of pilgrimage I had ever easily been able to call to mind was Canterbury Cathedral. My friend explained that the annual Anglican pilgrimage involved a Mass and a formal procession of vicars and bishops through the streets of Walsingham. It didn't sound terribly interesting until she said, "And then there are these other people who come to shout at them in protest."

The pilgrimage was small and brief; it took place on a single day. I would not have to explain or identify myself, nor would I be expected to do anything. The idea of people shouting in protest at the Anglican clergy was enticing, and thinking that Walsingham would be a simple way to ease into my investigation I decided to go.

Setting off that day from Fakenham I had met a woman who was nailing a homemade sign to a telephone pole. Arms stretched upward, tapping at the nail with a small hammer, the tail of her slip showing below the hem of her skirt, she had informed me, around a cigarette wedged into the corner of her mouth, that the manor house in East Barsham was the spot where Henry VIII had spent the night on his several pilgrimage journeys to Walsingham. "And from Barsham," the thin woman had said, lowering her arms and smoothing her hair, "fat old Henry walked the remaining two miles of his journey on his bare feet to show how holy he was!" She laughed richly, sucked at the dying cigarette, flicked it into the gutter, and reached up to give the nail a finishing blow. "Holy, me arse!" She pronounced the name of the town "Bash 'em." Her sign read: "Missing: marmelade tabby. Name: Wink. Reward: for return."

"You lost your cat?" I said.

She tucked the hammer under her arm. "Wink's me 'usband's cat. Never liked the creature meself, but me 'usband'll go insane if the bleeding thing don't get found."

After walking an hour or so I came to East Barsham. It was tiny — the manor house, a church, a pub. The manor house and the pub were closed; I went to look at the church. Nearly seven hundred years old, the little stone Church of All Saints sat alone in an overgrown field bristling with nettles and slatted with a handful of skinny, tilting tombstones. Inside, it was musty and crumbling, and there were mouse droppings and cobwebs in the corners, but its simple appointments and advanced age gave it a melancholy sweetness and dignity. The ceiling was high, the arched doorways graceful. The ends of the rotting wooden pews were delicately carved with images of poppies; the arched windows were made up of a thousand tiny diamond-shaped panes. I wandered around in the dim windowlight looking at the ledgers and lozenges hung on the cracked and moldy walls, the heraldic escutcheons and memorials, the sparse altar. A large wall monument showed a carving of a wimpled woman, one Mary Calthorpe, who died in 1640 at the age of twenty-eight, rising up out of her tomb in response to the last trump, blown by a plump musical cherub above her. The plaque below the monument said, "James Calthorpe dedicates this monument to the pious memory of Mary, his wife, by whom he had issue 2 sonnes who all, in this chancel, lie together interred."

Instead of being reassuring in its insistence on an afterlife, Mr. Calthorpe's 359-year-old memorial to his wife somehow cast doubt on the entire paradisiacal proposition. For all their hopeful stretching toward God, memorials in a damp and disused church like this have a way of making death seem horribly final. The church was full of Calthorpes and Fermors, many of whom had died young. It seemed clear to me that their souls would languish forever in this dusty little church. It was not they who had left the world behind but the world who had left them behind. I was alive and able to leave here. I could shift my view and return to a fresher breath of air. But the Calthorpes and Fermors had no such luxury. They were "together interred" here and would stay that way. Looking at their names on the wall, I couldn't deny that I would one day be as dead as they were, the world's colorful activity hidden from my view. And eventually, when the explosively dying sun reduced the earth to a cindery crust, even that colorful activity would die, extinguished by the cruel sweep of nothing. Churches aimed to show us that with God we could surmount that ugly insult, but this quiet church seemed to illustrate just the opposite: there would be no life and no color after death. Death found its way into every corner. And wherever it went it stayed.

I grew short of breath thinking this way, and to distract myself I dropped a one-pound coin into the church's donation box and sat down in a pew to study the church visitors' book. The pages were damp and mildewed, and between them a potato bug had been flattened to a gray flake. The book was filled with comments and messages from people who had stopped at the church. "Cold. Smelly," said an entry from 1991. Another said, "Gary found it a bit spooky after an hour or so. But nice place." I skimmed through the entries.

> The lack of paint. Pity about.
> 8/3/92 Small but nice.
> Uspoilt.
> I will not hit my sister. 13/6/92
> Why is this beautiful little Church left so neglected? <u>Shame on East Barsham</u> and its residents. <u>Disgraceful</u>. Ruth Abrahams 14/8/92
> I love it very mush.

Sad.

Peaceful, beautiful, bliss, blessed, tranquil, nice, good, old, full of history, the most wonderful church in Norfolk!

Could do with a lick of paint.

I love Willy, from Aggie

Don't write in this book, Aggie, you cow.

Horribly church. 11/2/94

A very shitty church — from Willy

Bitch from Flazel.

Lovely pilgrimage stop.

Grounds need work.

Dear God, it has been great couple of seconds in your holy church but I'm board so I'm off. Yours faithfully Ann Mitchal.

Reading these comments was like listening to the free-associative thoughts rippling through the heads in a restless crowd. I was most interested in two entries written in ragged handwriting and marked obsessively about with radiating lines of ink:

Gregory Martin Sewell. God, please heal my mind. (born E. Barsham 8/12/61) Ward 20, Hellesdon Hospital Norwich (Sorry for taking up so much space) 16/9/95.

and

Greg (Sewell) (Mum + Dad's for xmas.) God loves me. I love God. 29/12/97.

I sat in the cold light of the little church with the book in my lap and thought about Gregory Martin Sewell. He was a mere eight months younger than I was and was locked up in Ward 20. There was something the matter with his mind and he knew it, which seemed to me worse than having something the matter with your mind and not knowing it.

I returned the book to its table, went out of the church, and headed off again on the road to Walsingham. That Gregory Martin Sewell had asked God to heal his mind stayed with me for the rest of the walk. It had been many years since I had thought to ask God to fix anything in my life.

AS I CAME into Walsingham, a whiskery old man swaying at the side of the road crooked his finger at me and said, "Come 'ere, love. Where you going?"

I told him where and continued walking.

The man dropped his hand in disappointment. "Oh, do not run off!" he cried. "I only want to tell you somefing noice!"

I went over to him. He was tiny and rheumy-eyed and stinking of whiskey. Each of his beige eyebrows was the size of a healthy mustache. On this warm day he was dressed in an oilskin slicker and a peaked cap.

"I'm sorry," I said. "Please tell me."

"Do not hate me," he mumbled sadly.

"I don't hate you."

The man shifted the cap on his head, took a step backward, put one freckled hand against a brick house for support. He blinked a little at the hand, then looked down at his Wellington boots and blinked at them. "Me name is Mike," he said. He scratched at the white velour of whiskers on his chin, stepped with one foot, then retracted the step, orienting himself. Behind him I could see the perfectly preserved medieval façades of Walsingham, the whitewashed half-timbered houses leaning cozily into each other, the rambling pink roses creeping up the freshly painted window casements, the brick chimneys, the red and black tiled roofs, the windows hung with white lace; it was all so pretty and so old it looked fake.

Mike found my face again and stared a long time at me, his red eyes blinking with the slow deliberation of an owl's. Behind him a score of sparrows socialized in a shrub. I waited, but Mike said nothing. Finally I said, "What was it that you wanted to tell me?"

He raised the index finger of his free hand and said softly, "You are the best vision I have seen all day."

"Thank you," I said. "That's a very generous thing to say."

He found my hand and crushed it sincerely in his.

As I continued across the Friday Market, Walsingham's main square, I saw a sign in the window of a house that said: SUNDAY AT 9:45 ASSEMBLE IN FRIDAY MARKET FOR PILGRIMAGE PROCESSION. I had been told that the pilgrimage procession would take place on Monday. I went into Elmham House, the guesthouse where I had reserved a room, and as I was checking in I mentioned the sign to the man at the reception desk and asked if the day of the pilgrimage had been changed.

"No," he said, "it hasn't been changed. That sign refers to the Catholic procession to the Slipper Chapel in Houghton Saint Giles."

"But isn't this an Anglican pilgrimage?" I said.

The man was shuffling through his reservations book. He had a vivid pink scar on the side of his forehead and one wandering eye. "Catholic," he said. "The Anglican pilgrimage takes place on Monday."

"There are two pilgrimages?"

"Indeed."

"Two separate pilgrimages?"

The man — his name was Stephen — folded his hands on the desk and smiled at me. The wandering eye made it very difficult to tell where he was looking. "I know it's confusing," he said, "but, yes, of course they're separate."

I learned that Elmham House, a Georgian mansion that had once been a grammar school, was a Catholic guesthouse. I had found it through a travel agency and had neither asked nor been told about its religious affiliation. The place had several outlying brick buildings, a large dining hall, and its own chapel. It was well maintained, bustling with guests, and clearly thriving.

Stephen showed me to my room, a spare little box like a nun's cell. It was tidy and clean, had a gleaming sink in the corner and a view of a privet hedge and a small garden with a statue of the Virgin Mary in it. Before he went away I asked Stephen if there was anything to keep me from attending both the Catholic and the Anglican pilgrimages.

"Nothing but your own conscience!" he said. And then he laughed loudly to show it was only a joke. "You can attend both, of course. But the Anglican pilgrimage . . ." He hesitated, studied the freshly vacuumed carpet, then smiled in apology and sighed, "Well, I don't mean to be irreligious, but the Anglican pilgrimage does have sort of an air of a . . . well, an air of a fiesta about it!"

When Stephen was gone I sat down on the bed and looked out the window. I hadn't expected to find any Catholics in Walsingham, let alone a whole colony of them. For some reason I had thought that Catholicism in England was virtually extinct. Sitting on the bed and staring at the statue of the Virgin I realized that as surprised as I was to find myself among Catholics I was also inordinately pleased.

AT FOURTEEN I went to an Episcopal boarding school in New Hampshire, not for religious reasons but because my mother believed it was a good school. The school had its own chapel ("chapel" seemed a misnomer; it was a huge Gothic building that was, to my mind, as elaborate and magnificent as any cathedral), and students were required to attend morning services four times a week. The first thing my mother did when she delivered me to the school was to inquire where the nearest Catholic church was. "We're in luck," she said when she'd got her answer; "there's a Carmelite monastery right up the road. You can walk there." My mother was delighted. She liked the Carmelites nearly as much as she liked the Capuchins. They were intellectual and ancient and more sensitive, she thought, than the authoritarian and provincial diocesan priests.

All that September and most of October, out of love for my mother, I walked every Sunday morning through the gates of my school, up Pleasant Street, past the onetime residence of Mary Baker Eddy, and on to the Carmelite monastery and its little chapel to attend the eight o'clock Mass. The congregation was a mix of elderly couples and very young families, which was a relief. I didn't want to see other students from my school there. With my confusing new life at boarding school and my not entirely welcome independence, the Mass had become both very intimate — a familiar thing from home — and more difficult. It had become uncomfortably real. For the first time I had no parental proxy at my side to sop up its sanctity on my behalf while I daydreamed and toyed with the hem of my skirt. Because I knew my mother took the Mass seriously and listened carefully to it, without her I suddenly felt that I should listen carefully too.

Left to listen on my own, I heard a new gravity in the Mass, a new sorrowing, a new tone of warning; there were threats and admonishments, desperate pleas, the tears of this one, the despair of that one. There were smitings and suspicions, betrayals and mockeries, rending of garments and gnashing of teeth. And I was vexed by all the biblical paradoxes. The prodigal son, for example, seemed to me like kind of a prick, but when he returned home his father treated him like a king, and when the good son said to the father, "Hey, I stuck by you all this time and you didn't even offer me one tiny goat to eat with my friends!" his resentment seemed justified. Occasionally I was amused or uplifted by something in the Scripture, some miracle or phrase or story that caught my attention, as when Jesus spat on a blind man's eyes and touched him with his hands and said, "See anything?" and the blind man said, "I see men, but they look like trees, walking." But mostly I found the Mass troubling. I didn't want to listen, and after a few weeks I turned the priest off and went back to daydreaming, restively and with the flavor of worry. I picked at my hangnails and adjusted the straps of my comically inessential bra and longed for my next visit home. Every Sunday I received Communion because I knew my mother would have wanted me to.

Until one Sunday when I arrived at the monastery and found the chapel empty. It was five minutes to eight. The church was usually full by that time. I sat in a pew and waited. No one came. Ten past eight and still not a soul in the place. I flipped through the tissue-paper pages of a missal, counted the panes in a stained glass window, looked around the church, and at twenty past eight I got up and waded back to school through drifts of brittle brown leaves. I was puzzled but hardly disappointed.

Later I learned that daylight saving time had gone into effect the night before. But for my school and its five hundred students the time change would not go into effect until that night, a trick the school administration had devised in order to give the students an extra hour of sleep on a school day. Out of step with the world, I had arrived an hour early for Mass. I never went back. The mistake marked the end of my Catholic practice.

I didn't tell my mother, for I knew that her greatest fear in sending me to this boarding school was that I might get sucked into the Episcopalian quicksand. In my mother's view the Episcopal Church was unrigorous, inferior, based in pomp and society, a frivolous imitation of its Catholic parent. Though many of her friends were Episcopalian, she made little effort to disguise her distaste for the entire spurious organization. Her greatest praise for an Episcopalian was "She has it in her to convert," and her sliest dismissal "Who would want to be a member of a church founded on divorce?"

In fact it was not solely the Episcopal Church that irked my mother but Anglicanism in general, with the strong whiff it carried of the British Empire, which had twisted its tentacles around Ireland and its people — her people, whose identity was synonymous with Catholicism and whose Catholicism had been vilified and marginalized by the British Crown. (Even now my mother's animus for Henry VIII is as fresh as her animus for Margaret Thatcher. That pair sit together in her mind like a callous, hypocritical married couple.)

Later in the school year, when I told my mother that I had joined the school's Acolytes' Guild, there came from her end of the telephone line a silence as profound as if I had said "I've written a mash note to the pope." Belonging to the Acolytes' Guild meant only that once in a while, wearing red and white robes, I would carry a fancy cross or a church flag during ceremonies in the school's chapel services. For me it was an extracurricular asset and was in no way motivated by religious feeling, but in my mother's mind the gradual leaching of my Catholicism had begun.

The truth was that the leaching of my Catholicism *had* begun, but not because of any Episcopalian influence. I had inherited my mother's view that Catholicism was superior and had no intention of becoming Episcopalian. I just didn't have a particular desire to be Catholic either.

THAT SATURDAY AFTERNOON in Walsingham I went for a walk and discovered that the village had two public squares virtually side by side, the Friday Market and the Common Place. In the middle of the Common Place was a stout little octagonal pump house of very old red brick, its conical roof like an overturned funnel. A number of the houses around that square were medieval. Some were half-timbered, with diamond-patterned windows and steep roofs, and some were of bright red brick. Some had façades carefully fitted with thousands of smooth beige stones the size of hens' eggs, and there were sidewalks cobbled in the same way. Some houses had been turned into shops that catered to the pilgrims' interests — a bookstore called the Pilgrim's Progress, a place called the Shrine Shop, which was full of religious literature and artifacts, and the Shirehall Museum, which gave a brief history of life in Walsingham. There was a tourist information office and an ivy-covered brick pub called the Bull Inn. Everything was spotless and tidy and cinematically quaint. It didn't look like a town that anyone actually lived in.

I went to see the Anglican Shrine of Our Lady of Walsingham. At Elmham House I had found a book called *Walsingham: Pilgrimage and History* and had read up on the place. According to its legend, the holy shrine was founded some time during the eleventh or twelfth century by one Richeldis de Faverches, a noble widow of Walsingham, who experienced several visions of the Virgin Mary. In one of the visions the Virgin brought Richeldis to the house in Nazareth where the Angel Gabriel had appeared to her at the Annunciation, and asked the wealthy noble-woman to build a replica of the holy house in the town of Walsingham. A devout woman, Richeldis could hardly deny the Virgin's request. She hired some carpenters and, uncertain as to where exactly she should lo-cate the house, waited for another miraculous sign. One morning, in a meadow wet with dew, she discovered two plots of ground that through the night had mysteriously remained dry; both dry spots were the ap-proximate size of the projected holy house. Richeldis chose the spot that was near a pair of holy wells and instructed her carpenters to build the house there. The carpenters set to work but eventually found them-selves bedeviled by technical mishaps; nothing they produced fit prop-erly. For some reason the small house was impossible to build. Con-founded, Richeldis spent a night in prayer to the Virgin, and the very next morning the workmen were shocked to find the holy house beauti-fully completed two hundred feet away on the other spot of dry ground. The general conclusion was that the Virgin herself had intervened, cor-rected Richeldis's mistake, and miraculously finished the job.

Soon after the establishment of the shrine house at Walsingham, other miracles began to occur there, miracles believed to have been worked directly by the Virgin Mary. (In one miracle a young boy fell down one of the holy wells in Walsingham, drowned, and by the inter-cession of the Virgin was brought back to life. In another the young King Edward I was playing chess at a table, when a strange and power-ful urge caused him to stand up suddenly and move away from his chair. Moments later a large piece of stone fell from the ceiling onto the chair.) People who visited the shrine and drank the water from its holy wells at-tested that their petitions and prayers were being answered. Drawn by these reports, pilgrims of all classes began to resort to Walsingham in great numbers to express their faith, to seek divine intervention, to beg for cures, for salvation of the soul, and for the Virgin's good favor in a host of other material matters.

The Walsingham phenomenon seems to have fit the trends of its time. During the late eleventh and early twelfth centuries the increasing focus on Jesus' human qualities spurred a new devotion to his mother, and with a greater interest in the Virgin came a widespread surge in the number of miracles supposedly worked under her authority. At roughly the same time the Muslim occupation of Jerusalem and the subsequent Crusades had made the traditional medieval pilgrimage journeys to

Rome and the Holy Land difficult and dangerous. Deterred from their usual destinations, European Christians began creating safer points of pilgrimage closer to home. Unable to travel to the Holy Land, they simply brought the Holy Land to Europe. Across the continent shrines began to spring up boasting relics from Palestine: pieces of the true cross and garments, bones, and various body parts reputed to have belonged to long-dead saints. (The great volume of "pieces of the true cross" that proliferated in Europe in the Middle Ages would, if puzzled back together, have made Christ's cross an impossibly huge device.) Under the circumstances, the Marian shrine at Walsingham became one of the most important holy places in all of medieval England, for what it offered the faithful was no mere relic but Nazareth's own holy house reconstructed at the request of the Virgin Mary herself. (According to Desiderius Erasmus, the Dutch humanist and philosopher who visited Walsingham in 1514, the shrine was also in possession of one of Saint Peter's fingers. Like pieces of the cross, saints' fingers appear to have been particularly popular and plentiful in medieval times.) Walsingham became widely known as "England's Nazareth."

Some of Walsingham's fame derived from its popularity with British royalty. In 1226 Henry III made the first of thirteen visits, and his gifts, favors, and enthusiasm for the shrine firmly established its national reputation. Edward I visited the shrine some twelve times. Edward II and Edward III went to Walsingham to pray, as did King David of Scotland, Queen Anne, Queen Joan, and Edward IV. The list of royal and noble visitors to Walsingham is long, and their offerings and donations — jeweled crowns, gold statues and chandeliers, candles, silver and wax models — eventually made it one of the wealthiest shrines in England.

The shrine flourished until 1538, when King Henry VIII systematically dismantled it. Henry, who by all appearances was a believer in the Catholic sacraments and the supremacy of the papacy, had in preceding years been a great devotee of Our Lady of Walsingham. He had visited the shrine three times and had given it valuable gifts. But with the machinations of his desired divorce from Catherine of Aragon, Henry made his infamously self-serving turnaround, broke with Rome, appointed himself the supreme head of the Church of England, and began the dissolution of the nation's important religious shrines and houses. In 1534 the prior and twenty-one canons who ran the priory at Walsingham signed the Act of Supremacy, renouncing papal authority and accepting Henry VIII as head of the English church. Those who refused to sign —

the subprior and sixteen canons — were executed. As part of the effort to enrich Henry's religious authority as well as his coffers, the priory and shrine were razed, the land was sold, and the much revered statue of the Blessed Virgin was brought to London and burned as an instrument of idolatry. For the next four hundred years the pilgrimage to Walsingham lay dead.

But the Catholic Emancipation Act of 1829 and the Oxford Movement's subsequent push for a return to the pre-Reformation church (with its ancient Catholic liturgy and doctrine, its hierarchical order of bishops, priests, and deacons, its devotion to the Virgin, its ritualistic style — incense, vestments, processions, holy water, and weekly celebration of the Eucharist) paved the way for the twentieth-century revival of the Walsingham pilgrimage.

VISITORS WANDERED ABOUT the Anglican shrine's fifteen small chapels, filling water bottles from the holy well in the floor and admiring the replica of Richeldis de Faverches's holy house. The holy house was lit in such a way that its golden altar seemed to glow from within. Above the altar stood the sacred statue of the Blessed Virgin and child, a replica of the statue destroyed on the orders of Henry VIII. The Virgin's shoulders were draped with an enormous cape of heavy yellow silk, its folds spread out at her sides like the wings of a moth. Her crown was tall, its filigree as fine as lace, and above her head a radiant sun fanned toward the ceiling. Within the cape the Virgin and infant looked suffocated and small, like two wooden dolls cloaked in an empress's trumpery. The statue was merely a reminder, a way of focusing the imagination on a historical being who was now invisible, but for centuries people had focused their hopes on it as on a lucky charm. In 1526 Erasmus published his colloquy "A Pilgrimage for Religion's Sake," mocking the religious excesses of the Middle Ages: the superstition, the fixation on relics, and the hypocrisy and corruption of the clergy. Singling out the pilgrimages to Walsingham, Canterbury, and Compostela, the colloquy contains a letter from a beleaguered Virgin Mary, who professes herself "all but exhausted by the shameless entreaties of mortals."

They demand everything from me alone, as if my son were always a baby (because he is carved and painted as such at my bosom), still needing his mother's consent . . . Sometimes they ask of a Virgin what a

modest youth would hardly dare ask of a bawd — things I'm ashamed
to put into words. Sometimes a merchant, off for Spain to make a fortune, commits to me the chastity of his mistress. And a nun who has
thrown off her veil and is preparing to run away entrusts me with her
reputation for virtue — which she herself intends to sell . . . And if
they lose at dice, they abuse me outrageously and curse me, because I
wouldn't favor their wickedness.

Mary was one of the few fully human individuals believed to have
been asked by God for a favor. Why wouldn't those who believed in
God in turn believe in her and ask her for favors? (Pope John Paul II,
who is particularly devoted to the Virgin Mary, believed that she had
intervened to save his life during the 1980 assassination attempt. In
gratitude he had requested that a bullet that had lodged in his car during
the shooting be fitted into the crown of the statue of the Virgin of
Fatima.)

I studied the statue a while and then went into the shrine church, sat
before the high altar, and tried to feel God's presence. Behind the altar
was the tabernacle, where the Eucharist was kept. I thought about what
the Eucharist was: a bread product formed into paper-thin disks; a symbol of Christ. And then suddenly my mother's voice was at my left ear,
correcting me: *It is not a symbol of Christ. It is Christ.*

My mother had said this many times, her eyes widening and her
voice dropping low to convey the import and mystery of transubstantiation. For support in the matter she always appealed to the testimony of
a writer she admired whose name, as she grew older, she found increasingly difficult to conjure. "What's that Milledgeville woman in Georgia
with the crutches and the peacocks?" she would say, stirring the air with
her free hand to hurry me along. When I said "Flannery O'Connor," her
eyes and mouth would snap shut in recognition, and her head would
bob tinily with impatience at the useless husk of her own memory, and
then she would ask if I knew what Flannery O'Connor had said about
the Eucharist. "Yes," I would say, "I do." (My mother had told me a
hundred times what Flannery O'Connor had said about the Eucharist.
How could I not know?) Ignoring the fact that her punch line had been
preempted, my mother would raise her chin and her voice and tell me
anyway. "Flannery O'Connor said, 'If it's a symbol, to hell with it.'"
(O'Connor said this to Mary McCarthy, who had left the church at the
age of fifteen, joined the Episcopal Church, and did not believe the Eu-

charist to be anything beyond symbolic.) Of the Eucharist Flannery O'Connor had also said, "It is the center of existence for me; all the rest of life is expendable."

Though my mother couldn't remember Flannery O'Connor's name, she had no trouble remembering these lines, which showed, I think, where her priorities lay. If you were a true Catholic, the Eucharist was the center of your existence and was not merely a symbol. Thomas Merton had devoted an entire book, *The Living Bread,* to the subject. Not long before my visit to Walsingham my mother had given me a copy of this book that had belonged to her father, who had nearly joined the Catholic priesthood. It startled me a little when I opened the book and saw my mother's inscription: "To Rose: You were right, you will live forever."

When had I said I would live forever? I had no memory of it, but it had the flippant, precipitate ring of my teenage self. With the same felt-tipped pen she used to write the inscription, my mother had drawn, for my benefit, two shaky arrows pointing to the book's epigraph: "I am the living bread that has come down from heaven. If anyone eat of this bread, he shall live forever" (John 6:51–52).

I had always been impressed with Christ, easily moved by his words, and tempted by the concept of the Incarnation, but that self-flattering pronouncement that I would live forever was predicated not on Christ and the Eucharist but more likely on what had always felt to me like a fundamental unquenchableness of the soul, a soul that may or may not have been granted by a merciful God. If he existed, I thought, he would probably forgive me for not having quite made up my mind about him.

About God I was forever uncertain, suspended, teetering. I wanted very much to believe. I saw that belief had given my mother strength and reason, that it supported her, that to her it came if not tamely then at least unbidden. Belief was in her; she had only to tend it. I wanted it to come to me that way. And it did come, in bursts, but went away again, driven off by the inevitable questions. What if this was all just an elaborate accident of atoms? What if we, with all our steaming consciousness and self-importance, were unplanned and insignificant? If God existed, what in fact was he? Was he that personal, biblical God who choreographed the events of the universe, judging, selecting, and rejecting? Wasn't there something perverse about a God who was always hiding out and setting people up? In his stubborn invisibility he reminded me of Wakefield, the creep in the Nathaniel Hawthorne story of the same name, who said goodbye to his wife one day in an ordinary way, said, "Be back soon," and disappeared for twenty years, having taken up residence in a house the next street over, from which he kept a morbid eye on his unwitting "widow." And the sadistic way in which the Hebrew God tested poor Abraham's fealty struck me as appallingly low. He wanted us to believe without a stitch of hard evidence, yet, like a jealous lover, he himself needed constant proof of our belief. If he was not this sort of personal God, was he simply the mystical essence of all matter? What if my mother was fooling herself? What if her faith was merely an elevator in free fall with her in it, stitching at her rosary with her long fingers and smiling up at Nobody?

I was a rationalist, a realist, attached to proof and justification. Since the age of twelve or thirteen I had had one eye on the scientists. It made me uneasy to ignore what appeared as truth, however frightening a truth it might be. If there was no God, then all creation was random and brutish and would end in final blackness. That possibility was a plummeting elevator of its own sort, but at least in that one you'd be prepared for the eventual impact. Preparation seemed important. I didn't like surprises. Faced with a rope footbridge that had to be crossed, I was always certain that the bridge would snap while I was on it.

And yet I always plunged across the bridge anyway. I was drawn to danger with a recalcitrance sometimes inexplicable even to me. Thin ice beckoned me in the most seductive way. The desire to take risks was less a rational choice than an overwhelming impulse toward action, and though it was headlong, it seemed rooted in affirmation. I had a suspicion that my seeming recklessness and my volatile faith in God were branches of the same strange tree. The bridge will snap. *I'll live forever.*

Not long after she gave me the Merton book, I asked my mother when I had said I would live forever. "About a year ago," she said.

It was not a facile thirteen who had said she would live forever but a ruminative, hopeful thirty-seven.

I got up from the pew and went down the narrow flight of steps to the holy well located in the middle of the shrine's foundation. It was said that if you made a wish while drinking this water your wish would come true. An attending deacon held a large spoonful of the well water to my lips, and as I drank it I wished for a sign, however small, from God.

BY 9:15 the following morning the Catholic pilgrims had begun gathering outside Elmham House, excited and squinting in the brilliant sunshine that flooded the Friday Market. The cloudless sky was royal blue and the air was fragrant and still. Big tour buses swung into the square and deposited more pilgrims. A thin, gray-haired man wearing a reflecting yellow safety vest lifted a megaphone to his mouth and called the group to attention. The pilgrims would sing the *Ave Maria,* then recite the rosary while they proceeded the one and two-thirds miles to the Slipper Chapel at the Roman Catholic shrine in Houghton St. Giles. There would be a Mass at noon in the Chapel of Reconciliation. Everyone should mind the cars and kindly walk in lines of two.

Feeling self-conscious, I fell into line beside an elderly woman in a white cardigan, and off we went down the narrow street that led out of Walsingham. The marchers were mostly middle-aged and older. They were white-haired and casually dressed in sleeveless blouses, T-shirts, sunglasses, and comfortable walking shoes. The women wore their handbags slung across their chests like mailbags. Some of them walked with canes, many carried rosary beads. At the head of the procession of some two hundred people, a pair of pilgrims carried a large banner that said OUR LADY, PRAY FOR US. Like a shepherding collie, the group leader hurried back and forth alongside the procession singing, "Immaculate Mary our hearts are on fire" with the megaphone raised to his mouth. The pilgrims joined in, meekly at first, but as the parade moved out of the town and into the blazing green countryside the voices gained confidence and strength. I couldn't quite bring myself to sing, but, like the rest of the processionists, I knew the hymn by heart. On Sundays of my childhood I had heard it sung with a Boston accent. It was odd to hear the song here among the lush fields of Norfolk. I knew that in the seventeenth and eighteenth centuries in England public displays of devotion to the Virgin were punishable as a form of treason; under the Penal Laws against Papists and Recusants, the very trappings of Marian devotion — the rosary, iconography, shrines, even the mention of Mary in the liturgy of the Mass — were forbidden. But that morning, in the open air, the hymn sounded lighthearted and happy.

My neighbor shielded her eyes from the sun with her hymnbook and sang with great feeling. She was spry and well groomed, her white hair carefully teased and shellacked, her lips generously daubed with crimson gloss. On her feet was a new-looking pair of white sandals. She had a wooden cane, but instead of using it to walk with, she carried it hooked over her forearm. She walked in an eager, loping way, her broad forehead pressing forward through the air, the cane swinging. The hymn came to an end, the rosary began, and as soon as she said "Hail Mary, full of grace," I realized that the woman was Irish. It made a familiar kind of sense to me, for one of the most distinct characteristics of Irish Catholicism is its focus on the Virgin Mary; the rosary was always stored in an Irish cabinet in my mind. My Irish grandmother, whom I did not know but had heard a great deal about, was so devoted to the Virgin that she had named her four daughters Ellen Mary, Mary Elizabeth, Nona Mary, and Elizabeth Mary. On my office wall I had tacked her personal copy of "The Memorare," a special prayer to the Virgin. It wasn't the prayer that drew me but my grandmother's faith in it, that she had bothered to type it out flawlessly on a sky-blue notecard, that she had carefully affixed it to her kitchen wall. ". . . To thee I come, before thee I stand, sinful and sorrowful. O mother of the word incarnate, despise not my petitions, but, in thy mercy, hear and answer me." Because my grandmother was Irish, the Virgin Mary was nearly as important to her as Jesus.

In a break in the prayers the Irish woman turned to me and asked me where I was from. I told her. "Did you come all the way for this?" she said.

When I told her I had come for the Anglican pilgrimage, she looked a little startled. "But that's tomorrow, you're aware."

"Yes," I said.

The woman's name was Fran. She had a long, fine-boned face, a small mouth, and heavy eyelids. In the heat of the day her pale skin looked damp and slightly distressed. "Now just a warning," she said affably. "Tomorrow the Anglicans will charge you three pound to go in and see the holy spot where the statue is inside that house of Nazareth. But the Catholic shrine is free. Anyone at all can come and visit us. Even those like yourself who are not Catholic."

At Fran's words I felt the pinch of surprise. I wasn't a practicing Catholic, it was true, and therefore couldn't call myself Catholic, but it struck me to hear my status so baldly defined by a stranger. Even as a child who regularly attended Sunday Mass, I had felt that I didn't truly belong to the Catholic Church. As devout as my mother was, I had never attended Catholic school, was never confirmed in the church, and my first Communion, at age seven, was a strange and solitary event. In the conventional Catholic childhood, seven-year-olds prepared for first Communion with formal classes and rehearsals; then, wearing their special white first Communion clothing, a group of thirty or forty paraded into the church and received the Eucharist as a team. Afterward, there were family celebrations. Like first confession and confirmation, first Communion was a communal event, a rite of passage in which the child had a comforting crowd of comrades to buoy her and verify the event. In contrast, my Catholic education had been private, a kind of rough home-schooling. I did not attend Christian Doctrine classes and never learned the catechism. (My mother had coaxed and pushed my six older siblings through the religious education process. I was the last; by the time it was my turn she had run out of indoctrinating steam.) It was my mother and not an official teacher who hurriedly prepared me for first Communion.

When the day came I had no crowd of children with me. At a regular Sunday Mass the priest announced to the congregation of our small church that Rosemary Mahoney would be making her first holy Communion that day. I was a shy child and hated being singled out; I ducked my head at the sound of my own name ringing through the church. I went to the altar rail in a fog of embarrassment, wearing white gloves and a flowered, slightly too big dress instead of the traditional white. I knelt down at the far right end of the rail, the way I had seen people do every Sunday. But since I was the sole communicant, the priest — Father Donatus, with his foreign Brooklyn accent — had gone to the middle of the rail to receive me in a blaze of ceremonial glory. I looked to the left. There he stood, waiting patiently for me, golden chalice in hand. With a cold seizure of horror I realized I was kneeling in the wrong spot. I got up and proceeded to the middle of the rail at the very moment that the priest, seeing that he would have to come to me, began making his way to the far end. We blew past each other. Naturally there was laughter from the congregation and even a little laughter from the priest. It was kindly laughter, of course, but at the time it seemed only to confirm the illegitimate and impromptu nature of the event as well as a certain unworthiness of my person. The priest held out the Communion wafer and said, "Body of Christ." I choked out, "Amen," and stumbled back to the pew, mortified and derided, the host dissolving in my mouth with the unpleasant taste of ash, my cheeks two hot coals of shame.

My first confession, too, was a solitary, dubious event. Without preparatory classes, I stumbled through the strange event, embarrassed and disoriented, kneeling in a box and speaking to an utter stranger sitting behind a dark screen. I recited, "Oh, my God, I am heartily sorry for having offended thee . . ." as my mother had taught me. But I was not a bit sorry. What had I done to offend God? Because I couldn't think of any sins that I had committed, I blithely made them up: . . . *hit my brother/ stole candy from my sister/ disobeyed my mother* — all of it untrue. In confessing these "sins" I felt I was committing a sin. The whole practice of confession struck me as cryptic, confusing, and unnecessary, and my first confession, tainted with another taste of shame, was both the beginning and the end of my participation in that particular sacrament.

Looking at Fran, I realized that I had always felt something amiss in my Catholicism, something regrettably askew. I had a fleeting urge to say to her, "I am *too* Catholic." Instead I asked her if it was true that three thousand people would attend the Anglican pilgrimage the next day.

"Yes," she said. "But we have three thousand coming to the Roman Catholic shrine all the time!"

The small road to Houghton St. Giles passed through a stand of tall oaks that cast us all into a purplish shadow. Ahead of us the pairs of white heads bobbed and weaved. Proud of her Catholicism, equally proud of the Slipper Chapel shrine, Fran told me that she participated in every pilgrimage that took place here. When I asked her why, she said, "It is one thing to believe, but another thing to *show* your belief."

Thirty years of residence in London had given an English cast to Fran's Irish accent. "The Slipper Chapel shrine," she said, "is all that the Catholics have left in Walsingham. Everything else here is Anglican. But it *used* be all Catholic. Long ago. Many royalty came."

Fran shifted her cane from one arm to the other, and, as if to set the schedule straight in her own mind she said, "Now today the Catholics proceed. Then tomorrow the unCatholics proceed. The vicars and the canons and the whatnot. They will carry the statue of the Blessed Virgin through the streets, as you know. And then the Paisleyites and such will come from Northern Ireland and protest against them for doing it. How they hate the Virgin." With her pale, slender fingers she touched my forearm in warning. "Imagine hating the Virgin! They are fierce. Do not get involved with those people, darlin', for they are very vociferous and there has been violence in past years. The Reverend Paisley — you know him, of course. He is evil."

Having once lived in Ireland, I knew that Ian Paisley was a defender of the union between Northern Ireland and Great Britain, that he was the founder of the Free Presbyterian Church, and that he was a member of both the British and the European Parliaments. I knew that he was a bigot who incited violence in Ulster and that he despised Roman Catholicism. In 1988 Paisley had disrupted Pope John Paul II's speech before the European Parliament by standing up and shouting, "I refuse you as Christ's enemy and Antichrist with all your false doctrine," the last words of Thomas Cranmer, the sixteenth-century archbishop of Canterbury who was burned at the stake for his Protestant beliefs.

I pictured Paisley's fleshy, florid face, the big eyeglasses, the big teeth. He was always full of incendiary rhetoric.

I asked Fran if she really believed that Paisley was evil. She leaned away from me and gave me a dire look. "Oh, he is indeed!" A sudden electric-blue dragonfly hovered momentarily near her glittering white hair. Fran ducked her head and swatted feebly at it. "Every year those old Protestants come and shout down the Anglicans," she continued, "because the Anglicans are very high church. They all used be Catholic, you see, before Henry the Eighth. And plenty of the Anglicans've grown almost Catholic again. And the Protestants fear the Church of England will submit to Rome and go back to being Catholic."

"Do you think that will happen?" I said.

Fran said eagerly, "I would like to think it will. 'Twould be grand to see the two churches united again. But the Protestants hate the idea. Oh, how they hate the old ARCIC!"

ARCIC, the Anglican–Roman Catholic International Commission, was established during the 1960s to promote Christian charity and to heal the ancient division between the Anglican Communion and the Catholic Church. Just a few weeks earlier the commission had published a controversial statement proposing that the Anglicans of the world accept papal authority over one "reunited" church. The rift of the Protestant Reformation had caused not merely animosity and anxiety but thousands of deaths perpetrated in Christ's name by both Anglican and Catholic monarchs. Heretics, unbelievers, and those who wouldn't submit to the latest religious decrees of Henry VIII or his daughters, Mary Tudor and Elizabeth I, were executed. (In the four short years of Mary Tudor's Catholic reign, three hundred people were burned at the stake for religious nonconformity.) With the bad feeling that had grown up between the two churches, a modern-day reunion would be a monumental, almost unimaginable, event.

I asked Fran why, if Rome was the perceived enemy, the Protestant protesters did not simply go directly to the Catholic shrine to voice their complaints.

"Ah, well," Fran said with a shrug, "they do sometimes, but usually they wouldn't bother. They know they don't have much influence on people who are already Catholic. It's the ones tottering on the edge they want to prevent."

After fifty minutes of walking, we came into Houghton St. Giles, a hamlet so small I marveled that it had its own name. Fran gave me a nudge with her elbow, pointed into the distance with her cane, and said with jaunty, childlike pride, "Now, Rose, do you see that field over there? Rome owns it, but they will loan it out to the Anglicans now and then so that their pilgrims can camp out there and play games and what have you."

The idea of Rome showing the Anglicans this bit of noblesse oblige seemed to please Fran immensely, and as we neared the Catholic shrine her step grew almost coltish. My mother, I thought, would surely have cottoned to Fran.

THE SLIPPER CHAPEL in Houghton St. Giles was the centerpiece of the renewed Catholic pilgrimage to Our Lady of Walsingham. Built in the thirteenth century, the chapel was dedicated to Saint Catherine, the protector of the holy house of Nazareth. Medieval pilgrims on the road to Walsingham had developed a tradition of stopping here, saying a prayer, removing their shoes, and walking the remainder of their journey barefoot, but after the demise of the Walsingham shrine, the pilgrims stopped coming and the Slipper Chapel fell into decay.

At the end of the nineteenth century, Charlotte Boyd, a wealthy Catholic convert with a vision of a renewed shrine at Walsingham, bought the Slipper Chapel (after a failed attempt to buy the original abbey grounds at Walsingham) and restored it. The first modern pilgrimage to the chapel took place in 1897, and in 1934 the chapel was declared the National Catholic Shrine of Our Lady of Walsingham. At roughly the same time the Anglican vicar of Walsingham, Alfred Hope

Patten, successfully reestablished a shrine in Walsingham proper for Anglicans who wished to honor the Virgin. The two shrines had a shared origin, yet for many years neither shrine officially recognized the other. Though the mood had recently warmed due to the efforts at a rapprochement between the two churches, in my weekend visit to Walsingham I felt a slight undercurrent of resentment from the Catholic pilgrims. The unspoken sentiment seemed to be that the Walsingham pilgrimage tradition was rooted in Roman Catholicism and that in modern times the Anglicans, with an unfair advantage as the state religion, had usurped it.

The Catholic shrine at Houghton St. Giles was pretty and tidy and well equipped with a gift shop, a shrine office, a tearoom, a holy water font, and a large, modern church. But the shrine itself was much smaller than the Anglican shrine, and, situated outside the heart of Walsingham, where the pilgrimage history had unfolded, the place felt a touch secondary, a touch forlorn, like an unpopular booth relegated to the distant edge of a large state fair.

The Slipper Chapel was small — a mere twelve feet by twenty-eight — and beautiful. Inside, a bank of flickering votive candles and the filtered light of the stained glass windows gave the room a warm glow. On a pedestal in the corner was an elaborate statue of the Blessed Virgin similar to the one at the Anglican shrine. In her blue robe Mary sat on a throne, knees spread, bare feet firmly planted, a Saxon crown on her head, a lily of purity in her right hand, and the infant Jesus on her left knee. The infant, too, wore a crown. He had a Bible in his hand and an authoritarian look in his infant eye.

Bells rang to announce the start of the noon Mass. As I was going into the Chapel of Reconciliation, a familiar face appeared in front of me. It was Mike, the man who had stopped me the day before on the street in Walsingham. Clean-shaven, sober, his big beige eyebrows tidily combed, and dressed in a jacket and tie, Mike looked like a different person. He had a stack of hymnals in his arms and was handing them out to the congregants as they entered. With no indication that he had ever seen my face before, he smiled kindly at me and asked, "How many will you take?"

"Just one," I said.

He drew a hymnal briskly from the top of his stack and handed it to me. "That'll be three pence then, please."

I looked at him in surprise. After a moment he grinned slyly and, leaning close, whispered, "Not to worry, miss. That is only a joke!" And he winked and dipped his big head and tittered at his own naughtiness.

I sat down in a pew and watched the pilgrims streaming into the church. The Chapel of Reconciliation was an airy structure and, like so many modern Catholic churches, the point of its blown-open design was informality. It was a bright gathering place for the masses, not unlike a gymnasium. Its bare wooden beams and overt geometric shapes appeared to say that everyone and anyone was welcome here. It had none of the fussy, intricate, darkly symbolic detail of traditional Gothic or Renaissance churches; instead it was bland and soothing. The Mass, the chapel seemed to say, was a meaningful enough event that it could be celebrated in a horse barn without losing its purpose.

I watched the pews filling up and could hear Mike behind me in the aisle passing his joke off on a succession of newcomers. "How many will you take?"

"Three."

"That comes to nine pence, please." And then the gratified laugh followed by "Not to worry, folks . . ."

A white-bearded priest appeared at the altar, and the congregation reflexively stood. Pressing the air down with his hands, the priest said, "No need to stand at this moment. Please sit," and speaking off-the-cuff he welcomed the congregants, praised the shrine, the beautiful Slipper Chapel, the beautiful May weather. He cracked a few jokes and gestured with his hands. With the friendly informality of a host at a summer cookout, he was breaking the ice, letting us know who he was, encouraging us, putting us at ease. He seemed to be saying that the Mass should be neither daunting nor difficult but an enjoyable event.

Very little in the priest's demeanor was traditionally priestly, and it seemed fitting that his homily was centered on the meaninglessness of image. Crossing his arms and leaning back on his heels, he said, "Now I am reminded of a story that Tip O'Neill, the former U.S. speaker of the House, used to tell about a man named Jake. Jake was a shopkeeper in Boston who decided to get a complete makeover in his appearance. When the makeover was finished he flew to Miami to ask a woman he liked out on a date. But guess what? At the airport Jake was struck by lightning and died. Unfortunately, his makeover had been so complete that when Jake arrived at the gates of heaven, even God didn't recognize him!"

The congregation laughed heartily at this.

"Now we all know that Christ's image was wrong," said the priest. "Christ was a carpenter's son from Nazareth. Nobody was expecting a Messiah like that. They were expecting somebody very majestic. Likewise, we don't see ourselves as prophets. But by our baptism we have been called to be prophets and saints. If we don't recognize ourselves as prophets, maybe God won't either." The sermon was a warm boost to the ego that ended with "When you go home today, look in a mirror. That is what a real prophet looks like."

It had been some years since I had attended a full Catholic Mass. Listening that day I realized that the language of the liturgy had become so accessibly colloquial that it now had the ring of a self-help seminar. That, together with the priest's breezy manner, had the effect of making God seem terribly current, like a thoroughly modern man in touch with his feelings. It was no surprise to me that over the years the once formal Catholic Mass had been reworked in a way that was calculated to diminish the gap between God and us. In the early 1970s my mother took, briefly, to attending the folk Masses put on by some guitar-strumming Catholic priests in a church in Harvard Square. In these Masses the Our Father and the sober words "I am the Resurrection and the life" were set to the rhythms of Dylanesque rock songs; the Eucharistic wafer was exchanged for whole-grain bread; the sign of peace was not a handshake but a hug; and Christ was transformed into a tie-dyed conscientious objector. Increasingly it seemed the Catholic God was kindly, encouraging, and applicable, a God that people could *relate* to. The modernity adhibited to God by the Catholic Church seemed to me, in theory at least, a good idea, and yet to one who had trouble believing at all, his ever-evolving style also made God a little suspect, a too malleable creation of the human imagination. And, oddly, though from decade to decade the church subtly switched the hat on God's head, it was easy to forget that after John XXIII the Vatican itself remained adamantly unchanging.

THAT EVENING the little town of Walsingham had grown crowded. The streets were busy with Anglican priests and pilgrims, busloads of marching bands swung into the square, laypeople here for the Monday pilgrimage wandered about or browsed in shops or sat in cafés, and the guesthouses were filling up. There were Indian, Chinese, and Arab

Christians here, people in wheelchairs and on crutches, people wearing pilgrimage medals, nametags, and scarves. The Anglican shrine and the abbey grounds connected to it were crowded with visitors. Some people sat drinking in the town's two pubs. In the Friday Market a vendor was busy constructing a large outdoor grill; tomorrow there would be a hog roast. Everyone seemed happily excited. Old friends called across the streets to each other in greeting: "Haven't seen you since last year's pilgrimage!" And the Anglican shrine authorities hurried about in preparation.

I sat down at an outdoor table at the Bull Inn pub and ordered a sandwich. At the next table a group of schoolteachers, five women and two men, were drinking beer and talking about their students — the discipline problems, the fashions the students wore, the ones they liked and didn't like. I felt a small thrill listening to them; it was like being back in school again and eavesdropping at the door of the faculty lounge. One boy was a particularly bad article. A plump, pretty woman said, "'Is mother 'as a bunch of kids, but 'e's the only one she doesn't want."

"Right, and that's what's wrong wiv 'im," said another. "'E knows 'is mum don't love 'im."

"I think 'e's dead clever, really."

Though the sky was still bright, the sun had just slipped behind the roofs of the town, and in the shadow of the pub the air had grown chilly. The women, in their sleeveless summer blouses, rubbed at their pale, goose-pimpled arms. Their table was littered with empty glasses, dirty ashtrays, cigarette lighters, and spilled beer.

A fat man with a gravelly voice and a cigarette in his fist was talking about the school soccer team. "We've got a couple of girls on the team, but I'm not sure whether they really are girls. They're tough, and they've got names like Sam and Pat."

The teachers laughed at that. Then one of the women, realizing that I was sitting alone, said, "Here for the pilgrimage?"

I felt myself hesitate, then said, "Yes."

"We're here too," she said. "It's a brilliant outing, isn't it? We do it every year."

I explained that I had never been here before, but so far, yes, it was a good outing.

"Where you from?"

When I told her I was from the United States, the teachers fell silent, and when I spoke again I saw them listening to the sound of my voice with an amused and slightly mistrustful look on their faces, distracted by all that they associated with an American accent — Hollywood and television and war.

"You came from America to see Walsingham, did you?"

"Yes."

"All alone?"

"Yes."

"God, I wouldn't come here all alone. Wouldn't you be a bit afraid?"

This inquisitive, friendly woman had rings on four fingers, a blond shag hairdo, lashes clogged with mascara, and a laugh like a mallard's. Her name was Annie. Her cozy curiosity made her easy to talk to. When I said that compared to America, England was a relatively safe country, the teachers nodded their heads in knowing recognition. The fat man said, "We've seen it on the telly. Children getting shot in America when they go to school."

I told them that Walsingham with all its idyllic charm felt typically English.

Another man said, "You haven't been to Blue Water!"

That made the teachers howl with laughter.

"What's Blue Water?" I said.

"It's the typical idyllic England!" said the fat man, slapping his knee.

"It's a big shopping center in Kent!"

"The biggest shopping center in Europe!"

The teachers found the very idea of the Blue Water shopping mall terribly funny.

Annie sat up suddenly and said, "Now, listen, I'm glad you're come from America. You can help us. We're doing this thing in school for the kids, and we need someone to tell us about the —" she paused and raked at the air and winced at her colleagues for help, "what's it called, that day in July, the um . . . the first of July in America . . . ?"

"Fourth," said a dark-haired woman named Lizzie. "Fourth of July."

"Yeh, fourth of July. Now what is that exactly?"

"Independence Day," I said.

"Independence?"

"The American revolutionaries defeated the British and gained their independence," I said.

"Right, so in school, what should we do to celebrate it?"

I looked at her to see if she was kidding. She wasn't. I told her that in theory the British probably shouldn't celebrate the Fourth of July. "The British Crown lost the American colonies on that day."

The woman didn't care who lost what. "Well, okay. But we want our kids to know about it."

I explained that the American colonials wanted independence from the Crown.

"How do you tell it to four-year-olds?"

Before I could answer, another of the teachers, a tall redhead with narrow eyes, lifted her glass to her lips and said fatalistically, "You can't! It's too complicated." She took a deep drink of her beer, settled the glass back on the table, and wiped her damp fingers on her freckled arm.

I said, "Well you could start out by telling them that many of the colonists originally left England because they wanted religious freedom."

The redhead flapped her hand at me. "Nah! Those kids don't believe in religion."

"Well, you could tell them that the revolutionaries were sick of being taxed by a distant monarch," I said.

"*I* am sick of being taxed by a distant monarch!"

The teachers howled again. They shook their heads and grinned into their beer glasses. Their camaraderie was old and deep. They were as familiar with one another as the members of a family. They had that English habit of self-reference; their own nation, with its traits and quirks, was a topic of great interest. Someone mentioned the approaching wedding of Prince Edward, Queen Elizabeth's youngest son, as though he were a nephew of them all.

"Didn't that girl he's marrying say right out she was not going to obey him?"

"No, Lizzie, she said she *was* going to obey him."

"I think Eddie's a little light on his feet," said the fat man.

Annie said, "Poor old Diana wouldn't obey, and look where it got her! Oh, look, there's Father Pickering! Hello there, Father!"

Father Pickering, a tall, thin figure in a black robe, waved vaguely in our direction from across the street and hurried away.

"And Fergie, too," said Lizzie. "She wouldn't obey."

"The royal family has had to face up to it and come to terms with life. I think they'll change their ways," said the redhead.

Annie said, "I still wonder about Diana, personally. I wonder did they kill her. I think it was deliberate. She spoke her mind and they didn't like that."

"Who do you think killed her?" I said.

"The royals," she whispered. She pronounced it "roles" — her accent, like that of the other teachers, made her sound a little like a medieval henchman. "I think the roles had something to do with it. The queen and Charlie and them. Diana knew too much and the roles had to get rid of her."

The fat man grinned. "That's heretical, what your sayin', Annie!"

A round-shouldered, long-haired woman appeared in the doorway of the bar and called the teachers in. As they clambered up from the table, Annie said, "Well, I'm going to think of you now." Actually, what she said was "Om gonna fink of yew nayw. Om gonna be finkin' of yew comin' all the way to Woe-singum from America. Peepoo like yew fessynoite may."

The teachers disappeared into the pub, and I got up and headed back to Elmham House, wondering why I had hesitated when Annie asked if I was here for the pilgrimage. In high school, just around the time that I had stopped going to Mass, I had assumed the posture that God was for geeks and losers. For years I pretended to think this, although in my heart, even as a teenager, I respected spiritual people and was curious about why they believed. I had quit going to Mass not as a result of any struggle I had had with God but to deter unwanted attention. Among my peers religion was generally considered uncool, and I felt there was already enough uncoolness in my life.

In college I was fascinated by the Christian literature required for one of my classes — Søren Kierkegaard, Thomas Merton, Simone Weil, Thomas à Kempis, Julian of Norwich, Saint Augustine, and others — and was prompted by those writers to reconsider my teenage apostasy. In a small red notebook (the one that years later showed up in the trunk in my basement), I recorded my thoughts about their work. And I began, furtively, going to Mass again. On Sunday mornings in my sophomore year, I crept out of my dormitory and hoped that nobody I knew would see me entering the Catholic church on Bow Street. Far from giving me strength, my interest in God made me vulnerable and secretive. I had five roommates that year, only one of whom was religious; that the religious one happened also to be the unhip, unpopular one seemed no coincidence. Though I was curious about God, I continued to protect myself with the pretense that God was for squares. It was, I suppose, my doubt and uncertainty about God's existence that made me secretive — had I fully and confidently believed, I would have needed no social shield. But I had doubts, and, worrying about what my friends would think, I kept my notebook, my churchgoing, and my spiritual thoughts to myself. I knew it was a bit cowardly to hide what mattered to me, and I experienced an unpleasant moment of self-recognition when I read in Merton's *The Seven Story Mountain,* "The logic of worldly success rests on a fallacy: the strange error that our perfection depends on the thoughts and opinions and applause of other men. A weird life it is, indeed, to be living always in somebody else's imagination, as if that were the only place in which one could at last become real!" The impulse to disown spirituality had somehow become reflexive in me, and even now, when asked if I was here for the pilgrimage, I reflexively hesitated, though in fact I felt no shame whatever about saying yes.

THE NEXT MORNING was gray and cold, the sky like a blanket of thick gray flannel. Twists of smoke rose out of a few of the brick chimneys around the Friday Market, and in the middle of the square the hog roast had begun. I saw the vendor busily basting the hog's bald head with a fat-soaked housepainter's brush. Greasy white smoke lifted from the grill into the still air. In the Common Place, a brass band of uniformed teenagers, the Brighton Sea Cadets, were stamping their feet and huffing experimentally into their trumpets in the chilly morning light. The drummers beat out tattered drum rolls in practice, then blew warm breath onto their hands. A big man with little feet and a potbelly paced up and down the pavement, idly banging at a huge bass drum.

Parade spectators and Anglican priests milled outside the Bull Inn pub, and though it was early, many were already drinking. I had never seen so many priests in one small place, nor had I seen such ecclesiastical finery — they were dressed in linen cottas, lacy copes, surplices of purple velvet, stoles of rich maroon, and long black cassocks with crimson piping and a blaze of crimson buttons down the fronts. There was great variety among the Anglican priests: some were gay, some were women, some were gay women, some were quite young, others very old. Some wore shoulder capes, some wore zuchettos, some wore Roman collars beneath leather motorcycle outfits. A few wore their hair in ponytails, a few had shaved their heads. They smoked and chatted and laughed. They held hands with their wives. Some held hands with each other. Two women priests came down the street in black robes, their heads shaved, both with tiny rat-tails at the base of the neck. As I passed by the pub I heard one powdery priest tell another that his antique stole was beautiful enough to be hung on a wall.

Some thirty feet away, in the cobblestoned triangle around the pump house, another group had begun to gather. They had placards and signs, Bibles and lunch bags and umbrellas. They were serious and ruddy-faced and spoke very little to each other, which gave them all an air of harbored resentment. They stood patiently on the cobblestones and leafed through their Bibles, waiting for the Anglican procession to begin. Their clothing, in contrast to the finery of the clergy, was dowdy and outdated, stalled somewhere in the mid-1950s. Some of the men were in shirtsleeves and wore socks with sandals and broad, short neckties. The women wore long skirts and low-heeled pumps and, on their heads, tams or straw boaters or woolen caps with furry pompons. The pockets of their misshapen cardigans bulged with tissues and bunches of keys. Like the Catholic women in the procession the day before, they wore their handbags slung securely across their chests. They stood with their feet apart and their signposts firmly planted, their breath unfurling faintly in the damp air. Their lack of style was so marked it looked almost calculated.

I sat down on a stone wall and read their signs of protest; some were quotations from Scripture, some expressed personal opinion, some recalled the names of Protestant martyrs. One man's homemade sign showed a colorful drawing of a man being burned at the stake. The words below the image said DID I DIE IN VAIN FOR REFUSING TO FOLLOW CROSSES AND IMAGES IN PROCESSIONS OR BOW DOWN TO THEM? WILLIAM ALLEN FOLLOWED CHRIST. Another sign said THOU SHALT WORSHIP THE LORD THY GOD & HIM ONLY. WHY DO YOU WORSHIP MARY? ADORATION IS WORSHIP, AN IDOL AN OBJECT OF WORSHIP. MARY DID NOT DIE FOR YOU AND CANNOT SAVE OR PRAY FOR YOU. One man held a sign in each hand: BIBLES NOT BEADS! and NO POPERY! A woman in a dirty ski parka raised a banner: A.R.C.I.C. URGES TO ACCEPT THE POPE. JESUS URGES: COME OUT OF HER MY PEOPLE. SHE IS DOOMED FOR DESTRUCTION. CALL NO MAN YOUR FATHER ON EARTH FOR ONE IS YOUR FATHER IN HEAVEN.

The signs were colorful, some professionally printed, others made by hand, and seeing them in that medieval square, I had a strange sense of being knocked back in time. Here was the tradition of the Protestant Reformation reduced to a selective summary, four-hundred-year-old sentiments expressed with crackling currency. The signs formed a crude montage of John Wycliffe's fourteenth-century insistence that the Bible was the supreme authority and the Eucharist a mere symbol, Martin Luther's doctrine of faith alone as justification, his rejection of papal authority, and his objection that the power attributed to an ordained ecclesiastical hierarchy was a usurpation of God's authority. The signs proclaimed the Protestant insistence on a direct communion with God without intermediaries, rituals, or images of any kind — the protest was clearly a bitter rejection of the practices of Roman Catholicism.

The parade was scheduled to begin in fifteen minutes. I got up and wandered toward the protesters. A white-haired woman wearing a blue tam, a red cardigan, and a long, flowered skirt held a sign with a picture of the Virgin Mary and the words: THE WOMAN DRUNK WITH THE BLOOD OF THE SAINTS AND MARTYRS OF JESUS, INCLUDING WILLIAM ALLEN 1555. SHE IS MYSTERY BABYLON THE GREAT MOTHER OF HARLOTS ABOMINATION OF THE EARTH. WHAT IS NOT OF CHRIST IS ANTICHRIST. As I approached, the woman smiled pleasantly at me. I asked her what her group was. She said, "You could call us the Walsingham Witnesses."

Her cheeks were so red they looked slapped. Her voice was very soft. By her feet sat a gray-muzzled old poodle with a bluish tint to his filmy eyes. The dog looked up at me, sighed, then stared into a gutter garnished with brilliant green weeds. "Are you a Protestant organization?" I said.

"We are Christian," the woman said softly.

I stepped closer to hear her better. "Are you part of the Church of England?"

She pointed a finger at the priests drinking outside the Bull Inn pub. "Not that Church of England. The true Church of England."

I took a stab. "Are you Lutheran?"

"Protestant."

"Presbyterian? Calvinist?"

Vaguely she said, "We believe in the true Protestant doctrine."

The term "Protestant" was nebulous; it meant so many things. At its inception its only certain definition had been anti-Catholic.

"What do you protest?" I asked.

"Right. We protest Rome and its superstitions. These people are engaging in the Romish practice of worshiping false idols."

There was no venom in the woman's sighing voice, no shred of defensiveness. Though her sign declared that the Virgin Mary was a whore and the Catholic Church the mother of harlots and the abomination of the earth, her words sounded sweetly passive. She spoke with a slow, bland certitude.

"What are the Anglicans doing that you don't like?" I asked.

A tall, bearded man passed behind her holding up an enormous banner that read: THOU SHALT NOT MAKE UNTO THEE ANY GRAVEN IMAGE. The priests began to make their way down to the Anglican shrine for the start of the parade. The parade would begin at the shrine, pass through the square, and thread its way to the grounds of the abbey for the afternoon Mass. More spectators streamed into the square or settled on the sidewalks to watch.

"They are leaning toward Rome," the woman said. "They are reversing the work of the Reformation. They do not adhere to the Thirty-nine Articles, which are the foundation of the Reformation."

"What is it that you don't like about Mary?" I asked.

"I do not dislike Mary, but she is taken for an intermediary. She is worshiped as though she was God. That is not right. So we are here saving souls."

"From what?"

She straightened her tam and said sweetly, "Damnation. The pope is the emissary of Satan and Roman Catholicism is a superstitious diversion from the way of God. We are part of a long tradition that has been against the activities here at Walsingham."

The poodle stood up, stared at a stone, limped to the pump house amid the legs of the protesters, and sat down again. I asked the woman if the activities that day were hurting her interests in Christ.

"Right. It is all part of a scheme to spread Catholicism in this Protestant country," she said. "The Anglican leadership is hoping to bring Britain back to Rome. The ARCIC want Anglicans to accept Rome." She looked across the street at the people laughing in front of the Bull Inn and said as an afterthought, "And Tony Blair's wife is Catholic."

The woman answered all of my questions freely, as though accustomed to being interviewed in this way. She had plenty of time and

knew what she needed to say. She was affectless and mild, and the into-
nation of her voice remained unchanging, like a person slightly depressed. The words flowed recitatively from her tongue, and though
they were dire, her bland demeanor suggested no emotion whatever
about her subject. She seemed almost bored. She looked idly about the
crowded square as she talked, very rarely looking at me, yet after each
of my questions she gave a polite nod of recognition and occasionally
acknowledged the questions by saying, "Right," which had the odd effect of making it seem that I was agreeing with her.

I said, "Why would it be bad for the Anglicans to accept Rome?"

She nodded. "Right. It would mean slavery again. Idolatry and superstition. That is why the Catholics were kicked out of England by
Henry the Eighth. Rome would like to get us back. Like the Arabs and
the Muslims, they will do any underhanded thing to spread their religion. Catholicism is a religion of cannibals. They call the host the flesh
of Christ."

I looked at the woman's flaming cheeks. "What don't you like about
the Mass?"

"Superstitious ritual."

"Are you English?"

"That's right. Yes. In Northern Ireland, where I live, Rome is mur-
dering innocent Protestants. Just like the Muslims do."

"How do you feel about the pope?"

She stifled a yawn and her blue eyes watered. She shifted her sign.
"That's right. The pope is the Antichrist."

I looked again at her sign and realized that the image of the Virgin
Mary was actually the cover of a book called *The Principality and
Power of Europe: Britain & the Emerging Holy European Empire.* I
asked her what the book was about.

"Oh, yes. This important book reveals the plot that is afoot. The European Union is an attempt to make Europe a Catholic nation, a Roman
Empire. That is the pope's wish. Now . . ." she shifted the sign so that
we could both look at it. "Do you see that halo around Mary's head?"

A halo of twelve gold stars encircled Mary's crowned head.

"Yes."

"Does it remind you of anything?"

"No."

"Those twelve stars in a circle are the design of the flag of the European Union."

So they were. Precisely.

"That is deliberate," the woman said. "The design for the flag of the European Union was taken from the halo of Mary. They want to offer the union to the Virgin Mary. Eventually the pope would be the head of all Europe and the head of Britain. Christians like us are treated as a minority in the E.U. We are considered a sect because we are not Roman Catholic." She rummaged in her purse and produced a copy of the book that was depicted on her sign. Opening it to a previously marked page, she said, "Now this part explains why the signers of the European Treaty are guilty of treason and should be arrested." She began reading in the same soft voice. "Queen Elizabeth the First said: 'To no power whatsoever is my crown subject save to that of Christ the King of Kings.'" She closed the book. "And the treason act of 1848. We have a treason act in this country which says that if anybody tries to take power away from the queen, they should go to prison for life." She recited the treason act from memory. "The European Union is treason against the queen."

It was a novel idea. "So this is a political protest," I said.

"It is religious. There is no difference."

"No separation of church and state, then?"

"Why should there be? Jesus Christ is our ruler. The queen, who is the head of our state, is also the head of our church. European Union hands our country over to foreign powers."

It was a political protest as much as a religious one, and with its xenophobic paranoia it encapsulated much of the history of religious conflict. Religion was a source of identity, an antidote to the fear of obscurity, a bright banner behind which to stand. It created a sense of belonging. In defining God we defined ourselves; whatever didn't conform to our view of God was a threat. Sacred texts were open to interpretation and therefore could be twisted to prove anything; anyone who didn't agree was the Antichrist. I asked the woman what exactly was the queen's authority.

"She is the keeper of the faith. The European Union is Catholic. It has vowed to abolish everything Protestant."

When I asked her who William Allen was, her pale blue eyes suddenly came to life. "That's right. William Allen. In 1555 he was burned at the stake here in this town for his Protestant beliefs. Bloody Mary slaughtered many of us."

I had to think for a second. "Is that Mary Tudor?"

"That's right. The illegitimate daughter of Henry the Eighth. She tried to reinstate Roman Catholicism in this land."

"For the first part of her life she wasn't illegitimate," I said.

"That's right, but then she was by decree." As if speaking of a close relative's failed marriage, she added, "That union with Catherine of Aragon was invalid."

When I said I didn't think anyone would be damned to hell for carrying a statue of the Blessed Virgin, the woman said, "You are a very misguided person," but in such a sweetly agreeable tone that I had an impulse to thank her.

There was a stirring down the street — the parade had begun and was winding its way toward the square. In the distance I heard the faint screech of trumpets, the rumble of drums. A dozen or so police officers in Day-Glo yellow entered the square, positioning themselves between the protesters and the parade route. They had truncheons and walkie-talkies and helmets. Suddenly a stocky, powerful-looking little man stood up on a short wall of bricks near the pump house and began shouting with the formal insistence of a preacher. The moment his booming voice rang out, the poodle lifted its head and began happily drumming its short tail on the cobblestones. The man held a Bible bound in red vinyl and waved it as he spoke to the crowds gathered along the sidewalks. Behind him the protesters hoisted their signs in support. "The Immaculate Conception has no basis in the word of God and is contrary to the word of God," he cried. All the heads around the square turned to look at him. "You pray to the Virgin Mary here! But the Virgin Mary would need to be omnipresent to hear the prayers of those praying to her from all over the world! Secondly, she would need to be omniscient to know the prayers we have in our hearts. Omnipresence and omniscience are attributes that belong to God alone and cannot be communicated to Mary or the vicars and priests here today."

The man shouted slowly, his words drawn out and evenly spaced, as though he were reading from a prepared text. He had bushy white eyebrows and a dense helmet of steel-gray hair. A flap of shaggy bangs covered his forehead. His accent was the choked, whining drawl of Northern Ireland. "And I'll tell you something else," he bellowed. "If you pray to Mary and to the saints you are directly contradicting what God commands in the Old Testament, wherein he forbids communication with the dead! Praying to the dead is a form of necromancy."

At the mention of necromancy two men standing nearby shook their heads and giggled into their glasses of beer, but the woman I had been talking with nodded approvingly at the preacher and softly said, "Yes, that's right."

The parade was just entering the square. At its head the Brighton Sea Cadets were performing an official salute with a lot of intricate formations. Behind them a long stream of clergy stretched back toward the Anglican shrine. The far sidewalk on the north side of the square had filled with protesters waving their Bibles and their signs: JESUS IS THE AUTHOR AND THE FINISHER OF OUR FAITH. BY WHAT GOD AND AUTHORITY DO YOU FOLLOW AND WORSHIP THIS IDOL? GOD'S WORDS DECLARE THIS AS PAGAN NOT CHRISTIAN.

I left the pump house, crossed the street, and stood with the crowd on the sidewalk. Above the tune the band had struck up, the preacher ranted on. "There is nothing in the Bible to substantiate what you're doing here today! As for the priests! There is no mediator between God and man."

A plump, smiling priest in a black velvet cassock with sleeves of scarlet came up the street leading the parade. The gold-tipped crosier in his hand was the size of a cheerleader's baton. A large gold medallion depended from a ribbon around his neck. His brilliant zuchetto matched the color of his sleeves. Behind him an altar boy carried a brass crucifix, and behind the altar boy followed two lines of choirboys in blue and white surplices. They approached the pump house, while from around the corner of the Bull Inn a band of stately vicars appeared. The vicars wore long black robes; over the robes they wore white albs, over the albs they wore small shoulder capes of lavender fitted with tiny pink buttons, and over the capes they wore white stoles embroidered with gold flowers and fringed with long strands of gold threads. Many wore gold medallions or crosses on ribbons around their necks.

As the front of the parade approached the pump house the gray-haired preacher, in an unbroken stream of rhetoric, was crying, "Now, dear friends, what you are doing today is not according to the law and the testimony. If it was, you would be up here with your Bibles open, arguing with us, saying, 'Look, this is what the Bible says to support our actions.' But you are not up here! Why? Because, as far as Mariolatry is concerned, the Bible's a blank book."

None of the priests appeared interested in responding to the preacher or refuting the boldly provocative signs, and the spectators seemed to take it in stride. I turned to the man standing next to me and asked him why they were all so unpurturbed. "The Witnesses are just crackers," he said with a shrug. "No point dignifying such silly nonsense with a response."

The Witnesses looked confident and proud. "Now listen!" the preacher roared. "Spurious miracles and delusions do not authenticate the word of God. No man has the ability to forgive sins. We don't need priests — vicars or whatever they call themselves — to forgive our sins when we have Jesus Christ to forgive our sins."

A dazzling flock of bishops in white robes and gold stoles entered the square. Their starched miters were brilliant in the gray light, like fresh linen napkins artistically folded to stand upright on a table. Hundreds of priests in hooded white surplices followed in rows of two, smiling and singing a hymn. A grand bishop appeared in an alb of canary yellow, a bold blue stripe down his front and a gold miter on his head. On either side two identically dressed assistants protected him. A woman standing beside the preacher wagged her sign at the bishop: BURNED ALIVE HERE, 1555, WILLIAM ALLEN BY THOSE OF THIS TRADITION WHO DESPISE THE BIBLE, GOD'S WORD. Behind him came an even grander bishop wearing a heavily embroidered cape and carrying a silver crosier. Draped in velvet and gold and with Maltese crosses sewn into the shoulders of their capes, his two assistants, like a pair of servants, held out the heavy wings of the bishop's cape as he walked. I turned to the man standing beside me and asked him who the bishop was. "That is the Right Reverend David Thomas, the provisional assistant bishop of Wales." I watched the Right Reverend go by; a mere assistant bishop, yet he was dressed more colorfully than the pope.

With their magnificent finery the Anglican clergy made a Technicolor rainbow under the gray sky. I couldn't remember ever having seen Catholic priests dressed this beautifully. The priests walked proudly, chins lifted, hands pressed together in the position of prayer. Filling the small street, they smiled benignly at their admirers. Toward the back of the parade I could see the statue of the Virgin entering the square on a palanquin.

"Tell me something," the preacher cried, his head a foot or two above the parade. "Did Jesus Christ set himself up in fancy dress or separate himself from the rest of the people the way the vicars and priests are doing here today? He did not. The Pharisees did. Those who are false did, but Jesus Christ dressed as the ordinary people dressed. Jesus said about the Pharisees: They like to be called Father. Is that working for you? They may be fathers, but are they *your* father?" He waved his Bible at the heads passing by the pump house. "These priests, are they here to honor Jesus? No! Are they trying to raise the name of the Virgin Mary higher than Jesus? Yes! Is this just a day out so that they can show off their fancy clothes and drink a few beers? That's certainly how it looks."

Between the passing pairs of priests I could see the cuffs of the preacher's baggy trousers sagging over his feet; he was wearing black sandals and white socks and a tweed jacket two sizes too small. His double chin billowed and shook as he waved his Bible at the parade. Behind him his frumpy colleagues nodded and raised their Bibles and signs, while the Anglican procession, like a peacock parading among pigeons, flowed slowly past them and then turned the corner toward the Friday Market.

Some bystanders listened to the preacher with obvious scorn and irritation, others snickered and shook their heads and made disparaging jokes about Bible thumpers. Now and then someone in the crowd shouted at the preacher, "Go home, ya barmy bugger," or "Why don't you shut up!" To which the preacher calmly replied, "No papist will shut the mouth of the Lord!"

Eventually the statue of the Virgin arrived at the center of the square, preceded by two priests with flaming torches and four priests in blue velvet robes. Her palanquin was carried on the shoulders of four yellow-robed priests. Over the Virgin's head was a canopy fringed with gold, and an enormous bouquet of roses and poppies had been arranged at her feet. Behind the statue came more priests in crimson, violet, cream, black, and purple. The procession was flanked on either side by the cadets in their black uniforms and white caps and belts, while at the outer edges of the parade the police hurried along, escorting the Virgin and keeping the peace.

In the daylight the statue of the Virgin and child looked more than ever like a doll, and the sight of her borne on the shoulders of these grown men in their dandy clothing, heralded by bishops and protected by police, suddenly gave the event the feel of an extravagant satire. I tried to feel the seriousness in it, to think about the woman behind it and what she represented, but the story was obscured by the pageantry of the parade, the shouting voices, and the jeering signs. The whole thing seemed a bit absurd, and in the Virgin's arms the infant Christ looked thin and rigid. On the far side of the street a huge red sign with white lettering said CHRIST JESUS CAME INTO THE WORLD TO SAVE SINNERS!

A second Protestant preacher stood up on the wall and began to shout at the parade in the same ranting way as the first. He raised his Bible. "That image that you carry through the streets today, command it to speak to you! If that image has any spiritual significance, then let it walk by itself. Why do you carry it? You have defiled the words of God today!"

The priests, blithely smiling, began a new hymn, and the protesters answered with a hymn of their own, a thundering version of "Rock of Ages," accompanied by an accordion. The hymns collided and clashed, the voices rising aggressively and overlapping until it was one big hair-raising cacophony of religious sentiment. The aged poodle paced back and forth at the foot of the pump house and became so agitated that he howled and barked at the disturbance. The protest signs swayed and bobbed: MASSES ARE BLASPHEMOUS FABLES & DANGEROUS DECEITS . . . ARTICLE 31. The police peered nervously left and right, and the onlookers seemed both stunned and thrilled.

As soon as the hymn singing ended, the preacher started in again. "Have you found what you're looking for, people? I see many of you have glasses in your hands. I thought this was supposed to be some kind of pilgrimage! You can't think of anything better to do on your pilgrimage than to have a few glasses of ale? You should be worshiping Jesus. Instead, you worship yourselves."

The spectators and some of the priests laughed at this, yet the preacher's words had a touch of truth to them. The Anglican priests were celebrating the Virgin, but they were also celebrating themselves. They were preening. I scanned the procession — it was a parade only of priests; the lay Anglicans watched from the sidelines. In the Catholic Mass the day before, the casual priest had said, *Look in the mirror, it's you.* The parading Anglican priests seemed to be saying, *Don't look in the mirror, look at us.* Watching the parade I thought of the English writer Alan Bennet, who, after attending a Catholic funeral full of gormless, ill-dressed characters, wrote, "It reinforces what I have always known: that I could never be a Catholic because I'm such a snob, and that the biggest sacrifice [John Henry] Newman made when he turned his back on the C. of E. was the social one." (I once read this line to my mother; she laughed and said, "Social! Christ cared nothing for society. Alan Bennet *is* a snob, and his calculated admission that he is doesn't exonerate him a bit! Newman left the Church of England because he knew it was hollow. What, in fact, do they actually *believe* in beyond dressing up?" My mother, by the way, never bothered to criticize the low Protestants — they were too exotically far-fetched. It's those most like us who vex us the most, and therefore her obsession lay with the Anglicans. Once, when I asked her what she thought of the Unitarian Church, she said with light disdain, "Well, I don't know, really. I think that's one of those feely-good places where they swing and sway.")

My mother's enmity for the Anglicans had nothing to do with what they did practice and everything to do with what they didn't. In her view the Anglican Church contained none of the difficulty of Christian realism; it was a tepid, watered-down faith. The Anglican God was genteel, antique, and passive, like a piece of fine furniture. And yet for the Protestant protesters in the square that day the Anglicans, with their too-Catholic ways, posed a terrible threat.

New signs appeared around the pump house: THIS PROCESSION & MASS DENIES THE WORD OF GOD WHICH FORBIDS IT and CHRIST'S REAL PRESENCE IS NOT IN THE MASS.

I felt some sympathy for the Anglicans; everyone seemed to dislike them — the Catholics because they weren't Catholic enough, the Protestants because they were too Catholic. They were vilified because they were neither here nor there but at the same time managed to emanate an air of superiority. Gliding along, smiling imperturbably, singing their praise of Mary, they represented the state religion and the power of England. (Though only half of the British population now professes any religious affiliation at all, and only a quarter adheres to the Anglican Church, it is still the most populous church in the kingdom, followed at some distance by Roman Catholicism, then Islam, then Presbyterianism.) For my mother, for Fran in the Catholic procession the day before, for the Walsingham Witnesses with their strident, condemning signs, the issue was political. It was also personal and psychological. It was a struggle for a name, for a place, for power and recognition.

"There are some of you here today who haven't found rest for your souls, and you're looking for it in pageantry and Masses and buying trinkets and holy water and all sorts of countless representations of paganism! You have the apostate spirit of Rome that would silence anybody who disagrees with them. But this is a Protestant country. No papist will shut the mouth of the Gospel in this country. We were burned at the stake in this town many years ago and we are determined not to let that happen again."

Dour, humorless, far outnumbered, the protesters managed to be the center of attention in Walsingham that morning. Though they did nothing more than express their opinions, they were a remarkably disruptive presence. And they were persuasive — some of what they said made sense. God was powerful enough that he needed no intermediary; why not pray to him directly? And what was the point of all these elegant ecclesiastical robes but to glorify the self? As for the clergy, why should any man be above another in relation to God? And Rome, with its roving history and its converting bent, *was* imperialistic.

Nevertheless, as reasonable as parts of their message were, why was it so easy to dismiss the Witnesses huddled around the pump house? Why did they, with their spare religion, come off as cockeyed? It was, I thought, the constant references to Satan and the Antichrist. It was their paranoia, their extremism, their clenched nationalism. One picketer's sign, which had drawn my eye all morning, said: A.R.C.I.C., W.C.C., ECUMENISM, N.W.O., E.U. = MOTHER OF HARLOTS, HARLOTS, WHORE, FALSE PROPHET, BEAST, CHURCHES TOGETHER, MULTI FAITH. It was like the ravings of a lunatic. The protesters were frightened of extinction and certain of a conspiracy run by a devil dressed in a pontiff's robes. The Bible had been diluted by science, archaeology, anthropology; in the face of so much contradicting evidence, their literal interpretation of the Scripture seemed like a form of dementia. Who could say that the protesters were wrong? Except for the anxiety visible in them. If religion was a balm, they did not seem soothed by it. The heart of their religion seemed to lie in disproving the religions of others.

Standing shoulder to shoulder with the other spectators, I realized that although I did not embrace the Catholic Church, when presented that weekend with its Christian alternatives I had been tilting weakly toward it. The Catholic Church was the church I had inherited and the church I knew best; its familiarity asserted a subtle gravitational pull.

Long ago I had rejected it, first out of shame and later by active disagreement. But, like the childhood scars that faintly remained on my elbows and knees, Catholicism was still with me. For all my own dismissals of it, when the soft-spoken woman in the blue tam had said, "Catholicism is a religion of cannibals," I had momentarily felt the words as a personal insult, had inwardly winced and wanted to knock the silly tam from her head. I could criticize the Catholic Church freely but, as with criticisms of one's own parents, when others did the criticizing it stung. The innate impulse to defend Catholicism (and its all-important Eucharist) was, I knew, an impulse to defend my mother and, by extension, myself.

Religion, like ethnicity, is an emotional issue and is similarly passed from generation to generation. Under the circumstances objectivity and reason can be easily eclipsed. It was no great discovery to realize that an unexamined religious inheritance can be a source of conflict and strife. For me the unsettling discovery was that that truth applied not just to other people but to me as well. My religious history, slight and skewed and rejected as it was, still had the power to set me at variance with those who didn't share it.

As the tail end of the parade glided through the Common Place, I saw an elderly man with a glass of wine in his hand squeezing his way up the crowded sidewalk. He positioned himself so that he could see the parade, his eyeglasses halfway down his nose. He had reddish eyes and a heavy face. As he gazed at the noisy scene, he drew a small comb out of his pocket, raked it idly through his fine white hair, then tucked the comb away again. He sipped at the wine and smacked his lips. He surveyed the crowd, drummed his fingertips on his chest in satisfaction, listened awhile to the shouting preacher, sipped again, then shook his head and said jovially to anyone who would listen, "Fancy one of those fanatics in your car all day yapping at you! I'm afraid I'd be out the window before very long." And with that he continued on up the sidewalk, sheltering his glass from the jostling crowd.

· 2 ·

LOURDES

Mrs. Stenswick, the elderly British woman sitting beside me, wore a black eyepatch over her right eye. She seemed to be sniffing her rosary beads as she prayed. With her two hands, brown and knotted by arthritis, she held the beads just below her nostrils, like a squirrel worrying an acorn. Her visible eye was shut tight in concentration as she prayed along with the other women.

The prayers were led by a pair of Italian nuns, and for those of us who didn't speak Italian, they were difficult to follow. We sat, perhaps two hundred pilgrims — Spanish nuns in Reeboks, Indian women in saris, Chinese schoolchildren, African nurses, Irish teenagers — outside the famous holy baths at Lourdes, waiting our turn to go in. I had been sitting for an hour, the women at the front of the line had been sitting at least two hours, but the line seemed to move swiftly. Every three minutes or so Mr. Thomas Neill, the red-haired Irish man supervising the line, gave us all a hearty wave of his hand and the woman at the end of each bench advanced to the bench in front of her, while the rest of us slid over one seat to fill up her empty space. The baths closed at four o'clock. I had arrived at two and was assured that I would make it inside before closing time. The predominating nationality seemed to be Italian. Most of the attendants — nuns and nurses — were Italian. The three stout women in black in the pew in front of me were Italian. The two Italian nuns leading the prayers summed up each decade of the rosary with a little hymn of praise sung in voices so off-key that some of the pilgrims couldn't help but titter.

The line moved like a sidewinder snake, threading through the benches, while on the opposite side of a low barrier, several hundred men moved toward the bathhouse in the same slow way, praying and shifting seats. The holy baths were segregated due (one Italian nurse had informed me) to certain unavoidable moments of nakedness during the bathing process. The bathhouse, a long, low, stolid-looking building of gray stone, looked grim, like a structure in a concentration camp.

In an interval of the prayer Mrs. Stenswick's friend, Mrs. Stumpf, who was also English but had a faint German accent and a deaf person's hollering way of speaking, again said, "What a miraculous coincidence, Molly, that I have met you in this fashion today in Lourdes! I'd no idea you were back from Kampala."

Mrs. Stenswick lowered her beads and turned her good eye toward Mrs. Stumpf. "Aye. Tuesday last."

Mrs. Stumpf had questions about Africa, which Mrs. Stenswick patiently answered, confirming that she had seen many wonderful things there. She had, for example, seen a leopard.

With one hand cupped behind her ear, Mrs. Stumpf squinted up at her slightly taller friend. "Good God, Molly, a *leper?!*" she shouted.

"No, dear," Mrs. Stenswick said, "only a leopard."

Mrs. Stumpf's long face fell. "Oh. A leopard. Well, equally dangerous, Molly. Equally dangerous."

On the other side of me, sitting with her mother, was Carla, a slightly retarded girl of perhaps fourteen. Earlier they had been reciting the alphabet for amusement, and now that her mother had gone back to praying, Carla leaned toward her every so often with a mischievous grin and whispered, "Guess what, Mum. A, b, c," then giggled and covered her mouth with her hand. The mother, handsome and gray-haired, had a kindly face and wore a strand of pearls. She was saying the Hail Mary.

"Hi, Mum," Carla said. "Guess what. A, b, c, Mum."

Carla was fat and pretty. She had delicate eyebrows, thick black hair, a gap between her two front teeth, and an adorable snickering laugh. The even paleness of her skin was interrupted only by a sudden squall of camel-colored freckles across her nose and the tops of her cheeks. In her lap was a box of animal crackers. A loose rubber band hung like a bracelet from one plump wrist, and on her small face she wore a pair of eyeglasses nearly the size of ski goggles. When she wasn't talking to her mother or smiling and blinking through her finger-smudged lenses at me, she scanned the pavement beneath her feet, her mouth open and her hands folded neatly in her lap, or inspected the backs of the heads of the women in front of us. All the while she rocked slightly and wore a pleasantly distracted expression, blinking and smiling, as if reminiscing fondly about some amusing thing in her short past. Her curious, expectant way of staring at the world gave me the eerie sense that at any moment the fog she seemed to be peering through would lift. She blinked a great deal, as if trying to clear her head.

Pointing a short finger at me, Carla said to her mother, "Mum. Am I sitting by her then?"

"Yes, love," said the mother with a smile. "You are."

Carla grinned shyly at me, plucking at the rubber band on her wrist. "The sky is nearly gray today, isn't it?" she said.

The September sky was deep blue, and the day was very hot and calm. "Well, it looks kind of blue to me," I said. "But I could be wrong."

Carla shortened her neck, raised her pale hand to her mouth, and snickered. With devilish delight she said, "Har! I was only testin' ya!"

I laughed. Pleased by my laughter, Carla turned to her mother. "Mum, I talked to that lady. Look at her laughin'."

The mother smiled, nodded, and prayed on with the rest of the women.

As we sat there amid the murmuring women, large groups of pilgrims passed by on their way to the grotto, tramping like livestock across the hot pavement. Most were middle-aged or elderly, and each group carried an identifying flag, a beacon that herded them together. The flag of Italy went by above a sea of moving gray heads. The flag of Ireland. The flags of Spain and Portugal and several countries I didn't recognize. Beyond them was the shallow River Gave and on the far side of the river an open lawn ringed with tall, leafy oak trees. Except for the masses of people and the huge numbers of wheelchairs, the shrine at Lourdes looked like the well-tended campus of a wealthy college. The grass was groomed, the shrubs were pruned, the gardens healthy, the pavements swept, the windows of the eleven or twelve buildings sparkling.

The shrine has not one but three basilicas, a crypt, four chapels, an information center, a pilgrims' shelter, a picnic area, a central kitchen equipped to serve 7,500 meals per day, five conference rooms, a hospitality bureau, a family center, two museums (one called the Museum of Precious Objects), a bookshop, two cinemas, a youth camp, three accommodations for the sick, the grotto, the baths, and its own printing press. It has 400 employees, 100,000 volunteer helpers, 60 priests and other religious, 1,304 beds for the sick, 1,000 wheelchairs, 1,000 fire extinguishers, 707 telephone points, and 22 places of worship. It serves 700,000 meals and burns 800 tons of candles annually. An average of 52 Masses are said each day; some 400,000 people take the baths each year.

As if reminded by the passing armies of devout Christians, Carla said to me, "Well, we're only in Lourdes now." Finding a piece of candy in the pocket of her blouse, she drew it out, unwrapped it carefully, and popped it into her mouth. After chewing for some time she said, "These sweets are nearly nice then, aren't they, Mum?" She chewed slowly and noisily, with a lot of graphic smacking and drooling. Her mother put her arm around her and kissed her head and said affectionately, "Carla, close your mouth when you chew, darling."

Carla did not close her mouth but turned to me again. Daintily, with her ten fingers spread, she used the tips of her index fingers to raise the huge glasses slightly higher on her nose. She stared and blinked at me, her mouth hanging open. "Come to think of it," she said, "I saw a giant mosquito in Lourdes."

"What did he look like?" I said.

"Priest or mosquito?"

"What priest?" I said.

Carla raised an impatient hand at me. "That old priest I saw in Lourdes!" She seemed to be wishing that I would try just a little harder to keep up with her.

"Well, first tell me about the mosquito," I said. "What did he look like?"

"Stringy legs." She thought a bit. "And wings. And terrible big."

"How big was he?"

Carla widened her eyes and raised her hands before my face, making the shape of a football. "Something fierce."

"Did he fly?"

"'Course he flowed! Straight by my head."

"And what about the priest?" I said. "What was he like?"

Carla blinked and thought. Her eyes looked sore behind the thick lenses, and her lips, eyelids, and fingernails had a pale bluish hue, as though she had been swimming too long in a cold sea. Having thoroughly reenvisioned the priest, she said in summary, "Stringy legs."

"You're not testing me, are you, Carla?" I said.

Carla laughed so hard at this that bits of spittle and candy landed on the back of the bench in front of us, and she hunched over in her seat and cupped her hand over her mouth and hooted. Her whole body shook with the comedy of it. A string of drool slid down her chin. At the sound of this irreverent laughter, the Italian women on the bench in front of us turned to look at us, but when they saw Carla's face they looked quickly away again and went back to their prayers. The smiling mother tsked in mock disapproval, and with a tissue she wiped the back of the bench.

Mr. Thomas Neill waved his hands at us and cried, "Come along, ladies!" He had the potbelly and skinny legs of a robin. The whole group began to move in a blurred frenzy of motion. Mrs. Stenswick, Mrs. Stumpf, Carla, her mother, and I all slid obediently along the bench in our procession toward the bathhouse. I watched the people who had finally reached the entrance disappear behind a blue-and-white-striped curtain hung over the doorway.

I had no idea what to expect of these baths. In 1891 Émile Zola, who was virulently anticlerical, published the novel *Lourdes,* in which he described the shrine's infrequently changed bathwater as a frightening cesspit. "As some hundred patients passed through the same water, you can imagine what a horrible slop it was at the end. There was everything in it: threads of blood, sloughed-off skin, scabs, bits of cloth and bandage, an abominable soup of ills . . . The miracle was that anyone had emerged from this human slime."

Settling herself in her new seat, Mrs. Stumpf said eagerly, "We're making progress now, Molly! 'Twon't be long!"

I HAD NOT PLANNED to visit Lourdes. There are innumerable worthy pilgrimage sites in the world: thousands of wells, hundreds of sacred trails, scores of weeping icons, moving statues, and mystical shrines — I couldn't possibly visit them all. Size and popularity, which Lourdes has more than almost any other pilgrimage site, did not appeal to me. In truth, the bigger the place, the less I wanted to see it. Furthermore, I had long viewed the miraculous and the supernatural with impatience and doubt. As an adult I had heard the reports of scoffing skeptics: Lourdes was hokey and tawdry, a commercial circus full of ranting faith healers, superstitious cranks, plastic Vatican-approved souvenirs, and an unending river of the sick, the dying, the crippled, and the deformed, whose tender hopes were preyed upon by a disingenuous, avaricious municipal machine. I felt that I had heard enough about Lourdes. But on my way to St. Jean Pied-de-Port in southern France, where I would begin walking the medieval pilgrimage trail across northern Spain to the Galician city of Santiago de Compostela, I looked at a map and realized that a mere fifty miles separated Lourdes and St. Jean.

At the sight of Lourdes on the map I recalled that as a child I used to urge my mother to go there, hoping that she might be cured by the miraculous power of its holy spring water. I had heard the stories about the numerous ill and infirm people who had bathed at Lourdes and had emerged healed and whole. It struck me that the healed always left their crutches and canes behind in testimony.

My mother, whose left leg had been paralyzed by polio, couldn't walk without crutches and a leg brace. Science had all but freed the world of the polio virus, yet there was still no cure for the paralysis suffered by those who had been damaged by it. My mother's leg would be paralyzed for as long as she lived. She knew that. Not prone to fantasy and generally insusceptible to the supernatural, she regretfully accepted her paralysis. The one time I had seen her submit to the possibility of a cure was at the invitation of a Chinese acupuncturist, who insisted that his Eastern medical skills could help her.

I accompanied my mother to the Chinese man's house (until I was twelve I accompanied my mother everywhere) and watched while he and his tiny, smiling wife twisted long silver needles into the back of her useless leg. It was disconcerting to see my mother lying flat on her face while two strangers involved themselves so minutely with her body. I hated the whole thing. I hated the man's short-sleeved shirt and hairless arms; I hated the way their ill-lit house smelled of boiled onions. Throughout the ordeal I consoled my morosely staring self with the Hershey's Kisses that the Chinese couple had set out on a table beside me. Nevertheless, I felt that the spectacle and the vulnerability would be worth it if my mother could walk again. If there was a cure for her, I wanted it regardless of the cost. I wanted my mother, a dynamic woman, to be free of what had held her back. Once or twice when her leg was pierced just so with a needle, it twitched in a shocking way, and on seeing this I felt enormous hope. But after six or seven visits to the "office" of Dr. and Mrs. Wu, my mother's lame leg remained unchanged. I knew it would take a miracle.

I was, at eleven, as excited as the next person by the prospect of the mystical, the supernatural, the unexplained. Religion in and of itself didn't have those qualities, but some of religion's wilder manifestations did. The fact that particular problems or worries could be soothed and solved with prayers to particular saints was eerily thrilling. Saint Anthony helped you find lost articles. Saint Christopher was good for a safe passage. Saint Jude straightened out hopeless causes. Saint Blaise would take care of your throat. Saint Barbara, the patron saint of fireworks and firearms, would grant you a happy death. That specific prayers could be answered at all was thrilling. At Lourdes, I knew, medical miracles were possible.

When I was eleven, twelve, and thirteen I would sit on the edge of my mother's desk and tell her that we could go to Lourdes together. I would help her; I would carry her suitcase and push her in a wheelchair. I liked planning it. We would have to go in summer, when she had time off from her teaching job and I had time off from school. *What if you could finally walk?* I would say. Thinking of it, my mother always laughed in a slightly scoffing way. *Imagine me throwing down my crutches and dancing off!* She liked the idea of going to Lourdes, and she too was captivated and tantalized by the idea of all those crutches left behind by the cured. But I knew that in her heart my mother felt a trip to Lourdes would simply be an interesting expedition from which she would return physically unchanged. When I asked her if she thought miraculous cures were possible, she said she had no idea, but she didn't think one should go to such a place and expect to be healed. It was more a spiritual matter, she said, a change of heart, a different view of one's life. "I don't think you can command or bargain with God," my mother would say. "And if you show up with a scont in your eye, you certainly won't be cured."

"Scont" was a word her parents had made up. A person with a scont in the eye was a skeptic, one who went about saying, *Prove it.* Though my mother had tremendous faith in God, she also had a scont in her eye. I suspect this was the reason she never went to Lourdes. She did not believe that miracles were worked in a conventional way or enacted on demand. As a child I sincerely thought that my mother would leave her crutches in the grotto at Lourdes alongside all the others, but as the years passed I developed my own scont, and Lourdes receded from view.

THE FRECKLES on Carla's cheeks were distorted and magnified by her powerful glasses. "A, b, c," she said meaningfully, expectantly to me.

"D, e, f," I said.

The corner of Carla's large mouth twisted upward in amusement. "D, e, f spells deaf."

Her mother said, "No, silly, it doesn't!"

Carla ducked her head and grinned. They had been through this before. It was all a test with Carla; she was checking to see who was on their toes and who wasn't.

She removed the rubber band on her wrist and hung it over her ear. "Can you do this?" she asked. I put my hand out for the band, she gave it to me, I hung it on my ear and said, "G, h, i." Carla nudged her mother and pointed at me. "Mum. The lady."

When Carla saw that I had a scab on my elbow, she pointed out that she had one on her knee. I noticed she had one on her shin as well, and together we counted up all the scabs and nicks and scratches we had between us. When I accidentally counted one of Carla's freckles as a scab, she cried, "Ah, no! Stop! That one is only a freckle!" And then we passed time by counting our freckles. I showed Carla the strange constellation of large brown freckles on my inner arm; she touched each freckle with the tip of her finger and remarked, astutely, that the pattern they made resembled the Big Dipper. I had never noticed this. We talked for some time, until Carla's eyes began to droop and she fell asleep, her head on her mother's shoulder, her mouth open, her bluish eyelids not quite fully closed, the box of animal crackers gripped loosely in her hand.

Carla's mother introduced herself. Her name was Agnes. They had come to Lourdes because Carla was unwell; a congenital disease made it unlikely that she would live beyond her seventeenth birthday.

I looked at Carla. Her small nostrils had a delicate paisley shape. Her breath came in short, heavy bursts. She had the beginning of breasts, the size of lemons. Carla's mother told me that this was their third visit to Lourdes. "I don't come to Lourdes for a cure," she said. "I come out of gratitude for the lovely girl I've been given."

At the end of one decade of the rosary the Italian nuns ran through the various incarnations of the mother of Jesus — Queen of Peace, Queen of Roses, Mother Mary, Holy Queen, Blessed Virgin, Queen of the Most Holy Rosary. Then they made their final plea: "Santa Bernadette de Lourdes, prega per noi!"

ON FEBRUARY 11, 1858, Bernadette Soubirous was sent with her sister and a friend to collect firewood on a barren piece of common land outside the town of Lourdes. Bernadette, the oldest of five children, was fourteen, malnourished, and suffering from asthma and the beginnings of tuberculosis. Her family, like many Lourdais families of the mid-nineteenth century, was desperately poor; they lived in a cold, dark, one-room cell in what had once been the town's prison. Her father, a failed miller who was fond of drink, had recently been arrested for stealing grain.

As she foraged in the woods along the banks of the River Gave, Bernadette heard a murmur like the wind, although the day was quiet and the trees very still. She looked up, and in a crevice in a stone grotto she saw a soft, glowing light and within it a beautiful girl dressed all in white but for a blue sash at her waist. The girl wore a white veil over her head, and atop each of her bare feet was a yellow rose. Bernadette grew fearful and tried to reach into her pocket for her rosary beads but found that she could not move her hands. The girl in the grotto seemed to be signaling her to come forward. As soon as the girl lifted her own rosary beads, Bernadette was able to move her hands and make the sign of the cross on her forehead. The apparition disappeared without speaking. When Bernadette told her sister and the friend what she had seen, the girls protested that they had seen and heard nothing. Upon hearing the story, Bernadette's mother gave both daughters a beating and forbade them to go to the grotto again.

That didn't stop Bernadette. Compelled by a pressing desire, she returned to the grotto a few days later with some friends. The vision appeared to her again in the same spot. Bernadette asked whether it was a sign from God. The vision remained silent, and when Bernadette tossed holy water at it, the girl did not disappear or protest but seemed to appreciate the gesture.

Over the next three weeks Bernadette saw the vision in the grotto some eighteen times, and although no one else who accompanied her saw it, all agreed that in the presence of the apparition Bernadette seemed to fall into a beatific, trancelike state, becoming nearly immobilized, that her face became beautifully radiant, and that indeed she spoke and acted as though she were communing with a real person. The story of the visions spread. Each time Bernadette went to the grotto (the vision had politely requested, in the patois used by most Lourdais, "Would you have the goodness to come here for fifteen days?") she was accompanied by increasing numbers of onlookers, including, on separate occasions, the village priest and the local police. Although Bernadette did not identify the vision in any way, the villagers began to believe it was the Virgin Mary.

Fearing the unrest that these fantastical visions might cause among a poor and fervently Catholic population, the police commissioner forbade Bernadette to return to the grotto. But feeling an inexplicable urge to go there, she disobeyed him. The girl in the apparition revealed several wishes to Bernadette: she wanted prayer, penance, and the conversion of sinners. She said, "I desire that people come here." At one point she asked Bernadette to kiss the ground. Another time she asked her to drink from the spring and eat the grass around it for the sake of sinners. There was no spring in that area that anyone knew of. Onlookers watched in astonishment as Bernadette scratched and scrabbled at the muddy ground with her bare hands, eventually revealing a natural spring beside the grotto. They watched as she drank the dirty water and pulled up grass and weeds and chewed on them. Some people thought she had lost her mind. Some insulted her. Her mother and aunts, shocked and embarrassed by her bizarre behavior, beat her and quickly took her home. But others believed it was the work of God.

Over the next few months the spring that Bernadette had revealed blossomed into a freely flowing stream. On one visit, while entranced by the vision, Bernadette held her hand over a candle flame, but her flesh remained unburned. During the thirteenth apparition, the glowing white figure asked Bernadette to tell the local priests to come to the grotto and build a chapel there. Finally, when Bernadette went to the grotto on the Feast of the Annunciation, the vision revealed her identity, saying, "I am the Immaculate Conception."

The doctrine of the Immaculate Conception had been officially adopted by the Catholic Church a mere four years before, in 1854. At that time, with secularism on the rise and Roman Catholicism under seige, Pope Pius IX declared that Mary, the mother of Christ, had been conceived without the universal blight of original sin. The concept of original sin essentially maintains that all of humanity is tainted, born guilty, restricted in the ability to give and receive of the self in the manner of the divine. The theological necessity of the Immaculate Conception rested on the identity of Jesus and his relationship to God. In short, if Jesus was divine and anointed by the Holy Spirit, how could he have been born to a sinner? In the papal bull *Ineffabilis Deus,* Pius IX decreed that he had not been:

> We declare, pronounce, and define that the doctrine which holds that the most Blessed Virgin Mary, in the first instance of her Conception, by a singular grace and privilege granted by Almighty God, in view of the merits of Jesus Christ, the Savior of the human race, was preserved free from all stain of original sin, is a doctrine revealed by God and therefore to be believed firmly and constantly by all the faithful.

The concept, though accepted by Roman Catholics, was still relatively new and unfamiliar to the average worshiper in 1858. The term "Immaculate Conception" (often confused with the Virgin Birth) was a description of Mary's own conception and was not a defining title. At no time before or since the visions of Bernadette has the Blessed Virgin herself been referred to as the Immaculate Conception. To the local priests of Lourdes, the statement "I am the Immaculate Conception" was distinctly odd, as odd as if Jesus had referred to himself as "the Virgin Birth." (Jesus did not refer to himself thus, but in a semantically parallel fashion he did say, "I am the Resurrection.") The priests of Lourdes insisted that the vision must have said, "I am the *fruit* of the Immaculate Conception." But Bernadette Soubirous steadfastly insisted that the vision in the grotto had called herself the Immaculate Conception. Further, the uneducated and reputedly slow-witted young woman insisted that she had never heard the term "Immaculate Conception" before. When pressed about the meaning of the apparition, Bernadette declared with characteristic impassivity and calm, "I am not responsible for making you believe in it. My responsibility is to tell you about it." Bernadette was firm about what she had seen, never once changing her story, even though she was hounded and interrogated by clergy hoping to fit her view to the traditionally accepted image of the Virgin. They insisted that the vision must have been a grown woman and must have stood in a certain pose, but Bernadette rejected their assertions.

Despite the skeptical protests of the local authorities, who feared public unrest, of a clergy ever wary of superstitious hysteria, and of an intellectual elite trying to shape and order an increasingly scientific and secular world, within twenty years Lourdes had been transformed from a quiet village to an immensely popular place of Christian pilgrimage, especially for the incurably ill.

Wedged into a little valley in the Pyrenees, the crooked streets and stout gray buildings of Lourdes seem to have landed there haphazardly but peacefully, like snowdrifts against a fence. The town, dominated by tall mountains dotted with scrubby pines, has that thin-feeling mountain air in which sound seems to travel faster and echo louder. With a population of 17,000, it is still only a village, yet with more than 5 million pilgrim visitors a year from over 150 countries, Lourdes is the second most visited place in France. The town has 360 hotels, 75 restaurants, and 20 camping sites. Each year more than 7 million postcards and letters are sent out to the world from its post office. Its train station looks like that of any small French village, except for some rooms called Halles des Malades, which were designed to receive the tens of thousands of sick and handicapped pilgrims who come to the town each year.

Soon after Bernadette's visions, the local faithful began to speak of miracles and cures taking place at the grotto and its neighboring spring. When a woman with two paralyzed fingers placed them in the spring water, the fingers were cured; a woman who had been barren for years drank the water and eventually gave birth to a healthy child; an infant on the verge of death was touched with a piece of the rosebush that grew in front of the grotto and was instantly cured; a blind man's vision was restored. Word of these miraculous healings spread, and people came from across France to drink or bathe in the water and to pray. Although the figure in the apparition had at no time promised that physical healing would take place here, and though Bernadette's own asthma and early signs of tuberculosis were not cured, the cures at Lourdes multiplied.

In the mid-nineteenth century, apparitions of the Blessed Virgin were common, particularly in the Pyrenees. Lourdes was situated along several major European pilgrimage routes — to Montserrat, Rocamadour, and Santiago de Compostela. As a result, Lourdes and neighboring towns were steeped in traditional pilgrim stories of the miraculous. Since the Middle Ages, many local peasants had professed to have exchanges with the Virgin Mary, and the area was scattered with numerous shrines in her honor. Yet no other French visionary experience caused the national — and eventually international — explosion of piety and fervor that Bernadette's did.

In her superb history *Lourdes: Body and Spirit in the Secular Age,* Ruth Harris examines the many factors that conspired to produce the Lourdes phenomenon. One important element was France's defeat in the Franco-Prussian war, which was understood by many as a punishment from God. Napoleon's Second Empire had been dismantled, and in an uncertain political climate royalists and papists were eager to reinstate the Christian monarchy. The Assumptionists — a fiercely nationalistic Marianist Catholic order that was offended by the increasing secularization of the world, the revolutionary developments of modern science, and the diminished role of religion in state authority — championed the doctrine of the Immaculate Conception. Responding to Bernadette's assertion that the Virgin had described herself as the Immaculate Conception, and in a pointed affront to secular rationalism, the Assumptionists promoted the pilgrimage to Lourdes. The focus of the pilgrimage would be Catholic unity and the intervention of the Virgin in the affairs of the lowly and downtrodden. Pilgrims of means would serve the poor, the well would serve the sick, Christianity would triumph over socialism, and religion would, in a sense, triumph over science. As Harris writes, "Pilgrimage became a public, even a theatrical manifestation of Catholic piety in the face of godlessness" (p. 222).

Local authorities built a shrine around the grotto, baths and hostels were constructed, and under the aegis of the Assumptionists volunteers began operating a hospice for the sick. In 1872 the Basilica of the Immaculate Conception was built in response to the Virgin's request for a "chapel." Towering over the grotto and the river, the enormous Gothic monstrosity looks eerily out of place in this small town; standing in its shadow along the river, one almost has the feeling of having been dropped onto the set of a horror film.

In 1858, the year of Bernadette's vision, Dr. Pierre Romain Dozous registered more than a hundred cases of healing, and by 1880 Lourdes was booming. Between 1858 and 1914 another 4,445 cures were declared. A medical board was established to determine the authenticity of cures. At present, according to Lourdes authorities, for a cure to be deemed genuine it must be clear that "the fact and the diagnosis of the illness is first of all established and correctly diagnosed; that the prognosis must be permanent or terminal in the short term; that the cure is immediate, without convalescence, complete, and lasting; that the prescribed treatment could not be attributed to the cause of this cure or be an aid to it." The sick person must be accompanied to Lourdes by a doctor with the appropriate medical records. Upon claiming a cure, the pilgrim presents a file to the medical bureau, which, after careful consideration and repeated examinations of the patient, forwards the case to the International Medical Committee, comprising physicians from thirty countries who consider the details of the case and observe the patient's further development. If the committee deems the case worthy as well as inexplicable, it is forwarded to the cured person's local bishop, who gathers a Canonical Commission of priests, canonists, and theologists for its final consideration, following guidelines defined in 1734 by the future Pope Benedict XIV in his treatise *Concerning the Beatification and Canonization of Servants of God.*

Since the establishment in 1947 of the International Medical Committee, thirteen hundred files have been opened, twenty-nine have been presented to the church, and nineteen have been judged to be miraculous. (Before the international committee was established, the church had already deemed forty-six cures miraculous.) In the one hundred forty-four years since Bernadette's visions in the grotto, there have been sixty-six documented, inexplicable, and officially recognized cures at the shrine at Lourdes. (Many more pilgrims have claimed miraculous cures but have not submitted to the rigors of official documentation and verification.) The following cures are a selection from the official list:

Twenty-year-old injury to the right eye; blind in the eye for two years; cure recognized by the diocese of Tarbes, January 1862.
Lumbar Pott's disease, with neuropathic clubfoot; cure recognized by the diocese of Tours, October 1907.
Fistular lymphangitis of the right arm with enormous edema; cure recognized by the diocese of Paris, June 1908.

Cachexia and lupus of the face (probably tuberculosis); recognized by the diocese of Perigeux, July 1908.

Blindness, paralysis of the lower limbs, recognized by diocese of Aix-en-Provence, May 1949.

Hodgkin's disease, recognized by the diocese of Vienna, Austria, May 1955.

Arachnoiditis of posterior fossa (blindness, deafness, hemiplegia); recognized by the diocese of Rennes, August 1956.

Sarcoma [cancer] of pelvis; tumor so large that his left thigh became loose from the socket, leaving his left leg limp and paralyzed. After taking the waters he was free of pain, and could walk. [Nine months later] the tumor was gone, the hip joint had recalcified, and he returned to normal life. Recognized by the diocese of Trento, Italy, May 1976.

The most recent verified cure took place in 1987, when Jean-Pierre Bely, bedridden and severely debilitated by multiple sclerosis, was made well in a "sudden, unexpected, and unforeseen way." In a document posted on the Lourdes Web site in February 1999, Patrick Thellier, the resident physician at the shrine, described Bely's cure:

> After having celebrated the Sacrament of Reconciliation on the 8th October in his sick room, he received the Sacrament of the Sick the next day during the Mass in the Rosary Square. Mr. Bely then felt himself overcome with a powerful sense of interior liberation and peace that he never before experienced. Then, that same Friday, at midday, when he was lying down in the sick room, he experienced a feeling of cold which grew stronger, almost painful, which gave way to a feeling of warmth, also more intense and overwhelming. He found himself sitting on the side of his bed, and was surprised to be able to move his arms, to feel contact against his skin. During the night that followed, although in a deep sleep, Mr. Bely woke up very suddenly and had the surprise of being able to walk for the first time since 1984. The first steps were hesitant, but it quickly became normal . . . From then on he had regained the use of his physical faculties. Objectively, his cure, twelve hours afterwards, appeared complete and stable . . . Mr. Bely no longer shows any symptoms or clinical signs of attacks to the nervous system.

In verifying Bely's case the international committee wrote:

> It is possible to conclude with a good margin of probability that Mr. Bely suffered an organic infection of the type Multiple Sclerosis in a se-

vere and advanced stage of which the sudden cure during a pilgrimage
to Lourdes corresponds with an unusual and inexplicable fact to all the
knowledge of science.

It is impossible to say any more today in medical science.

It is however to the religious authorities to make a pronouncement
on the dimensions of this cure.

When the religious authorities make their "pronouncements on the
dimensions" of cures at Lourdes, they are bound by the requirement
that there is no "valid explanation, medical, scientific, natural or
usual," for the cure. According to the administration at Lourdes, "Having established this, it remains for the Canonical Commission to determine that this cure comes from God. Furnished with conclusions
reached by the Commission, it is the responsibility of the Bishop to
make a defining pronouncement and to suggest to his diocese and the
world that they see this cure as a 'sign from God.'"

In order to see the cures at Lourdes as signs from God, one must first
believe in the existence of God. Skeptics and those who do not believe
prefer to explain the cures in terms of the powers of the unconscious, of
hypnotism, and of mass persuasion. But to the majority of pilgrims
at Lourdes — who come precisely because they believe — these cures
are undeniably miraculous signs from God. The two main streets of
Lourdes and the shrine itself are filled year-round with people whose
failing and imperfect bodies have left them with chronic suffering, people in wheelchairs, people on stretchers and gurneys, people leaning on
crutches and canes. Rows of pilgrims in wheelchairs and hospital beds
line up at the foot of the basilica stairs for the outdoor Masses — walking among them is like walking through an outdoor hospital in the af-
termath of a war: the deformed, the blind, the palsied, the maimed, the
gaunt and skeletal figures rendered short of breath by AIDS or cancer,
the oxygen tanks and bandages and traveling IV tubes, the limbless, the
autistic, the psoriatic, the deaf, the mute, the horribly acned, the child
on crutches dragging his legs after him, the infant born with no eyes, the
teenage girl with a bad heart.

Despite the great crowds of people, the shrine at Lourdes was remarkably quiet. There were no raised voices; people spoke in the
hushed tones suited to libraries and churches. No one hurried or did
anything abruptly. The crowds flowed harmoniously, and in the huge
open square in front of the basilica people milled in a thoughtful, rever-
ent way. The place resembled a crowded fairground with none of the

noisy hilarity. In the streets of the town pilgrims sat in cafés drinking tea and staring out of the window or quietly examining the religious artifacts they had purchased. Though Lourdes had aspects of an enormous sickroom, I didn't find it depressing.

Seeing so many ill and disfigured people from varied nations gathered in one place, like immigrants to a promised land, was humbling, but seeing so many with a shared hope of having their suffering eased, or at least with a hope of finding a way to bear the suffering, was ineffably moving. Hope has always struck me as the most tender of human emotions. It has no guarantee, it requires bravery, it makes the soul vulnerable, and when dashed it can inflict the gravest of wounds.

EARLIER IN MY DAY at Lourdes I had waited in a long line at the edge of the River Gave to see the famed grotto of Bernadette's visions. In front of me was a flock of white-haired, bowlegged, serious-faced Polish women. When the line moved, they tottered forward in their sensible, low-heeled lace-up shoes. The tops of their kerchiefed heads were level with my collarbone. Earlier I had seen these women going up the pebbly Scala Sancta, the elaborate way of the cross that had been constructed on the hill beside the basilica, on their bare knees.

The sun was hot on our heads, but a little breeze lifted up from the shallow river. Tall oaks and spruces along the banks cast shadows over the water, and in these shadows I could see the river's muddy bottom and now and then a large fish idling in its current. As we neared the grotto some of the pilgrims began to look frightened, others began to cry. In a small alcove in the steep rock face that rose from the river was a statue of the Virgin Mary dressed and veiled in white, a rosary dangling from her arm, hands clasped near her heart in prayer. Around her waist was the blue sash Bernadette had attested to, and on her bare feet the two yellow roses. The statue, approximately the height of the Polish women in front of me, had been constructed to fit perfectly within the stone alcove. She stood on a plinth engraved with the words *Que Soy Era Immaculada Concepciou,* the identifying phrase she had spoken to Bernadette in the local patois, which looked to me more Spanish than French. Just below the statue was a larger cave, in the floor of which the famous flowing spring was visible through a piece of plate glass that looked bulletproof. In front of the spring was a simple marble altar. Pilgrims passed between the altar and the wall of the cave, dragging their hands along the stone in a way that over the years had given it the greasy smoothness of wax and the shine of fine china. The line of pilgrims appeared endless. All day they flowed through the grotto in an unbroken stream, leaving flowers and candles, coins and written messages on its floor. Above our heads the many discarded crutches and canes of the cured dangled from a wire like weird stalactites, just as they had hung in all the photographs of the grotto I had seen as a child. Some of the crutches were wooden, some were metal like my mother's. Some of the metal crutches had been here so long they had rusted to a dull copper brown.

I stood in the grotto, watching the spring flow. If my mother had come here and been cured, would she have cast her crutches up on the wall like this? And what exactly was it that Bernadette had seen? Was it real? A calculated invention? A psychotic episode? A neurological disorder? A cry for attention? By extension, were these dangling crutches a hoax, just phony props? Or were they the real thing? I tried, as I had done a million times in my life, to see my mother walking without brace and crutches. It was difficult. I had great trouble seeing her left leg move at all. It had been lame since before I was born, and in my mind it was so much a part of who she was that I seemed to have developed a sympathetic weakness in my own left leg. Two childhood swimming instructors had noticed that I swam without kicking that leg, and the left shoe of every pair I own has had its sole worn away at the toe, the result of a slight dragging of that foot.

Whether real or not, Bernadette's visions had brought to this spot millions of the faithful from all over the world. On the walls of the shrine hundreds of messages of gratitude addressed to the Virgin had been left by those whose wishes had been granted. And whether or not they had been cured, most pilgrims left the town with what they invariably described as "a sense of well-being."

The town and the church had benefited, many pilgrims had benefited, but whether Bernadette had benefited was debatable. In the years following the visions she herself became a celebrated object of worship and curiosity. Visitors clamored to touch her, to snip off pieces of her veil as mementos. The authorities at Lourdes came to feel that her presence was a distraction from the sanctuary and the worship of the Virgin. Bernadette had ceased to be useful; in fact had become a liability. Eventually she left Lourdes to join a convent in Nevers, where she spent the rest of her life in seclusion. When she died of tuberculosis at thirty-four, the town of Lourdes rejected the suggestion that her body be returned to it, again fearing that Bernadette would become the shrine's central object of veneration. In 1933 she was elevated to sainthood, and her embalmed, waxed, and perfectly preserved body is on view in a reliquary in the cathedral in Nevers.

AS I SAT in line for the baths, a photograph slipped out of my notebook and fell to the ground. Carla, who had woken from her brief nap, bent down and picked it up. Before returning it to me she held it close to her glasses and examined it. It was a five-by-seven black-and-white of Bernadette Soubirous sitting on a stool looking grave and slightly ill and darkly beautiful, with big eyes, high cheekbones, fine brows, a broad forehead, and full lips. I had bought the photograph in one of the many shops that lined the two main streets of Lourdes. The shops sold the usual religious articles — plastic holy water bottles, statues of the Virgin and of Bernadette, rosary beads, holy medals, miniature models of the basilica, books, and postcards.

"That's Bernadette," I said to Carla.

"I know it," Carla said. "Why's she angry?"

I could see why Carla might think her face was angry. "To me she just looks sad," I said.

Carla's mother leaned over to see the photo. "To me she always looks like Isabella Rossellini."

Mr. Thomas Neill waved ten of us into the bathhouse. Once inside, I was separated from Carla and her mother. With eight or nine other women, I was led into one of seven small changing rooms and instructed to undress. The room was dimly lit, with hooks on the walls and wooden benches lining its walls. The marble floor was wet. A blue-and-white-striped curtain at one end separated the changing room from the bath. Every now and then from behind the curtain I heard a tremendous plunging splash followed by murmuring voices, and presently a wet-haired woman would emerge from behind the curtain. Attendants in white coats and blue aprons moved quickly about, disappearing behind curtains, passing from one changing room to the next.

As I was undressing I saw a young Spanish woman slip behind the curtain for her bath. An attendant came into the room and spoke to the old woman standing beside me, saying, "Italiana?" The woman shook her head no. The attendant said, "Polacca?" The woman answered,

"Slovacca." Beside the Slovak was a fattish French woman with a scarf on her head. Across the room were two Polish women in girdles. Mrs. Stumpf, who had been separated from Mrs. Stenswick, stood in the corner on one foot, sighing and grunting as she struggled out of her skirt. I was the youngest person in the room.

When I had undressed to my underwear, an attendant stood before me with a large sheet of Marian blue and held it up like a blind while I removed my underwear. Once I was completely naked the attendant briskly wound the sheet around me and then, with tender efficiency, began organizing my possessions. I had carelessly dropped my bra and T-shirt on the bench; she picked them up and hung them on a hook. She folded my trousers and laid them on the bench. The boots I had removed from my feet lay helter-skelter on the floor; the attendant slipped them tidily under the bench. With its efficiency and spareness, the place had the feel of a hospital, and like a hospital it inspired in me an infantile feeling of surrender and vulnerability. I heard another great splash behind the curtain, a Spanish shriek of shock that made all the women look up in alarm, then murmuring voices. When I moved to take off my wristwatch, the attendant held up her hand to stop me and said, "No. C'est okay!"

The Spanish woman reappeared from behind the curtain, beaming and saying to anyone who would listen, "Muy frio!"

I was next. The attendant quickly ushered me through the curtain into a small space like a kitchen pantry sealed off from the baths by yet another curtain. The attendant, who was blond and olive-skinned and short, turned me toward her, put her hands firmly on my shoulders as if to keep me from lifting off through the ceiling, and looked at the floor. We stood that way, silently, for perhaps a minute, she staring at the marble floor, I staring at the part in her hair. She wore tennis shoes and smelled of toothpaste. I thought of Zola's gruesome description of the bathwater; just as I felt myself growing apprehensive, a small hand reached from behind the curtain and flung it wide, and there in a very small room stood three white-coated Italian women around a stone tub set into the floor. The room, smaller than a squash court, was garishly lit by a fluorescent wand in the ceiling. The tub, long and narrow like a coffin, was made of beautiful stone and had three stone steps at one end.

One of the women stepped forward. "Italiana?" she said without smiling.

"No, American."

"American! We do not see many Americans. Is this your first time?"

I marveled at her perfect English. Like many of the attendants at Lourdes, she had come here as a volunteer for several weeks; the languages she spoke were indicated on her lapel with little flags: Italian, British, French, and Spanish. Feeling like a small child, I said yes, it was my first time.

"Do not worry," the woman said, holding my bare elbow and steering me to the top of the steps, while the two other attendants stepped back to make room. "Take it slowly and please step down one step."

I stepped down and was up to my shins in icy water. The water looked clear and clean, but I had no idea how often it was changed or how many people had entered it before me. Suddenly and without warning, the attendent ripped the blue sheet from my shoulders, lifted my arms above my head, and for perhaps half a second I stood on the step stark naked until the two other attendants came up behind me and slapped a cold, wet sheet around my body, the shock of which was so assaultive that my jaw dropped and I actually staggered.

The attendant smiled in wan apology and told me to offer a prayer. I think that was what she said, though it may have been "Make a petition." I was finding it very difficult to concentrate or to respond appropriately. The whole thing had the mood of a twisted Nazi experiment. All three of the Italian women seemed to be staring at me with what suddenly looked like a zealous gleam in their eyes. I could really pray only when no one was looking, when no one expected me to. Under the circumstances, I found it nearly impossible to pray. I lowered my head and pretended.

"Now," said the woman, "before you go in you can make the sign of the cross if you want."

I made the sign of the cross.

"And before you exit you can please kiss the statue of the Blessed Virgin."

I looked for the statue. Seeing nothing, I said, "What statue?"

She pointed toward the far end of the tub. I peered across the icily glittering water and in the dim light I saw a tiny statue of the Virgin Mary in her usual blue and white robes. The statue was half the size of a Barbie doll. I might as easily swallow it as kiss it.

The two assistants stood on either side of me, held my wrists, raised my arms above my head, and led me down the slippery steps into the water. When I was in up to my waist the woman whom I had come to think of as Matron said in that careful classroom English, "Sit down, please."

I craned my neck around to look at her, "Sit down?"

"Yes, please. Sit." The patiently stern look on her face seemed to say that I had broken the rules, and perhaps the spell, by speaking in the middle of my important bath. This was not a time for idle chatter.

I thought, *Christ Jesus,* and, rigid with distaste and still handcuffed by the two attendants, I sat down up to my yawning armpits in the startling water, my body displacing enough water that little waves splashed over the edge of the tub and onto the stone floor. All three attendants leaned over me and said softly together in a sort of incantatory chant, *"Notre Dame de Lourdes, prega per noi. Santa Bernadette, prega per noi."*

I sat there, my mind racing, in no way thinking about the Blessed Virgin. When it was clear that they were not going to say anything else I struggled to my feet, walked to the end of the tub, and, feeling a little insane, kissed the statue, which was only slightly bigger than my own nose. She teetered and fell over as my lips bumped into her. I stood her upright, hoping the attendants hadn't noticed the insult. After standing there for a respectful amount of time I turned around, waded back to the steps, and climbed out of the tub. The two attendants removed the wet sheet, put the blue one back on me, and sent me out through the curtain. As I was leaving I saw them wringing the sheet out by twisting it like a length of rope over the tub, preparing it for the next person.

Back in the changing room a woman unfastening her bra was sobbing softly. I dressed quickly and went out, and as soon as I stood in the hot sun my legs began to tingle pleasantly. Suddenly overcome with fatigue, I, who find it nearly impossible to sleep anywhere but in my own bed, crossed the river on the footbridge, lay down in the middle of the neatly mown lawn, and with my face pressed into the hot grass and the droning sound of prayers from the grotto in my ear, fell into a sound sleep.

AN HOUR LATER I went to collect some holy water from the fountain near the cathedral and saw Carla and her mother filling their own little bottles to take home with them. Carla's hair was damp. I asked how her bath was. She told me that she had cried in the bath because it was frightening and cold. "And my specs got awfully wet," she said. "And coming out of the bath I took a fierce tumble on the steps, and the lady and Mum had to catch me. But afterward, when we came out to the sun and the people, I felt nearly special."

"Me too," I said.

Carla and her mother went off to their hotel, and I went off to the post office, where I placed a note and a small plastic bottle of Lourdes holy water in an envelope and addressed it to my mother.

WEEKS LATER, after returning from my trip, I went to see my mother, who was then seventy-seven. She was sitting in her bedroom dressing when I arrived, fastening the brace to her leg. When I came in, she pointed to the table beside her bed and said, "Open that drawer, Rose, and give me the ruler in there."

I opened the drawer, which for thirty years has been filled with the same collection of amazing and useless artifacts. The ruler was a new addition. I handed it to her.

"Not that one," she said, "the *thin* one."

I went back to the drawer, and as I dug through its contents I realized that there were three foot-long rulers there, all of them plastic. They all looked the same to me. Why my mother needed three rulers by her bed was a mystery. With no idea what she wanted it for, I handed her a second ruler. I had learned not to ask. My mother knows her own methods so well and relies on them so heavily that no one can deter her.

"No, Rose. Not this one. The thin ruler."

There was only one ruler left. I gave it to her.

"That's it."

My mother moves slowly in her old age, has become precise and meticulous in her way of doing things. I watched as she used the tip of the ruler to tuck the long ends of the three leather brace straps between her thigh and the metal side bar of the brace. I marveled at how she had developed this method, and how important tidiness was in her physical appearance. She was battling matter, gaining control over it, ordering her world.

As she worked I asked her whether she had received the holy water I had sent. She had. "What did you do with it?" I said.

She shrugged. "I put it on my leg, just as you told me to do."

"And what happened?"

With that deadpan gaze of hers that was as much a sizing up as a cutting down to size, my mother, sitting in her wheelchair with the ruler in her hand and the brace securely fastened on her lame leg, said, "I flew up the chimney."

"Come on," I said. "What really happened?"

"Do you think, Rose, that if something had happened I'd be sitting here in this chair right now?"

"Why do you suppose nothing happened?"

"You know why."

"The scont."

She laughed and nodded, as if to say, *Of course.*

Though I knew the answer, I asked my mother what she believed in. She pointed to the small crucifix that hung over her bed. Never particularly fussy about the placement of furniture and pictures in her house, my mother had been adamant that that wall hold nothing but the crucifix. "I believe in God," she said. "I live by the cross."

"Do you think God has done anything for you?"

"I can't know if he has done anything for me, but I hope so."

"What about polio? Why did he let that happen to you?"

"Every single night that I'm alone here I think *Why me?* like they do in the comics. Why was *I* paralyzed? And yet polio could have killed me. But it didn't kill me."

Two of my mother's sisters had died of polio. "Was it God who saved you?" I said.

"I can't answer that. I don't know that he involves himself so minutely. But I do believe that God is love. And when I get into bed at night my last thought is a prayer. I say to God, 'See me, hear me, know that I am here.'"

"Do you think he sees you?"

She didn't hesitate in her answer. "Without question."

My mother's future has grown short; a cure at this late date would probably not change many things for her, and she seems now to have little interest in one. She, who is fond of quoting Jesus' phrase "Where there is love, there also is your treasure," has found her health elsewhere.

· 3 ·

EL CAMINO DE SANTIAGO

The night train from Lourdes to St. Jean Pied-de-Port was only one car long. It was an old car, with leather seats and ashtrays that flipped up on the armrests and windows that opened. It smelled pleasantly of dry dust and rusted metal. We were posting briskly through the deep countryside of southern France, but the ceiling lights of the train were so bright and the September night so dark that all I could see out the window was the reflection of my own face. I imagined what we might look like to a shepherd standing nearby on a hill: a little carriage, mostly empty, glowing like a lantern as it wended its way west through the heavy thickets of trees. There were five other passengers on the train that night: a young, chain-smoking teenaged couple, a tall nun, and, across the aisle from me, two dapper British men sharing a bottle of wine. The men had spread paper napkins across their laps and were sipping discreetly from plastic glasses. They were discussing (or dissecting) a person named Ronald, whom they both hated. Ronald was "execrable," a "disgrace," a "parasite." He had despicable taste. He was — the dashing, white-haired man hated to say this about anyone — vulgar.

At the front of the car the nun sat stiffly in her raincoat and wimple, reading a French newspaper, her shoulders and head swaying with the jouncing rhythm of the little train. She seemed to be dancing quietly in her seat.

The shorter of the two British men lifted his glass to his lips, sniffed at the wine, and said loudly into the glass, "What time do we arrive at Saint Jean, Henry?"

His companion held his watch to his face and pursed his moist lips in calculation. "Well! We were to arrive at ten-oh-six, but we were twenty minutes late leaving out of Lourdes, so we'll be there about . . ."

The other man winced and banged his fist theatrically on his thigh. "I don't want *about,* Henry!" he cried. "I . . . want . . . precise . . . time!"

Henry looked slightly drunk. His teeth were yellowish in his intelligent-looking red face. He grabbed the wine bottle by its neck, said cheerily, "Oh, bugger off, Charles," and slowly, with his elbow bobbing, sloshed more wine into his glass.

We teetered our way through the dark. Now and then the long branches of trees slapped and scraped at the windows. Occasionally a lighted platform blurred suddenly by, or a string of streetlights, or the lighted windows of a farmhouse glowing in the distance like little fires in the woods.

In preparation for the walking pilgrimage I would begin the next day in St. Jean, I studied my guidebook, a tall, narrow paperback called *A Practical Guide for Pilgrims: The Road to Santiago* by Millán Bravo Lozano. The Camino de Santiago is a medieval trail that crosses from France over the Pyrenees into Spain, traverses the breadth of the Iberian Peninsula, and ends at the cathedral in the city of Santiago de Compostela. For centuries Compostela was one of the three great pilgrimage centers of Christianity; in its heyday it rivaled both Rome and Jerusalem in popularity and importance. The city gained its fame during the ninth century, when the remains of St. James the Apostle were rumored to have been found in a tomb there.

James (the Greater) was a Galilean fisherman and a close acquaintance of Jesus, but the Spanish legend that grew up about his person transmogrified him into a valiant and terrifying Christian soldier, Santiago Matamoros, the Moor slayer on horseback who helped to defend and recapture Spain from the grasp of the Muslim invaders. The legend was fantastical. How James's remains (he was executed by Herod Agrippa I) made their way from Jerusalem to northwestern Spain is a question without an answer; scholars and historians believe that in fact they didn't. Yet, like so much of religious "history," the legend held fast and grew, and by the time of the Crusades and Saladin's conquest of Jerusalem in 1187, Saint James had become a fighting symbol for a Christian Europe that felt threatened by the spread of Islam.

The act of pilgrimage was an important element of the medieval church, usually with a focus on relics and remains of saints. At the height of this pilgrimage's popularity, some half a million people annually traveled the famed routes to Santiago from all over Europe, intending to venerate the saint's remains. To serve the great numbers of travelers a pilgrimage industry developed all along the way — hospital complexes, churches, hospices, shrines, and monasteries. Anyone who considered himself a good Christian hoped to make the journey to Santiago. Saint Francis of Assisi had done so, as had the less than exemplary Wife of Bath, according to Chaucer.

In recent years the pilgrimage to Santiago has enjoyed a great resurgence of interest. In 1982 only 3,500 pilgrims received official documentation at Santiago, but in 1999 roughly 100,000 would complete the journey. Anyone is free to walk the Camino de Santiago, but only those who have obtained the proper credentials are considered official pilgrims who are welcome at the various pilgrims' hostels or *refugios,* some of them ancient, along the route. The average trip takes four to six weeks, but some people spend three months on the trail, while others walk it in stages over a period of years.

I had obtained my documentation, a six-page pamphlet, from the Confraternity of St. James in London. The pamphlet's first page read:

CONFRATERNITY OF ST. JAMES

Founded in 1983 to promote the pilgrim routes to Santiago de Compostela
President: His Excellency the Spanish Ambassador

PILGRIM'S RECORD   CARTE DE PELERIN
CARTA DE PEREGRINO

This is to certify that: Rosemary Mahoney of New York of the Confraternity of St. James (London) is making the pilgrimage to Santiago de Compostela *entreprend le pelerinage a Saint-Jacques de Compostelle sigue el peregrinaje "Camino de Santiago"*
From: St. Jean Pied de Port

Six blank pages followed, awaiting the official stamps that I would receive from refugios or churches along the way to verify my presence and my progress. I expected my trip to take approximately a month.

As I studied my book and my maps of the trail, the teenaged French girl sitting toward the back of the train suddenly let out a murderous shriek, causing the rest of us to wheel around in our seats.

"Qu'est-ce qui se passe?" cried the nun, clutching her newspaper, her pale face a mask of shock and horror.

The long-haired girl hunched low in her seat and tittered behind her hand. Her boyfriend, she explained through her fingers, had just poked her.

Charles, the shorter of the two British men, said gleefully, "Poked you with what, dearie?"

The girl, pouting now, fitted the end of a lock of hair into her mouth. "His stupid elbow."

The slouching, round-shouldered boyfriend smirked wolfishly at the window.

Charles raised his glass. "Well, that's grand, darlings! Keep it up."

Henry shut his eyes and sighed. "Must one always make an ass of oneself, Charles?"

With a disapproving cluck the nun returned to her newspaper. I returned to my guidebook.

THE FOLLOWING MORNING, with my pack on my back, I stepped out of my hotel in St. Jean Pied-de-Port and felt suddenly depressed. The town was tightly hemmed in by tall green mountains padded with dense forest and capped with mist. The sky was congested and dark, the bloated clumps of black cloud hovering so close to the ground it almost seemed I could reach up and stir them with a stick. It felt a bit like Vermont, closeted and close. I prefer wide-open spaces, long vistas, the sea, cornfields, the desert.

Why I had expected to find something different in St. Jean that morning I'm not sure. I knew that my long walk began in the Pyrenees, and I knew what those mountains looked like. Nevertheless, I was very gloomy starting out that morning. My trip across Spain was about 475 miles long, and the bundle of maps that I had for it — thirty-one little charts divided into 30-kilometer sections — was the thickness of a grilled cheese sandwich. The maps indicated the pilgrim's trail in a winding line of pink dots that intersected and sometimes paralleled the main roads. Sometimes the trail was the road itself, other times it was a trail through fields or plains or woods. I checked the first map and

headed out of St. Jean on a road that would wind south through the
mountains, cross the Spanish border, and travel over the Valcarlos Pass
and finally over the Ibañeta Pass and the Pyrenean divide to the Augustinian monastery at Roncesvalles, a distance of twelve and a half miles.

The start of this small road cut through a lush, narrow valley of
damp meadows and towering trees. It was steamy and still and overgrown with creeping vines and billowing, dripping greenery in every direction. Underfoot was long, wet grass and mud and pine needles.
Along the side of the road lay great piles of enormous logs. Occasionally
a huge truck blew by loaded with logs, but otherwise the road was
empty and there were very few houses in sight. The mountains ahead of
me, though not terribly high, were remarkably steep. I felt suffocated,
and I thought that if the landscape and the dark weather were like this
all the way across Spain, I would lose my mind.

I had been walking for less than an hour when the rain came, falling
in heavy, gray sheets from a sky that was a biblical turmoil of thunder
and lightning. Though I was wearing a brimmed hat, within thirty seconds my head, face, and boots were soaked. In my little backpack I had
a knife, a flashlight, batteries, two pairs of underwear, one pair of socks,
a pair of shorts, a T-shirt, a small, lightweight fleece blanket, an emergency aluminum blanket that folded up to the size of a deck of cards, my
passport, a camera, six pens, two small notebooks, a toothbrush, toothpaste, a tiny bar of soap, six Band-Aids, a film canister full of aspirin,
and a pair of sandals. I was determined to travel light; the pack — the
sort that children carry their books to school in — weighed five pounds.
(Later I was shocked to learn that most of the pilgrims on the Camino
carried some thirty pounds on their backs, and many carried much
more.) The bulk of the weight I carried was the clothing I wore: jeans,
socks, boots, a T-shirt, a long-sleeved shirt, a sweater, a lightweight
woolen jacket, a small shawl around my shoulders, and a windbreaker.
I had never heard of a serious hiker going on a trek with an umbrella, so
I had not brought one. Now I wished I had one.

Just over the Spanish border I came to a service station and went in,
hoping against hope that they might have an umbrella to sell. They
didn't, of course, but when I went out again into the rain I saw a small
black umbrella lying open on the pavement not far from the door. I
went back inside and asked the shopkeeper, an old man with greasy
hands and a cigarette behind his ear, if the umbrella belonged to him.
No, he said, in Spanish, it didn't. I stared at him. He stared back at me

with puffy eyes. He had the physique of a greyhound. My wet clothes were leaving a little puddle on his linoleum floor. He must have known what I was thinking, but he simply licked his greasy finger and went back to turning the pages of his ledger.

I couldn't think of anything else to say because I didn't speak Spanish, which I sensed was going to present something of a problem in Spain.

I went outside and sat on a wet stump beneath a tree and waited to see if anyone would come along to claim the umbrella. There was no one in sight. The station was empty and so was the road. There was nothing here but green trees with dripping leaves. The rain came down in torrents, blackening the air and splashing angrily on the pavement. I had tied the thin hood of my windbreaker tight around my face, but the hood was soaked through now, and the rain trickled down the back of my neck and inside the collar of my shirt. I had seven or eight more miles to go that day. Finally I struggled up from my stump, snatched up the umbrella, and hurried down the road with it, hoping that God would forgive me for beginning my holy pilgrimage with the sin of theft.

These dark hills were not my favorite landscape, but as I settled into the rhythm of walking and listened to the rain hurtling down onto my umbrella with the staticky sound of sizzling fat, I began thinking, *Well, I suppose it's pretty enough*. Clumps of lavender grew along the sides of the road, and tall reeds hung with giant, lacelike spiderwebs, and soon the road began to be littered with slugs the size of cigars, which would have been a hideous sight except that the slugs were the startling color of ripe tomatoes. Some were the bold orange of persimmons, and a few odd ones were onyx-black and patent-leather shiny. They had long, fleshy antennae, like fingers spread in a victory sign, and they slid along the wet pavement leaving thick slicks of mucus behind them. They were so startling and wondrous that it didn't occur to me to be disgusted by them.

Soon the rain let up, and I passed a beautiful stream. Two fat Spanish men in white jumpsuits pulled up in a little pickup truck and asked in French if this was the way to Pamplona. I had no idea where I was, but I knew that the road would eventually lead to Pamplona, so I said in bad French, "Yes, Pamplona is this way." The driver tipped his great bulk across his passenger's lap and peered up at me. He had the dry, singed face of a smoker. "Eet ees dees way?"

"Yes," I said.

"You like to take a ride?" He gestured at the two-inch stretch of seat that remained open between him and his friend. I saw myself squeezed in between them all the way to Pamplona. In my heart I wanted to take the ride, but I had vowed to travel only by foot. If I covered any mileage by other means I could no longer call myself a true pilgrim. The point, as I understood it, was to make the journey in the manner of the medieval Christians, to mortify the flesh and make oneself vulnerable in the service of a greater spiritual connection to God. Of course, no one else would know if I cheated and took a ride, but I would know, and I wanted to walk the entire trail from start to finish under my own steam. Besides, I liked walking. I said, "No, thanks," and the two men shrugged their fat shoulders and drove on.

After another two hours the pilgrim's path left the road and followed a narrow dirt trail through a deep woods. The entrance to the trail was marked with a scallop shell, the symbol of Santiago, which would appear several hundred times along the Camino. I followed the path down to a small stream, where a handpainted wooden sign said promisingly SANTIAGO. The yellow arrow on the sign pointed to an even smaller path that led up a steep hill. Santiago was 470 miles away; it was weird to see a sign for it here in this dense woodland in the middle of nowhere.

The trail climbed and grew rocky. Cobwebs broke across my face, and wet ferns slapped water onto my pants. I heard the tinkling of sheep bells in the deep ravine below me, and then the path grew incredibly steep. The beech and chestnut trees gave way to huge spruces that blocked out what little light there was from the hovering gray sky. This forest certainly was dense. And dark. And clearly the trail was not well traveled. In fact, it looked as though no one had walked this way for years. Where were all the pilgrims I had been told I'd run into? Close to a hundred thousand people walked to Santiago that year, and on that first day on the trail I saw not a single one of them.

The rain started again, but the trees were so close together that it would have been nearly impossible to use my umbrella. The tree trunks were black with damp. Sheep droppings appeared on the trail, and tiny purple flowers like crocuses. I crashed along the narrow path — it really wasn't more than six inches wide — fighting back the long arms of the spruce trees, panting, slipping in the mud, crushing the cabbagey weeds underfoot, grabbing at saplings to keep myself from falling backward. Steam began to rise from my cuffs and the throat of my jacket, and for the first time my pack felt heavy. Wet leaves slapped me in the face, rain dripped from the trees. The earth was spongy and mossy and muddy. My pants from the knees down were so wet they stuck to my legs. It was spooky and dark, and as the afternoon progressed it grew darker. Snapping sounds came out of the depths of the woods, and from a nearby stream the murderous rattling of kingfishers. A crow screeched. I hated the place.

I had always hated the woods. In the woods you can't see anything but what is directly before your face. You can't tell if something is creeping up on you, can't see any snakes that might be lurking near your feet. The sky is a tiny puddle above your head, and as you walk you have no sense of progress, for what lies ahead looks precisely like what is behind you. There is no horizon or liberating vista.

All the pictures I had seen of people walking the Camino showed wide-open plains and dry vineyards and smooth trails, and that was one of the reasons I had come. I loved walking, and I loved open spaces. But this forest was all cramped and desolate and old. It felt haunted, like the place Rip Van Winkle had passed out in — Creepy Hollow or whatever it was. People had been walking this trail for a thousand years, yet it looked as if I were the first person who had ever been here. That worried me. I had not once thought about possible perils, and since there is an inn to sleep in every night at conveniently spaced intervals along the Camino, I hadn't brought a tent. I hadn't even brought a sleeping bag. I had nothing warm with me but a blanket. This particular place was much wilder than I had expected it to be, and the very sound of my own footsteps was beginning to frighten me. Thinking I must be on the wrong trail, I stopped and looked at my map again. But I had done exactly what the map had told me to do; it had to be the right way.

I carried on. And then, as I reached the top of a rise, breathless and gasping and muttering, I looked up from the path and saw, not three feet from my face, two big yellow eyes staring at me. I jumped backward. A few terrible moments passed before I realized that the eyes belonged to a ram. He was standing by a raspberry bush and blinking in the rain. He tried to run from me, but something was wrong with his legs. When I went nearer I realized that a thorny rope of brambles had gotten wound around his two hind legs, creating a tangled hobble so complicated and complete that the ram was thoroughly trapped, paralyzed by a shrub. The harder he pulled at the brambles, the tighter they held him. He looked miserable. His long beige face was covered with mud, and broken strands of brambles were tangled in his matted wet hair. He blinked his big yellow eyes at me. It was impossible to know how long he had been there, but by the looks of it he would be stuck here until he died of starvation if someone didn't help him. I looked back down the trail. There wasn't a soul around, and it didn't seem likely that any souls would be arriving soon. If anyone was going to help this animal, it would have to be me.

I stared at him, not knowing exactly what to do. Each time I stepped closer he bucked wildly and threw himself back into the bush, his steaming nostrils flaring, eyes rolling wildly in his head. The very sight of me terrified him. He was only a sheep, yet, strangely, something about his being trapped and desperate and all alone in this gloomy place made him equally terrifying to me.

I took off my backpack, opened it, fished out my knife, and walked slowly toward the animal, trying to remember if I had ever heard of a sheep biting a person. Goats could bite, I thought. Why not sheep? As I approached him, he lunged at me with his two big khaki-colored horns, and I danced away with the knife slashing wildly at the air above my head. Three times I tried to approach him. Three times he butted me. On the fourth try I managed to grab one damp horn and hold him still. I sawed at the brambles with my knife until finally the whole mess came loose. The animal, free now, crashed crazily away from me through the dense shrubbery and down the side of the mountain, trailing long strands of thorny brambles from his legs.

I listened as the awful crashing noises receded into the glen, and when I put my knife away I realized that my hands were trembling. Trembling over a sheep.

AT FIVE O'CLOCK I reached the Ibañeta Pass, which marks the divide of the Pyrenees. The sky was growing very dark. According to my map it was less than half a mile to the monastery at Roncesvalles, where, according to my guidebook, I could spend the night. I hurried down a wide, muddy path, and when the huge stone building loomed up in the distance at the edge of an open field I was startled into stillness. Built in 1127, it was an immense castle with pointed towers and high walls and very small windows. Gloomy, dark, and solitary, it looked uninviting, but for eight hundred years it had served as a refuge for pilgrims traveling to Santiago.

I passed through a porte-cochère into the courtyard and found the pilgrims' registration office, a small, dimly lit stone cell where fifteen people in hiking boots and hats and dripping rain ponchos were milling about, looking exhausted and slightly worried as they waited to have their pilgrim records stamped. Both the officiating priest, a cranky, elderly Spaniard who looked as if he wanted to strangle someone, and the intense medieval gloom of the place had caused everyone to speak in whispers. I was puzzled by the sight of these people. Where had they come from? I hadn't seen any of them on the trail.

The priest took my booklet, turned it over in his fingers, slowly examined every blank page, muttered something that sounded like a protest to his assistant, dropped the booklet on the table in front of him, banged it sourly with the official Roncesvalles stamp, tossed the booklet aside, and waved the next pilgrim forward.

The priest's assistant gave me a registration form and a printed sheet that said:

RONCESVALLES

There're not any blankets or sheets into the shelter. It's obligatory to have a sleeping bag.

Just take the assigned bed.

Don't leave anything in another bed.

Keep the shelter claned.

Shelter clouses at 10:00 PM. Leave the shelter at 8:00 AM.

You can't smoke or cook into the shelter. To reserve dinner, before 8:00 PM in the restaurants showing pilgrim's credential.

No animals accepted.

You should give some donation. It well help to shelter conservation.

As I sat at the long wooden table with the other pilgrims, filling out my registration form, the lights suddenly went out, plunging the entire monastery into damp darkness. A momentary silence followed, and then I heard tiny gasps and frightened tskings, scuffling footsteps, the rustling of rain slickers, and the annoyed mumbling of the priest. I reached into my bag, found my flashlight, and set it up on the table. By unscrewing the lens cover you could turn this tiny flashlight into a kind of electric candle that illuminated the room in a general way. Several of the pilgrims slid down the bench toward the ghostly little light and resumed scribbling at their forms. Their faces and heads gleamed with rainwater. Some were young, some looked surprisingly advanced in age. The priest appeared at my side and, through a translator, asked if he could examine the flashlight. I gave it to him. With the same slow, skeptical attention that he had given my pilgrim's document, he turned the device over in his fingers, frowning in wonder; finally, with the tiny bulb illuminating his bony face, he smiled with approval at the ingeniousness of it.

A new pilgrim with an enormous pack on his back came staggering through the door in a shower of rainwater, a walking stick in his hand and a flashlight strapped to his forehead. The lights flickered on again, but only for a few seconds. They died, flickered back on, and died a third time. Remembering who he was, the priest handed the flashlight back to me and marched through the gloom toward the door, muttering something that sounded distinctly like *Goddamn it!*

AFTER THE ELECTRICITY was restored I followed the other pilgrims up some winding wooden steps to the dormitory, a big, open, dimly lit atticlike room with rows of bunk beds crowded into it. More pilgrims were lying on the beds, some in their underwear, some in the wet clothes they had been walking in all day. The room was filled with muddy boots and stinking clothing and wet backpacks, and the windows had steamed over with the dampness. In a small common room between the bathroom and the dormitory, people sat at tables studying their maps beneath a dim bulb. Some were changing the Band-Aids on their blisters, others were taping their ankles. One man was morosely eating tuna fish from a can with a plastic fork. In the bathroom a handsome young Brazilian was staring at himself in the mirror and shouting in Portuguese into a cell phone. Beside him a barefoot German woman with damp hair dangling in her eyes was furiously scrubbing her underwear in the sink.

I took a shower, dressed, went back to the dormitory, sat on my bed, and stared at all the high-tech hiking equipment. Some people had metal walking sticks that resembled ski poles, with straps for the wrist and a little disk at the base to keep the pole from sinking into quicksand or mud. There were large, serious-looking vinyl backpacks with metal frames, filled to capacity with who knew what. There were cocoonlike sleeping bags that compressed to the size of a football. Some people wore gaiters around the tops of their boots. Some of the boots were as tall and sturdy as ski boots. There were ultraviolet-protected walking shorts with sixteen zippers and hidden Velcro-secured pockets. There were water bottles that clipped to the tops of the backpacks with built-in plastic drinking straws positioned conveniently within reach of the mouth. There were inflatable bedrolls and mesh laundry bags that clipped to the backpack frames. Some people had headlamps like those that coal miners wear. It was the equipment of experts. Sitting on my bed, I reviewed the meager contents of my backpack and felt slightly concerned. The only new thing I had bought for this trip was a thirty-five-dollar pair of discount hiking boots.

As I sorted through my things, a woman from New Zealand and her French boyfriend in the bunks next to mine stripped down to their underwear and complained to each other about not being able to cook here. She spoke English to him, he spoke French to her, and as they clawed out the contents of their enormous backpacks — a pot, a little camping stove, bags of noodles — they fretted and grumbled about money. If they couldn't cook, they would have to pay to eat in the pilgrims' dining room. The priest had asked for a donation of a thousand pesetas. The Camino was costing more than they had expected.

I mentioned to the woman from New Zealand that I hadn't seen a soul on the trail that afternoon. "That's funny," she said, "we saw loads of people. Which way did you go?" I took out my map and showed her. "Oh," she said knowingly, "*that* way. Well, we asked about that trail in Saint Jean, and the guy at the refugio told us that hardly anybody goes that way anymore."

"How come?" I said.

She shrugged to show that the answer was obvious. "It's harder?"

THAT NIGHT, in the thirteenth-century Royal Collegiate Church, the priests of the monastery of Roncesvalles held a service and blessing for the pilgrims. I arrived early and sat in a pew toward the front, next to an elderly local woman and her adult son. The dimly lit church was beautiful, with spare wooden pews, a smooth stone floor, an incredibly high vaulted ceiling, and tall, intricately designed stained glass windows in the delicate purples and pinks of orchids. The altar was decked with an abundance of brilliant flowers.

The town of Roncescalles is tiny — a smattering of red-roofed houses, an inn, a restaurant, and a bar, all situated around an open square. But the history and legend attached to the place are huge, immortalized in the *Chanson de Roland,* the early French epic poem that recounts the feats and defeats of the Carolingian king Charlemagne and his heroic commander, Roland. In 778, after invading Spain, Charlemagne and his troops were making their way back to France when their rear guard, said to be led by Roland, were cut off at a pass and slaughtered by the Basque army. The *Song of Roland* puts this pass at Roncesvalles and turns the Basques into the dreaded Muslim Saracens, who at that time dominated much of Iberia. It was here at Roncesvalles that the great Roland was said to have died after blowing his magical horn — too late — for help.

The pilgrim trade had also helped to bring fame and wealth to the town, with donations from the faithful pouring in from all over Europe. As a result the church, though it sat in the middle of a vast and unspoiled countryside, had the opulent feel of a cathedral in Paris.

The Spanish woman next to me had a kind of uncontrollable nasal tic; every thirty seconds or so she sniffed loudly, and her head jerked slightly backward with the effort. She and her son both wore black. They watched with keen interest as the pilgrims gathered in the pews for the service, many still dressed in their hiking clothes and some still wet from the trail. Seven elderly priests in white albs appeared and stood behind the altar.

During the Mass, in Spanish, the celebrant announced where each of the pilgrims had come from: New Zealand, France, Germany, Spain, Belgium, England, Switzerland, Italy, Ireland, Australia, Brazil, Holland. The only North Americans in the group were a Canadian nun and me. There were perhaps thirty pilgrims in the congregation, and all were sleeping in the dormitories that night. It was a standard number of guests at that time of year, but I had heard that during the summer the number could multiply into the hundreds.

Eventually the pilgrims were asked to come forward to the altar to be blessed. As we crowded together and bowed our heads, I thought about what we were doing. We were embarking on a long journey on foot in an ancient tradition begun, effectively, in defense of Christianity against the spread of Islam. The earliest recorded pilgrimages to Santiago took place in the mid-tenth century. Our goal was a thirteenth-century cathedral at the far end of 750 kilometers. We would pass through the provinces of Navarre, Rioja, Castille, Palencia, Léon, Lugo, and La Coruña. Along the way we would cross over five mountain passes that rose above 3,300 feet, the highest being more than 5,000 feet.

As the priest said his benediction, I looked at my feet and knew that I could not explain why I was about to walk all the way across Spain. The original Christian pilgrims, those who had transformed this route into a historical and international phenomenon, knew exactly why they were doing it; they wanted to pay homage to the martyred bones of the great Saint James. It was a religious endeavor. They walked because they had to; for most, it was the only way to get to Santiago. Anyone who had a horse or a donkey would make the journey on an animal's back. Santiago was not far from the coast of Spain, and many pilgrims went by ship from points along the coast of Europe and the Mediterranean. The pilgrimage journey was taxing and arduous because it had to be, not because the pilgrims wanted it to be. If automobiles had existed in the eleventh century, the pilgrims most certainly would have hopped into their cars and driven to Santiago, just as pilgrims do now when they go to Rome or Jerusalem or any of the other destinations of pilgrimage.

That the early pilgrims had traveled to Santiago the hard way was in large part what made the journey interesting. It was a long trip with many hazards; there were bandits and charlatans, kooks and cheats, festivals, toll bridges, romances, sideshows, and natural, architectural, and cultural phenomena that must have been marvelous to the foreign eye. If you walked or rode a donkey across a great distance, you couldn't help but become intimately engaged with your surroundings and fellow pilgrims. Upon returning home, the pilgrims found themselves enriched; they saw things in a new way, they had stories to tell and memories to entertain and perhaps chasten themselves with. The religious journey became a form of adventure.

In *Chaucer: His Life, His Works, His World,* the historian Donald Howard writes of medieval pilgrimage in general as having been, in addition to a religious exercise, "a form of vacation or travel."

The institution had its dark, unrespectable underside, against which moralists inveighed and both church and state passed restrictive laws, quite in vain. Pilgrims not only told tales to keep themselves amused, they flirted and gambled, ate and drank to excess, swore, misbehaved even in the shrines themselves: we read of sexual escapades in dark corners, of pilgrims by the thousands carving their names or coats of arms on the tombs of saints. The sin of "curiosity" was an inevitable temptation to which almost all pilgrims gave way; moving from place to place, especially in strange countries, the traveler saw sights that were a distraction to worship. [p. 403]

Standing in the church in Roncesvalles that night and looking at the faces around me, I doubted that any person there had a burning desire to reach the city of Santiago and the crypt of Saint James. We were going not for the arrival but for the experience of getting there. Our journey would be arduous because we wanted it to be. It seemed to me that walking to Santiago by choice in the twentieth century was — among many other things — a reenactment of sorts, not unlike the efforts of American Civil War buffs who dress in period uniforms and stage mock battles at Antietam.

AFTER THE SERVICE the pilgrims were served an inexpensive dinner in a small dining room attached to a bar. We sat at seven or eight round tables and ate fried trout, French fries, bread, barley soup, and vanilla ice cream. Carafes of meaty new wine went around the room, and hanging lamps threw a soft yellow light onto the pilgrims' journey-reddened faces. Like the dormitory, the room was steamy with dampness and heat.

I sat at a table with three French people from Cognac who were traveling the Camino on bicycles. They spoke very little English, they said. Quickly I realized that in fact they spoke *no* English. I told them that if they spoke slowly, I might be able to speak French with them.

Claude, the older of the two French men, was still in his riding suit: tight black shorts and a tight nylon jacket with a zipper that traveled to his chin. He had a beefy face and a dense five o'clock shadow. He was an engineer who designed, from what I could make out, either bottles or buttons. He was traveling the Camino, he said, for fitness. The younger man, Jacques, and his wife, Pauline, were both math professors. They were here on holiday and were not sure they would go all the way to Santiago, which they referred to as Saint-Jacques de Compostelle. Jacques was genial and gentle and a little bit giggly. The gaps between his very small teeth gave him the innocent, dissolute-looking grin of a happy jack-o'-lantern. His eyeglasses were normal in every way but for dime-sized, remarkably thick magnifying lenses set into the middle of the bigger lenses. They were very distracting, like two soap bubbles that had been blown there on a breeze, and when Jacques raised his head to look through them, his eyes were grotesquely magnified.

In his spare time Jacques was a beekeeper. That night he wore a T-shirt that said SI TCHERNOBYL VOUS A FAIT RIRE, ESSAYEZ SUPER-PHÉNIX. Beneath the lettering was a deadly-looking skull and crossbones. Superphénix, Pauline explained, was the controversial French nuclear power plant.

Jacques lifted his head, giving me a positively scientific view of his hugely magnified retinas, and told me in French about the beauty of honeybees. I would have found that subject interesting, I think, but Jacques spoke very quickly, and I could follow only half of what he was saying. Claude, who until then had remained silent, began to tell me about the beauty of bottles, the difference between green glass and clear glass, molded glass and blown glass, why some bottles have a seam in them and some don't. That too would probably have been very interesting, but not only did Claude speak too quickly, I couldn't understand his accent. He might as well have been speaking Japanese.

I ate my soup, ripped at my bread, drank my wine, nodded with what I hoped were appropriate expressions of curiosity and interest, and listened to the rising volume of conversations around me in French and Spanish and Portuguese. I was sure that I would go all the way to Santiago like a deaf-mute. Suddenly I was ready for bed.

BY THE TIME I climbed onto my creaking bunk, a huge storm had settled over Roncesvalles. Though it was "obligatory to have a sleeping bag" I did not have one. I thought, "Tant pis," and laid my little fleece blanket and my shawl over myself and my slightly damp wool jacket over that and tried to sleep. But the wind rattled the windows and hurled the rain against the roof, and great gouts of rainwater shot out of the gutters and went smashing down onto the cobblestone courtyard below with the clatter of aluminum pie plates. From several indistinct points in the room came snoring so loud the place sounded like a construction site. There was teeth grinding, creaking bedsprings, a musical array of loud farts, and the smell of sweaty socks.

Several hours later, as I was finally drifting off, someone cried out in his sleep, "Il n'y a pas de design!" In the darkness the cry sounded particularly despairing.

THE NEXT EVENING, in the hostel at Pamplona, I asked a young Spanish woman if she spoke English. Clearly and glumly she said, "No, I am very sorry I do not speak English," and continued to doggedly unload the contents of her pack.

I had seen this girl several times that day on the road, and each time she looked miserable. Once I had said hello, but she didn't answer me, so I kept walking. She was very small. Though it wasn't raining, she wore a yellow rain slicker with the hood pulled up over her head. Her face, a tiny, dark-eyed oval in the shadows beneath her hood, was the pale and doleful face of a medieval saint. Her chin was faintly whiskery. She wore small glasses, riding jodhpurs with leather patches at the insides of the knees, and a pair of high and rather delicate-looking lace-up boots. At some point I stopped to eat a sandwich in a café along the way, and when I neared Pamplona I saw that this girl was ahead of me again. Her pack was very big for such a small person. To the back of it she had tied a pair of sneakers, which dangled and rocked and banged against the pack as she walked. For twenty-five minutes I watched the sneakers swinging crazily in front of me. That the girl wasn't bothered by them fascinated me. Big nuisances I could tolerate — running out of gas and having to walk fourteen miles for help, dealing with a roof leak in the middle of the night, needing an emergency appendectomy. But little nuisances irked me: a crooked picture on a wall made me itch to straighten it, the rumbling of a refrigerator motor made me want to yank the plug out of the wall. A newspaper flapping in the wind, the static of an ill-tuned radio, my own hair hanging in my eyes, the sound of a fly buzzing against a windowpane — all those little things could drive me mad. If my sneakers had been swaying and banging on my pack like that, I would have stopped and hurled them into the bushes. But the Spanish girl walked on, seemingly undisturbed. In fact, she kept up a quick pace, and we arrived at the refugio in Pamplona at the same time.

Now she was sitting on her bunk and rooting in her pack. Her T-shirt said in English BROWN BEARS HAVE BEEN SUCCESSFUL IN THE PLAINS AND FORESTS, which seemed like a laconic commentary on the vulnerability of the pilgrim.

I said, "Okay. But can you just tell me how to say 'post office' in Spanish?"

"In Spanish," she said, "the word for post office is *correo*."

I thanked her. She said without affect, "You are most welcome," and put her face into the bag.

I looked at her. She still looked very unhappy. "I thought you didn't speak English," I said, trying to be friendly.

She lifted her head again and stared glumly at me. "I do not."

Her English sounded fine to me. I sensed that if I asked her how to say "fishing pole" in Spanish, she could tell me. I was tempted to say, "Are you *sure* you don't speak English?" but I recognized the inward-looking aspect of someone preoccupied with a deep unhappiness, and I feared that my silly chatter would annoy her. All day long she had been alone, and here in the hostel she seemed to be avoiding contact with the other pilgrims. She spoke English; she simply didn't want to speak in any language.

I, too, liked being alone, but that evening I was so happy that I couldn't help wandering through the hostel glad-handing everyone I met, whether or not they spoke English. After the night in Roncesvalles the sky had cleared and the countryside, glittering in the sunlight, had improved; the mountains had receded, the trees began to thin out in a thrilling way, and fields and farms appeared. I was happy that after getting slightly lost outside of Pamplona, I had made it here safely. And I was very happy with the dormitory. It was a huge seminary, the Seminario de Pamplona, and the pilgrims were housed in a large auditorium full of bunk beds, all neatly made up with crisp sheets and woolen army blankets. It was like a military infirmary, and the moment I saw it I loved it. Something about the great size of the room, the hundreds of beds, the highly polished floor, satisfied a weird desire in me for institutional order.

I wandered around the room and stopped to talk with a friendly young Belgian man sitting on his bed. He held his right foot in his lap and was using a sewing needle to guide a length of black thread through the enormous bubble of a blister on his heel. All around the room other pilgrims were engaged in the same strange pursuit. It looked awful to me, but they all claimed it was the best remedy for blisters.

"Want to sew some thread through your blisters?" the young man said to me. I declined the offer and said that my blisters weren't bad, which was true. I had no real blisters yet.

"Where you came from today?" he asked.

"Roncesvalles."

He lifted his head and let out a long, low whistle.

It was far — twenty-four miles or so — farther than I had planned to walk. Many pilgrims leaving Roncesvalles made their next stop at Larrasoana, some thirteen miles away, but I was so happy to be out of the woods, and I felt so well and so free that I plowed on, marveling at the slugs, which outside of Pamplona had suddenly become a dark greenish blue, and taking in the Basque separatist graffiti that I began seeing past the town of Zubiri — EUSKAL and ETA and one in German in big violent-looking red letters: FREIHEIT FURS BASKELAND. Before I knew it I was crossing the Puente de la Magdalena into Pamplona.

I slept soundly that night and didn't wake until eight o'clock the next morning. I was surprised and then pleased to find myself alone in the huge dormitory. Everyone else was long gone.

ON MY THIRD DAY on the trail I was thrilled to be walking through precisely the sort of deserty landscape I had hoped for. The weather had turned clear and cool, the sky was high and breathtakingly blue, and the air held the first touch of autumn. I heard the early autumn sound of crickets in the brownish grass. Leaving Pamplona I had climbed a short ridge and seen a row of slender power-generating windmills. And after the town of Puente la Reina, the earth was the rich brown of chocolate cake, and there were olive trees and apple trees and pear trees heavy with fruit, and small vineyards full of ripe grapes. I was in my element. It was warm enough now that I was able to wear shorts. The air and the blackberry bushes were full of yellow butterflies. Just outside the little town of Cirauqui (according to my guidebook the name meant "vipers' nest" in Basque) the trail followed a Roman road flanked by small cypresses. The huge stones of this road had been worn concave, like shallow bowls. The trees were filled with tiny birds with tufted heads and dusty green backs and orange streaks on their pointed beaks, and high above me white-bellied buteos hung in the air, their barred tails fanned open as they teetered and waited for mice. Everything was new to me, I could see for miles, and I was alone and walking, following the helpful yellow Camino arrows. Singing a little song as I walked down the Roman road, I could hear the happiness in my voice.

BY THE FOURTH DAY my life as a walking pilgrim began to take on a pattern and a rhythm. Despair and elation both passed, and I settled into a more reasonable, less hysterical mood. In the hostels some pilgrims began stirring before dawn, flushing toilets, packing their bags, folding up their sleeping bags, and putting on their windbreakers with a lot of noisy rustling and zipping. Then off they would go, clawing their way down the path through the dark at five-thirty or six. I was quite happy to leave the hostel by seven-thirty with the just-risen sun creeping up behind me and helpfully illuminating the road. Every morning I limped to the bathroom gingerly so that the excruciatingly painful blisters on my heels — the size of Kennedy half-dollars — which had dried and hardened during the night, wouldn't split open and bleed. Stiffly, I put my stinking clothes back on, spent close to twenty minutes getting my boots back onto my brittle feet, peeled another little map from my by now very untidy packet, and roughly planned the day's trip — where I'd have breakfast and lunch, where I'd buy water, where I would sleep that night. Then I packed my bag, brushed my teeth (and sometimes didn't), said goodbye to the innkeeper and whomever else was still at the hostel, and went off through the town. Each morning, because of my blisters, I started out limping like an old woman. After an hour the blisters grew moist and flexible, the pain dissipated, and I was able to increase my speed. I would find a café in which to have coffee and bread, and then, five or six hours later, I would find a place for lunch, usually a bar, where I'd bleat an approximation of a Spanish greeting at the bartender, have two or three bottles of water, a can of Coke, two glasses of orange juice, three chorizo sandwiches, a weird array of Spanish garnishes (for example, two gherkins, two green olives, a sardine, a hunk of tuna fish, and a piece of pickled onion, all stabbed through with toothpicks), some nuts, and some chocolate. If there was a worthwhile sight to see in the town I was passing through, I saw it. In the first four days of my trip I had seen the Cathedral of Pamplona, the ruined Palace of the Counts of Guendulain, and the Iglesia del Crucifijo in Puente la Reina, where a skinny-armed Christ hung on what looked like the branch of a tree.

More than once, as I walked into a small town toward the end of the day I was unable to locate the yellow arrows. Confused about which way to turn, I'd stop to squint at my map. Without fail, each time I looked up from the map two very old Spanish women fifty yards down the road would be wildly waving their canes at me and pointing vigorously down a dirt track, as if to say *You want to go to the right! To the right! To the right!!* though I had never seen them before and hadn't said a word to them. The Camino de Santiago had become so popular and heavily traveled that of course the old women knew where I wanted to go.

The people who lived in the towns along the trail were used to seeing people like me — dirty, sunburned foreigners with backpacks and maps traipsing through their streets. Without speaking to me they knew where I had come from and where I was going. I had become a part of their daily life, as they had now become a part of mine. I thought about how strange and tiresome the pilgrims' presence might be for them. When I heard that in recent years one or two pilgrims had been accosted or robbed, and that one had been murdered, I wasn't terribly surprised. But I came to realize that the local people in these northern Spanish towns were exceptionally patient, tolerating the pilgrims' hoboish gear and often unintelligible requests with grace and generosity.

Along the trail I saw a man carefully sweeping the ancient cobblestones of a village street with a twig broom; a kestrel swooping down to snatch a grasshopper out of a vineyard; black-and-white magpies with long tails as stiff as the handle of a frying pan; Spanish policemen wearing hats like overturned tin pots; a one-eyed dog with sixteen teats dangling from her belly barking at a trashcan in a senile, halfhearted way; giggling nuns with marine-blue veils and blue-and-white-striped pinafores sitting by a well and practicing their English; old people roasting red peppers in a barrel; a pack of Spanish teenagers in shiny vinyl tracksuits hanging about the central square of a small medieval town, smoking, throwing cigarette butts into the ancient and delicately ornate municipal fountain, and saying *mierda* and *puta* to each other with casual violence.

After about eighteen miles my pace would begin to slow, mostly because my toes had become incredibly painful, as though they had been smashed many times with a hammer. I realized with astonishment that I was actually developing blisters on the insides of my upper arms from the swinging of my arms against my ribcage. I had never walked so many miles in one day, let alone day after day. As I neared my destination for the evening, with the powerful sun in my eyes, I began catching up with other pilgrims. Sometimes the people ahead of me in the distance seemed to be standing still, yet they remained the same distance away, like the resurrected Christ on the road to Emmaus. And once in a while, in a weird and inexplicable illusion, they appeared to be walking toward me, like a bicycle wheel that at a certain speed suddenly looks as though it's spinning in reverse. When I finally caught up to the others, I got a full view of the brand name of their backpacks, with drying underwear dangling from them and the pilgrim's scallop shell tied to them. Some packs looked as big as refrigerators, and their owners struggled to carry them uphill. As I passed by, everyone would smile and nod knowingly and say *Hola!* in a hearty way to show that we were all in this bizarre endeavor together.

Finally, I would stagger into the hostel — a church run by a religious society, a schoolhouse run by the municipal government, a monastery or convent, a town hall that didn't seem to be run by anybody, or a brand-new building constructed by the provincial government expressly for the pilgrims. I had my booklet validated with the hostel's own little rubber stamp imprinted with some significant image — a walking staff in Roncesvalles, a scallop shell in Pamplona, a bunch of grapes in Viana — and paid for my lodging, usually a dollar or two, but sometimes nothing at all. Then I went in and flopped down on a bunk until I thought I could stand again, whereupon I went to the showers. By the time I arrived (I tended to arrive later than others because I left later and walked longer) the water was usually cold. I washed my underwear and socks, put new Band-Aids on my feet, and went to look for something to eat.

Many of the towns I passed through had no conventional restaurant, just a little market or a bar where you could eat more curious garnitures and drink beer from a tiny wineglass. Sometimes the bar had a Pilgrim's Menu, and then all the pilgrims would sit together, drinking wine and introducing themselves and giving their reasons for walking to Santiago. One was doing it for fun, one to recover from a bitter divorce, one to meet a husband, one to heal her karma and find inner peace, one to lose weight, one to find himself, one because he had just been released from jail. They would offer how far they had walked, how many days it had taken, how many pains and blisters they had, how much their pack weighed, what hostels they had slept in. As the wine took effect and the pilgrims grew comfortable with each other, the opinions and complaints and criticisms of other pilgrims began: that one was carrying far too much weight, this one walked too fast, that one walked too slow, one had the wrong boots, another had the wrong attitude, another knew nothing of the history and significance of the Camino, this one was not spiritual enough, another was too spiritual, there were far too many Brazilians on the trail, and (my favorite) the Camino had been much better ten years ago because there were fewer people on it.

After dinner everyone went to bed. The lights went out at ten, the doors were locked at eleven, and the creaking, grating snoring began at ten after eleven. And the next morning we'd get up and do it all again.

I TALKED with many unusual and diverting people on the trail, but for me the best parts of these long days were the stretches when I was alone, thinking and listening to the steady rhythm of my own footsteps trailing me like a heartbeat. That spring I had walked the hundred and fifty miles from Winchester to Canterbury along the medieval pilgrimage route that roughly followed the North Downs Way. It was a beautiful trail and well marked, but what I liked most about it was that I was completely alone. In modern times that route is not considered a pilgrimage trail, and few people walk its full length. I seemed to have the whole of the English countryside to myself. Here in Spain, as in England, I liked walking through new territory, through sunwashed towns and villages whose simple beauty I had never imagined.

Walking this way I felt freed from the troubles and concerns of my life at home. A long relationship with a man I loved wasn't going well; there seemed to be no solution. For some months I had been alternately angry and sad about it, and on this long trip I had time to think without being faced every day with the problem. It wasn't why I had come to Spain, but I found that walking cleared my mind. I felt more relaxed than I had in a long time. I felt I was getting a taste of what it would be like to be on the run, escaping. I had no responsibilities, no telephone calls to make, no promises to keep. Nothing could reach me, and that made me feel calm. My feet were my vehicle, and everything I needed was on my back. The self-containment, anonymity, and compactness were liberating. My life as a pilgrim was reduced to days of constant movement. I had always liked being alone, but being alone and moving was a pure joy. As a writer I spent my days at home sitting at a desk, cut off from the world, trying to depict with specificity and precision the very world I was cut off from. I find writing difficult for many reasons but especially because I have a great deal of physical energy. I hate sitting. Here on the Camino de Santiago, I was outside, moving through the world and expressing very little. I loved not talking and was glad to be alone.

By the fifth day of my trip I was walking an average of twenty-one miles daily, more than I had planned to do. As I got into the rhythm of it, I found that the more I walked, the more I wanted to walk. At the end of the day, exhausted, I had the illusion that I could go on forever. The trail was well marked and well maintained, and for the most part the walking was easy. The trail varied from hard-packed dirt to cinder tracks to country roads to brief stretches of highway to big-city sidewalks to cobbled village streets bordered by ancient stone walls. The landscape was so varied, with so many magnificent churches and castles and ruins along the way, that it was like wandering through an enormous living museum. The Spanish villages I passed through looked much the way the medieval pilgrims had left them. Here was a Visigothic ruin, a mile down the road a thirteenth-century Moorish fountain, a Gothic cloister, or a Romanesque baptismal font. The Roman influence was visible everywhere, for the Iberian Peninsula had been one of the most important provinces of the Roman Empire. If I didn't feel like stopping to see a famous ruin, it didn't matter because there would be many more ahead, and the sepia-colored fields, violet skies, and yellowish stones of the villages were sights as thrilling as any church.

Many of the villages I passed through were engaged in celebrations. The town squares, often strung with banners and pennants, could be raucous with the sound of church bells and clarinet music, clapping hands and tin drums. Sometimes a holy parade came lumbering down the narrow, ancient streets: a bald-headed priest followed by sixteen children dressed in medieval velvet costumes followed by a thirty-six-inch statue of a saint or a Virgin mounted on a silver plinth proudly borne along on the shoulders of the stout local men. One Virgin wore a jeweled crown and a wig of long crimped hair, which in the jostling excitement got knocked askew, giving her a slatternly, slightly come-hither look. In one celebrating town a banner strung across the street said (as far as I could make out): *There is no man as holy, generous, hard-working, devoted, and genial as Father Gonzales.*

With nothing else to do and no purpose but to move forward, my walking took on a meditative rhythm. I didn't really care about getting to Santiago de Compostela as long as I could keep walking every day with no other responsibility. The concerns I had had before I came to Spain seemed to have receded, and I stopped my habitual worrying about what would happen next in life. The landscape — as well as the fact that I didn't speak Spanish — had a soothing, muffling effect on my nerves, and my thoughts became reflective and musing rather than teeming and anxious.

OUTSIDE OF VIANA I had a huge view of distant purple mountains to the west. They looked very big, professional almost, like the Rockies. The countryside was beautiful — dry, wide open, graced with gently rolling hills, and nearly treeless but for shimmering little stands of olives. There were grasshoppers everywhere, some the color of fuchsia, some robin's-egg blue. I passed a farmer who was burning his field, walking along with a big pitchfork that had a flaming rag tied to the end of it; he dragged the rag along the ground, striping the field with fire. There were walnut trees here, and grapes, and what looked like chestnut trees. I wandered into a vineyard, plucked a bunch of red grapes, and ate them as I passed from the province of Navarra into the province of Rioja. Rioja was famous for its wine. The grapes were certainly the most delicious I had ever eaten — full of juice and as sweet as raisins.

Around a bend, the road passed directly in front of a ramshackle little house. A dog in the weedy yard barked at me, and at the sound an old woman came out of the house with a broom, smiling and waving at me and saying, "Hola, peregrina!" Many more dogs appeared, and an impressive assortment of cats. I stopped to greet the woman, and she grinned at me and threw down her broom. She spoke rapidly and held my hands in hers, as though I were an old friend. She was tiny — no higher than my sternum — and had white hair and very large glasses with dense black frames. "Venga, venga," she said and led me by the elbow to a table set up in her yard. On the table was a dish of fresh, ripe figs, a dish with coins in it, photographs of pilgrims posing with the dogs in front of her house, and some maps. She offered me the figs; I ate two, and then she said, "Quieres sello?" and held up a rubber stamp. I dug in my bag for my pilgrim's document and gave it to her. She held it in her brown hands, admiring the stamps I had already collected, smiling and nodding in recognition at the various towns I had stopped in. She talked a toothless blue streak and asked me questions, though I had told her I didn't speak Spanish. (Most of the time I didn't mind that inability, but sometimes when I met someone who seemed lively and interesting, I was so desperate to communicate that I just made words up as I went, grabbing a Latinate English word and throwing an *e* or an *o* or an *a* onto the end of it. I had discovered that by this method I could sometimes convey an idea. One day, taking a wild stab, I had asked a pharmacist for some *filamente dental,* and though this was in no way the term for dental floss in Spanish, the pharmacist knew exactly what I meant and quickly produced a package of Johnson & Johnson waxed.)

I smiled and nodded at the old woman and looked in amazement around her yard. A great many dogs and cats lounged in front of the house, scratching, snapping at flies, snoozing, or rolling in the hot dirt. Several of the dogs lay on their backs with their paws in the air, as if drying them. In a cage by the front door an unusual game bird, like a grouse, was stretching its fabulous feathers and pecking at grain. A handwritten sign attached to the cage said CONSTRUCION POR RUBEN GONZALES and gave the date of Gonzales's death.

The woman asked me where I was from, and when I told her, she pressed her hands to her cheeks in astonishment. She said, "Bueno," then laid my pilgrim's document on the table and carefully pressed her stamp onto it. It was a pretty image of a scallop shell, a fig leaf, a water jug, and a cross, and around the edges of the picture were the words CAMINO DE SANTIAGO, FELISA, HIGOS — AGUA Y AMOR, LOGRONO. I guessed that Felisa was her name, and I knew that the other words meant figs, water, and love. Felisa had been enterprising enough to set up her own little Camino de Santiago welcoming office, offering figs, water, and love for a small voluntary consideration. Everyone else seemed to be benefiting financially from the renewed popularity of the trail — why not Felisa? Along the route entire towns had been economically revived by the pilgrims' custom; new restaurants and hostels were going up, and shopkeepers carried an array of items geared toward hikers. Sometimes in the evening a local woman would appear at the hostel to cook an evening meal for the pilgrims, and when her work was done she would cheerfully wave goodbye and go off with the money she had earned tucked safely into the heel of her shoe.

I loved Felisa for her industry, her good nature, her figs, the grouse. I put two hundred pesetas into the dish on the table. She kissed my hand, and as I went down the path she waved with great exuberance and blew more kisses through the air.

TOWARD THE END of that day, nearing the hostel in Najera, I came up behind the unsmiling little Spanish woman I had met at the hostel in Pamplona. I recognized her jodhpurs and her brittle way of walking. She stepped lightly on her delicate booted feet, like a cat in a hurry. I had seen her many times along the road, always looking dour, and had come to think of her as the Spanish Saint. I realized that in my five days of walking she and I had been keeping the same pace. I was twice her size; for each step I had taken she must have had to take two. After her insistence in Pamplona that she didn't speak English, I hadn't said much to her except hello. Coming up behind her that day I said hello in my usual way, and in her usual way she turned her pained face toward me, nodded once, and looked away again.

She was a tough one to engage. We were both on a trail in the middle of nowhere, we had been occupied by the same strange endeavor for the past several days, we had seen each other's face many times, had several times slept in the same room, and had stood side by side at sinks brushing our teeth, yet she showed none of the interactive facial expressions that human beings usually grant each other, even strangers. Her face was a wall.

Deciding that I had nothing to lose, I said chattily as we trudged along, "I know you don't speak English. Nevertheless, you taught me the Spanish word for post office."

The grim little face cracked with a strained smile of recognition and, shockingly, amusement. Her teeth, which I was seeing for the first time, were beautiful.

THAT NIGHT the hostel was a very old church building that had been restored and converted. The superintendent, a Brazilian woman, greeted me when I came in, stamped my booklet, and directed me to the bunks. The hostel was simply an open room with a high ceiling and walls of ancient stone, but it had new fixtures and amenities — a small bathroom and kitchen, new windows, and modern furnishings. Music with a cloying, distinctly New Age feel was playing at one end of the room. At a long wooden table two handsome Brazilian bicyclists, one still wearing his helmet, were using a large hunting knife to shave slices from a large ham and stuffing the slices into their mouths. I had come to like the bicyclists on the Camino. They talked less than the walkers and had few pretensions about being spiritual. It was fitness for them, and sightseeing, a healthy holiday on wheels.

My toes were killing me, but after so much strenuous walking it seemed marvelous that they were the only part of my body that hurt. I lay down on a bunk near a woman whose husband was massaging her calf muscles and engaged in my usual twenty-minute end-of-the-day blank stare at the springs of the bunk above me. I had been wearing the same clothes for five days. I raised my leg to stare at an almond-sized blister on my big toe, lowered the leg again, and thought, *You smell like a donkey.*

Then the little Spanish Saint came in and sat on a bunk not far from mine and began — in that methodical, tidy, unhappy way of hers — to empty her backpack. I watched as she withdrew from its depths a small suitcase full of makeup and health care products; lipstick, powder, a loofah sponge, a large bottle of shampoo, a hair dryer, a bottle of perfume, a pumice stone, a bath towel, baby powder, a bag full of clothespins, a small tin mug. It was fascinating and baffling. My only grooming supplies were a toothbrush, a sliver of soap, and a broken comb. Because I couldn't imagine dragging a bath towel across Spain, I had not brought a towel; I dried myself with my dirty shirt, then washed the shirt and let it dry overnight. But I was satisfied with what I had brought. So far my fleece blanket, my shawl, and my jacket had been enough to keep me warm in bed at night. And I didn't care how I smelled.

I got up, went out, and bought some bread, sausage, fruit, and wine and returned to the hostel. I sat down at the table next to an English couple in their early sixties who were sharing a hunk of cheese. They were both lanky and tall and remarkably fit. For much of that day they had been ahead of me on the road; I kept seeing them in the distance, their two long shadows trailing behind them. They walked briskly and Britishly with long strides, chins held high, and few pauses.

I introduced myself to them. They were Susan and Karl from Nottingham, though he was originally from Germany. I sliced my sausage, and Susan said, "Did you see Jennifer on the road?"

"Jennifer?" I said.

"The Canadian."

By now I had met several Canadians.

"Jennifer's got a problem with blisters," Susan said.

Karl grimaced. "*I* have a problem with blisters."

Karl was slightly deaf, wore wire-rimmed glasses, had a small mouth, and a deadpan, punning sense of humor. He told predictable jokes and made corny associations. When he saw the little bag of peanuts I had bought he said, "I see you're a friend of Jimmy Carter." When he saw my aluminum blanket he said, "Looks suitable for roasting a very large turkey." When I remarked on the large backpack he was carrying, he said, "That's right. Har-har, they don't call me Karl the Mule for nothing!" I offered them some wine. Filling Karl's glass I said, "Tell me when to stop." He chuckled and said, "Tomorrow!" His humor was like a tall hedge he was peering over.

Like Karl, Susan had a long face, though hers was very English-looking, with a long Roman nose, a long chin, deep-set blue eyes, sturdy, strong teeth, and very red cheeks. Her gray hair was knotted in a bun, and loose strands flew about her face and neck, giving her a harried, scatterbrained look. She had long, fine hands and the game, tomboyish manner of a Girl Scout leader. The front of her sweatshirt said CROMPTON REGATTA. I asked her if she liked to sail. She shut her eyes bashfully, grinned, and said, "Mucked about some in boats when I was a kid." Susan was a botanist. She had a plummy accent, and when she said "botany" it sounded to me like *pottery*. She said "blimey" and "crikey" and "telly" and "brolly" and "ever so nice." When she got up to use the bathroom she said, "Excuse me; I've to go spend a penny."

Karl and Susan liked to travel and to hike but were not, they said, terribly religious. When I told them I had just come from Lourdes and had taken the bath there, the corners of Karl's mouth turned downward in a roguish smirk. "I heard a miracle about a woman who came out of the bath at Lourdes totally dry," he said. "Now if that was me, I'd've demanded a refund from the Virgin herself!"

More pilgrims arrived, and soon the table was crowded. A French man from Brest was walking the Camino because a few years back he had lost his job and was doing nothing with his life but drinking and smoking. Beside him sat a silent Belgian priest with a wooden cross around his neck and a black beard meticulously shaved to a dense fringe along the very edge of his jaw, like the beard of a gnome; his mustache had been whittled to a tiny black strip, and from where I sat it looked like a line of ants marching single file across his lip. At the end of the table was a twenty-five-year-old ginger-haired French girl named Odile, with a very red face and small eyes with long, pale lashes. A lawyer, Odile had just spent six months with a volunteer peacekeeping effort in Kosovo, where she had had to drive a large dump truck. She had left Kosovo just five days before and had immediately begun walking the trail to Santiago. I asked her why. "To clear my head," she said gravely. "Because Kosovo was not funny."

I realized that many of the people I met on the trail were walking alone.

A Basque woman from Bilbao sat down next to me and began to explain Basque nationalism. She said the Basques were the oldest extant ethnic group in Europe, but Spain had bullied and oppressed them. In 1936 two Basque provinces gained independence, but because the Basques had supported the Republicans during the Spanish civil war, Francisco Franco vengefully revoked their autonomy, bombed Guernica, the center of Basque nationalism, and finally banned the language. During the early sixties a splinter of ETA, a group that supported Basque freedom, began resorting to terrorism to achieve their goal of an independent state. In 1980 the Basque region regained its autonomy, but ETA was still fighting for self-rule and separation from Spain. The Basques I met on the trail were proud, kept to themselves, and bristled if you mistakenly referred to them as Spanish.

The Spanish Saint was also at the table, eating noodles and looking aggrieved and saying very little. Before I went to bed I wrung out of her that her name was Olatz, that she lived in Barcelona, and that she planned to walk thirty miles the next day.

THAT NIGHT the Spanish man in the bunk next to me snored unceasingly. The noises he made sounded variously like the dregs of an ice cream soda rattling through a straw, an outboard motor, and a woodpecker worrying a sycamore. I wanted to throttle him. At one point during the night I reached over and tapped on his forehead with the handle of my toothbrush to make him stop. He fluttered and flapped his lips and rolled over. But twenty minutes later the snoring started all over again, and from across the room another man chimed in, snoring so loudly he seemed to be choking to death. I listened to this for a long time, and finally I found two aspirin tablets in my bag and threw them across the room at the wall above the choking man's head. It worked. The noise startled him into silence.

It was a bad night, and in the morning the Brazilian hostelkeeper called us awake with more New Age music and the smell of burning incense. Not long before, she had walked the Camino and, like a number of people, had become infatuated with the experience and had returned to spend some time as a volunteer. She had personalized the hostel to fit her sensibility; resultantly the place had a slightly moony feel.

As I packed up my things that morning I saw Karl and Susan sitting at the table looking exhausted, as if they too had had a hard night. They seemed to have lost their good-natured ease.

"I'm going to have some of that cheese for breakfast," said Karl.

"Why don't we save the cheese for lunch?"

Karl frowned at his wife. "I don't think we're so hard up, Susan, that I can't have a bit of cheese and bread in the morning." He unfolded their map. "Now, which way do you want to go today?"

"Well, I'd like to save some miles today, Karl."

"But that wasn't the question," he said testily.

My mood wasn't great either, so I said goodbye and hurried out the door, eager to be alone again.

BEFORE LONG I reached Santo Domingo de la Calzada, and because I liked its old houses, with their wrought-iron window balconies and immense carved wooden doors, I sat down in the square and looked the place up in my guidebook. The town was known for its native son, Saint Dominic, and for the legend of the roasted rooster that returned to life. According to the legend, in the fourteenth century a couple making the pilgrimage to Santiago with their son stopped for the night at an inn in Santo Domingo. The innkeeper's daughter fell for the son, but because the boy showed no interest in her, she framed him by hiding one of her father's silver goblets in his luggage. The boy was accused of theft, arrested, and hanged. But as his parents were leaving the inn they heard their son's voice calling out to them that he was not dead — Saint Dominic had saved his life by holding up his feet as he hung from the gallows. The parents went to the house of the local judge to tell him that their son was alive. The judge, who was just about to eat his dinner of roasted rooster and chicken, replied, "That boy is no more alive than this cock and hen." Whereupon the birds flew up from the plate, crowing and cackling, proof that the boy was innocent.

I went into the great Cathedral of Santo Domingo to see the famous chicken coop erected in honor of the story. There in the transept was an ornate grilled cage containing a pair of chickens clucking and strutting and winking through the bars. It seemed to me a humorous and lovely device to have set up in a cathedral as venerable as this one.

OUTSIDE OF SANTO DOMINGO I came up behind a man I had seen in the hostel but hadn't spoken to because he had kept to himself and had gone to bed early. The man was in his early sixties but looked much younger; he was fit and very handsome in a severe and tidy way. He wore reading glasses secured by a thin chain around his neck, and he carried one of those fancy aluminum walking sticks that so many of the pilgrims seemed to have — a light aluminum wand with a rubber hand grip and a wrist strap, like a ski pole. He had stopped to look at his map. I said hello and carried on down the trail, which in that particular spot wound along the edges and corners of some newly mown wheat fields. The man didn't return my hello, but as I proceeded I heard him say to my back, in French and with an unmistakable edge to his voice, "Are you going to stop and take an aperitif when you get to Santiago?"

By that time in my trip I had heard enough pilgrims criticizing the walking style of other pilgrims that I knew he meant I was walking too quickly for him. This meddling concern with how other people walked the trail was both puzzling and annoying. And after the town of Belorado it had, for some reason, grown worse. Irritability and a chafing competitiveness seemed to have affected everyone; it was as if, having come this far, the previously well intentioned pilgrims had grown prideful. Some exhausted walkers had dropped out, which appeared to give others a kind of satisfaction — *Poor old thing, glad it wasn't me.* With our lives reduced to this narrow scope, personal opinions had begun to clash.

I ignored the man and walked on. But a few minutes later I realized that he was cutting diagonally through the fields in a mile-saving short-cut that put him ahead of me again. He wasn't interested in walking with me or in talking to me — he wanted only to race against me. Attractive as he was, he seemed a little crazy, and I wasn't eager to catch up with him. I slowed down in order to lose him. But half an hour later, outside the next town, I found him sitting on a stone wall at the edge of the trail, almost as if in ambush. My heart sank when I saw him. As I walked by he said haughtily, "I thought you would be ahead of me by now." I shouldn't have responded, but my own mood was sour and the remark was aggressive enough that I couldn't keep myself from saying, "And I am surprised that you have come this far so quickly. Did you take the bus?"

"Of course not," he huffed.

His name was Luc, and for several miles I was stuck with him. He walked in a stiff-spined way, rhythmically stabbing the ground with his ski pole, his reading glasses perched on the end of his nose. Each time his arm swung forward for another stab he gave an unnecessary little flourish of the wrist that came off as a slight challenge. Luc had the air of someone used to being watched and admired. He didn't smile and he expressed no surprise or emotion. When he told me he was retired from the military, it made sense. He spoke with the infallible authority of a commander. His two grandfathers and his father had all had careers in the military. His two sons were in the military, and he hoped his grand-sons would join as well. When he said that this was the second time he had walked the Camino and that he had begun his trip in Le Puy, four hundred miles north of St. Jean, his superior attitude made a little more sense: he was an expert now. He had been here and seen it all before.

We were walking on a small paved road. I was walking with a stick I had found that morning on the road. Luc said, "I see that you know how to use the walking stick. Most people don't. They might as well throw it in the ditch or carry it on their shoulder. You must have done some walking before."

Knowing how to use a walking stick seemed a strange thing to be proud of. I told Luc that I usually walked six miles a day at home. He said, "At home I walk twenty a day."

When I said, "You must like the Spanish people very much," he said, "I don't care a bit about the Spanish people." He began complaining about Spain, stabbing at the road with his stick. "You see this cow shit on the road? You would never see that in France. The police would stop and give the farmer a ticket, because cars can slide on this stuff." He mimicked a cop writing a ticket; the posture suited him.

Luc spoke no English at all, so I was forced to speak French. Under the best of circumstances I found it difficult to speak French, and walking down a road with a testy crank like Luc, I could think of little to say. He told me he read a great deal of military history, biographies of soldiers and generals ("for example," he said, "the great Napoleon"), and narratives of contemporary wars. As we walked through a stand of birch trees with Luc's stick clinking on pebbles, I tried to imagine what it would be like to spend one's life thinking about fighting and killing.

LATER THAT DAY I met Olatz walking through a field on a low plain. The day was clear and bright and windy, with shredded white clouds skittering low across the sky. Gusts of wind stirred the fields in shimmering waves. My mood had improved a little, and with bald persistence I was finally able to engage Olatz in conversation. Her English, as I had predicted, was very good, and before an hour had passed I had learned that she was twenty-six years old, one of five children, and that her mother, who had been well educated, had abandoned the children when Olatz was six, leaving her father to raise them. But then "all came to change," when her father met another woman and, for some cataclysmic reason that Olatz would not elaborate upon, the children turned against the father and went to live with the mother.

"Now," she said gloomily, with the wind pressing at her eyeglasses and her feet stepping lightly over the stones in the road, "I have no contact at all with my father."

"None?" I said.

"Not one."

I asked her what she did for work. With a heavy sigh she said vaguely, "Office." Recently she had been angered by something that had happened at the office and in her pique she had simply left. And now she was here, walking to Santiago. When she returned from the trip she would "pick up the telephone and see if I still have a job."

I asked Olatz why she was walking the Camino. "For fun," she said grimly.

From a woman who seemed to have had not a moment of fun while on the trail, it was a surprising response. A moment later, as if realizing how absurd her answer had been, she added, "And to test myself sportingly." And then, with a degree of self-consciousness, she confessed, "Well, and also to think."

That was more like it. Across a hundred and thirty miles it had been evident in Olatz's face that she was thinking hard. Whenever I saw her she seemed not to be seeing the trail and the landscape at all, her expression an abstracted stare of misgiving.

I told her what the crazy handsome French man had said to me, and she laughed loudly. Coming from her, the laughter was startling. "He has said the same to me!" she cried, and laughed some more. "I think he is angry at anyone who can walk fast than he can. Especially girls. I can walk fast than him. He did not like me about this."

Olatz did walk fast, and far. Every day she arrived at the hostel ahead of me. She was tenacious. Behind that brooding face was a will of iron.

ONE DAY after a week or so of walking, I began to experience worrisome pain in the muscles of my shins. I had been walking very long days, but I had been sleeping fairly well — in spite of the snoring — and aside from the blisters, which still bled in the morning, I had felt well. But that day my shins felt tight, and every so often a sharp shooting pain traveled up my legs. I slowed down, hoping the pain would disappear.

At lunch time I stopped in a tiny, treeless town in the middle of a vast plain. The town was poor and looked abandoned. It consisted of a few houses, a bar, and a barn with a patchwork roof made out of twisted tin, frayed carpeting, wooden planks, hay, and a couple of red tiles. The buildings were plain and sparse, and the dry fields around the town stretched away for miles. A lone cow stood lowing at the side of the road. The two o'clock sun had baked the stone walls and the dusty pavement to a kind of furnace, and the brown earth at the edge of the street was so parched it showed fissures and cracks. Everything was exposed and desiccated. Angry flies stirred in the dirt and crawled along the dusty windowpanes of the houses. Hungry and thirsty, I went into the town's one bar.

The bar was small and so dark I had to stand blinking in the doorway for a minute before I could see anything. Eventually I could make out a few rickety wooden tables and a dirty man in a torn shirt sitting at the bar drinking beer and patting an elderly beagle that was sprawled on the bar top. A television flickered above the bar. The bartender, a teenaged girl with huge brown eyes, was sitting on a low stool, her forehead level with the counter. She was staring up at the television and holding a baby bottle to the mouth of an infant lying in a basket on a shelf beneath the bar. I asked her for a glass of water and something to eat. When I spoke, the girl looked startled, dropped the baby bottle, jumped up, and hurried through a door. I took off my backpack, sat on a barstool, and waited. In the darkness of the bar I realized that my wrists and neck were stinging with sunburn.

At one of the small tables two men, pilgrims, were silently drinking beer and looking exhaustedly at the television. At another table a local man in a tweed jacket and beret was drinking a glass of wine and reading a newspaper. And at a third table a very old woman with arthritic hands and a tape measure around her neck was sewing a seam in a pair of trousers by the light of a little lamp on the table. Like most of the older Spanish women I had seen, she wore a dark skirt, a white blouse, and a black cardigan draped over her shoulders like a cape, its top button fastened at the throat. She had short gray hair and ruddy cheeks and thick eyeglasses. But for the television and the brilliant wands of daylight that leaked in around the edges of the one shaded window, the old woman's lamp was the only light in the place. Cats wandered languidly about, rubbing their haunches against the legs of the tables. Flies landed on the beagle's back, the old woman's hair, my hands. A few of them walked across the TV screen.

After a minute or two, the man patting the beagle grinned at me and said, "Hola, mujer."

He was probably fifty. When I said, "Hola, señor," my response seemed to please him a great deal. Eagerly he said again, "Hola, mujer." His voice was reedy and high. He had a jowly, whiskery face and was missing a front tooth, but his thick, greasy hair had been carefully combed against his head.

Having run out of things to say, I smiled at the man. He smiled back at me, sipping at his beer and smacking his lips. His left hand never stopped stroking the beagle's head. Now and then he glanced at the pair of pilgrims at the table behind us, smirked strangely at me, and turned back to the dog. I had met the two men once before on the road. They were a Brazilian father and son. The father wore his gray hair in a ponytail and had very white teeth. The son was an ice climber who had spent a year in Ohio and had learned a little English. His favorite English phrases were "Damn, man!" and "It was a hell of a good time!" and "Oh, boy, that sucks!" They were both rugged and rather quiet and very well equipped for their trek. When the pilgrims saw me looking at them, they nodded their heads in recognition and went back to staring at the television. Every bar and restaurant I had been in in Spain had a television going, and the program was always either a soccer match or dramatic flamenco dancers with jet-black hair or the kind of sensational American-style talk show in which bad things happened to good people. On this particular television it was the talk show. A big-busted teenaged girl wearing spaghetti straps and too much makeup was being interviewed by a man in a suit. The girl was weeping. A boy sitting beside her was staring at his hands with a guilty look on his face.

The man with the dog asked me where I was from. I told him. He asked if I had come to Madrid in an airplane. I said I had walked from France. "France!" he said loudly. "Ha! Very far!" He turned to the seamstress and said, "Mama, this one walked from France." The seamstress lifted her eyes at us, nudged her eyeglasses higher on her nose with her thimbled finger, said, "You don't say?" and returned to her work, thoroughly unimpressed. She had heard it all before. She frowned at the trousers, her white hair and crooked hands glowing yellow in the lamplight.

The bartender, who looked no more than fifteen, came back through the door with a glass of water, a bowl of olives, and a ham sandwich for me. Then she sat down again, put the bottle back into the baby's mouth, and stared at the television. She looked depressed. As I began to eat, the two Brazilian pilgrims got up from their table, put their packs back on, said goodbye, and went out the door. The man with the dog watched them go, and the moment the door closed behind them he turned to me and said, "I don't like Brazilians."

"You don't?" I said.

He made a face. "I hate the Brazilians the most."

Now that the Brazilians were gone, the man became very talkative, his strange voice piping through the gloom, his left hand ceaselessly patting the dog's head, his right hand reaching for my olives. I tried to follow what he was saying. He seemed to be saying there were too many Brazilians on the Camino de Santiago; Brazil was a primitive country full of primitive people; Brazilians lived the way Spanish people lived a hundred (maybe it was a thousand) years ago; they were lazy and stupid and one other unpleasant-sounding thing that I couldn't understand; their country was terrible and dirty; anything good about Brazil had come from Europe. As he talked he kept cupping his dirty hands around his mouth and blowing, as if through a tube, and then jabbing himself in the neck with his index finger to indicate that he had been shot with something. I gleaned that he was showing me the primitive manner in which Brazilians hunted for their food, like jungle people with poisonous darts spat through a straw. "I hate them," the man said, popping two olives into his mouth. "They are dirty. And so many of them are coming here now." He chewed the olives with noisy satisfaction and reached for more. "It is very bad."

As the man talked I felt something tapping me on the back. I turned around to see a cat sitting on the stool behind me and stretching its paw at me. In a sudden and unprovoked flash the cat lunged forward and bit me on the arm. Seeing this, the old man in the beret suddenly came to life. He jumped up, shouted, banged the door open with his booted foot, and, brandishing his cane, he chased all the cats — five or six of them — out of the bar and into the hot street, kicking at their rear ends as they scurried past him. Then he slammed his cane mightily down on the bar near the beagle's rear end. The shocked dog shrieked in fright and was on the floor in an instant, his nails scrabbling on the linoleum tiles. He skidded and skittered between the legs of the barstools and shot through the door. Provoked by the violent disturbance, the infant in the basket began to wail. The bartender turned her depressed brown gaze from the television to the old man and back to the television again, as if accustomed to this sort of sudden disturbance from him. Her big eyes glittered in the glow of the television, and the seamstress never looked up from her work.

Angry words passed between the two Spanish men, and then the older one went back to his wine and his newspaper. On the television King Juan Carlos and Queen Sophia suddenly appeared, a pleasant, genteel-looking couple. It was impossible to imagine either one of them losing their composure.

I ate my sandwich in a hurry, paid the girl, said goodbye, and went back to the hot trail. The muscles in my shins were very stiff, and I realized that I had begun to limp slightly with the pain.

ON A DIRT ROAD in the forest of the Montes de Oca I met a woman named Christine, whom I had talked with briefly the night before in the hostel in Belorado. We walked together through spruce trees and heather wet with dew. Christine was quick, curious, and intense; the night before, she had asked me a hundred questions with an unnerving directness. She was small, with short blond hair and sharp blue eyes, and though she was fifty, she looked thirty-five. Her English was so close to perfect that I thought she was Dutch or German. Later I heard her speaking Spanish and was sure that she was Spanish. Still later I heard her speaking French and realized that in fact she was French. She could shift from language to language with enviable ease.

As we walked, Christine told me that she came from a very Catholic family from Rouen. In the late 1960s, when she was in her early twenties, she had traveled to Africa and ended up as a guide leading people on safaris. Months later, at her mother's command, she returned to Rouen for Christmas, passing through Amsterdam on her way. Realizing that she had no warm clothes with her, she went to the flea market in Amsterdam and bought an old moth-eaten fur coat. "My hair was very long then," she said, "like a hippie. And I had brought an American boy home with me."

When she showed up at the train station in Rouen, her older brother was so horrified at her appearance, at the American boy, and at her carefree demeanor that he said, "You are no longer my sister," and turned on his heel, leaving her there on the platform. Christine and the boy made their own way home.

Christine said, "When my mother saw the boy, one of the first things she said to me was, 'Are you engaged?' She was horrified that I had brought this American boy home, and we were not allowed to be alone together in a room in my mother's house for more than thirty seconds. And yet, my sister was allowed to be on holiday in London alone with her boyfriend, whom she was not engaged to. But it was different for my sister, because that boy was studying at Oxford, so he was like God!"

Though Christine was philosophical about her mother's reaction, and even laughed at the story, thirty years later pain and resentment still lingered in her voice. I asked her why she was walking to Santiago. She told me that several years earlier her husband, to whom she had been married for only a few years, had died suddenly. They had been sitting together talking about a trip they had planned to take together, and suddenly he said: "Christine, why don't you go on this trip by yourself?" Minutes later he fell over and died. Shortly after that a good friend of hers committed suicide. Badly shaken by these events, Christine was at a loss for how to proceed, and she, like so many others I had met, had come here to walk and to think about her life.

Christine carried a prayer book in her pack and had attended Mass all along the route. There were countless Catholic churches along the Camino de Santiago, yet aside from a group of Brazilian women walking the trail with a priest, who set out every morning murmuring the rosary together in Portuguese, I hadn't heard many pilgrims asking where they could go to Mass. I hadn't heard many people talking about Christianity or, for that matter, religion in general. The longer I walked, the longer and more varied the list of pilgrims' motivations grew, but most seemed to have a psychological focus. Most people I talked to wanted to feel better about life, more comfortable with their existence. Many came to break out of some unhappiness — a depression, a bad relationship, a bad marriage, a bad job — or to muddle through conflicted feelings or recover from some disappointment. People said, "I'm looking for meaning" or "I'm trying to get in touch with myself." They wanted "to try to remember what's important in life" or "to work on myself." They said, "I want to regroup" or "because Kosovo was not funny." There was some talk of God, but for most the main purpose of walking the Camino was to strip away the clutter of life in order to better see the self.

There was, too, a small but pungent New Age presence on the Camino de Santiago. I met a number of people touched with an astrological, homeopathic, reincarnated, crystal-and-wind-chime aesthetic, and I saw that for some of the repeat pilgrims and volunteer hostelkeepers the Camino had become a little religion all its own, a mix of Christianity, mysticism, psychic healing, self-help, selective elements of Buddhism, and a romantic perception of poverty and the divestiture of worldly possessions. In one hostel I stayed in, the keeper had hung pictures of the Dalai Lama on the walls and placed crystals on the windowsills. This Camino religion had its own rituals, its own brand of spirituality, a pre-Christian belief in sorcery, a post-Christian belief in incense, and its own sometimes dubious history. (One legend maintains that the route of the Camino de Santiago is really the pre-Christian route to the lost city of Atlantis, another that the Camino lies directly beneath and parallel to the Milky Way, giving the trail a certain force that draws its energy from the stars. Shirley MacLaine and the Brazilian writer Paulo Coelho had walked the Camino precisely to avail themselves of this energy, and both have written books about it.) But for all their protestations of peace and harmony, the New Agers struck me as the most defensive, least mellow people on the trail.

In 1999 the Camino de Santiago had elements of a fad. The number of pilgrims had multiplied radically during the preceding fifteen years. Coelho's book had drawn the many Brazilians who were here, and MacLaine's presence had drawn others. (MacLaine's fantastical book about her 1994 journey, published in 2000, prompted one Pamplonan priest to say, "It was the worst thing that ever happened to the Camino.") The word spread, and the seekers and the curious came. During the months of June, July, and August the underequipped hostels were woefully crowded, forcing many pilgrims to sleep in fields. In some places toward the end of the trail the Spanish army resorted to setting up tents outside the hostels to shelter the overflow.

The pilgrims I met were predominantly people of means. They came overwhelmingly from prosperous countries — Holland, Germany, Britain, Belgium, France, Switzerland, Austria, New Zealand, Australia, Brazil, Canada, and the United States. They could afford to take a month off to do this whimsical thing, to pursue what Shirley MacLaine calls "resolutions regarding conflicts of self." They had credit cards. Many carried cellular phones so they could call the office or the children or the broker. Many could afford to stay in a comfortable hotel now and then if they wanted a break from the spartan hostels. I met no truly poor people walking the trail — no Spanish peasants, no one employed in the mines of West Virginia, no hard-up Portuguese fishermen, no Irish farmers. It was for the most part a white-collar pilgrimage, an interesting and enriching pursuit for the educated and the affluent. Though a difficult undertaking, it was also a self-indulgent one.

In her book *The Camino* MacLaine records such thoughts as: "My brain and consciousness became the rainbows" and "I reveled in the antiquity of this magnificent Gothic structure, thinking I had probably been here centuries before that!" She also writes, "The experience of complete surrender to God and self is the motivation behind most people's attempt at the Santiago de Compostela Camino," as if surrender to God and surrender to self were one and the same. Spirituality and self-interest appeared to have become interchangeable. One man I met on the trail told me he was here "so that I can brag to my friends that I did it." That seemed as good a reason as any of the others I had heard.

One day on the trail I made a telephone call to my mother to see how she was. She asked, "Now this pilgrimage to Santiago is a Catholic one, right?"

I said yes.

"So everyone there is Catholic."

I thought about how to put it. "Well, a lot of them were born Catholic, yes, but many aren't Catholic in a conventional sense."

I could hear my mother sifting through that remark, suspiciously examining the word "conventional." I knew she was thinking *You either are a Catholic or you're not.*

I had met Protestants, atheists, agnostics, and Buddhists on this trail, as well as a Jewish couple from Brazil. I told my mother that. A long silence followed. Finally she said, "Oh, well," in that amused and airily ironic tone that meant the topic was too strange to honor with a protest, "I can make no sense of it, Rosemary. But good luck anyway!"

For my mother, who believed we were at God's mercy and for whom religion was a discipline, the world had grown slaphappy — too compromising, too unexacting, too slipshod and unconsidered. On the brink of the twenty-first century, it had lost its seriousness. As I walked, I thought about my mother's viewpoint and found it hard to disagree with her.

CHRISTINE WAS the first person I met on the Camino de Santiago who seemed interested in talking seriously about the Catholic Church. When I asked if she considered herself Catholic, she said, "Yes," with a quickness that surprised me, considering that she had just recounted some disappointing experiences with the church. In her early thirties, pregnant by a married man and uncertain whether she wanted to keep the child, she had gone to a priest, a family friend, for advice and counseling. The priest was so affronted by her sin and by her bold request for help that he refused to speak with her. When I explained to Christine why I had difficulty with the Catholic Church, citing its rigidity and hypocrisy, its sexism, authoritarianism, and historically punitive approach to human frailty, Christine flinched and said with wounded interest, "Oh, such strong words!" Sounding remarkably like my mother, she went on to say that the church could be run only by people and that people were flawed, but that the core of the church, the reason for its existence, was spiritual and transcendent, and therefore it would prevail and endure beyond the mistakes made by its human superintendents. Such an optimistic and forgiving attitude had to be the result either of incredible naiveté or of an admirably true belief.

IN THE VILLAGE of San Juan de Ortega, Christine and I ran into Olatz. I was surprised to see her; I had imagined that she was way ahead of me by now. The sky had grown overcast, and a cold wind was yanking leaves from the sycamore trees and bringing brief but bitter flurries of rain with it. Though it was only one in the afternoon, Olatz was stopping here for the day. Heading into the hostel, she looked stricken and pallid and exhausted, and when she took my hand to shake it, her hand, though she had just walked miles, was shockingly cold. The wind buffeted her huge backpack, making her stagger, and pushed her brown hair into her face, entangling it in the earpieces of her glasses. She made no move to clear the hair out of her eyes. I told her that I was sure we would meet again before we reached Santiago, but Olatz said sadly, "I think that I cannot reach Compostela."

I knew from the way she said it that it was true; she had made up her mind to quit. Her words stunned me. Of all the people I had met on this trail, Olatz seemed the most determined and most certain to arrive in Santiago de Compostela. At times I had taken inspiration from her glum persistence. But I understood her discouragement. So many days of constant walking had begun to take their toll. My own legs had become very painful, and I feared that I, too, might be unable to continue if the pain got worse.

I told Olatz that I had enjoyed meeting her and talking with her on the road, we said goodbye, and she disappeared forlornly into the hostel. It made me strangely sad to see her go.

Christine and I went into the little bar next door to the hostel and drank coffee and *orujo*, a strong Galician liqueur the color of urine. The bar was full of Brazilians. Christine told me that a few days back, in a crowded hostel in one of the towns along the road, she had seen a terrible fight between a Brazilian man and some Spaniards. The Spanish hostelkeeper had promised the pilgrims that he would provide them with dinner, but the food came slowly and was served to the Spanish pilgrims first. The Brazilian, who was becoming drunk, complained to the hostelkeeper that he and his countrymen were being ignored and mistreated because they were Brazilian and that the Spanish resented and disrespected them. Words flew, the hostelkeeper shouted, "Are you saying bad things about Spain?" and within minutes a fistfight broke out. The hostelkeeper called the police, who arrested the angry Brazilian and took him to jail.

I had sensed the tension between the Spaniards and the Brazilians, but since I didn't speak either language, most of what they said went over my head, and I assumed that the conflict had more to do with the great numbers of Brazilians on the trail than with anything else. The Brazilians in the bar that day were having fun, laughing loudly and speaking their Russian-sounding language.

Christine and I left the bar and went to look at the twelfth-century monastery church at the edge of the square. The church, small but beautiful, contained the tomb of San Juan, who had established the village as a stopping place for pilgrims, which it remained. The village sat in the middle of a plain of dry grass and nettles, with nothing around it for miles. That such a beautiful church had sprung up here and had survived for so long was astonishing. The Romanesque capital in the church showed pictures of the Annunciation, the Visitation, and the Nativity of Jesus. According to my guidebook, "Each equinox at precisely 5 P.M. solar time, a single shaft of sunlight strikes this capital, illuminating it alone in the surrounding gloom and creating the marvellous illusion that the Holy Ghost is alighting on Mary's belly."

As I was leaving the town I saw Olatz again, a lonesome figure in jodhpurs and red jacket hanging wet clothing on a line strung between two trees. As she limped back to the hostel across the square, the abusive wind slapped at the clothing and finally ripped one or two items clean off the line and hurled them to the ground.

WHY I DIDN'T STAY in San Juan de Ortega that day I don't know. It was a mistake, but it was still early afternoon, the weather was clearing, and I was so used to walking until evening that I ignored the pain in my legs and decided to continue on to Burgos. Christine, who had a pain in her heel, took a ride in a passing car. My map indicated that Burgos was about twenty-three kilometers — fourteen miles — away, a fact that did not register in my head. I had already walked nearly fifteen miles that day, and my shins hurt badly. By the time I arrived at the outskirts of Burgos I knew I was in trouble. I had never felt physical pain so unalloyed and consuming. A torn cornea I had once suffered was very painful, like having crushed particles of glass rubbed firmly into my eye, but it was nothing compared to the pain I experienced that day on the road. I felt as if my legs had been sawed off at the shins and I was walking on the stumps of them. Every step brought an excruciating electric shock. I was unable to focus on anything but the next step. I tried to remember a time before this pain had existed, but there didn't seem to be such a time. I tried to imagine a time when it would be gone, but that was impossible too. My whole being consisted of the pain in my legs.

Just outside of Burgos I found myself on a strip of highway called the N1, which in ambience was not unlike U.S. Route 1. The road was lined with gas stations and factories and places that looked like furniture outlets. Eighteen-wheelers full of potatoes sailed by with a taunting whine of ease, and the long stretch of uninviting highway seemed unending. I waited for the city proper to appear, but after half an hour of dragging my feet along a hard sidewalk I was still surrounded by gas stations and cinder-block buildings. The sun was beginning to set, and by the time I reached the city it was difficult to see. I missed the guiding yellow arrow, made a wrong turn, and spent the next hour lost, limping up and down tangled streets in the dark, asking everyone where the hostel was. They knew, but they found it hard to explain to a person who didn't speak Spanish. A man who had had a tracheotomy answered me with an electronic device held to his throat; I understood none of what he said.

Under a streetlamp I met an old woman in black. She had a kerchief tied onto her head and no teeth. Her skin was olive-green in the gassy light. I told her my predicament, trying not to cry, and she patted my arm and said, "Pobrecita." I asked her if there was a restaurant or a hotel nearby. She shrugged and shook her head no. I said I was hungry. She said, "Peregrina, tienes hambre? Te puedo hacer un bocadillo." Her willingness to take me into her house and make me a sandwich caused the tears I had been struggling to hold back to suddenly spring to my eyes. A man came along who spoke English. He told me that the hostel was a half-mile away, not far at all in the greater scheme of things, but at that moment half a mile sounded like a thousand. He pointed me in the right direction, I thanked them both, and I stumped very slowly up a little hill and down again, past stone houses and shuttered shops, with bats skittering above my head.

Finally, after hobbling around the city in a wide and unnecessary circle, I ended up at the door of a government building, where a pimple-faced soldier fiddling with a radio answered my question about the hostel by pointing across a dark field of knee-high grass to some buildings and lights on the far side. I headed across the field, but in the dark I tripped over a rock and fell forward onto my face, and the sudden, unexpected motion caused the pain in my legs to shoot all the way to my throat. I lay in the grass for a minute or so, my pack feeling very heavy on my back. Then I righted myself and moved on, weeping and feeling for the first time lonely and afraid.

When I reached the hostel, a long, low building like a military bunkhouse, the hostelkeeper said he had been expecting me. Christine, who had arrived earlier that afternoon, had written my name in the guestbook. It was 9:15. I had walked thirty miles.

Christine sat with me in a small restaurant while I ate bacon and eggs, the only thing the restaurant had left at that hour. I told Christine how difficult my trip had been. She said, "How did you continue?"

I thought about it. I had gone on walking out of an ancient fear of quitting. I hated giving up, even when giving up was the intelligent or generous or brave thing to do. It was an irrational fear of defeat. At one point in my long walk I had also, unexpectedly, thought of Jesus dragging the cross through the streets of Jerusalem. It was rare that I thought of the suffering of Christ in connection with my own suffering. But the image had come to me and shamed me into continuing. Sometimes that seemed the point of Jesus. If you felt desperate and sorry for yourself, if you thought your life wasn't going well, all you had to do was think of his suffering and by comparison you were forced to realize that you were hardly suffering at all. When I told Christine that I had thought of Christ with his cross on his back, her eyes, ice-blue, spontaneously filled with tears. She slapped them away with a napkin. "But he was God," she said.

I said, "Wasn't he human?"

Again sounding like my mother, she said, "He was fully human, but he was also God."

THE NEXT DAY I was severely crippled. It took me twenty minutes to hobble the quarter-mile from the hostel to the hospital. At the hospital's front steps I had to hold onto the railing with both hands and work my way up sideways.

The hospital offered its services to pilgrims free of charge. A sympathetic but unsmiling doctor named Yolanda, who had luxurious auburn hair and a generous wash of blue eye shadow on each lid, poked at my shins and worked my feet back and forth like the levers on a one-armed bandit. I sat on her examining table and howled in pain. "Tendinitis," Dr. Yolanda said, raising her carefully plucked brows and twisting her mouth to the side in a way that suggested she had seen more cases of pilgrim tendinitis than she cared to remember and that while pilgrims were very well-intentioned people they were also rather dumb.

The doctor gave me some painkillers, some anti-inflammatory pills, and some cream to rub into my shins and sent me off, saying, "You must not walk for three days. And slow your pace. Perhaps it is God's will that you should slow down."

FROM THE HOSPITAL I made my limping way to a hotel on the cathedral square, stopping at every step to take a deep breath of pain. In the hotel room I sat in a bathtub for four hours, talking to myself. The bathmat had the name of the hotel embroidered on it: El Cid. The Christian warrior El Cid (Rodrigo Díaz de Vivar) was born near Burgos in 1043. He was, I knew, a questionable character and not a terribly loyal warrior, fighting both for the Moors against King Alfonso and for Alfonso against the Moors. Spain's great epic poem *The Song of El Cid* contains the line, "So many white banners turn red with blood and so many good horses, riderless, roam, while the Moors call 'Mahomet!' and the Christians 'Santiago!' respond." Washing my neck for the third time, I realized that epic poetry was always about bloody battles fought in the name of religion.

I climbed into the clean bed, elevated my legs on pillows, and stared at my feet. So much walking had turned four of my toenails the dark purple of Concord grapes. I was uncomfortable, and the constant pain in my legs had made me irritable. Sunlight streamed through the windows and onto my face, blinding me and overheating the room. Just outside my window a hundred pigeons pecked at the ledge; I could hear their submarine noises, a watery gurgling like the sound of a tape rewinding. The sound annoyed me. If I had been able to walk to the window, I would have clapped the birds away and shut the curtains. But just traveling from the bathroom to the bed had been a ten-minute adventure that involved leaning with both hands on every piece of furniture along the way. Now that I was in the bed, I refused to get up again. Through the windows I could see the tops of the magnificent spires of nearby Burgos Cathedral, tall Gothic stalagmites of golden-yellow stone, ornate with statues of bearded saints, grinning gargoyles, angels, griffins, trefoils, rosettes, and curling leaves. The spires glowed in the morning light, looking as frilly and confusing as lace against the pale blue sky behind them. Each spire was as crowded and intricately worked as a Fabergé egg. That, for some reason, irritated me too.

I lay there in the hotel room, hot with frustration. Irritated by one thing, I had become irritated by everything. I wanted to murder the nattering pigeons; the room was too hot; I had left my bottle of water in the bathroom and couldn't get it. I thought enviously of all the pilgrims who had set off merrily down the trail that morning. I thought of glamorous Dr. Yolanda saying, "Perhaps it is God's will that you slow down." Her words had struck me, not just because I disliked the fatalism of the phrase "It's God's will," but also because I knew that I was an impatient person, always in a hurry.

Sometimes while my dinner was cooking (on the rare occasions that I actually took the time to cook it), I would eat my dessert to save time. I was extreme. Once, when I started out to make a simple backless bookshelf, I ended up making a twelve-foot double-ended, hard-chined dory instead. After buying a house that I didn't like, I pulled down walls and ceilings, replastered the remaining walls and ceilings, replaced joists, ripped up the wall-to-wall carpeting, resanded the floors, rebuilt the front porch, dug up the lawn and reseeded it, planted twenty shrubs, and painted the exterior. When I lived for a time on an island in Maine, I spent several months ridding a meadow of poison ivy and sumac trees taller than myself. I was compelled, whether or not it benefited me personally, to take what was rough and make it smooth. It was a disease,

I knew, a kind of insanity. I hated to leave things unfinished, would work obsessively on a project, no matter how pointless or silly, until it was complete. The sight of Olatz surrendering less than halfway to Santiago had left me not just sad but worried. Her defeat was like a warning. Having said I would walk to Santiago, I dreaded the possibility that I, too, might not complete the promise.

Flat on my back, in pain in a strange city with no one to talk to, that promise suddenly seemed absurd. Why was I walking across Spain? Why was anybody walking across Spain?

In his colloquy of 1526 "A Pilgrimage for Religion's Sake," Erasmus criticized the pilgrimage to Compostela. Greeting his gullible friend Ogygius, who has returned from his holy trip draped in pilgrim symbols, Erasmus's scoffing character Menedemus asks mockingly, "But what's this fancy outfit? You're ringed with scallop shells, choked with tin and leaden images on every side, decked out with straw necklaces, and you've snake eggs on your arms."

> OGYGIUS: I've been on a visit to St. James of Compostella . . .
> MENEDEMUS: Out of curiosity, I dare say.
> OGYGIUS: On the contrary, out of devotion.
> MENEDEMUS: Tell me, how is the excellent James?
> OGYGIUS: Much colder than usual.
> MENEDEMUS: Why? Old age?
> OGYGIUS: Joker! You know saints don't grow old. But this new-fangled notion that pervades the whole world results in his being greeted more seldom than usual. And if people do come, they merely greet him; they make no offering at all, or only a very slight one, declaring it would be better to contribute that money to the poor.
> MENEDEMUS: A wicked notion.

I felt foolish. I felt like Menedemus and Ogygius both. I was a skeptic, and yet I was stumping my way across Spain to see a holy shrine. I had curiosity but not a shred of devotion. Suddenly I disliked even the word "pilgrim." It sounded pious and creeping, and it made me think of the early American Puritans, with their austerity and their dire punishments. I began to scorn the Camino de Santiago and everyone on it.

My temper was like a fever. I lay in the hotel fretting and fuming, cursing nearly everything I could think of. And eventually my fit of irritation turned, as it always did, to self-criticism. Having driven my temper into a muddy cul-de-sac, I could do nothing but start over and ask myself why everything suddenly annoyed me: the New Agers on the trail, the nagging, chattering experts, the wealthy pilgrims. From the moment I first heard it, the statement "It is easier for a camel to go through a needle's eye than for a rich man to enter into the kingdom of God" sounded wrong and unfair. The notion that people who lived in poverty were more spiritually authentic was ridiculous, and yet here on the Camino I was falling for it. The wealthy pilgrims struck me as insincere, their vague "seeking" an excuse. I had expected to find poor pilgrims with an old-fashioned belief. But why? Belief had no style or era, its quality was constant and ageless. The banker's soul was no different from the peasant woman's. And the New Age pilgrims, with their incense and crystals and piping wooden flutes, were simply trying, like everyone else, to survive. They were all, in their own manner, manifesting an ancient need in a modern age.

That was the difficulty: the modern age was not amenable to spiritual concerns. The New Agers seemed to me to have passion but little reason. Their religion was a kind of emotional pantheism — they appeared to have faith in anything that smelled or sounded good, anything comforting. It was a religion based in the placebo effect. But in the end, was that not true of all religion?

"Imagination does not breed insanity," Chesterton wrote in his defense of orthodox Christian theology. "Exactly what does breed insanity is reason . . . How much happier you would be . . . if the hammer of a higher God could smash your small cosmos, scattering the stars like spangles, and leave you in the open, free like all other men to look up and down." If religion was not simply blindly inherited, then it was a matter of choice, and Chesterton was suggesting: take the leap, choose to believe; you'll feel better. My thoughts about Chesterton were like my thoughts about God — I wanted to believe in him but found it difficult. His clever sentences, which have apparently consoled any number of twentieth-century thinkers, did not entirely persuade me. Everything he said had a tautological ring and his God was like an imaginary friend. I didn't want an imaginary friend; I wanted a real one.

I shifted my right leg and gasped in pain. Just by moving my toes I could send an excruciating electric shock all the way to my teeth. The hot sunlight crept slowly down the bed. With the sandcastle spires of the cathedral in my peripheral vision I — not sure I believed in God in the first place — asked myself out loud what form of belief would satisfy me. I was interested in other people's cosmic theories and philosophies of life but was anxious about forming my own. I admired those who believed, but kept deflecting belief myself. Anglicans, Protestants, Catholics, New Age pilgrims — their systems all struck me as cluttered and clubbish and obscuring, a junkshop of tribal fears, of rituals and rules and the impulse to convert others.

Would belief alone ever suffice? At home I had been reading the Bible, Emerson, Chesterton's *Orthodoxy,* Theresa of Ávila, the anonymous *Way of the Pilgrim,* and other spiritual texts. I admired Theresa for the fierceness of her belief — she was nearly as fierce as Jesus. In writing to her sisters, she said that their vow of poverty offered greater protection than any "sumptuous edifices" and adjured them to maintain it. "If I may say what my conscience bids me, I should wish that, on the day when you build such edifices they may fall down *and kill you all.*" I was drawn to Emerson, who believed that God was within us, whose view of the soul was generous and open, who could say, "Belief consists in accepting the affirmations of the soul. Unbelief in denying them."

The Way of a Pilgrim is a nineteenth-century account of a homeless Russian peasant who, upon hearing Saint Paul's words "Pray constantly," was forced to ask himself "how could it be possible for a man to pray without ceasing when the practical necessities of life demand so much attention?" The peasant set off across the country struggling to find a practical answer. Along the way a spiritual teacher instructed him to read the *Philokalia,* a compilation of texts on prayer and spiritual life written by the spiritual masters of the Greek Orthodox Church. The *Philokalia* was a guide for all those who, at the prompting of God, hoped to develop their powers to "overcome fragmentation and achieve wholeness . . . attain contemplative stillness and union with God." Saint Simeon, one of the composers of the *Philokalia,* taught that those interested in achieving knowledge of God should practice the Jesus Prayer. "Sit alone and in silence; bow your head and close your eyes; relax your breathing and with your imagination look into your heart; direct your thoughts from your head into your heart. And while inhaling say, 'Lord Jesus Christ, have mercy on me,' either softly with your lips or in your mind. Endeavor to fight distractions but be patient and peaceful and repeat this process frequently." The pilgrim was instructed to say the Jesus Prayer three thousand times a day in the beginning. He did this, and the number was raised to six thousand a day. For a week he stayed in his hut and did nothing but pray. He found that prayer became easier and easier, that when he wasn't praying, all he wanted was to pray. Finally he was saying the prayer twelve thousand times a day. "I was joyful the whole day," he reported, "and seemingly oblivious to everything else." He had begun without knowing how to pray, but simply by beginning he had learned. "I walk in a semi-conscious state without worries, interests, and temptations."

I envied the anonymous pilgrim, for he had, through belief and prayer, attained a kind of ecstasy, though he walked miles every day and ate little more than bread and water. On my pilgrimage I had so far attained no spiritual ecstasy. I had attained little but a bad distemper and two ruined legs. It was no surprise; I lacked the two main ingredients: belief and prayer. I hardly ever consciously prayed.

Saint Simeon wrote, "We cannot speak in the abstract of any one form of life as higher than another — of the hermit life, for example, as superior to the cenobitic — for the best and highest form of life is, for each one, the particular way to which he or she is personally called." His words passed through my mind like an admonishment, but that didn't stop me from thinking, *I will strangle the next person who tells me it's God's will or that I'm walking too fast or that the Camino is the path to the stars.* It did not stop me from praying to God that I would not have to stay in another hostel bedecked with burning joss sticks and tinkling wind chimes or from recalling with annoyance the pilgrims who spoke airily of their spirituality, criticized materialism, extolled generosity, and then elbowed their way into the hostel hoping to get the hottest shower and the best bed. It did not stop me from wondering miserably why I had chosen to write about faith, a topic that seemed very distant from me.

I put my forearm over my eyes, sighed, and said, "Lord Jesus Christ, have mercy on me." Coming from me, the Jesus Prayer sounded like a vulgar curse. My map lay on the table near my bed. I opened it and stared. I was only halfway to Santiago. I folded the map up and threw it across the room so that I couldn't reach it. I fumed a while longer, then went quiet, because I knew that what was really upsetting me was that love was failing in my life. At its core, love, like faith, was not a product of reason. Reason ignited it, but for love to survive, something else, some form of trust, had to take over. Real love required a risk, an act of daring. In my relationship there was not enough trust and too little daring. Walking to Santiago I had tried not to think too much about it, but it was the most important thing in my life at that time, and it kept cropping up in front of me and blocking my path.

I SLEPT most of that day and the next night, fitfully and in pain and wishing I were in my own bed at home. During the night a tempestuous rainstorm began, and when I woke in the morning the encrusted cathedral spires were dripping and dark against the mouse-gray sky. The wind whistled and thudded against my windows and lashed ropes of rain against the hotel. As if extinguished by the rain, my hot temper was gone. I was still unable to walk, but my mood had lightened.

The pilgrim trail went directly past the cathedral, and as I hobbled to the bathroom I saw through the window a few hearty pilgrims tramping through the puddles, hoods up and heads lowered against the storm. It was the first rain since the day I had started walking in St. Jean Pied-de-Port, and I was glad not to be walking. I sat down and looked out the window as I waited for someone from the hotel kitchen to bring me coffee and bread. The wide, open square was surrounded by shops and very old buildings. How many pilgrims had walked past this cathedral over the centuries? And what were they thinking as they walked?

The medieval pilgrims came from every class of society; they were bishops and kings, saints and peasants, and they had come from approximately the same places the pilgrims came from now. Some made the journey inspired by true faith and devotion to Saint James. Others came as representatives of their village or town. Some came in penance, others to fulfill a sentence for a crime. Many traveled in groups for safety. They left from Paris and Le Puy and other designated points. The standard medieval pilgrim to Compostela wore a wide-brimmed floppy hat and a shoulder cape, carried a satchel, a gourd for water, a walking stick, and a scallop shell, the symbol of Saint James. Many pilgrims kept records of their trip, detailing the sights, the cities, the hospitals, and their own experiences. Most famously, an anonymous French priest wrote a detailed five-volume account of his pilgrimage known as the *Liber Sancti Jacobi,* a kind of medieval Camino guidebook. The flow of pilgrims, at its height during the eleventh and twelfth centuries, began to wane during the sixteenth century, and by the eighteenth century it had dwindled to near extinction. The modern pilgrimage is a recent development. In the 1970s hardly anyone walked the trail to Santiago, and the trail itself was all but lost. The old route and its landmarks had to be rediscovered by historians and interested amateurs.

Looking out the window at the pilgrims below, I thought about the people I had met on the trail. I had met Jorge and Juan, the Brazilian father and son. I had met a shy twenty-two-year-old German boy named Robert, who was walking the trail for "the silence." He told me, "In Germany, if you give somebody the finger when you're driving, you have to pay a fine of five hundred dollars. And if you touch your finger to your temple to show that the other driver is a stupid idiot, that's a four-hundred-dollar fine."

I had met Enrique, from Pamplona, who had a thick black mustache that ran all the way to his jaw on either side of his chin, like a furry horseshoe hung below his nose. Like all Pamplonans, Enrique said, "You know Ernest Hemingway?" He had a harmonica with him. I played "Camptown Races" on it, and he cried, "Oh, that's the song my cell phone plays when I have a call!" When I told him he had a face like Don Quixote, he was delighted and said, "Want to see the rest of me?"

In one hostel I had met sententious, gray-haired Pat Trench from Texas, who lay on her bed in a nylon running suit and crowed about her advanced age. "Ahm sevn'y-one!" she exclaimed. "If you can prove that anyone older than me has ever done the C'meeno ah'll give you one thousand peseters!" Pat looked like Peter Ustinov, the little eyes, the hanging cheeks. She often said, "It is a desecration!" and "It is the wee-yull of the Low-erd."

And then there was handsome Manuel, a translator from Brazil. When he was a teenager, his parents discovered that he was gay and took him to a psychiatrist. "It was the only time in my life that I was ever depressed," he said. Manuel was puzzled by the world's weird perceptions of homosexuals. Once, when he asked his mother to sew a button on his shirt, his mother said, "Isn't your boyfriend the woman in the relationship? Ask him to do it."

I had met Mario, a wealthy retired Italian businessman, who loved the United States and big cars and hated India because the people were "too poor." He hated poverty. "I don't want to see it. I know it's real, but I just don't want to see it. It ruins my day." He also hated Padre Pio, the stigmatized Italian friar, calling him a "nasty woman-hating mafioso." Mario was hoping to fix his son up with a nice woman. The son had only one problem: "He does not see well." From the way Mario said it I had the impression that the son was stone-blind.

I had met a skeletal Japanese boy named Takuo, who was so bow-legged that he looked as though he were holding an invisible beer keg between his knees. Takuo wore neon-green socks. He had long, sparse stubble on his chin like newly sprouted grass. He was a curiosity on the road because Japanese pilgrims were very rare. Takuo spoke no Span-ish, no French, and so little English that no one bothered to talk to him. Behind his back people made fun of his huge, saucerlike eyes. One morning, I had walked with him for a few hours and he managed to tell me he was a hairdresser and lived alone in Tokyo. When I asked why he was walking to Santiago he replied, "To get new ideas for hairstyles." That morning there happened to be a lot of dead frogs on the road, and at one point we came upon a headless snake. The snake was big and the brilliant green of a Wellington boot. Flies buzzed around its wound. Takuo gagged and hurried on. Later we saw a farmer throwing a dead lamb to his dogs, and Takuo cringed and covered his eyes. "I think that the road is very difficult," he had said. "Sometimes I want to cry."

Outside, the pilgrims pressed on through the rain in a thin but steady stream. Some jackets I recognized, having met their owners days before. The trail of people on the Camino was like an amoeba. You met peo-ple, got separated from them, met again, and separated. Everyone was thinking about their bodies, their pains and hungers and wishes for what they had left behind. When you met someone and asked how he was, he would say, "Well, fine, but my right foot." Or "Limping along!" Or "Lost five pounds so far!"

My coffee arrived, and as I sat drinking it I wondered about the souls of the medieval pilgrims. Had they found what they were hoping for? Whatever had set them on this arduous road, whatever hopes or wor-ries they had, they were free of now; the search had been passed on to the new pilgrims, who exercised it in a new way. I had been reading A. N. Wilson's *God's Funeral* and Karen Armstrong's *A History of God* and was learning that the course of religion was like the course of natu-ral selection. We took what existed and adapted it to our present reality. The relative ignorance of the medieval pilgrims had made a fantastic, miraculous, world-ordering God plausible. When science made it clear that God did not create the world in a week, people who still wanted and needed to believe didn't stop believing but simply altered their understanding of God. The more we learned of the human body, of the universe, of the laws of nature, the less believable the old religious explanations became and the more God seemed not to be separate and above but present and within. The tenets and assertions of all religions become outdated. In modern times the once mighty Roman Catholic Church has stumbled and staggered, its five-fingered grip reduced to a trembling thumb and forefinger. Saint James and what he represented seemed insignificant now; it was the road created by his name — its length, its variety, its difficulties — that drew us. Most of the modern pilgrims existed in a culture of ease. In the twentieth century we could travel all the way from Jerusalem to Santiago in a day if we chose to. The more we learned about our physical existence, about the hard facts of our world, the more we were able to accomplish, but the less room there seemed to be for us here. We were moving so quickly now that moving slowly had become a struggle. As I watched the pilgrims below in the square, it struck me that we had come here in an effort to slow down.

THE DOCTOR had told me not to walk for three days, but on the morning of the third day my legs felt better, the sun was shining, and when I went to the window and saw the pilgrims crossing the square I felt lonely and left behind. I was so eager to get back on the trail that I ignored the doctor's advice, packed up my bag, and put my boots back on. In a contrite, chastened mood I left the hotel and began walking west through the city, vowing that I would slow down, try to be a better person, try to be accepting, try to control my irascibility, and try to let the hammer of a higher God smash my small cosmos.

Burgos smelled pleasantly of coffee and sausages. Street sweepers swatted the pavement with straw brooms. Everything looked clean and bright. Walking out of the city, I met pilgrims I hadn't seen in days, people who were traveling at a slower pace: the Canadian nun, the Swiss medical student, the Brazilian Jews. Though my legs still hurt, I found that by using a stick as a cane I could move forward slowly. That I could walk again seemed a tremendous gift, and that morning the marvels of the human body struck me as reason enough to believe in God. The concatenation of corpuscles and cells, cartilage, follicles, enzymes, bone, and brain was no less staggering than the cosmos, and when it all blinked out upon the body's death, no less than a universe would come to an end.

SEVEN OR EIGHT MILES outside of Burgos, in the high plains, the landscape became a wide expanse of nothing, a brown, rolling sea of badlands. There were hanks of yellow and brown grass, a few white rocks, some gargling flocks of larks, and nothing else — just a huge sky crowded with clouds. After the rain the thick clay along the trail had grown sticky; with each step I gained another quarter inch of it on the soles of my boots, until after ten steps I was walking on platform shoes of mud. When I stopped to knock the mud away with my stick, I saw something bright in the grass and picked it up — the torn remains of a rubber helium balloon with a piece of paper attached by a length of butcher's string. On the paper was a child's pencil drawing of a house with a river of blue sky above it, and at the bottom, in crooked hand-writing, the words *Timor para Paz*. The drawing was signed *Inês*. The peaked roof of the house was like a tall duncecap, the two windows like eyes, the door an astonished mouth. I put the drawing in my pocket. There was nothing around for miles. The child's balloon, with its message of peace for Timor, had carried into the badlands from God only knew where.

APPROACHING CASTROJERIZ, the road passed under a double archway of stone, part of the fourteenth-century Monastery and Hospital of San Anton. According to my guidebook, the main distinction of the French Antonine order was "the ability to cure erysipelas or 'St Anthony's Fire,' a contagious skin disease producing burning red blisters, which scourged Europe in the 10th and 11th Centuries." Saint Anthony was also the patron saint of swineherds, "which is interesting as the same disease affects pigs in the form of swine erysipelas, which the followers of St. Anthony also cured."

The monastery building was beautiful but decrepit. Scores of little statues in the arched doorway of the church had had their heads neatly broken off, and that obsessively systematic destruction reminded me of temples I had seen in China, where the faces of a thousand Buddhas had been drilled down to blank holes by Mao's Red Guards.

Castrojeriz sat in the middle of a pretty, umber-hued plain of farm-land. Like so many of the villages along the way, it had an amazing collection of ancient churches and monuments. On the top of the hill above the town was the daunting form of a ruined castle. During the ninth and tenth centuries fierce battles between the Christians and the Saracens had taken place here.

I went into the Church of San Juan and was met by a short, watery-eyed, slow-witted man with an official-looking booklet of tickets. The church was big and dark and cool and empty, but from somewhere in the columned recesses I could hear a choir singing. The small man made a formal show of selling me a ticket: leaning over a desk, he slowly wrote the ticket number in a booklet, closed the cover, fastened it shut with a rubber band, licked the tip of his index finger, carefully tore the pink piece of paper from its stack, and proudly presented it to me. I peered at the ticket in the dim light. The man stood at my side and read out loud what was printed on the ticket: "Parroquia de Castrojeriz! Burgos!" His voice was a shout that rang out in the big church. He stood with his arms held slightly away from his body, like a person whose clothing was soaking wet. His shirt was buttoned all the way up to his throat, which made him look choked. I asked him how much the ticket cost. "Nada!" he cried. "Es gratuita!" He addressed me as "peregrina" and asked where I was going, and suddenly his arm was around my waist. I removed it and told him I was going to Itero de la Vega.

He said in Spanish, "Today, pilgrim?"

"Yes," I said, "today."

"It's very far." That was what villagers always said, even when the destination was a mere two kilometers away.

The church's high, dusty windows strained the sunlight to a pale mist. The singing voices echoed against the bare stones, and gradually I realized that the voices were recorded. The ticket man insisted on walking around the church with me. I didn't want his company but didn't know how to tell him this politely in Spanish. His name was Salvador. As we walked he pointed his short fingers at objects and told me what they were. He put his arm around my waist. I removed it. He said, "Es un convento que . . . Mira, San Francisco aqui . . . La ventana es piedra." I understood very little but nodded my head anyway. "Santiago en Caballo," he said, slipping his arm around my waist again. It was a statue of Saint James on his horse, wielding his sword and trampling on some particularly Arabic-looking black men. I removed Salvador's arm again and kept walking. I had seen along the Camino a hundred depictions of Santiago slaying the Moors. His sword was sometimes covered in blood, and the Moors, often dressed in Arab clothing, were always depicted in indign postures: upside down with their feet in the air or cowering or with their turbaned heads thoroughly severed from their bodies. And the horse always looked muscular and vicious and wild. I was growing a little weary of all this triumphalism. But this brutal murderer, Saint James, was ostensibly the reason I was shuffling across Spain.

I made my way through the big church with Salvador grinning and chasing after me. I stopped to look at an amazingly detailed handmade diorama of Christ's life, but it was difficult to concentrate on the gruesome depiction of the slaughter of the infants with the mooning little man sneaking his hand toward my breast. He seemed dim and harmless; it was not worth protesting. The poor fellow spent his days alone in this empty, echoing church waiting for a pilgrim or two to show up. As I was leaving he gave me a kiss on each cheek and patted my hair. I made a donation to the church; he slipped the money into his shirt pocket. He said, "I won't forget you." I went off down the path and he stood in the doorway of the church crying, "Peregrina! Don't go!"

I was rubbing anti-inflammatory cream into my shins in a field outside of Castrojeriz when two old men approached across a field with an enormous flock of sheep and nine or ten dogs. The dogs skulked and darted, and the wild-eyed sheep trotted in a nervous huddle, cackling in fear and kicking up a cloud of yellow dust. One of the men wore a brown hooded cape made out of a woolen blanket. With the hood up he looked like the Grim Reaper. He walked slowly toward me, chewing on a piece of straw and peeling a fig he had plucked from a tree. Squinting in the sunlight, he looked curiously at my hiking boots and backpack. Flies hurried around his hooded head. He pointed to a steep ridge at the edge of the field, and said, around the straw, "You have to go over that hill, you know."

A FEW DAYS LATER I arrived in the town of Carrion de Los Condes, limping heavily again. Early in the day my legs were fine, but toward evening the pain returned. The hostel was big and utilitarian and so crowded that the hostelkeepers had spread mattresses on the floor. The closer we got to Santiago, the more crowded the hostels were. Pilgrims were hanging their wet clothing on strings across the tiny windows. A group of college students was sitting around on the mattresses looking dirty and tired. A pale-skinned Austrian girl was wandering about playing a medieval tune on a wooden recorder. At the kitchen table a man with very thick glasses was sitting in his underwear eating a dinner of raw hot dogs and sipping a glass of water.

The place depressed me, but I was happy to have found a bed. I took a shower and went to a little restaurant nearby for supper. The restaurant was noisy and narrow and lit with dim yellow lights. It was crowded with both pilgrims and local people. Above the bar a television showed a soccer match on a fuzzy screen.

I found a seat at a table of pilgrims, several of whom I had met before. Gilbert, a fat, bearded Frenchman, was there. So was Odile, the French lawyer who had driven a dump truck in Kosovo. Next to Odile sat the Belgian priest with a gnome's tiny beard. Juan and Jorge, the Brazilian father and son, were at the end of the table, and there were a few others I didn't know. They were all eating chops and French fries and salad and drinking wine. The air was smoky, and in the poor light everyone looked tired and a bit sickly. Jorge was drinking brandy and saying, "Damn, man, that brandy is *strong!* Now in Italy me and my daddy drank something —" He turned to look at his father. "Daddy, what was that guy called that we drank down there in Italy?"

Without looking away from the television, the reticent, ponytailed father said, "Grappa."

"Grappa! Man, that guy was strong, too! It sucked tasting! But we had a hell of a good time, didn't we, Daddy?"

Odile introduced me to the man I had sat down next to. His name was Eduardo. I said, "Nice to meet you, Eduardo," and held out my hand, but he made no move to shake it. He peered over his shoulder at me, not turning his body toward me, his elbows on the table. He was drinking red wine and smoking a cigarette. He hadn't touched the food on his plate.

"So!" he sneered. "You don't remember me, eh?" His English was very good.

"No, I'm sorry," I said. "I don't."

"We have met two days ago!"

"We did?"

Eduardo raised his wineglass in front of his nose with both hands and smirked contemptuously at it. Baffled, I stared at him, trying to remember. I had met so many people on the road and been through so many towns that it was all becoming one long day in my mind. Eduardo didn't look at all familiar. "Ha!" he cried. "You do not remember!"

It was unmistakably an accusation. And then I realized that he was drunk; the whites of his eyes were the color of maraschino cherries and his teeth were maroon from the wine. He had a watery smoker's cough, a broken front tooth, and what looked like the remnants of a black eye. He was handsome, but the vindictive look in his eye made him rather menacing. He looked very unhappy and was clearly harboring some resentment toward me. He was bristling, looking for an argument. His anger seemed utterly unreasonable, but I didn't care. My legs hurt, I was very tired, and my high hopes for calm, transcendence, and an even temper were crumbling. I was hungry and a little sad, and tired of my stinking clothes. All I had wanted was to find a quiet place to eat dinner and then go to bed.

"I'm sorry," I said again. "I guess I don't remember." I looked at the menu.

Odile began to say something, but Eduardo brusquely cut her off. "We met on the trail. I took a wrong turn and you called to me and sent me on the right trail. When I asked you if you were traveling alone you said yes. I said, Too bad. You said, It's not so bad because I love myself so much. And you went away!"

Now I remembered. He and another man had taken a wrong turn, and when I looked back and realized they were going the wrong way I called to them, indicated the right way, and kept walking. The exchange, from a distance of perhaps thirty feet, had taken all of three seconds. I had been wearing a broad-brimmed hat on my head. That he remembered me was astonishing. "I didn't say that," I said. "I said I liked walking alone, but that if I really hated myself it might be unbearable."

Eduardo put his face close to mine. "I love myself!"

I saw that it was silly to argue with him. Drunkenness had made him deaf. His speech was slurred, and he was weaving slightly in his seat. He pointed the stub of his cigarette at me. "I love yourself. You said."

He wasn't going to give up until he had provoked a response. I looked at the other faces at the table. They had all fallen mute with apprehension. Odile blinked her pale lashes at Eduardo. Her face was very red. Gilbert stroked his beard nervously with his fingers. The priest shoved lettuce into his mouth. They all seemed to know something I didn't know.

"I didn't say that," I said.

Eduardo slitted his red eyes at me. "Where are you from?"

"United States."

It was the wrong answer. He suddenly sat straight up in his seat and, giving the air a good stir with his wineglass, he roared at the top of his voice with malicious glee, "Aha! I knew it! Fucking Americans! All egomaniacs in love with yourself!" He sipped angrily at his wine. "And always unfriendly!" He sipped again. "And all of you so stupid!"

The bar went very quiet. All the heads — not only the other pilgrims but also the elderly local people — turned to look at us. The bartender dried his hands on his apron and turned down the volume of the television. I tried to ignore Eduardo and to remain calm, but the little engine of ire that sits stored away in a cabinet of my self had been clicked on. My scalp and my very fingertips were hot with anger. I stared at the menu and struggled to contain myself.

Eduardo put his nose an inch from my shoulder. "American! *You* are full of shit!"

I put the menu down and turned toward him. "I don't know who you are," I said, "but you should be grateful that I put you on the right road. You'd be in Morocco by now if I hadn't."

"You stupid Americans, you have a presidente who bomb Kosovo because Monica suck his dick!"

That one was hard to refute. The bar was very quiet. Everyone in it was listening. Nevertheless, I felt the need to say, "Shove it, you chimp!"

"You shove it, *American.*"

"*You* shove it," I said. "And fuck off, too."

Gilbert raised his pudgy hands at us. "Hey, guys," he said in his little-boy voice, "the Camino is love! Don't fight." Gilbert had skin the color of putty and a broad, freckled forehead. A bit of lettuce dangled from his fastidiously trimmed beard. I was so angry I wanted to turn to him and say *Oh, shut your silly French trap!* But Eduardo did it for me. He learned across the table and shouted at Gilbert, "You shut up about love, mister fat French divorced man talking about love!"

Odile blinked at her dinner plate in stunned wonder.

Eduardo said to me, "And fuck you, you stupid American."

I should have left then, but I couldn't keep myself from saying "Fuck you" back to him. And then, feeling like a pig and wanting very much to change the subject, I said, "Odile, tell me what it was like to drive a truck in Kosovo."

Odile opened her mouth to speak, but Eduardo interrupted her. "Clinton el Presidente ask you to suck his dick in Kosovo?"

Jorge put down his glass of brandy. "Hey, man. You don't talk damn shit like that to the people."

The father looked at Jorge in surprise and approval.

Eduardo glared at Jorge. "I hate America. And I hate fucking France too. And Spain. I am from Brazil. And I will tell you why the Spanish people don't like the Brazilians. They say we are backward third-world people. But really they envy us. We have freedom. Our country is very big. And we know how to have fun." He looked around at the people in the bar and said loudly, "The Spanish people hate us Brazilians because Spanish do not know how to have fun!"

The Spaniards, most of whom probably didn't understand what he was saying, looked fearfully at him.

"But pilgrims should love each other, man," Gilbert piped in bravely. "The Camino is love."

Eduardo grimaced at Gilbert, raised his voice two octaves, and, in a perfect imitation, peeped mockingly, "The Camino is *love*, man." Then he got up to go to the bathroom. He staggered slightly, and as he passed between the tables, the customers leaned warily away from him, as though he might lash out and knock their food to the floor. We all looked at each other across the table. Odile said, "Oh, Rose, you should not get into a fight with that man. He is very crazy! He fights with people wherever he goes. In one place he got in a fight and the police arrested him and put him in jail."

I realized then that Eduardo was the man Christine had told me about, the Brazilian who had caused a riot in a hostel. He was infamous on the trail now. I had heard about him several times, but I had had no way of knowing that this was the same man.

Jorge said, "Damn, man! That guy is schizo. I eat with him one time in a place, and when the food comes he says to the cook, 'Damn, this food is shit. This is the worst food I ever eat!' And then fifteen minutes later he is eating and telling everybody, damn, it is the best food he ever eat. He is a hell of a crazy. He is dangerous. You could get punched by him. He got in a fight and they broke his tooth and give him a black eye."

Gilbert, who was drunk, said, "He is drunk. He drinks and drinks. Then he gets mad."

I had had enough adventure for one day, and I got ready to leave the restaurant without eating anything. But Eduardo came back from the bathroom and staggered at me. I thought he was going to hit me. I stood up, and before I knew what was happening, he had flung his arms around me and was saying, "But really, Americana, I love you! You are a tough guy. I like tough-guy girls. I only wanted to walk with you."

I thought he would cry. He had me in a bear hug. Over his shoulder I looked at the other pilgrims. They were smirking and shaking their heads. Eduardo kissed me on the cheek and told me he loved me and was sorry for what he had said. He sat down, raised his greasy wineglass to his lips, and said, "And really I love America. I love the American people. And I love Monica Lewinsky."

Then he began devouring the pork chop that lay cold on the plate in front of him. He went silent, as if he were the only person at the table. In the course of a minute or two he had become a different man. But the sudden change only made me more wary, and after eating three pieces of bread and making polite talk with the others, I left the restaurant.

BACK AT THE HOSTEL Gilbert staggered up the stairs behind me. He was nearly as drunk as Eduardo. He held on to the post of a bunk bed for support and said, "I think you are great! You have stood up to that Brazilian asshole like a matador! When we reach León, you and I will have two nights. One night with friends and one intimate romantic night alone."

"We will?" I said.

The hostel was dark, and many people were already sleeping. Loud snoring came from three different parts of the room. Gilbert tried to kiss me. I pushed him away and went to bed, hating myself for losing my temper. I couldn't sleep. It bothered me that I hadn't been able to just ignore the silly insults of a drunk, and I realized I had been prepared to hit Eduardo if necessary. So much for my vow to accept and contain my temper. All my resolutions had dissolved.

I blinked in the darkness. My legs hurt and I was very wound up. I listened to the snores rumbling through the stinking hostel. I felt awful, filled with remorse. I couldn't deny that I had a temper and that when pushed far enough I could bore a hole through a manhole cover with the words that shot out of my mouth. It was, I thought, my greatest failing. In a rage I said things that felt right at the moment, but as soon as they left my mouth I regretted them and knew they were wrong. I wanted to be a calm, reflective person, like all those saints I had been reading about, like Theresa of Ávila and Julian of Norwich. They cared little for the opinions of others and stayed focused on a higher plane. I was too occupied by what was happening around me. I wanted to elevate my thoughts, but they were always sliding backward.

I slept very little that night, and in the morning I woke to the sound of the Belgian priest clipping his toenails on the bed beside mine, a steady clicking chatter. I rolled over and put my pillow over my head.

THAT DAY on my walk I was relieved to be alone again. In one town two little boys on tricycles saw me coming and rode ahead to a confusing fork in the road so that when I arrived they could point and tell me, "This way, this way, peregrina!" And in another little town I turned a corner under a stone archway and found that I was in the middle of a holy festival taking place in a small, enclosed medieval square strung with colorful pennants and crowded with women seated at many long tables. The women, all wearing red scarves around their necks, were eating, drinking wine, and listening to a group of singing children. When they realized, just by glancing at me, that I had no idea where to go next, they all raised their forks and without saying a word pointed to another stone archway at the far end of the square. I walked sheepishly between their tables. When I reached the archway I thought, *But my map doesn't say to go through a square,* and I turned and looked back, raising my hands at the women in a questioning way. They all lifted their hands and urged me forward with a collective shooing motion, nodding their heads in encouragement, the way they might for a small child hesitating at the door of a school bus.

As soon as I crossed the border from Palencia into the province of León, graffiti began to appear proclaiming that León, which was paired with the province of Castilla, should become autonomous. The angry scrawlings said LEÓN SOLO SIN CASTILLA! and PAIS LEÓNES! and

PUTA CASTILLA. Spain is divided into administrative districts called *comunidades autónomas,* of which Castilla y León is one. Much later I asked a Spanish friend why León would want to be independent from Castilla; she told me that certain right-wing factions wanted the province to become its own autonomous community, because although most of Castilla was poor, León was quite rich, and many of its residents resented paying taxes to support the rest of the *comunidad.* The separatists justified their agitation with the fact that León had been an independent kingdom during the Middle Ages. "All this," my friend told me, "is dressed with the horrendous appeal that nationalism is having more and more all over Europe."

León may have been rich, but it struck me as the least attractive province so far. The landscape was flat and rather dreary, the towns looked depressed, and even the Camino seemed a bit shabby here; the yellow arrows were scarcer and the trail not quite as well maintained as it had been. Graffiti of all stripes began to appear. On a signpost someone had scrawled SEX POR PEREGRINOS. On a wall someone else had written ONLY BRAVE HUMAN SOULS CAN SURVIVE. A third person marked a fence with NOW IT'S THE TIME TO HEAR THE ELFS SINGING LIKE THE STARS. I saw SATAN in several places, and the LEÓN SOLO messages popped up everywhere, one of them with the refutation ES MIERDA! following it.

After the city of León the trail became crowded. In order to receive a *compostela,* the official document identifying the walker as a true pilgrim, one was required to walk at least the last sixty miles of the Camino. To satisfy that requirement many people used León as their point of departure. I noticed many more Spanish people on the trail now, and many were here for a weekend excursion. They ambled along in tennis sneakers and sandals, smoking and drinking from wineskins as they walked. They were friendlier and more relaxed than the hard-core pilgrims who had walked hundreds of miles, and they stopped to sample the local wine and to shop for clothing and trinkets in the town they passed through. In one hostel I met a group of people from Valencia who were here on just such a casual excursion. Their names were Purification, Lourdes, Immaculata, Jesús, María, José, and Ángel. They carried their meager possessions in shoulder bags and eyed the serious, professionally equipped hikers with wary wonder. They got drunk in a bar and mocked, with great comedy, the rules and conditions of the hostels. All night long they talked loudly and giggled in their beds and repeatedly slammed the bathroom door. And in the morning the women carefully applied full masks of makeup before they set off on the trail.

MOVING WEST during the last week of my walk, I could feel September growing old; I smelled it in the air. The mornings were chilly, the willow trees had begun to turn yellow at their tops, and the grape leaves too were turning. Greenish yellow chestnuts and ripe walnuts smacked down onto the road as I walked. I saw very old houses with porches stacked with orange corn and barns full of onions and drying tobacco. I passed through Villadangos del Páramo, Astorga, Rabanal, and Ponferrada, and each day a shrinking half moon hung in the sky in front of me as if leading the way to Santiago.

Outside of Villafranca the farmland was rich. Anise grew along the road, and blackberries, and the apple and pear trees were ripe with fruit. The trail went through the middle of a large vineyard, and all around I could see people picking grapes. Their yellow, red, blue, and white jackets, clustered together and bent over the vines, made bright spots of color amid the green leaves. Tractors pulling trailors rumbled slowly through the field, and the pickers dumped their baskets of grapes into them. When I was halfway across the vineyard, a woman picking grapes stood up to look at me. She had a newspaper on her head and a straw hat on top of that. Wearing a cardigan draped over her shoulders, a skirt, and heeled shoes, she looked like a librarian. She smiled, and I could see lipstick on her teeth. Around her feet were many baskets of grapes. "Pilgrim, good morning. Are you going to Santiago?" she said in Spanish. The tractors full of grapes rumbled by. Already crushed, the grapes had begun to smell like wine.

"Yes."

"Alone?"

"Yes."

"Very good! Would you like some grapes?"

I said I would love some. With a curved knife she cut me a huge bunch. "Eat them today," she said, waving her knife across the field. "Because tomorrow this will all be wine!" She laughed.

I thanked her.

"Don't thank me! But please say a prayer for me in the cathedral when you get to Santiago!"

The landscape grew mountainous, and in the chilly mornings the high towns were covered in mist. Passing from the province of León to the province of Lugo, the trail climbed a long, steep hill — a small mountain, really — up to the town of Cebreiro. The hill was deeply wooded, and the trail was studded in places with ancient cobblestones. I could feel the air pressure changing in my ears as I climbed. The morning was quite cold, and steam puffed from the cuffs of my jacket as I struggled up the hill. Abandoned shoes began to appear along the trail — a loafer stuck in a mud puddle, a sneaker stripped of its lace, the sole of a hiking boot. Before I reached the top of the hill I counted five or six single shoes and one lone sock scattered about the trail in these dark woods. Though I tried to explain this strange phenomenon to myself, I could come up with no good answer. The trail was very steep and difficult in that spot, and I was left with the strange impression that these stray shoes had simply abandoned the pilgrims' feet in exhausted protest.

At the top of the hill in Cebreiro, I had a view of a vast green valley to the west and realized that from here it would be all downhill to Santiago. The trip was nearly over; I had less than a hundred miles to go. Looking west toward the Atlantic Ocean, I had a great sense of anticipation and a great sense of the distance I had already come.

ON OCTOBER 4, twenty-three days after leaving the French town of St. Jean Pied-de-Port, I arrived in Santiago de Compostela at noon, just in time for the Pilgrim's Mass. When I entered the vast Plaza del Obradoiro outside the cathedral, the church bells were ringing in an exciting, galloping way. I went to the Pilgrims' Office, declared myself, had my name registered in a record book, and received my official *compostela*, certifying that I had been a good pilgrim and had arrived at the cathedral to pay my respects. The document was written entirely in Latin; it stated in part: *"notum facit: Rosam Mariam Mahoney hoc sacratissimum Templum pietatis causa devote visitasse."* I was thrilled to have it, and though I was still uncertain about why I had walked all this way, I felt I had accomplished something strange and monumental.

The cathedral was crowded with tourists and pilgrims. Every seat was taken, and many pilgrims stood in the aisles with packs on their backs. Standing near the sanctuary, I was surrounded by pilgrims who had just arrived and were still sweating from the effort. I realized that the woman who had slept in the bed next to mine a few nights before in Palas de Rei was standing beside me. Anna came from the far north of Italy on the border with Austria. She had deep-set eyes and wild red hair and wore a headband that was always slipping down into her eyes. She looked like a Gypsy. We had spoken only a little that night in the hostel, but now, in her delight that we had both made it here safely, she hugged me as though we were old friends.

One by one the pilgrims began to sit down on their backpacks during the Mass. I sat, too, surrounded by hiking equipment and dirty boots. On the baroque altar a blind pilgrim, with his white walking stick and pack, sat beside the priest, who wore a miter and held a crosier. I couldn't understand a word the priest was saying. A short distance away I saw Manuel, the gay Brazilian translator, and at the end of the aisle I could see Juan and Jorge.

The cathedral was so big and so crowded that television screens had been set up to allow the pilgrims at the back of the church to see what was happening at the altar. In the great dome above us an eye was painted within a triangle, similar to the image on a dollar bill. Two French pilgrims stood at the altar and sang a beautiful medieval duet about the pilgrimage. When the priest instructed us to make the sign of peace, all the pilgrims hugged each other.

The city of Santiago de Compostela itself was a bit of a disappointment. It was crowded with shops selling Santiago trinkets and souvenirs — scallop shell ashtrays, brown felt pilgrim hats festooned with shells, walking staffs with fake gourds tied to them, little statues of Saint James on his horse, and thousands of red Santiago crosses. In the cathedral square a man who had dressed his dog in the costume of Saint James invited pilgrims to pose for a photograph with the dog for a small fee. The sad-eyed dog stood patiently on the stones in a brown felt hat and a brown cape bedecked with shells and pilgrim's medals.

The city felt no more holy than any other city, but the ceremony in the cathedral was exceptionally moving. The priest stood at a microphone and began to read the names of the pilgrims who had arrived in Santiago in the past twenty-four hours and where they had walked from. Some pilgrims, hearing their names, cried out, "That's me!" and began to cry. When I heard my name, it sounded a little unreal. I had never walked so far in my life and had never imagined that I would. It was the strangest thing I had ever done. But I was proud of myself for having finished the journey.

At the end of the Mass the church went very quiet as eight men began to swing the *botafumeiro,* a huge, ornate silver incense censer, like a sports trophy, which was suspended from the ceiling by thick ropes. The cathedral was built in the shape of a Latin cross, and the botafumeiro, with a fire of hot coals blazing inside it, swung in a great and frightening arc across the church, parallel to the altar. The swinging of the censer was an ancient tradition, established as much to rid the cathedral of the stink of newly arrived pilgrims as to call forth the Holy Spirit. The eight men worked the device with ropes and a pulley, swinging it so heavily and so high that I grew breathless watching it. Smoke perfumed with the piny smell of frankincense billowed out into the sunlight that filtered through the high cathedral windows. The organist played a dark and rousing hymn to accompany the censer.

Anna, sitting next to me, began to cry. She held my hand. "I am so happy it is over," she shouted over the noise. I smiled at her and realized that although I was satisfied to have completed the trail, I was sorry it was over. I wasn't finished yet. I had a great desire to keep walking.

· 4 ·

VARANASI

With the fountain pen he held in his delicate fingers, the tallest of the four young Indian men pointed to the rum-brown ear of the fellow beside him and said, "This friend is wanting permission to shake your hand." The proposal triggered a hot-faced panic of giggles in the other three — he might as well have said, "Madame, my friend would like permission to feel you up."

The four men were taking a break from their studies to air themselves along the banks of the Ganges under the fuming Varanasi sun, a sun that was less a distinctive disk than a throbbing stain in the pus-yellow sky. The thick air caught the sunlight like a gauze net. The wide brown river crept by a few feet from us. The men were not pilgrims or tourists or touts trawling for tourists' money. They were thin and sharp-shouldered, and their cotton clothing hung around them like drapery. Two were barefoot. All four had brown eyes and black hair and wore heavy-lensed eyeglasses with square black frames. Though their skin was far darker than mine, they seemed pallid and drawn, as if they had been sitting too long in a dimly lit library. They had a rural artlessness. Their lips were chapped, and the crevices between their bright white teeth were stained the color of acorns. Their smiling lips trembled when I spoke to them. Although most Indians who had any education at all spoke English remarkably well, they spoke haltingly and in a sweetly warped way. The tallest, their self-appointed spokesman, had a fat textbook tucked under his arm; his jutting buck teeth made him look slightly bewildered.

I shook his friend's brown hand; it was damp and fragile and surprisingly small. I shook the hands of the other three, and so much wanton handshaking brought on more fits of giggling. They covered their mouths and slapped their skinny thighs and stepped loosely about in the tepid sand and peered at me with an air of having lucked into an unimaginably exciting adventure.

There are close to one hundred ghats along the west bank of the Ganges in Varanasi, and in the two hours that I had just spent walking up and down them, a host of arresting sights — intimately human, coarsely animalistic — had unfolded before me. I had seen a solitary, naked, potbellied toddler wallowing in a pile of cow dung the consistency of applesauce. The child lay back in the spinach-green slush, kicked his feet, rolled over onto his stomach, laughed, and with a gentle spanking motion smeared dung on his face. I had seen scores of Hindu pilgrims standing waist-deep in the Ganges fervently praying, chanting, and bathing, ringing bells and burning incense and reaching into their loincloths to soap their crotches. I had seen a stunned-looking man having an attack of diarrhea behind a bamboo shed, had seen a Japanese tourist screaming so violently at his girlfriend that his floppy cotton hat flew off his head and his spittle hung in the thick sunlight. The Japanese girlfriend cried bitterly. I had seen barefoot *dhobis,* hired washermen, beating heaps of wet clothes against stones in the river, and women in vibrant saris spreading it all out to dry on the railings and steps of the ghats, on makeshift lines, over mud walls — bright strings of bras and underwear, scores of socks, dozens of white shirts, bedsheets, countless diapers, long spills of silk sari cloth spread like carpets upon the sand. I had seen two monkeys copulating furiously on a window ledge — the male, in his effort, baring two long white incisors the shape and color of peeled garlic cloves. I had seen a dog gnawing greedily at the carcass of a goat floating at the edge of the river. At the cremation ghat I had seen a man with a cigarette dangling from his lips pluck up a charred human leg with a pair of bamboo tongs and fling it into the river. A number of ghostly young men with rags wound around their heads had veered at me out of dark doorways, waving their hands, frowning and moaning, then quickly disappearing again. Not until they were gone did I realize what they were saying: *hashish, heroin, opium.*

At that moment, some ten feet away from us, an ascetic wearing nothing but a pink *lungi,* a sarong of cotton cloth tied around his waist, was standing on one leg and staring unblinkingly at the sun. He appeared to be in a trance of excruciating pain. His eyes, leaden and congested, streamed hot-looking tears, yet he did not blink or flinch or move. He held a tin pot in one hand and a bunch of yellow marigolds in the other. His forehead had been painted with the three horizontal white stripes of Shiva, representing truth in thought, word, and deed. At his feet were many tiny clay bowls filled with fine powders in bright colors. I had seen him standing at the same spot in the same posture at sunrise, five hours earlier.

On the other side of us, not seven feet away, an elderly *sadhu*, a Hindu holy man, with copper bracelets around his biceps, was fussily making tea on a little portable stove in a three-sided bamboo hutch decorated with many photographs of himself. His fingernails, as long as door keys, were warped and yellow. A Namadhari, a follower of Vishnu, he wore his hair in a conical bun dressed with mud. His cheeks, long white beard, and arms were marked with the yellowish ash of burnt cow dung. The way he and the other sadhus sat, an extreme form of cross-leggedness in which their heels managed to extend behind them, looked impossible and painful to me. I had spoken to this sadhu several times (this was my fourth day in Varanasi and my eighth walk along the river), and now whenever he saw me passing by he stared long and hard and snickered into his hand, as if he and I were in grand cahoots. Perhaps he was simply laughing at me. The look he gave me was both cowering and aggressive, the malevolent leer of an impostor. Perhaps his spiritual getup was merely a masquerade. It didn't help that the long tufts of white hair growing out of his ears gave him the look of a devil. Like all the other holy men up and down the river who had renounced material things, this sadhu had many possessions: little bags and tiny pots and bowls full of potions and unctions, a copper urn, a bell, strings of beads, garlands, incense, a highly polished walking stick. And like the other holy men he was forever rearranging and tidying them.

As the four young men and I stood talking in the soft sand at the edge of the mud-brown river, a very old woman wearing the white sari of a Hindu widow bathed nearby, scooping water up with her hands and letting it trickle over her withered arms. Her shoulders shook at regular intervals in a way that indicated she was either weeping or snickering. Varanasi was full of unwanted widows banished here by their families.

With so much to look at, I found it difficult to concentrate on the four mild scholars, but they stared so intently at me and seemed so thrilled at having shaken my sweating hand that I was forced to focus. Now and then the tilting lenses of their eyeglasses clashed with the sunlight, turning their eyes into blinding squares of white light.

Our conversation was halting and fragmented — *what name, where live, food, weather, how many days, good, bad, happy, sad* — the elementary information on which language classes everywhere are founded. The men had grown up in Allahabad, sixty miles from Varanasi, and had been friends since childhood. They wanted to know my religion, my nationality, my age. I was thirty-eight.

"You is looking young," said the tall, buck-toothed spokesman.

"Young enough to be your mother," I said.

"Not. Not. You is not. You can be my sister!"

"I have a lot of gray hair," I said.

"You is looking nice."

"And I have wrinkles," I said.

The shortest man stepped forward. "And I am eldest one of all."

The spokesman explained that this short one was married and lived in the house of his father-in-law. He had one child. "Santosh is the son of him's name. It mean satisfaction. Child is two years old." And then, with English-class precision he said, "Madame, what you are qualified in?"

I had to think about that. "Writing, I suppose."

"Are you come here with friends?"

"No."

"You are very brave."

"Not really."

A third man said, "Not really. You are right. You are not brave. Because you are with us. We will mind you."

And then the man who had wanted to shake my hand, whose voice was very high and whose English was very poor, blundered forward and said loudly, "Actually, Indian men do not believe in sex!"

It was difficult to tell what had inspired this sudden unsolicited outburst, which had the ring of a Freudian slip. It reminded me of a boy I had met in New Delhi who had followed me through the streets ominously repeating, "I do not want your money."

"What do you mean they don't believe in it?" I said.

As if afraid that his friend might say something else shocking, the tall one said quickly, "He is not good at English!" Anxiously he added, "Interaction with other people is the most important."

"Yes, of course," I said.

"And interaction with the brain is important. Just like exercise." It was the voice of reason and tact; he was backpedaling, trying to temper his friend's too-familiar outburst and perhaps prevent another. "According to the Indian society norms, before marrying people don't like going with girlfriend courting."

"Not allowed," the eldest piped in.

The tall one continued, "In India ninety-nine percent of the people has to marry before age of twenty-one."

"They have to?" I said.

"Usually, most."

"Are you married?" I said.

At this question the high-voiced friend with sex on the brain cackled inexplicably.

"Not so far," the tall one answered

A gang of long-tailed, red-bottomed monkeys suddenly ran down the steps behind us and cantered up the beach. "Why are these monkeys here?" I said.

"They are commonly," said the eldest. He waved his hand at a magnificent red stone castle above the ghat behind us and said, "That is their abode place." Later I discovered that this was the eight hundred-year-old observatory of Jai Singh, one of the few early Hindu buildings that hadn't been leveled by the Muslim ruler Aurangzeb.

Across the river I could see scores of people climbing out of boats and trudging slowly up a barren sand bank. In sharp contrast to the architecturally overburdened side of the river we were on, there was not a single building on the east bank, just a vast and lonely expanse of sand and beyond it a hazy line of low green trees that looked like the edge of a dark jungle.

I asked the young men what the crowds of people across the river were doing. The tall one considered the question, a thumbnail raised to his beautiful teeth. Recognition slowly surfaced behind his big glasses. He turned and squinted across the river, visoring his face from the sun. He stared a long time, seriously, then dropped his hand and turned back to face me. With a hint of impatience at having the conversation interrupted by such a mundane sight, he said, "Madame, they are enjoying funny."

It did not look funny. It looked like a barefoot exodus of saris and lungis, everyone banished to a steaming wilderness.

The men explained that they were studying for the license to sell insurance. When I asked what kind of insurance, a long and heated conference followed in Hindi as they argued over the correct word in English. Their hands flew, they shook their heads, they tsked and sighed, shushed each other, and struck their own foreheads in exasperation. Finally the spokesman raised a hand to silence his chattering comrades. Triumphantly he said, "Life."

"You'll be selling life insurance?" I said.

The speaker hugged his textbook to his chest. "Life, madame. Yes."

VARANASI SEEMED a strange place in which to be selling life insurance. This Hindu holy city was, in its way, a ceremonial factory of death. Considered the most sacred spot on the Ganges, it was the city to which Hindus came to die and was full of elderly people crouched at the edge of the river eagerly waiting for death to bear them away. Many who came to Varanasi were already dead, their bodies delivered to the train station and rushed through the city and down to the riverbank at Manikarnika Ghat for final rites and cremation. All day long through the city streets the dacoits, men of the lowest caste, carried bodies on stretchers on their bony shoulders. The rigid, cloth-bound bodies bounced as the men hurried along, rythmically chanting "Ram nam satya hai" — the name of God is truth. In this city the impatient elderly had been known to wade into the river and deliberately drown themselves. To the Hindu faithful it was a great boon to visit Varanasi on pilgrimage, an important step toward ending the tedious cycle of reincarnation. But to die and be cremated here, in the earthly domain of Shiva, was the most meritorious thing that could happen to a Hindu. It was the final assurance of *moksha,* the liberating enlightenment that brought the cycle to an end and released the soul into Shiva's heaven.

Death, too, was one of the pressing reasons foreign tourists came to Varanasi; in addition to its long history and its flavorsome culture, Varanasi was one of the few places in the world where one could freely witness a human cremation. Sanitized and closeted in the West, death and all its ghoulish secrets were openly on display here, a fact that proved nearly as compelling a draw as the Great Wall, the Eiffel Tower, and the Parthenon. Hindu pilgrims came here to pray and die; the world's tourists came to watch them doing it.

The eldest insurance scholar said, "In this country only twenty percent of people is insured."

With a correcting flourish of his fountain pen the tall one said, "Fifteen percent. And we have many plans. Five year, ten year, twenty. If you are very financial job, you can earn many money. If you are earning very money then you can take many plans."

The high-voiced one began speaking very quickly in Hindi, and again the men appeared to be searching for a word in English. But before anyone could find it, a small boy appeared at the edge of our circle, uncrossed his slender arms, and said softly, "Consider," then gazed out across the river.

Without acknowledging the boy, the buck-toothed spokesman said, "Yes, yes. Consider. We consider that insurance is very important."

I looked at the boy, who was listening intently, an index finger pressed to his lips, the elbow of one arm delicately cupped in the hand of the other, head inclined toward us to catch our words. He listened with a concentrated yet distant expression on his face, as if listening to voices unfurling from a radio. His black hair had been shaved to within a half-inch of his scalp, except for one long lock the length and thickness of a lollipop stick that drooped from the back of his head down to his shirt collar. His too-big trousers were cinched tight at the waist with a plastic belt. He looked nearly weightless in his rubber flip-flops. When he caught me looking at him, he moved to the far side of the circle, away from me, and turned his back to us.

"Marriage is also important. And we are partners long, long time," the spokesman continued, "because when we was last time born we was also partners. What the thinkings in your country?"

I said that in my country many people did not believe that there was more than one life on earth, that Christians believed there was an afterlife but not a process of many lives.

The tall one shifted his textbook to the other arm and stirred the air with his pen. "We have a . . . what is the . . ." Unable to find the word, he again asked his friends for help.

Without turning to look at us, the young boy said softly, as if to the river, "Distinction. The word in English is distinction."

"Distinction! That is correct."

Impressed, I said to the boy, "Your English is very good."

He didn't respond. He stood in the gray sand and continued to scan the river, hands clasped behind his back, like a lonely wife waiting for a ship. Though he seemed to be ignoring us, I could feel that his interest was keen.

The students noticed me looking at the boy and suddenly, as if answering the call of some internal bell, they looked at their watches and said hurriedly, "We have wasted our time! Sorry. And goodbye," and in a flurry of roiling sand and flapping trousers they retreated down the ghat. I was left standing between the sun-gazing ascetic and the ashy sadhu.

It always seemed to happen this way in Varanasi; if you were talking to one person and another approached and drew your interest, the first would quickly disappear, like a wounded suitor whose dance had been cut in on. I thought it had something to do with the small opportunities that engagement with a foreigner might afford: a tip, an invitation, a gift, a purchase, a chance for a new experience. In Varanasi in particular I was aware of an unspoken competition for the attentions of visiting foreigners, a competition governed by a code of ethics rooted in polite conciliation. Poverty and need applied an unrelenting pressure, and without this willingness to concede, the streets of Varanasi might have erupted in anarchy.

The boy showed no interest in the students' departure. He continued to stare at the river. Gradually I realized that he was singing softly to himself. I watched the scholars leaving the beach, and to catch the boy's attention I snapped my fingers and said to myself, "Off they go, just like that." At the crisp pop of my snapping, he glanced over his shoulder at me, then turned away again. I hesitated to approach him for fear that he would leave. I sat down on the sandy steps of the ghat and asked, "What are you singing?"

After a long silence he said, "I am singing some music that thanks God. And if you sing this song to a sick person, he will get cured."

"Are you a doctor?" I said.

"It is obvious, I think, that I am not a doctor. This is only a simile. It is given for the beauty of the music." He continued to speak to the river, his back firmly toward me. I asked him his name.

"My name is Jaga. What is yours?"

"Rosemary."

"From America," he said.

"How do you know that?"

"You are talking this way. Your accent I understand."

"Your English is very good."

He shrugged and stared at the river. "Not good not bad. Neither here nor there." His shadow was a dark, rumpled strip in the sand. I asked him how old he was. "I am unsure. Sixteen, maybe. I will have to ask my mother which year I was born. 1983, I think. I do not care about these things."

The boy was shockingly small for sixteen; he looked no more than ten years old. He wore a knotted black strand, like a shoelace, around his neck, and as he spoke he wound a long piece of discarded kite string around his wrist with a slow cranking motion, like a man reeling in an exhausted trout. Up and down the river, scores of colorful paper kites steered by barefoot boys plunged and darted in the air above the ghats. There was no kite at the end of Jaga's string, just a small lump of wood that dragged and hopped through the sand some yards away.

I noticed the sadhu with the teapot watching us, stroking his beard and smiling sardonically, his eyes half closed. He seemed to be making plans. With his long fingernails he picked flecks of burned sugar from his stove and rolled them into a little brown ball, which he popped into his mouth. He grinned creepily at me. His teeth were black stumps.

I asked Jaga why he wasn't in school.

"I never have seen the inside of a school," he said, still showing me his back.

"Never?"

"Not ever." A tiny child wandered up the beach, and as she passed, Jaga bent down and greeted her with a gentle pat on the cheek.

"How did you learn English?" I said.

Language, he said, was easy for him. And he had a guru who helped him with English. When he didn't understand a word he went to the guru and asked him what it meant. The guru had a book of words in English — a dictionary, actually — that he looked into now and then. I asked if the guru taught him other things, like mathematics.

"Everything he teaches me. But I can do mathematics by myself. Difficult mathematics I cannot do yet. However, if any person asks what is ten plus ten I can say that it is twenty. I believe that my mind is quite good. I don't like to say this, because people would say that I was boasting."

I said it was often that way: if you praised yourself, people called you a braggart and a cheat, but if you said how pathetic you were, they would say you were honest and brave.

Jaga stopped winding his kite string and turned around. He winced in the damp sunlight, trying to see me. His teeth were a brilliant white. "That is funny," he said. "I know what you are talking about. They will say, 'Bragging jackass.' But God, I think, would like us to love ourselves."

"I think so too," I said. "Can you do multiplication?"

"For example?"

"Six times six."

He dropped the kite string and spanked the sand from his hands as he thought. "Is it about thirty-six, madame?"

"It is exactly thirty-six."

He smiled and waggled his head in pleasure. "Actually, I know that it is."

I asked him why he hadn't gone to school.

"This was not the way in my family. I must learn from Guru-ji and from the foreign visitors."

Higher up the steps of the ghat in the dappling shade of a pipal tree, a man in a lungi began ferociously beating a very small donkey, hollering and spitting and bringing his bamboo staff down on the animal's skinny haunch with all his might. The donkey, who had been staring contentedly at the roots of the tree, lifted his head in pained surprise. Hindi words flew angrily from the man's mouth. When I asked Jaga what the man was saying, he cocked his head and listened to the snarling voice. The bamboo stick cracked smartly against the donkey's ribs. "He is saying, 'You wicked donkey. Try that again, my sweetie, and I will make my dinner of you.'"

The donkey stood perfectly still, his head lowered, staring at the dirt and taking his beating like a donkey. I said, "Don't Hindus believe in treating animals with respect?"

Jaga nodded. "But he is not Hindu."

"He isn't?"

"No, madame. I think that one is a Muslim man."

"Muslims are supposed to respect animals too. What did the donkey do to make the man angry?"

Jaga watched keenly as the man badgered and berated the donkey. He barked and screeched and howled, pummeled it mercilessly with the stick, and kicked pointlessly at a stone near his foot. His elaborately wound headcloth slipped askew with the effort. Finally Jaga said, "Nothing, I think."

"That's a lot of anger over nothing."

Jaga raised a finger and said in a quoting way, "Yes, madame, but anything going wrong is always the fault of the donkey."

This made me laugh, and the boy watched me with a studious expression on his face. Suddenly, as if remembering his responsibilities, he said, "What will your program be in Varanasi?" He wanted to know if I had been to the various important sites: the Monkey Temple, the Golden Temple, the silk market, the cantonment, the old city, the cremation ghat. He spoke as though it were his duty to make sure I took in all these sights but didn't like to ask. Shyly he said, "I can show you them."

Nearly every man over the age of ten whom I met in India had asked me if I needed his services as a guide, but it was usually the first thing they said, and none had asked as diffidently as Jaga. I had a vague fear of guides, a fear that my experience of a new place would be colored by the guide's character and preferences. I liked to see things alone, to learn what I could just from watching. I explained to Jaga that I wasn't in the habit of making a plan, that I liked to see what would happen if I set out walking in a strange city. "I like to be free," I said. "And if I happen to find the Golden Temple, I'll go in."

A look of understanding came into Jaga's face. He said, as if confessing something he shouldn't, "I also like to do this. But some visitors prefer to make a program. They carry a book and ask to see the places they saw in the book. They say, 'The book has said we should.' Sometimes that is how I make my money. I take them to places that are in the book."

I had one of those books for India. It was nearly as thick as a birthday cake, and it was precisely its thickness that put me off. The new breed of guidebooks, *Lonely Planet* and *Let's Go!* and the rest, are full of highly detailed information. They contrive to reveal for the tourist the most unique adventure, the one that, deep down, travelers always feel is eluding them, that authentic experience of real life that lies just around the corner, if only they knew which corner. The books tell you which corner, mapping it out with the precision of a pirate's chart ("Take a right at the winding stair where the one-eyed cobbler sits mending shoes"). They pride themselves on knowing where the best meal can be found, the best temple, the truest Hindu, the crankiest crone. Instead of happening upon the cobbler, you go looking for him, and when you find him you can feel satisfied that the experience was real. As a result, in places like Varanasi hundreds of travelers end up having the same unique adventure. The books can be very useful, especially in a country like India that is so confusing and complex. Nevertheless, too much information leaves me anxious and confused, and I agree with E. M. Forster's idea that "only what is seen sideways sinks deep." I had torn the map of Varanasi out of my guidebook and thrown the book back into my suitcase.

"I don't care where we go," I said to Jaga, "but I'd like your company."

He looked pleased. "We can talk about subjects," he said.

We arranged to meet the next morning at the tea stall at the top of Dasaswamedh Ghat. Before I left I asked Jaga about the long strand of hair at the back of his head.

"It was cut this way because my grandfather has died about two months ago."

"I'm sorry," I said.

Jaga raised his eyebrows and dipped his chin, a palliative little shrug. "No problem. Death is happening with everyone. That is the truth of life. Who is born on earth will surely die."

I stared at him. He was tiny, yet for one so young, he spoke like a sage. Though his face had a prepubescent roundness and his cinnamon-hued skin was as smooth as porcelain, there was something almost elderly in his serious brown eyes.

We sealed our goodbye with a formal handshake. I climbed the steps to the top of the ghat, and before I slipped into the web of narrow alleys that led away from the river, I looked back and saw that the boy was standing in the same spot. He was staring at his hands and trying, over and over, to snap his fingers.

I CANNOT PRETEND to have any proficiency in India or Hinduism. My knowledge of both before I went to India was vague, and my feelings about both were tainted early on by the Hare Krishna devotees who, in the late 1960s and early 1970s, danced regularly outside the

Boston and Cambridge subway stations that I frequented in my youth. I had no idea then that the Hare Krishna movement was a Hindu anomaly, that Hindus did not preach or proselytize. I was a self-conscious teenager muddled by daydreams, oblivious to God, and eager to avoid a spectacle. The leaping Krishnas, with their saffron robes, their jingling tambourines, their fulsome wheedling and moony chants, filled me with skepticism and fear. Their shaven scalps looked faintly obscene in the Massachusetts sun, and their efforts at conversion seemed a threat to my parochial consciousness. That the Beatles had dressed up in paisley and beads and gone to India was baffling to me, and later, when John Lennon announced that the Maharishi was a sham, I, in my adolescent wisdom and scorn, thought, *I could have told him that.*

The Hindu religion seemed a tangle of preposterous, violent mythology, full of strange creatures with supernatural powers. I had seen those statues of Vishnu with a surplus of arms radiating from his torso, those pictures of red-eyed, black-faced, snake-haired Kali lewdly biting her own red tongue, with a passel of skulls slung around her neck. Literal-minded, I was more accepting of the religions centered in historical figures who had two arms, two legs, and predictable human hearts. Christ, Muhammad, even Joseph Smith and the Angel Moroni made more sense to me. Whether I believed what they said was another matter.

In 1978, when I was seventeen, I went to live in Ireland, where I met a pale-faced Irish woman named Ma Anand Shayla, a twenty-four-year-old devotee of the Indian guru Bhagwan Shree Rajneesh; she had traveled all the way from Killarney to Poona to see him. Shayla dressed only in orange clothing, and every day she wore a necklace of wooden beads not unlike rosary beads. In the middle of the necklace, instead of a crucifix, was a round wooden frame containing a photo of the slightly pop-eyed guru with his beard of grizzled tinsel. Liza Mitchell, the seventy-three-year-old woman from whom Shayla and I rented cottages on her property in County Kerry, one day settled her eyeglasses on her nose, lifted Shayla's little medallion to her face, stared a long time at the picture, and finally said, "'Tis a queer-lookin' priest."

Liza took the words out of my mouth. I was enchanted by Liza; Shayla was not. In Shayla's estimation, Liza was too European, and therefore too suspicious, too greedy, too defensive, too generally ridden with aggressive Christian karma. Like Dusty Springfield, Shayla's real name was O'Brien. When I asked her what the rest of her real name was, she said with defiance, "Ma Anand Shayla is my real name. I'm not O'Brien. Those feckin' bogtrotters in Ballybaleen put that on me."

I, for one, had some genetic affection for the bogtrotters in Ballybaleen, and Shayla's dismissal of them did little to improve my internal relationship with India and its culture. Shayla, smart and likable, was touched with that inevitable byproduct of being a Western student of Eastern religions: a somewhat dictatorial scorn for those who didn't follow, a scorn never evident in the native Hindu or Buddhist. When a farmer whom Shayla had lured into the subject of religion told her that of course he believed in a God who answered our prayers directly, she said with a patronizing lift to her dark eyebrows, "Well, that must be very comforting." I felt for the farmer. Her remark made him seem superstitious and foolish, made his belief seem an embarrassment. I sat in Kruger's Pub with Shayla and drank beer and tried to avoid altogether the subjects of religion and India.

IN TIME I learned that Hinduism was one of the few religions that had found a way to accept all other religions as equally true, a refreshing notion that seemed to reflect an admirable confidence and generosity. Hinduism has a great respect for storytelling and interpretation. The myths of the Hindu gods recorded in the Puranas show a universe governed by an endlessly repeated cycle of creation, flowering, and destruction. The myths are full of magical and impossible feats. (For example, the Ganges River is believed to flow directly from heaven and with such force that it would knock the stuffing out of the earth if Shiva did not tame it by filtering it through his matted hair. Or take the origin of the elephant-headed god, Ganesh, who often trots about on the back of a rat. In one version (and that's another thing: every Hindu story has multiple versions) Shiva's wife, Parvati, sitting in her bathtub one night, decides that she needs a guard to stand watch in front of her house. From bath oils and her own sweat she creates the boy Ganesh for this purpose and immediately puts him to work. When Shiva shows up, Ganesh, merely doing his job, denies him entry. Suitably annoyed, Shiva cuts off poor Ganesh's head. The head somehow gets lost. That sends Parvati into a tailspin. (When Parvati goes into a tailspin, dishes fly across the kitchen of the universe.) Hoping to mollify his wife, Shiva orders his messengers to hurry out and bring back the head of the first creature they see. The messengers return with the head of an elephant, stick it on Ganesh's shoulders, and happiness is restored to the household.

If I found these myths a bit outlandish and difficult to embrace, I had also to ask what made the Virgin Birth, the Resurrection, the Ascension, the Assumption, or the concept of transubstantiation any less outlandish. People in Hindu stories are always dying and coming back to life — but what about Lazarus? Hindu images are often bloody and repellent, but so is the Sacred Heart. Hindu myths are full of violence, but what about the Inquisition, the Crusades, Santiago rattling his bloody sword and trampling the Moors beneath the hooves of his wild-eyed horse? *Who eats my flesh and drinks my blood shall live forever.* One doesn't have to stretch the imagination terribly far to hear a Hindu god saying that. Some Hindu believers have adopted bizarre personal habits in honor of their faith (more about them presently), but how much more bizarre are they than Bernadette of Lourdes munching on grass and rolling about in the mud because the Blessed Virgin appeared in a grotto and advised her to? At a certain age I began to think that if one is going to be skeptical, it is only fair that one should be skeptical all around.

That Hinduism is one of the oldest religions in the world seems of itself to command a certain respect. It had no primary founder but was a conflation of various regional religious practices. It was influenced by the invading Aryans who traveled to the Indus Valley from the Middle East approximately 1,500 years before the birth of Christ. It has many sects and no real hierarchical organization. The Upanishads, the sacred scripture, teach that all reality is united and supported by one powerful, pervasive, nebulous force: Brahman, which exists in each individual and yet cannot be identified. In the Kena Upanishad, Brahman is "that which is not seen by the eye, but that by which the eye sees." The truth is incommunicable, and the more you think about truth, the farther away from it you get. Perhaps the most important Hindu belief is in the importance of *moksha* and *samsara,* liberation from the tedious cycle of reincarnation.

Hinduism is a religion of wondrous excesses. It has 330 million gods doing impressive things, but in the end they are all representations of the one true god. There are gods for every imaginable thing: the god of Wednesday, the god of tin, the god of milk. The Ganges has 108 names. Sometimes it has 1,000 names. Vishnu has 1,000 names and once was incarnated as a boar and got into a fight that lasted 1,000 years. Krishna had 16,000 girlfriends. Nothing on earth should be left out of the Hindu holy catalogue — not rats or ravens or roaches or ringworms — because you never know when you yourself might be reincarnated as one of them. I had read that the most pious form of worship a Hindu could enact was the journey from the source of the Ganges in the Himalayas to its mouth in the Bay of Bengal, 1,600 miles away. And then *back* again. That pilgrimage was said to take six years.

HISTORIANS AND TRAVELERS always describe Varanasi as being to the Hindu what Mecca is to the Muslim and Jerusalem to the Christian. Believed to date from the first Aryan colonization in approximately 1500 B.C., Varanasi is one of the oldest cities in the world. Since its beginning it has been revered as the center of the Hindu faith. The city is also extremely important to Buddhism, for Siddhartha Gautama, having achieved supreme enlightenment in 560 B.C., is said to have preached his first sermon in Sarnath, just north of Varanasi.

At home, studying up on Varanasi and trying to decide whether to go there, I had found this contention in a dusty Victorian travelogue titled *India: Past and Present* by one Charles Forbes-Lindsay: "Benares [Varanasi] is not a pleasant city. As the centre of Hinduism it is curious and interesting, but one is brought into too close contact with idolatry in its most repulsive aspects, and superstition in its grossest manifestations." That decided it. A month after returning home from Santiago de Compostela, I flew to New Delhi and took a train to Varanasi. I had no specific plan in mind, no hotel reservation, and no idea how long I'd stay.

BEING IN MY HOTEL ROOM in Varanasi was like being in a submarine deep below the waves. The room had no windows; inside it I heard nothing. It was permeated with the smell of diesel fuel and exhaust fumes. Occasionally the air conditioner in the room above me rumbled like an idling engine. The lights would blink out without warning. Though there was a telephone on the bedside table, and though I had expected several people to call me there, the telephone never rang. Now and then I lifted the receiver and held it to my ear to see if there was a dial tone. There always was. It was like a dial tone anywhere else in the world, that Cadillac horn pressed to life by the weight of a body slumped over the steering wheel. On the wall was a framed print of a North American blue jay who, marooned here in the Gangetic Plain, managed to look exotic and delicate and rare. The room offered no sign that it was situated in India except for a book on the bedside table called *Paramhans Swami Adgadanand's The Geeta in Its True Perspective,* Translated to English and with introduction by Vinod Narain Sinha of Jagatganj, Varanasi, India. (A little investigation revealed that, like the Gideon Bible, every room in the hotel had one of these books; not a single one was in Hindi.)

If I began to feel claustrophobic sitting in my room, I could step into the bathroom and peer through a jagged, fist-sized hole in the frosted pane of the narrow window there. This miniature view showed a sliver of the clamorous street outside the hotel and half of the rusted tin hut across the street, where two boys sold coffee and fruit. At night the boys slept on the roof of the hut, and early in the morning, if I looked through the hole, I could see them lying huddled under blankets there. They had a long-eared donkey tethered to a bamboo post; it stood all day chewing pieces of newspaper that blew down the street. When there was no paper left to chew, the donkey stared at the dusty pavement and moaned. There was a water pump next to the building across the street, and if I left my bathroom door open I could hear the boys cranking it at dawn. Sometimes, while brushing my teeth or drying myself with a towel, I could look through the hole and see a shrouded corpse sailing past the hotel strapped to the roof of a car. The bathroom was very small. The toilet was a hole in the floor. The soap was rough, like low-grade sandpaper. At dusk crickets chirped in the wastebasket under my sink, and each morning I entered the bathroom to find a couple of cockroaches tasting the mouth of my open tube of toothpaste.

The Hotel Ramamurthi was small and occupied by middle-class Indians and Europeans alike. The manager, P. T. J. Subramani, was fat and well groomed. He wore his oiled hair slicked back on his head, and his Western-style clothes were always very clean and tidy. He sat in a wooden chair behind a large desk in the lobby reading a newspaper and patting at his humid forehead with a hankie and sighing in a fatigued way. His wife, he told me, was Indian-American and was trying to secure him a green card so that he could go to America and "be done with it." The day I arrived in Varanasi I had asked Mr. Subramani if there were many guests staying in his hotel, and he had said nervously and a bit incongruously, "No, no. It is mostly foreigners here. Mostly westerns. Do not worry, Mrs. Mohini. No Pakistanis." He had a habit of tipping his chair back on two legs until the back of his head rested against the wall behind him, a trick he had performed so often his head had left an oily smudge on the wall. He was always counting money and changing money and totting up bills, moistening his pudgy fingers with his tongue to turn the pages of his ledger. He never smiled. The telephone on his desk was often off the hook, the receiver lying helplessly on its side on a pile of papers, and sometimes, if you were standing close enough to the desk, you could hear a voice coming plaintively out of it. I was convinced it was Subramani's wife.

Subramani had a reproving manner and was dangerously helpful. Dial tone notwithstanding, I found it impossible to make a telephone call from my room, so I would go down to the lobby and make my calls there. Near Subramani's desk was a glass telephone booth from which guests could make long-distance calls. The booth had no door, and when I was in the middle of dialing a complicated number, Subramani would come up behind me, take the telephone receiver out of my hand, and say, "I dial for you, missus." Or, when I was in mid-conversation with a person on the other side of the world whose dim and staticky voice I was straining, at great expense, to hear, he would creep up and tap on the glass and wave at me and offer me a cigarette in the most distracting way. Sometimes, bafflingly, he would decide that this was a good time to chat, and he would put his sleek head into the booth and ask in a voice of utter boredom, "Mrs. Mohini, which country you are calling now? I can find it on the map for you." If I told him what country I was calling — France, Egypt, the United States — he would say dismissively and unconvincingly, "I been there, missus."

Subramani was nosy, but only superficially. He would ask as I went by his desk how many days I had been in Varanasi and how old I was and how much money I had spent, and if I tried to answer his questions he would yawn at me and vaguely nod and begin flipping through his ledger in the middle of my sentence, or he would pick up the dangling telephone and speak into it in a rush of irate-sounding Hindi. He had no interest in listening, as though the very act of talking with a foreigner was a necessary formality and a thorough waste of time. Nevertheless, I liked the Hotel Ramamurthi because I slept well there. The bed was huge and comfortable, and at night, after miles of walking, I would take my cold shower and fall into bed and sleep for nine hours without waking once. The room was utterly black. I could talk out loud to myself at length, secure in the belief that no one could hear me. At five-thirty in the morning someone would begin banging on the wall; a series of three knocks with pauses in between, like the sound of a sculptor at work, stopping between blows to see what he had wrought. But I was glad of it. I had no alarm clock and was eager to get up early. Every morning I had my breakfast in the hotel dining room before going out.

In Varanasi I walked every day — from one end of the ghats to the other, to the temples, the cantonment area, and into the markets. I walked through the streets to the northern end of the city, to the train bridge, and then back along the river. I walked parts of the Panchakroshi Road, which encircles the city. Walking was almost as good as asking questions; it was a way of understanding the city. It gave me time to take in what I saw and allowed me to think. And by walking the same route more than once, I became familiar with people and places.

I SPENT MOST of my time in Varanasi with Jaga. I liked that he walked quickly, speeding through the streets on his little legs with a sober yet peaceful expression on his face. He knew every alley and sacred well and ancient keystone in the city, as well as every shopkeeper and boatman. I was always a pace or two behind him. One afternoon I was on the verge of telling him that one of the things I liked about him was that he walked fast, but before I could say it he turned to me and said, "Madame? What I like about you is that you can walk fast. Most foreign visitors walk slow." When I told him I had been about to say the same thing to him, he strode on and said in his laconic way, "That's right, madame. Telepathy."

Jaga began each day with a visit to the tea stall. The stall was little more than a bench and a Bunsen burner set up at the top of Dasaswamedh Ghat at the open end of a short lane of bamboo huts where Indian farmers sold vegetables and Tibetan refugees sold underwear and scarves. The Tibetans, mostly women, had ruddy cheeks and glossy black hair and very high cheekbones. Though they were generally fierce-looking, they were always laughing and showing their brilliant teeth. (When I first arrived in Varanasi I had asked a group of them if they were Chinese, and they, nationalistically drawing themselves up at the affront, had cried, "No! We are Tibetan!")

The tea stall was run by two peripatetic teenage brothers who made their living brewing tea. They made it with boiled milk instead of water and served it in brandy glasses and cracked jam jars. The tea, the rosy brown of an egg, was strong and very sweet and hot, and their customers, mostly other young boys, sat shoulder to shoulder on the bench and gazed down at the river, raising the motley glasses appreciatively to their lips. To protect their burner's little flame from the wind, the brothers had made a rectangular shelter out of sticks and tattered squares of cotton, an ingenious structure that resembled an upright canvas coffin. They worked at a tiny table, stirring and measuring and pouring, snatching wooden spoons out of each other's hands and telling each other what to do in the hushed and hurried tones of car thieves. A little wooden shelf supported glasses, bottles of milk, a bag of sugar, and a small radio that was always on, leaking faint voices through a hiss of static — a woman singing, a politician indignantly ranting, the undersea sounds of Hindu music.

After his morning glass of tea, Jaga set about what he referred to as his "business." Like most of the teenage boys who roamed the ghats while the rest of the world was at school, Jaga was industrious. He made money as an impromptu guide for foreign visitors and as a walking advertisement for a toy shop that had the misfortune to be located in an obscure alley. At the toy shop Jaga did odd jobs, swept floors, and helped pack merchandise for export, but his main task was to prowl the ghats looking for tourists and pilgrims, inviting them to visit this shop, then leading the way when they accepted the invitation.

In the hip pocket of his trousers he carried a little box that he called his "pocket business," a set of vials full of colored powders and steel stamps. When he found an interested customer he would sell the set for two hundred rupees. One day, as we sat on the steps of the Varanasi post office, he showed me how the kit worked. The stamps, like little branding irons, were dipped into the colorful powder, then firmly pressed to the skin; when they were withdrawn a bright tattoo of powder was left behind. There were pictures of a cobra, an elephant, the Hindi word *om*, a flower, a peace sign, a sun. Jaga gently applied a yellow flower to my wrist, then, holding my wrist up to his face he admired the result and said with genuine delight, "Instant tattoo, madame," as interested in the stamps as if he had never seen them before.

Jaga was straightforward and watchful in a way that made me trust him. Even when caught off-guard he looked faintly guarded, and sad. He had a dark mole just below his left nostril and a small scar shaped like a fishhook under one eye. A rudimentary fuzz darkened his upper lip, and a flat lock of hair grew downward in front of each ear in place of true sideburns, giving him the aspect of a helmeted fighter pilot. The gray serge pants he wore looked like the castoff trousers from a businessman's three-piece suit. He wore long-sleeved cotton shirts and every day the big brown plastic belt around his waist. The belt was a necessity rather than an accessory; without it the pants would have fallen to his ankles.

Jaga spoke confidently and was full of information, yet he had the slightly detached air of someone who knew far more than he was telling. The enigmatic shadow of a smile played constantly across his features, as if some inward amusement were steeping just behind his face. He was proud of his city, which he moved through with the self-possession of a diplomat. He looked directly at people when he spoke to them and rarely looked surprised. He was wry and controlled. Though he had never traveled farther than Allahabad, sixty miles away, to visit his aunt, he had a worldliness born of curiosity and imagination. One night, as I sat with him on the steps of the ghat, he gazed at the sliver of waxing moon and said ruminatively, "Biggest shadow in the world," and it took me a minute to register what he meant.

Jaga's speech was clear and precise, dotted with a number of Latinate words and colored with an accent that sounded half Jamaican and half Irish. He said "shtill" and "shtop" and "shtraight," like people in certain parts of western Ireland, and he said "al-most" and "al-ways," like people in Jamaica.

ON THE DAY Jaga was to take me to the Golden Temple, I arrived early at the tea stall and sat watching the river while the two tea brothers and several lepers attended me. The lepers had followed me from their usual begging spot at the other end of the little lane, where all day they crouched in the dirt at a busy intersection, elegantly lifting their slender arms at passersby. Sometimes more than ten of them were there at once, huddling in a row, their thin bodies wrapped in cotton rags. They touched their mouths to indicate hunger, then lifted their bandaged hands, repeating the gesture over and over, like people throwing kisses from a departing ship. Those who had no hands raised a tin cup pincered between the polished brown stumps of their forearms. Some of the lepers were noseless, some had no lips, all had quick brown eyes and bright pink gums. They were always cheerfully grinning and displaying their deformities like merchants promoting their wares. Those who were legless arrived at the begging spot in little barrows pulled by other, more fortunate lepers who had toes and feet to walk with and who looked as if they felt very lucky to have such a helpless cargo to haul. The legless lepers had a way of inspiring, without a word of entreaty, a shower of coins and bills from horrified foreign tourists. The lepers gathered in Varanasi hoping to appeal to the pilgrims' sense of charity and karma, and though they sat on the ground and dressed in rags, their begging cups were always full. Each time I saw them I felt a fresh shock of surprise. It was not just the disease that set them apart but something bold in their eyes, an animal intensity and quickness. It was the wild-eyed look of people with little left to lose.

That morning at the tea stall, the leper who sat on my left was half naked. From head to foot his skin was a palette of scabs and sores, like coins of rust on a sheet of steel; clothing would have hidden this horror and robbed him of revenue. The man had the brittle hands of a mummy and had wound them in a mummy's tattered bandages. The hands and feet of the man sitting on my right were necrotic. His stumpy fingers — the tips of eight or nine had been amputated — were like little black chess pawns. The two were an amiable pair; they grinned eagerly at me and admired my shoes and murmured urbane-sounding Hindi blandishments and patted the wooden bench to indicate that I should sit closer. When one of the brothers brought them their tea, the lepers complained that it was neither hot enough nor sweet enough and, like a couple of aristocrats, they sent the tea back.

"Madame," one of the tea brothers said to me, "what you like eating with tea?"

I thought for a minute, having seen nothing edible in their stall. "Well, how about a biscuit?" I said.

The barefoot boy rummaged about on the lower shelf of his stall and then, looking anxious, ran off down the lane, tripping over a legless leper who was lying on his belly in the middle of the dusty track, inching toward us on his elbows. The leper smiled and stretched his good hand at me, and that made the Tibetan vendors shriek with laughter.

Dasaswamedh Ghat was the busiest and most central of the ghats, and sitting at the top of it one had an excellent view of the river and the crowds that worried its edge all day. Though Varanasi had some wide boulevards riotous with traffic and pedestrians, the riverfront was its true main street. It was what made the city interesting, and people were drawn to it the way they are drawn to a bonfire burning in the woods at night. While the ghats had a palpable holiness, an ancient and important feeling, they also had the slightly corrupted atmosphere of a city beach. The air was stuffy, like the air at a crowded cocktail party, and the sun struggled through the brown haze and seemed to burn the hotter for its effort. Amid the bells ringing out from the scores of temples at the top of the ghats there were impious shouts and laughter, children running and crying and flying kites, idling pensioners in sleeveless T-shirts, and eccentric vendors muttering and squawking. On Dasaswamedh Ghat alone, scores of cloth umbrellas were set up along the river like great satellite dishes tilting on a rooftop, and in the afternoons beneath these sun-bleached shades Brahman priests and tired pilgrims lay about on wooden platforms with legs, like beds.

The wide, flat vista north and south along the river was all sepias and browns, flecked here and there with brilliant spots of orange and pink, the colors of the silk saris and the robes of holy men. The steps of the ghats — there were thousands of them — were dizzyingly steep and as crisp as accordion pleats, with risers painted in gay colors: red and white here, green, orange, and white there, blue and red in another place. In November the river flowed slowly, its surface undisturbed by wind or rocks. Scores of double-ended wooden rowboats sat lined up in the shallows at the edge of the river like shoes tidily arranged in a closet. Vultures and black kites wheeled in the hazy sky. (They wheel in New Delhi, too. And in Bombay and Agra and every place in between. They are to India what the pigeon is to New York.) Most of the ghats had a large terrace halfway down the steps, which then led down to the water or to a sandy beach at the water's edge. The ghats were stark wonders of architectural engineering and geometry, and the terraces had the stony vastness of Tiananmen Square or the Alexanderplatz. The steps of some ghats were collapsing into the river with age. At the tops stood ornate, towering palaces; some looked Gothic, some Venetian, with pinnacles and minarets. The minarets of the mosque of Aurangzeb stretched into the sky like needles, high above the rest. There were rickety modern apartment buildings six stories high that looked ready to topple. Everything here had the look of being carefully stacked, like a stone wall.

As I waited for Jaga, a skinny man washing laundry at the bottom of the steps waved to me to come down to him. I excused myself to the two lepers and descended the steps. The man, middle-aged and wrapped in a lungi, stood ankle-deep in the river bent over his work, smashing his wet clothes on the stones of the ghat, wringing them out, then dropping them into a tin bucket. His reflection rippled in the river. As I approached he straightened up and peered at me, his hands dripping with suds.

"Lady," he said, "you can go that place of the distinga tarvanga he is the red a dis house red of the Varanas."

I stared at him. Unable to untangle his statement, I said helplessly, "Goodness, you have so many rings." Indian men were mad for rings, and, like several men I had seen in Varanasi, he had one on every finger.

He lifted his glinting hands, pointed to the biggest ring, and said, "This is the original diamond."

"Is it?" I said. The ring was a chunky tablet of glass in a tin setting.

"Is," he said. He began to brush his teeth with his fingers and a cleaning agent of red powder. He nodded and grimaced and talked around his knuckles. "Mr. John, Bank of Boroda manager gave to me. And American leadership. Out far. The big. Twenty thousand."

He bent over and spat into the river, scooped up a handful of water, rinsed his mouth with it, gasped, spat again, wiped his mouth with his sleeve, straightened up, put both hands on the small of his back, drew his head back, and looked at me in a pleased way, as though he had just said something incredibly pithy. In his lungi, with his narrow hips and rod-straight back, he looked noble. A severed fish head, one eye staring, dangled in the shallow brown water near his feet. "You like to Varanas visit, lady? Most people thinks it beautiful. I already visit. My Panchakroshi is Varanasi. I am already going for all India. Hindu. And you can see Italy."

From this seemingly encrypted message a grain of sense glowed: the man was a pilgrim, one of the truly devout who came to Varanasi and performed the Panchakroshi. The Hindu pilgrimage to this city could take many forms, and while just to visit was considered sufficient homage, the good pilgrim's traditional ritual was to walk the fifty-mile Panchakroshi Road around the city. Pilgrims came from all over India, as well as from Tibet, China, Nepal, and Burma. To free himself from impurity and sin, the pilgrim would begin his worship with a bath in the river at Manikarnika Ghat, then proceed along this road, stopping to worship at the 108 appointed temples, shrines, and wells, making offerings, reciting prayers, and performing ablutions. The journey, which took five days, was traditionally made barefoot, and the pilgrim was to conduct himself as decorously and piously as possible, banishing anger and bad thoughts. At the end of his walk he would throw flowers and rice or barley on the ground as an offering to Shiva. The walk would end where it began, at Manikarnika Ghat, where again the pilgrim would bathe in the river.

"Italy?" I said. The fish head bumped against the pilgrim's ankle.

"Italy, Italy," he said helpfully. "Roma. Holy Italy. Pope."

I had no idea what this meant. Perhaps it was a comparison: as Varanasi was holy to him, Rome might be holy to me. The man yawned and stretched and twisted the water out of one last rag, then lifted his bucket and wandered off to hang his clothes on a railing to dry. The original diamond glittered almost convincingly in the morning sunlight.

I climbed the steep steps back to the tea stall. Jaga appeared, and as we greeted each other, the two lepers stared, mouths open, enchanted by the ease with which this Indian child was able to speak to me. The tea-stall boy who had run off down the alley came forward with a packet of cookies in his hand and offered it to me, and Jaga said, "Oh. A very special cookie he has brought. They come from Allahabad."

I opened the packet of cookies and offered them to the lepers and to Jaga and to the tea brothers, and we all stood there eating them silently. They were like shortbread and tasted delicious. Jaga examined the package. "Yes," he said, brushing crumbs from his mouth, "it is real. You can see by the label. You must be careful of duplicate with these cookies."

"Duplicate?" I said.

"The false cookie. Some rats sell a duplicate."

"An imitation."

"Yes, but it is much inferior." Jaga jerked his head to indicate the tea brothers and said, "They have fetched this specially for you." He seemed proud and impressed. He looked up at me, the top of his head level with my chin. "Are you finding it tasty, madame?"

I said that I was finding it very tasty, and the lepers, holding the cookies in their damaged hands, munched and grinned and nodded their deigning approval.

JAGA LED ME through the streets to the Golden Temple. In the Hindu pantheon Brahma is the creator, Vishnu the preserver, and Shiva the destroyer. Hindus are followers of either Vishnu or Shiva. Varanasi was dedicated to the worship of Shiva, and nearly every incidental thing in the city seemed to be about him. The Kashi Vishwanath, the Golden Temple, which sat above Manikarnika Ghat, was the city's holiest Hindu spot.

Jaga walked without speaking. The pavement was littered with rough-hewn clay teacups that had been discarded by tea vendors after one or two uses. The cups were eggshell-thin, and as we walked they disintegrated underfoot with a satisfying crunch. Near the post office I tripped over a man sitting cross-legged in the middle of the sidewalk in nothing but a pair of baggy cotton pants. He had a blood-stained bandage wrapped around his head and was eating a bag of roasted beans and, despite his state, looking quite content. Coal sellers stood in their shops, faces and clothes black with dust. The only bright thing about them was the whites of their eyes, which gave them an eerie look, as though their true faces were locked behind masks.

In the gutter in front of a butcher's shop a beautiful lamb lay dead, its throat slit. The butcher and his two daughters sat on the floor of the shop in the muggy sunlight, a goat carcass dangling between them. Long strips of fat on the skinned goat were the yellow of beeswax. I thought the butcher was wearing a polka-dot shirt until I came closer and realized that the dots were flies. The daughters' ears and bare feet were black with flies. One of the daughters lifted her hand at me and shrieked, "Gimmee lady one rupee!" which caused the flies to lurch upward into my face in a sluggish cloud.

Jaga hurried on. The streets became narrower and darker. They were lined with little shops selling objects necessary for worship in the temples: flower garlands and sweets, brass pots of Ganges water, oil lamps, small lingams, religious beads, clay figures of the gods, incense and wooden boxes, colorful cones of tikka powder with which to mark the forehead, and souvenirs that pilgrims could take home. Passing pedestrians and customers haggling with vendors made it nearly impossible to walk. Warm forearms brushed against mine, and I was jostled and knocked against the damp walls of buildings. In this part of the city the alleys branched and multiplied, and I began to have the sensation of being in a tangled forest. I had no idea where north and south were now. The alleys were so narrow in places that at times I could touch both walls at once with my raised elbows. The place felt medieval. Jaga was small enough that he could maneuver and feint and slide between people, but I could only crash along behind him like a blindfolded hippo. A wizened old woman carrying a basket of baby chicks on her head came barreling down the alley, pushing people aside with a flailing arm. When she saw my face she grinned and shoved a hysterically peeping chick up to my nose. "Chick! Chick!" she cried and then wetly kissed my ear to show that it was all in fun.

I tried to place my feet exactly where Jaga's had been as a way of keeping up, but other feet intervened, and finally the only way not to lose him was to hold onto the tail of his shirt. Feeling my fingers on his shirt, Jaga's head snapped around in alarm. When he saw that it was only me he smiled. "Small leads big," he said.

Abruptly, in a narrow alley, we came upon an entrance to the Golden Temple. Beside the entrance a barefoot woman with a cotton cloth draped over her head stood frozen, staring at her own hands, which were raised before her in a gesture of supplication. Jaga turned to me. "Here is the Golden Temple. And I am sorry, madame, but only the Hindu person can go inside. But if you stand here you can look in and see how it is important."

Just looking at its dome one could see how it was important. The temple, built in 1777, had later had its dome wrapped in almost a ton of beaten gold, some of it hammered into intricate designs and figures. The dome was as brash as the sun and nearly as painful to look at with the naked eye. I asked Jaga if he wanted to go in and pray while I waited, and he looked surprised. "Thank you, madame. I have been in it many times. I know the place. I would like to stay with you."

And so we stood in the doorway next to the barefoot woman and looked in. The temple, with its large, glassless windows, was airy and shadowy and surprisingly noisy. There were many recesses and inner courtyards beyond my view, but I could see barefoot pilgrims wandering about and pigeons fluttering near the high ceiling. The irregular clanging of small bells drifted out, along with the sound of chanting and tabla drums. The place had the busy yet somehow soothing air of a train station. As I looked in, a black cow ambled across my field of vision munching on a garland of flowers. On the far side of the temple a big-eared monkey sat on the floor scratching his head.

Jaga explained that four times a day the ritual *puja* would be performed here, honoring Shiva with prayer and offerings. As part of the ceremony the black stone lingam, denoting the energy of the creator, would be decorated and washed in a bath of Ganges water, curd, milk, butter, ghee, and oil. "It is a special bath for Shiva," he said.

I had been reading about Shiva. Like most aspects of Hinduism he was confusing, complex, and contradictory. He was both benign and malign. He and his wife, Devi, were worshiped in a variety of forms. He was often depicted as human, sitting in the lotus position with a crescent moon in his hair, out of which the Ganges flowed. In other depictions he had snakes draped around his neck, a necklace of skulls, a trident, a staff with a human head at the end. Shiva's wife could show up as Uma, a woman of great beauty, or as Durga, riding on the back of a tiger, or as Kali, the scariest deity of all, who danced on Shiva's corpse, her black face dripping blood and her shoulders bedecked with snakes and human heads. Shiva was the lord of all beings and the protector of cows. He was violent and cruel and craved sacrifice and blood. He was the ruler of evil spirits, ghouls, and vampires and in that capacity had a penchant for places where the dead were buried.

I asked Jaga what the people in the temple were praying for.

"They pray to God to ease their problems."

"What kind of problems?"

The look he gave me was faintly incredulous; it seemed to say, *The problem of life, naturally.* Diplomatically he said, "For example, if someone is sick."

I told Jaga that my sister was very sick and that I wanted to pray for her.

"I will take you to a place where you can pray, madame."

He led me to a shrine not far from the Golden Temple, a dark little stall with a small box in it, like a manger. In the manger was a ball of papier-mâché painted orange and decorated with a tin crown and two staring plastic eyes. The eyes had been crookedly set, which left one of them gazing at the ceiling and the other at the buckle of Jaga's belt. It was an inauspicious-looking figure. I said, "Who is this?"

"It is Hanuman, the Monkey King."

"Oh, good," I heard myself saying heartily, as if Hanuman meant something to me. In fact I knew nothing about Hanuman except that he was popular in China, where he was, among other things, the hero of a series of children's books with titles like *Monkey King Goes to the West.* On the covers of these books Hanuman was always depicted as a fiercely grinning little chimp, clever and on the move, a sort of Chinese Curious George with supernatural powers. In contrast, this particular Monkey King looked soused.

The shrine was attended by a boy in rags who was preparing tiny cups of oil with wicks in them. On a stool beside him was a tin plate with a scattering of coins in it. Many small candles had been lit around the manger, and flowers and grains of rice had been tossed into it. Jaga said, "It is up to you how many fires you would like to light. But you must light it and then say your prayer."

"How much money should I give him?"

Jaga, I had learned, disliked being asked to decide such things. He wagged his head from side to side and said vaguely, "Some or none."

I tossed all the coins and shreds of paper in my pocket onto the plate, a little pile that amounted to fifty cents, and as the coins clattered down, the boy's hungry black eyes fixed almost warily on them, as though he feared that this sudden fortune might leap up and flee from him. I selected two candles, placed them at the foot of the manger, and, putting my hands together as Jaga instructed me to, I prayed self-consciously to the Monkey King for my sister, making a mental note to read up on who the Monkey King was and what exactly he was good for. When I was finished I asked Jaga if it mattered what god I prayed to. "Different gods for different things," he said. "But in truth, madame, they are all as one."

From a rooftop above us a woman's voice suddenly shrieked, "Ramesh!" and Jaga and the shrine boy and I all looked up. The woman was leaning recklessly over the edge of the roof. Having caught our attention, she threw a handful of coins down with a queenly flourish. The money went scattering into the gutter, and the little boy scurried after it.

"Who's that?" I said to Jaga.

"The mother of this boy. She wants him to fetch her some *pan.*"

Pan is a pasty concoction of chopped betel nuts, spices, and lime wrapped in the leaf of the betel vine. The betel nut has a slightly narcotic effect; all over India you can see men stuffing pan into their mouths and holding it there, like chewing tobacco. Varanasi was full of pan mongers, who set up shop on the sidewalk, swiftly dicing betel nuts, spreading paste on leaves, rolling them up, and passing them to waiting customers.

A great many holy shrines were crowded into this small area of the city. There was the temple of Anapurna, the goddess of plenty and patroness of beggars and the poor, and the temple of Sakhi Bunjanka, the witness-bearer, where pilgrims, having completed their bathing and devotions, could obtain official verification of their pilgrimage. At Shunkareshwar Shrine pregnant women prayed for the gift of handsome sons. Close by the Golden Temple was the Jnana Vapi Mosque, built by Aurangzeb, the Mogul emperor who famously destroyed many Hindu shrines and turned others into mosques. In 1669 Aurangzeb demolished the original Vishwanath Temple, which was said to be one of the finest in Varanasi, and built this mosque in its place. Nearly a quarter of Varanasi's population was Muslim, and there were roughly one hundred mosques in the city. Over the centuries conflicts had erupted between the Muslim and Hindu communities in Varanasi. Reading up on the city, I was struck by this passage in *India: Past and Present:*

> About fifty years ago [c. 1850] two religious processions, one Muhammadan and the other Hindu, happened to meet in the street and a fracas followed. This quickly developed into a blood riot, involving the greater part of the population. The Musalmans overthrew a sacred monument of the Hindus, who retaliated by burning a mosque. The Muhammadans then slew a cow, and poured its blood into one of the temple tanks of the Brahmans. This outrage aroused every Hindu in the city, and, being in the majority, they would probably have annihilated the Muhammadans but for the intervention of the sepoys.

A growing Hindu nationalism had kindled more recent enmity between Muslims and Hindus, and the Jnana Vapi Mosque was now surrounded by an immense steel barricade topped with barbed wire. The entire area between the Golden Temple and the mosque was under constant surveillance by armed guards posted in military lookout towers. In a courtyard between the mosque and the Golden Temple was the sacred Jnana Vapi, the Well of Knowledge. When the old Vishwanath Temple was being destroyed, the temple's chief priest threw its prized lingam into this well to save it from ruin. Every Hindu pilgrim who came to Varanasi paid the well a visit, threw flowers into it, and drank its sacred, though incredibly fetid, water.

Jaga and I wandered to the Nepalese temple at the top of Lalita Ghat, a small building of brick and wood with a pagoda-like roof. The buildings here were crowded tightly together, and every inch of earth was paved with stone. On the steps of the temple sat an Indian guide and a pale, skinny English man who had painted his forehead with Hindu markings of orange and red. Sitting in the sun, he looked hot and sickly. Jaga and I walked around the outside of the temple, which was graced with myriad small carvings, which on close inspection were revealed to be erotic — an intricate and highly detailed riot of figures engaged in every imaginable sexual pursuit. Jaga made no comment except to say, "You can see, madame, the carvings," and studied his feet. He knew I needed no explanation. When we had circled the temple and reached the front steps again, the Indian guide beckoned to me. "Madame, you are understanding the carvings?"

"They seem very clear," I said.

With a guide's unfailing grasp of the facts, he said, "It is fuckings and anal sexings. Also blow-job and otherwise."

The sickly English fellow smirked. Jaga looked at the sky. A monkey on the roof of the temple shrieked. I waited for further enlightenment from the Indian, but he said nothing and began unabashedly picking his nose as he stared at us. We moved on.

Beside the temple was a building with many hand-tinted photographs of the Nepali royal family hanging across its front, showing a succession of rulers — fathers, sons, grandsons, great-grandsons — twelve or thirteen kings in all. At the end of the row was a color photograph of the present ruler, King Birendra, and his wife, Queen Aiswarya, a tidy-looking couple who, less than two years later, would be brutally shot to death by their own mad son. Each of the Nepali rulers carried a splash of orange across the forehead, like a little stain of tomato sauce. I asked Jaga what the mark was for.

"So that God will recognize you," he said.

I asked Jaga if he ever wore this symbol on his forehead. He gave me his mild smile, said nothing, and proceeded down the steps of the ghat.

YOU CAN SENSE Manikarnika Ghat, Varanasi's cremation ghat, long before you see it. The air grows thicker and quieter, and smoke hangs over the river in a bluish veil. Jaga and I stood on the stone porch of a tower overlooking the ghat. The floor of the porch was riddled with human excrement. When I first arrived in Varanasi I was surprised by the presence of so much human waste in places that were considered sacred, especially in view of the Hindu emphasis on purity, but the worshipers never seemed bothered by it, so I tried to pretend that it wasn't there.

Below us the burning pyres sent up a shimmering wall of air that formed a hot curtain in front of the balcony and carried with it great drafts of gray-blue smoke and the faint smell of sandalwood. On our way here Jaga had warned me, "Men will come and talk to you. They will try to get money from you for giving you information. They will say the money is for poor people. But they are not truth tellers. They are mostly robbers."

Sure enough, as soon as the soles of our shoes touched the top step of the lookout tower, Jaga's prediction came to life in the form of a gaunt fellow who meandered over and began droning at me. Excessive use of pan had stained his teeth and lips a garish Kool-Aid orange. He wore a dusty gown and a tattered yellow scarf, which traveled from his neck up the back of his head, around one ear, across his forehead like a triage bandage, and snaked down around his neck again. He rattled away at me, with no apparent interest in whether I was following him. ". . . I am officially working at burning ghat and can be telling you anything what you want to know and we say Mother Ganga holy river pilgrim come from all over India and why we do burn the body? We burn because . . ." He paused only long enough to hurl a mouthful of red pan juice onto the stone floor; it slapped down like a hank of wet hemp. He waved his arm listlessly at the river. "This river is very much profitable for this city. This is a religious part that is very holy for us since long times ago."

His voice, though flat, held a trace of anxiety, perhaps from having recited this monologue so many times. His mind, and one eye, seemed to wander as he spoke. He scratched at his ear, straightened the brass bangles on his wrist, rubbed his elbow, sighed heavily, and all the while words streamed from his mouth.

Jaga stood off to the side listening patiently, one elbow planted on the balcony railing and his cheek cupped in the heel of his hand. Waves of heat rippled up behind his head. Beyond him a pair of Dutch girls stood at the railing squinting down at the fires. They looked stricken and suspicious. Their pale faces had gone crimson in the heat. On the steps of the ghat groups of tourists had gathered to watch the cremations; sitting with their sun hats and cameras and binoculars, their bare knees roasting in the sun, they resembled fans at a football stadium.

I went to the railing and looked down. Within a small circle delineated by a wooden fence, seven pyres burned, and the human bodies upon them were in various stages of combustion. Several of the fires had dwindled to heaps of smoking cinders, while others were freshly lit stacks of neatly piled wood. Some bore the partially incinerated scraps of human remains. On one dying pyre I saw something that looked distinctly like a human heart. As far as I could see, nothing else was left of the person the heart had belonged to. An attendant poked at it with a stick in the idle, distracted way he might poke at a chicken breast on a hibachi. Cooked, the heart was coffee-colored. When the attendant poked it, it rolled over heavily. He left it there, and with his bamboo tongs picked up a fallen foot lying at the side of the pyre.

Hindus believe that the world began in this very spot and that it will eventually end here. Long rowboats piled high with firewood bobbed gently at the water's edge, hemming the beach in with their unruly stacks of logs and uncut branches. At one end of the beach, at the foot of some narrow stairs, five or six bodies lay on bamboo stretchers, their feet submerged in the river. They were wrapped from head to toe in shimmering, foil-like cloth. Some were wrapped in golden foil, some in silver, one in brilliant red, another in plain white cotton. The bodies looked compact and tidy, like rolled-up carpets carefully packaged for shipping. Beside them a bare-legged boy stood flying his kite through the smoke. Men in rags wandered up and down the stairs, while an attendant splashed Ganges water on the packaged bodies and another weighed out piles of wood. Between the rowboats three men stood up to their knees in the river, hunched over and passing shallow wicker baskets again and again through the water, like forty-niners fishing for gold.

In the corral, two men dressed in loincloths tended the fires with bamboo tongs, laughing and chattering and shouting happily to each other as they hustled about. Their faces were black with soot, and they sweated heavily in the immense heat. They sucked on stubby cigarettes that dangled from their lips and impatiently straightened the damp rags twisted around their heads. They moved quickly and efficiently, tramping through the drifts of gray ash, and when they laughed, which they did often, their teeth were a startling white in the coal-black fields of their faces. They stabbed at the fires, rearranged the charred lumps of wood and flesh, and kicked away the starving dogs that lurked greedily, pink tongues hanging, just outside the corral. I could see the bare feet and shins of a body that was fully aflame. The feet looked twisted and swollen, the toes unnaturally splayed. Eventually the fire gnawed through the shinbones and, like the ends of charred logs, the feet dropped suddenly to the ground.

I gleaned from what the guide was saying that the flame below us had been burning roughly since the days of Shiva, that it was the very fire, more or less, that Shiva had built when his wife died, that the prime ministers in New Delhi were sometimes but not always cremated with flame imported from Varanasi, and that all over India, when people died, their families went to great pains to bring the loved one here to be cremated. The guide was persistent, yet I found it difficult to listen to him, distracted as I was by the scene on the ghat below us. It was something I had never seen before. It was something I had never imagined I would see. It was spectacular and unnerving, and the raw reality of it momentarily overwhelmed its history and meaning.

I watched as two sons helped their aging father prepare for the ritual cremation ceremony for his dead wife. They wrapped a clean white dhoti around the father's waist, removed his glasses and sandals, and helped him pull his shirt off over his head. The father was toothless, big-eared, and frail. He looked dazed without his glasses. His head had been shaved utterly bald, and he stood staring uncertainly at the ground, wiping his eyes and gingerly testing his footing. When one of the sons placed the eyeglasses back on his face, a particularly coarse-looking attendant who had been poking at a charred skull with a stick came over and delicately adjusted the earpieces. One son wrapped a white cloth around the father's shining head, the other pulled the tails of the dhoti smartly up between the father's legs and knotted them. They worked with the dispassion of shopgirls dressing a mannequin. They led the old man by his elbows down the steps to the water, washed his feet, and, when he was finally prepared, guided him to the side of his wife's body, which lay waiting in its shroud on a pile of wood. The old man walked in a tottering way with his hands held up before him, as if in self-defense.

"When somebody is burned here with this fire," said the guide, "it is the end of reincarnation."

Jaga lifted his head and said in his oracular way, "The first time they will die is the last time they will die."

The guide muttered something at Jaga in Hindi; it sounded like a reprimand. Jaga ducked his head and smiled bashfully out over the river.

The guide stepped closer to me and raised his hands in a proprietary way, trying to hold my attention. The cuffs of his baggy black sleeves were torn, and one was encrusted with something pink, like a splash of Pepto-Bismol. His face was dirty, and the area around his right eye looked as though it had been roughly besmirched with a lump of coal. He was delicate and fey. "In Hindu religion we want to break the circle of reincarnation. We do not want to see the same life again. Person cremated in this place will not be reincarnated. That why it is special."

There were, he explained, five exceptions to this rule, five types of souls that because of their circumstances at death would require reincarnation and thus were forbidden to be cremated here: first, the infant who had not lived a full life; second, the pregnant woman who, for the sake of the fetus, must bring forth that life again; third, accident and murder victims; fourth, lepers and people with smallpox, who "like young baby has not seen the light yet so they are getting chance for again life."

I interrupted him. "Only leprosy and smallpox?"

"You are right."

"But people die of all kinds of diseases," I said. "Why would only those two prevent a person from seeing the light?"

Jaga glanced sidelong at me. I could see he wanted to speak but was deferring to the guide. The guide said, "In the blood of the leper man there is an animal. It is called bacteria bug. If you are burning the leper man, the smoke will carry that bug in it. Is dangerous for the living people here. Same with smallpock."

I asked why accident and murder victims were excluded.

"If somebody is getting an accident and getting killed or they is getting murdered it means they have no good karma and is not anymore Hindu and they are getting burned in electrical cremation."

That fascinated me. If you had the misfortune to die a violent death, you were no longer Hindu and they tossed you into the incinerator at the top of the river. I had seen the incinerator, an ugly cinder-block thing on stilts at the water's edge. From its chimneys slender strings of black smoke lifted into the windless air.

The guide droned on. I would have been happier to hear all this from Jaga, but something in Jaga's manner — that Indian reluctance to stir up conflict — told me I should let the guide speak. The fifth exception, he said, was the holy man, the sadhu who hoped to be reincarnated many times in order to achieve the purest possible karma. "For sadhu one life is not enough to become like Shiva, because you need to do good karma to become more pure from inside."

I asked how the bodies of holy men were disposed of. He stared at me, the dangling tail of his scarf obscuring one of his eyes. "Disposed?" He scratched at his whiskers. His teeth, approximately the color of candy corn, were very distracting.

Before I could explain the word, Jaga wearily lifted his head from his hand and translated for the guide, then turned to me and said, "Holy men are put in the river when they die, instead of burning," and he tipped his head gently back into his hand and looked out over the river.

The guide looked at Jaga with distaste. Taking another step toward me, he positioned himself firmly between us. "So!" he said. "In Hindu what they do when somebody die: they are washing the body with holy water at home."

At the edge of the ghat a little man began hacking at a stump of wood with a hatchet. The smoke and heat seemed to muffle the sound. His back was glossy with sweat. Stacks of split wood higher than his head lined a wall near him. I knew that most of the men who tended the cremation ghat were low-caste Doms. They inherited the job and were said to be very rich because they had no qualms about exploiting the ceremony of death and extorting high prices from mourners for the wood and for their services. Wood was scarce, and families unable to afford enough of it had to be content to have their relatives' bodies burned only halfway and the rest thrown into the river. The electric crematorium was cheaper, but the very poorest people simply threw their dead straight into the Ganges. I asked the guide how much wood was needed for a thorough human cremation.

"Two hundred kilogram."

Under his breath Jaga said, "Three hundred kilograms."

"How much would that cost?" I said.

"One kilo is costing one hundred ten rupee," said the guide.

Jaga looked at the river. "One kilo costs thirty rupees."

"Altogether, madame, the funeral fire it cost them twenty-two thousand rupee."

"It cost them nine thousand rupees."

The guide gave me a lopsided smirk, an appeal to my sense of reason. "Madame," he said, speaking softly to conceal his irritation, "little boy is not working here. He is not knowing."

Jaga gazed coolly at the horizon.

The guide said, "And next they make skin massage with the butter. Because when you put body in fire you are going to smell the skin burning."

I looked at him. "You mean if you put butter on the skin you can't smell it burning?" It seemed weird.

"You are right. You cannot smell it now. Can you?"

Mostly I smelled burning wood, but from time to time I could detect another smell, something disturbingly similar to the aroma of hot dogs frying on a buttery griddle. I had begun to wonder if it was my own nervous imagination. "No, not really," I said.

"That is right," said the guide. "Then they tie the body in different color cloth. Bright color like gold or silver or orange is older person. When you see somebody only in white is an young man. When you see only red is an young woman. If they are from very far away they come here by fast car up through the main road. And from the main road four people carry the bamboo stretcher on their shoulder."

"Who carries them?" I said.

"Usually family only. Because family they don't want other people touch body. That is why nobody is working here."

Jaga said, "Yes, people work here. And if there is not enough family, the dacoits will carry the body."

The guide spoke sharply to Jaga again, and Jaga responded with a mischievous grin. He seemed to be enjoying himself. He was wonderfully in love with his famous city and fully confident of what he knew.

Turning to face me again, the guide stepped still closer and continued in his grinning, plodding way. A desperate unctuousness had crept into his droning, as though he feared I would abandon him before he could ask me for money. "So, first of all they are washing the body in the river.

This is last purification of skin and soul. Then they go inside to police station . . ." he pointed to a building behind us ". . . to get death certificate. Because sometimes they found out that the dead person is not truly dead. So before they burn, the police check the body."

That interested me. I couldn't help picturing the police rapping on the corpse's forehead to see whether one eye, or both, might open in protest before they sent it up in flames.

"And then the police give the certificate, and the family gather here. Like, look, madame, this people."

He was pointing at a group of men standing near a pyre. They were all draped in fresh white cloths and their heads were shaven clean. They looked dignified and pure, and their nude brown heads glinting in the sunlight had a vulnerable beauty. One wore only a diaperlike dhoti and a prayer string over one shoulder, like the famous images of Gandhi.

"The man who is having the string is the son of his mother died. She is the body there in red and gold. Old woman. The one who makes ceremony must shave his hair off, and beard, and wash in the river to purify self."

We watched as the mother's body was placed upon a pile of wood. An attendant handed the son a bundle of reeds with a hot coal tucked into one end of it. The son began to walk somberly around the body with the smoking reeds held out in front of him. "This is the last ceremony we make," said the guide. "The first time he walks around means the body is not anymore human body. For example, if my father die is hard for me to burn him. He give me life, he give me food. How I can burn my father? So, before they burn they do ceremony. It means he is not anymore my father. He is going to turn into the five different materials. Like water, fire, air, and earth and spirit."

As he spoke, another body arrived at the bottom of the steps and was placed at the side of the burning circle. Attendants shouted to each other and hurled huge logs about, oblivious to the gravity of the ceremony now under way. The heat was nearly unbearable. My eyes had begun to feel toasted. A black goat skipped into the corral, but despite the chaotic atmosphere I found it very moving to see this nearly naked adult son circling his dead mother with the seeds of the flame that would presently consume her. I wished the guide would be quiet for a moment so that I could concentrate, but he went on lowing into my ear, his pumpkin-colored lips a few inches from my face. The sweetish betel nut on his breath smelled like Coca-Cola. "Then they start the fire," he said. The body would take three hours to burn completely.

The attendant took the bundle of reeds from the son's hand and swung it through the air, the hot coal ignited the reeds, and the attendant handed the flaming torch back to the son. The son bent and lit the pyre with it, then took a jar of ghee and began placing lumps of it on his mother's body. He scattered sandalwood shavings over the fire. Strands of smoke began to creep up through the logs, and flickering fingers of flame appeared. Eventually the fire began to roar. The young man stepped away from the fire and stood with his family, and they all watched, squinting in the heat and sunlight, as the flames transformed the woman's golden shroud to black. Beneath the flaming shroud I could see the gentle curve of her skull.

The guide informed me that the rib cage of a man and the hipbones of a woman were the densest bones in the body and slow to burn, and that these were often the parts that remained when the fire had burnt itself out. When the body had been consumed, a clay pot full of Ganges water would be broken over the cinders, signifying that the relationship with the dead person was finished. Some families carried the ashes back to their homes, others took them to the Himalayas and threw them into the Ganges there. Ten days after the cremation the family would have a feast at their home, to which they would invite the local poor.

Jaga watched the fire and said, with sympathy in his voice, "When the fire is getting hot it means the dead body is finding peace."

The guide said, "Here nobody is allowed crying near the fire."

The point of the cremation was to release the soul. The sound of crying would naturally call the soul back to earth and thwart the whole purpose of the ceremony. This was one of the reasons that women were not allowed within the cremation area. "Ladies is not coming here. Only mans, because lady coming emotional so she make the cry. When she make the cry, the soul is hearing it and wanting to come back."

"Men don't cry?" I said.

"Man do cry, but only away from the fire. And sometimes some women jump in the fire because she want to die with her husband. Before that was common. They got lot of honor for doing it. Now it is not legal."

Sati, the Hindu ritual in which a widow would immolate herself on her husband's funeral pyre, had been banned in 1829 by the British government. But a week before I arrived in Varanasi, a forty-five-year-old woman in northern India had thrown herself on her husband's pyre and burned to death, an event that had inspired great controversy in the Indian newspapers and had turned the woman's rural village into an instant site of pilgrimage. Thousands of people, mostly women, flocked there to venerate the dead woman. Government officials were quick to dismiss the incident as the spontaneous suicide of a depressed woman, but local villagers insisted that it had been premeditated and that the husband's family had urged the woman to do it. Sati, which means "faithfulness" in Sanskrit, was said to have originated with a consort of Shiva, who set herself on fire to protest his mistreatment.

I asked the guide how many people were cremated here in one day.

"Here more than two hundred people in one day. Fire is burning all times. Even in night. And every day also twenty or thirty people we throw in river."

"Entire bodies?"

"Yah."

"The bodies just go floating down the river to Calcutta?" I said.

"No. There are many fishes and dolphins, and they are eating the body before it is going too long."

"Any crocodiles?"

"Yes. We have."

Abandoning all efforts to disguise his disbelief, Jaga lifted his head and frowned directly at the guide. "Crocodile? No. Only dolphins and big fish."

The guide sulked and tasted his teeth. He leaned over the railing, spat, wiped his mouth with his crusty sleeve. "And the crocodiles can come here but is because they afraid people that they stay back to the bridge. There are many."

"There are none," Jaga said.

The guide stared at him. It was plain that he would have liked nothing better than to give this interloping child a good slap. I asked him what the men with the baskets were doing in the water.

"They are looking for riches."

"Riches?"

"Jewlies and golds that fell from bodies. What they found they sell it."

I watched the three men pawing at the water with their baskets, their

backs turned to the pyres. They chatted and laughed, plucked little objects from the dripping baskets, frowned at them in the palm of a hand,
then flung them back into the river. That they were doing this in full
view of the mourning families seemed thoroughly shameless to me.

The guide raised his hands at me again. "And now, madame. You are
knowing Mother Teresa in Calcutta?"

I nodded.

"She is died, but still her good work is going." He pointed at a building behind me. "Excuse me, look here. In this house is people waiting
for dying." It was a hospice for the terminally ill who had no money to
pay for medical care or for their own cremations. He put his palm to his
chest. "Like me, madame, they are poor people working here. My father
do this work. My grandfather do it. I born in this job. The man who
work here is untouchables. I work free for these old sick people because
these are having no family. Same like in Calcutta missionary society."

He was speaking slowly now and very softly; the words flowed out
in a cooing way, like the fearful murmurings of a person trying to pacify
an angry dog. He pointed at the ceiling of the lookout tower. "There are
old lady upstair. They are like a nun, you know. They are taking care of
dead body and sicks. So as every Western country come here. We explain them so they can understand. We collect the charity. Donations
for the wood because every day two three four people died and got no
money."

"Are you working for Mother Teresa's sisters?" I said.

The guide paused, his orange mouth hanging open. He stared at me,
and I realized I had given him a good idea. He was dying to say yes;
I knew the answer was no. "Yah," he said, "you are right. Mother's
sisters."

Jaga said nothing. He gazed down at the fires, his fine hands clasped
upon the railing, his solemn face a portrait of offended civic pride.

The guide bent at the waist and spat on the floor again. "Let me take
you upstairs to see Mother's sisters."

As we mounted the dark stairs, his chatter echoed against the walls
of the stairwell. In an empty room at the top of the stairs, four emaci-
ated old women sat on the floor looking weak with hunger, drawing
their rags about them and swatting halfheartedly at the flies that landed
on their faces. One wore a white dishrag on her head, another sucked at
a tiny black cigar, its yellowish smoke twisting into her eyes. They
stared impassively at me.

The guide said, "You can see by your own eyes that they are old lady," as though age were a guarantee of goodheartedness.

I looked at him. He was hollow-eyed. He looked depressed and weak and as though he weren't getting enough fresh air. In the end it made no difference to me whether he and the women were working for the poor. They all looked starved and hopeless and derided by want. I gave two hundred rupees to the woman with the cigar, said goodbye to the guide, and proceeded down the steps. He hurried down behind me, repeatedly moaning, "And for my services, madame?"

I fished another two hundred rupees out of my pocket and gave it to him. He snatched the money up and pressed it to his forehead in gratitude. As I left the building he stood on the stairs saying, "When you sleep, your soul will make you peace because you gave right money for good work."

Outside, Jaga stood waiting, his arms crossed in a barricade across his chest. We stood for a while staring at the river and the smoke and the steps of the ghat. Finally I said, "They aren't giving the money to the sick, are they, Jaga?"

Jaga studied his feet. "They are crooks."

"Maybe so," I said. "But they're the saddest-looking crooks I've ever seen. Will the old ladies keep the money?"

"I think that man will take most of it."

"And the crocodiles?"

Jaga tossed his head in disgust and spanked his hands together briskly. "None!"

As we made our way down, I noticed that the family who had just sent their dead mother up in flames were sitting at the bottom of the steps. The grown son who had performed the ceremony was crying softly, safely away from the fire and from his mother's departing soul, his bald head hung low, his shoulders bent with grief, his knuckles swiveling in his eye sockets. Beside him, his dry-eyed father was speaking gently to him. He seemed to be reasoning with the sorrowing son, counseling him, perhaps reminding him that this was not an end for the mother but finally a beginning. As he spoke, he lifted an explaining hand, as if to say, *Don't cry. She's free.*

I knew that in Hindu philosophy the great problem of life was that we cared too much, were too attached to this world, to things, and even to people, to our pain and our fears. Those attachments became a kind of imprisonment. If we could only find a way to see it all as fleeting and temporal, a finite state of mind, we would suffer far less. The Hindu texts said, *Let go,* but how do you tell yourself that it is all right, that it doesn't matter when the people you love with all your heart are gone? I knew so well what the son was feeling that his grief presented itself as a pain at the base of my throat, and I dreaded that feeling so much that I had to look away.

ONE MORNING I awoke in the Hotel Ramamurthi feeling as if I had smoked an entire pack of filterless cigarettes the night before. When I stepped out of my room I found that the hallways of the hotel were full of smoke. I went down to the lobby and asked Mr. Subramani if the hotel was on fire. He frowned and looked insulted. "No. Why asking, Mrs. Mohini?"

"Because the hallways are full of smoke."

Subramani shrugged and patted his satin necktie. "It is just like always, madame."

"No," I said, "I think it's worse than usual." The fumes smelled noxious, as though an eighteen-wheeler had been idling outside my door all night.

"Do not worry, Mrs. Mohini. You are on your vacation."

Mr. Subramani was always telling his foreign guests that they were on vacation. He made it sound like an admonishment. It was a way of subduing and disarming them. If they were on vacation they should be relaxed, and if they were relaxed, they should not be upset about anything, especially anything that might happen in his hotel. In Mr. Subramani's interpretation, being on vacation was similar to being in a coma.

I went into the dining room, a big, gloomy room appointed with a dusty chandelier and wall-to-wall carpeting the color of a basketball. The tablecloths were always freshly stained, whether you were the first person at a meal or the last, the milk was always a little lumpy, and here too was the ever-present smell of exhaust. All of the food tasted more or less of curry, even the marmalade and the toast and sometimes the bananas. But the waiters were good-natured and helpful and so similar in looks — hatchet-faced, dark-haired, black-eyed, and very short — that I was certain they were all members of one family.

Though the hallways of the Hotel Ramamurthi were always empty, the dining room always seemed to be full. I sat at a table with a Canadian car salesman and a Norwegian security guard. The Canadian, a stout, cross-faced redhead in a John Deere cap, had finished his breakfast and was drinking coffee and reading a copy of *The Statesman,* an English-language Calcutta newspaper. I ate two shingles of dry toast and a papaya, struck up a conversation with the Norwegian, and quickly discovered that he had a serious preoccupation with numerical facts and mathematical detail. When I asked him where he was from, he said, "I live forty-three miles north of Oslo. You can also say sixty-nine point two oh kilometers. As you probably know, there are point six two one three seven miles per kilometer. I am traveling with a group. We started as thirty-seven people, but two had to return because of insufficient visas, so we are now thirty-five people in total."

The man was cutting his toast into small pieces with a knife and fork and chewing each piece thoroughly and deliberately. He had a bushy brown mustache like Stalin's. His eyebrows were the color of wheat and his eyes were a glacial blue. Watching the patient way he chewed reminded me that I was a person who ate too fast. I was always in a hurry. I had arrived at the table after him, had finished my breakfast in three minutes, and was now ready to go out. But the Norwegian seemed melancholy and eager to talk, and since the Canadian was ignoring him, I felt I should sit with him a little longer. He spoke the way he chewed — laboriously and without emotion. He told me that he and his group had been in India for two weeks. They would stay in Varanasi for another four and a half days. The mean temperature during their visit was 27 degrees centigrade. He adjusted his glasses, wiped his chin with his napkin, tucked another morsel of toast under his mustache. He had started his job in 1969 and had nine years until retirement. He had been to America five times. To Minnesota, in fact. Minneapolis, population 368,383. He had stayed in a town approximately twenty-six miles west of Minneapolis. The first time he went there was in 1979. He went again in 1980.

He laid his fork across the edge of his plate and tapped uncertainly at his lips with a finger as he looked over my head. The Canadian turned a page of his newspaper, glanced doubtfully at him, and went back to reading.

And again in 1993, 1994, and 1995. Five times in total. He drove one time to Colorado with his first cousin, a drive of twenty-three hours and thirty minutes.

"America," he said, "has fifty states but only one language. I have been to Israel once. I am going to Israel again next year, so I will have been to Israel twice."

I sipped my coffee. I had begun to feel a dense oppression descending over the table. The man was like a gentle freight train rolling down a hill. Focusing on the corner of the table as he talked, as if on a blackboard covered with formulas and equations, his mind sifted through all the numbers that had passed through his life as he divided his toast into neat fractions. He did not appear to expect a reaction to anything he was saying. He asked me nothing. I had the eerie sensation that if I stood up and left the table, he would carry on talking in the same homogeneous way. And yet I respected him. The terrible unwaveringness of his interest was almost freakish; it was like a paralysis.

"I saw on TV just before I came here that there was a bombing in Netanya, Israel," he said. "Three people killed. Five people injured."

I told the man that I was soon going to Bethlehem and that people had told me to wear a bulletproof vest while I was there. He neither laughed nor protested but said without hesitation, "A bulletproof vest works quite well. I have used them in my job. At ten feet the vest is useles, because it is only two point five four centimeters thick. At a range of twenty feet the vest is of more use.

The Canadian cleared his throat loudly and rattled his newspaper. I sensed that like me, he had an urge to run out of the room. The Norwegian said. "In Minnesota there is a place called Minne-ha-ha."

"Yes," I said.

He peered at me. "Ha-ha is what we say when we laugh." And for the first time his calculating lips split open and he laughed, heaving his shoulders and putting his hand to his mouth to prevent chewed bits of toast from flying out of it. He patted his mustache and sighed and laughed some more.

The Canadian lowered his paper and stared warily at the man, then folded up his paper, tossed back the dregs of his coffee, and abruptly left.

The Norwegian said, "I am alone. My wife died three and a half years ago next week. We were married for thirty-five years." That one innumerate piece of information adrift amid the numbers struck me as very sad.

Behind the man's head, high up on the wall, was a small window, and through it I could see the Varanasi sky beginning to lighten, gradually assuming its pallor of yellow. It seemed especially odd that this Norwegian security guard was sitting here mulling mundane numbers when all of enormous, chaotic India was thrumming outside the window. But I thought I understood him. Muddling through a culture so different from my own sometimes made my head feel like a locked vault sinking deep into the well of my own experience. The point of foreign travel was to try to understand the culture, the religion, what the people were saying and thinking — but the stranger and more alien the sights, the deeper the vault sometimes sank, and the darker and more personally clouded was the water through which my vision was filtered. In teeming Varanasi I felt at times submerged in a strangely muffled space of my own making, and I had to struggle to peer out of my self-protective myopia.

"What do you think of Varanasi?" I said.

The Norwegian grimaced. "I do not like it."

Dirty, frightening, overcrowded, and poor were the words he used. He was not wrong. When I first arrived in Varanasi I was a bit overwhelmed by what I saw. I tried to cast my eyes beyond the desperation and the squalor and the suffering. I had seen awful, disturbing, horrifying sights in other countries, including my own, but it was the volume of suffering here that was so distracting, that made it impossible to rationalize or ignore. Wherever I cast my eye it fell inevitably on poverty, malnutrition, deformity, and disease, and each sight seemed more stunning or cruel or bizarre than the last. I found it difficult to keep from obsessing on the bizarre, for my eye was naturally drawn to what it was unaccustomed to seeing. (If one person in a group is missing the tip of his little finger, I will notice it immediately.) I don't think of myself as an easily shockable person, yet each day in India I saw something that struck me with the kind of shock that snaps at the face and sets the armpits aflame, and each day it was a relief to get that one shocking sight out of the way.

One day, as I walked down Kabir Chaura Road, I saw an object in the street that I thought was an old, empty leather briefcase. It was brown and dusty and flat and had creases and folds in its outline. It looked like something that had fallen off of a trash truck until, out of the corner of my eye, I noticed that the object had ribs, barely covered by a layer of skin, and was breathing. It was a dog. As I came nearer I saw that its eyes and mouth were open. At the back of its neck was a large red wound the circumference and depth of a soup bowl. Clearly the dog was taking its last few breaths. Cycle rickshas wheeled past, people hurried by on foot. No one noticed the dog. Why should they? The death of a dog was unremarkable and unimportant. I walked on and thought, "Well, there's my bad sight for the day." But ten minutes later I came upon a woman lying on the pavement in much the same posture as the dog, on her side, her head in the gutter, an assortment of rags covering her limbs. Her eyes, like the dog's, were open. A large flap of her scalp, the circumference of a tea saucer, was missing, as though sheared off by a machete. It was not a new wound; the film of a scab had begun to form over it. Little black blossoms of flies quarreled angrily in the wound. The woman had recently vomited and was now lying in the product. Her fingers were curled around a dirty bowl, which held a few tiny coins. I turned to a man standing in the doorway of a nearby shop and said, "This woman is very sick."

The man nodded and shrugged and said, "Sick, sick."

I said, "Can we help her?" and the man wagged his head in resignation and raised his palms at me and said, "How help?" which I took as an indication that any move to help would be utterly futile and anyway would not be forthcoming. A feeling of desperation came over me. The day before I had seen a man going down the street squatting like a rabbit and pulling himself along on his hands. Some malformation of his spine prevented him from walking upright. He wore nothing but a shirt and a pair of flip-flops on his hands, and as he proceeded his bare rear end and genitals dragged along the pavement.

It was clear that everything in life truly was relative. Here a dying dog and a dying woman were on equal footing. I tried to focus beyond them, to prescind from all that was famously brutal and inevitable about India. People often said that Varanasi was beautiful. Indeed, if you sat on a ghat in the evening or in a quiet place at dawn and looked at the buildings and the river from a slight distance, it was, in a dusty, aged way, somewhat beautiful. Kashi, the ancient name for Varanasi, means "City of Light," and at night, when the moon turned the river to silver and gave pale yellow edges to the passing blue clouds, it could be lovely. The sight of Indians dressing themselves after bathing in the river was lovely. The fresh colors in the open-front shops were lovely. But as I sat in the Ramamurthi dining room and listened to the Norwegian security guard evading all thoughts about India, I suddenly found it difficult to shake the image of the dying woman, the grinning leper, the starving baby, the sleeping bodies huddled under sheets on the sidewalks at night.

I finished my coffee and said goodbye to the security guard. On my way out of the dining room I made the mistake of telling the cashier that I liked his turquoise sweater. He jumped out of his chair and said, "And I am liking you too, madame. And am knowing you. You are a liar woman. You are abocate." He was beaming.

"Excuse me?" I said.

He made wild shapes in the air with his hands. "Abocate. For making the decisions. Very straight. Liar woman. For the law."

"You mean a lawyer?"

"Yes. I am knowing you are liar woman abocade."

"Advocate."

"Yes, you are abocate."

"No," I said. "I am not."

He flapped his hands. "Yes, you are. You are very sharp and straight and going strong around the world with a very good mind. I am wanting to use your mind. Nobody can trick you. Your face. You will tell them what to do. Your eyes look straight inside. That is why nobody will be liking you. But I am liking you."

I thanked him and made a move to leave, but he hurried out from behind his table and stood in front of me, grinning beneath his heavy mustache and wringing his hands. He had the holy red smudge of greasepaint between his eyebrows. "In life I have never seen a woman like you. In India we have woman abocate liar. But not like you. If you give me your address in your country, I will be using your mind. And liking you. A lot of tourist coming in hotel is silly and loudly and not knowing nothing. Subramani manager boss them what to do. You do own decision. And is quiet. That is why I am liking you."

I had only a vague idea what the cashier's interpretation of me was based on. In my own view I was a volatile, distempered, obsessive, garrulous woman, emotional sometimes to the point of being maudlin. I would have made a rotten lawyer, unable when crossed to refrain from telling the judge that he had his head up his ass. But I had heard myself described as being "very New England" so often that nothing surprised me anymore. I knew that "New England" meant that I appeared skeptical and taciturn and impatient.

Indian men had a compulsion to flatter, no matter who you were or how awful your behavior. They could create the illusion that you looked like an Indian movie star, that you were graceful, intelligent, generous, and above all *different* from the rest of the masses of tourists. But the illusion was only momentary, and rupees were always at the distant end of it. The flattery was a way of applying pressure to your pocket. This man had managed to make my sometimes saturnine demeanor seem stellar. Though uncertain whether I should thank him, I did so, and in my lawyerly fashion I moved along.

As I passed by Subramani's desk on my way out of the hotel that morning, the manager shuffled through his papers and said with complete indifference, "Excuse me one minute, Mrs. Mohini, what is your opinion: the Varanasi people is good people or cheating people?" and then began rooting for something in his desk drawer.

ON MY WAY to see the cantonment that morning, I stopped at the toy factory where Jaga worked. The factory was a large, ill-lit room lined with shelves that were crowded with toys: nesting dolls, Santa Claus dolls, pinwheels, toy trucks, children's lamps, and Christmas ornaments. Cardboard boxes were stacked up in columns about the room. A black-and-white television in a dark corner gave off a bluish light, like an illuminated block of ice, and lent a shiny pallor to the faces of three boys who were sitting on the floor in front of it, mouths hanging open as they painted faces on wooden dolls held in their laps. On the television screen two Indian lovers seemed to be doing a tango on a ship. The three boys and Jaga appeared to be the only employees there, and it was impossible to tell if one of them was in charge. The place smelled of dust and varnish.

Jaga greeted me with his formal handshake and said, "How do you do, madame? I am pleased to be seeing you." He showed me a few toys — penguins, frogs, trains, spinning tops. He handed me a wooden flute, and as I looked into its barrel, he put his hands on his hips and said, "It is similar to the Western oboe, if you are familiar with that instrument."

"A reed instrument?" I said.

"Believe it or not. You must soak the reed to make it soft. Now it is hard." He held up a wooden Santa Claus. Staring fondly at it he said, "Do you know this fellow, madame?"

"That is Santa," I said.

"I quite like him!"

When I picked up a toy man with a tin drum hanging from his neck, Jaga said excitedly, "Oh, that one I like too! But I will show you my favorite one!" He went to a shelf and took down a wooden polar bear on wheels, and, with the enchantment and delight of a young child, he rolled the hand-painted bear across the dusty cement floor, illustrating how the rolling of the wheels triggered a mechanism that made the bear's mouth open and close repeatedly. "Oh, he is jolly," Jaga said. "A resident of frosty places."

The excellent, old-fashioned toys were all made by hand for foreign markets; they would be packed in boxes and shipped out of India.

"I like him too," I said. "Where do you send these toys?"

"Every country. America. Europe. Many places."

"China?"

He gazed at the bear, his face aglow in the dark, musty room. "No. China does not need us to make toys for them. China makes her own."

I liked the nesting dolls and asked Jaga if I could buy some.

"If you like," he said. "They are sixty-five rupees apiece."

Seeing an opportunity to test his mathematical skill, I said, "So if I bought four, how much would it cost me?"

His round face went utterly still. He looked at his hands. From the television the two dancing actors, who had been speaking Hindi, broke into English to screech, "I love you!" and their tinny voices streaked across the room. For five seconds Jaga seemed to have stopped breathing, and then he said, "Two hundred sixty." To keep his colleagues from hearing him, he held a hand to the side of his mouth and whispered, "But, madame, I think it is too much money to spend."

BUT FOR THE ROVING BANDS of monkeys, Varanasi's cantonment was like an Indian Beverly Hills. The cantonment lay at the edge of the city and was quiet and thick with trees and the feel of imperialism and money. There were big colonial hotels and well-groomed gardens with grass trimmed as short as putting greens. The plane trees that lined the wide streets offered a shade that at midday was almost cool. Between the branches spiders had woven webs so dense they were like billowing clots of fog.

Passing down the street I had seen four or five monkeys leaping in an organized way out of the window of an army truck parked at the curb; ten more had occupied an empty city bus parked behind it, rattling the window latches with their hairy fingers, swinging from the steering wheel, and climbing over the seats. A few trotted jauntily along the window ledges of a building. A monkey perched on a hydrant gnawed at an orange; another sitting on the pavement yawned and scratched at his chest. They were langurs, with long black hands and wise black faces and stiff blond bangs and beards. Their resemblance to humans was astonishing. They snatched things the way children do. Walking past the army truck I had felt a sudden fervid weight on the front of my body, a warm paw on my forearm, startling but not unpleasant. In an instant the weight was gone and so was the small paper bag of peanuts I was carrying.

Outside Saint Mary's Convent School at the edge of the cantonment, I stopped to buy a Popsicle from a man who had cleverly parked his ice box at the gate to draw the children at recess in the schoolyard.

Beyond the school gates the grassless campus was tidy and controlled and had a civilization-in-the-jungle atmosphere. The students wore uniforms of white trousers or skirts and white blouses, and boys and girls alike wore orange-and-yellow-striped neckties tied in a Windsor knot. Several children careened back and forth on a rickety swing set. Across the schoolyard a nun wearing a white wimple was teaching a dozen girls a dance that looked for all the world like a hula. Other children ran hectically about, and several girls came over to buy Popsicles. When I said hello, they stared at me as though I had pulled a rabbit out of my mouth. A fat, sweating, very pretty girl with short black hair said hello back. Her necktie was knotted so tight it appeared to be choking her. Her name was Sujata. She sucked on a cherry Popsicle and grinned and stared at me with big black eyes.

"How are you?" she said, as though she had known me for years.

"Very well," I said. "How are you?"

"I am very fine." She waved her Popsicle. "This is our school, please."

"Yes. I see it's called Saint Mary's. Is it a Christian school?"

"Yah, it is a Christian."

"Are you Christian?"

"No. I am Hindu. But Christian and Muslim and Hindu can come here together."

Sujata was fat-faced and game. She spoke with breathless glee. Her blouse was too tight and strained at the buttons on the front placket. Her pleated skirt had spun crooked on her waist, and her shirttail had sprung loose. She was panting and sweating in the sunlight, and her fine hair was dusted with tiny white feathers and bits of yellow straw, as though she had just stepped out of a chicken coop. A brass bracelet on her wrist had left a ring of green tarnish on her plump forearm. She gasped as she sucked at her Popsicle.

Under an enormous mango tree in the center of the schoolyard a man in Nehru pajamas and a white cap was marshaling a ragtag marching band of children who sawed away at a military march. A gangly boy banged at the bass drum, a trumpet bleated wildly, an unruly trio of little horns screeched like chairs being dragged across a floor. Other children ran around in circles under the mango tree. They were healthy and plump — nothing like the children on the ghats, whose long, tangled hair was stained red by malnutrition. They were nothing like Jaga and the boys at the tea stall. These were the cosseted, well-fed children of money.

I asked Sujata if it would be possible to see the school. She peered nervously over her shoulder at the nun in the distance, giggled, said, "Um. Yah. Come along with me." I followed her through the gate. As we crossed the courtyard, Sujata muttered excitedly, "Oh, God, Sister will beat me!"

"Why will Sister beat you?"

Sujata said nothing. She walked on, dragging her flattened Mary Janes through the dust and peering anxiously over her shoulder. Her plump brown cheeks jiggled as she walked. The tops of her white ankle socks had slipped below her heels.

Across the schoolyard, Sister, her arms raised over her head, shouted something at the dancing girls. "Will Sister beat you because I am with you, Sujata?"

"Hee-hee," she said and ducked her head and held the Popsicle in front of her nose in a feeble attempt to hide her face.

"Well, when we get over there you can just pretend you don't know me."

"But, madame, that would be a lie."

That was true. Having exchanged pleasantries at the school gate, Sujata and I were now in this together. She had been willingly suborned. She could not deny it. "Well, yes," I said. "It would be a lie. In that case, you can just tell Sister that it was my idea and that you had nothing to do with it. That would not be a lie."

The girl lifted her red-stained, gap-toothed grin at me, giggled in a way that meant this foolish idea would never wash with Sister, and went back to sucking fatalistically at the Popsicle.

We passed the school building, a long, low brick bungalow like a Western trading post. The classrooms had no doors, and through the doorways I could see ancient desks of worn dark wood, blackboards, and chickens careering fretfully about the dusty floor. A goat pranced out of a doorway.

As we approached the little dance class, Sujata's Popsicle began to slump in the heat. The red liquid ran over her knuckles and down to her wrist. As she licked at her hand, a slushy clump plopped onto the front of her white blouse, leaving a stain like a gunshot wound. "Oh, Saint Mary, have mercy! Mother will beat me." She slapped hopelessly at the stain with her free hand, and the Popsicle disintegrated on its stick and plopped down onto her shoes. "Oh, for shame," she said fretfully. "And now I must practice for dance."

The dancers were marching in a circle, moving their raised arms languidly like enraptured worshipers at a gospel meeting, their pleated skirts twirling, their rep ties swinging.

"Can I watch the dance, Sujata?"

"Yah."

"Are you sure?"

"Yah."

"Will Sister be angry?"

"Can you ask her, madame?" Black ants had begun to pool around the sweetness at Sujata's feet; some had climbed onto her shoes.

"You want me to ask Sister?"

"Yah. Sister."

Sister looked stern and slightly irritated. I was beginning to be a little afraid of her. "Sujata," I said, "will Sister beat me if I ask her?"

Sujata let out a ripping screech of laughter at the thought of Sister beating — of all people — me. I was twice Sister's size. "Gosh, no, madame! Never. She will only beat me."

And then a sudden bell began ringing deeply over the school, and before I could say goodbye to Sujata, she and Sister and the other children hurried into the building with the urgency of people sheltering from an

impending tornado. As they poured into the building I tried to determine which students were Hindu, which Muslim, and which Christian,
but I saw no distinctions. They all looked the same, and they fled back
to class in the same sweetly frantic way.

WE SAT TOGETHER — Jaga, his friend Tarun, and I — on the elevated seat of a cycle ricksha on our way to visit the Monkey Temple.
The ricksha, driven by a man named Ahmed, jounced and rocked over
the broken streets. The seat was meant to accommodate two people,
but the boys were so thin that together they occupied little more than
the space of one person. They sat with their knees together and their
hands clasped primly in their laps. Twice Jaga said from below my left
shoulder, "Madame, you are always on time. And you keep your promise." The way he said it suggested that he had too often been stood up
and disappointed. His politeness, his gentleness, had a way of stifling
my usual impatience; as we rumbled along the streets I had an urge to
put my arms around both boys.

In the weeks that I had been in Varanasi the sky, never cloudy, was
also never quite blue. It was a muffled, mustardy color, like the color of
the river at evening. The air was always slightly humid, the temperature
always hovered near eighty, and the dampish sunlight had a tranquiliz-
ing effect. That afternoon Jaga was perspiring in a black turtleneck
sweater. Tarun, on my right, wore a similar turtleneck of cherry-red
wool and, around his neck, a silver chain strung with beads of amber
glass. As I praised Tarun's necklace he stared apprehensively at my
mouth, slowly making out the words. Then he lowered his chin to peer
at the necklace and said proudly, "My dear mother have give it."

Tarun was Jaga's best friend. He was handsome and agreeable and
terribly shy. With his long, thin legs, fine cheekbones, dark skin, long
straight nose, and the coal-black sweep of bangs that fell over his brow,
Tarun looked like a Hindu prince. He had amazingly strong white teeth,
and on his forehead he often wore a smear of red powder, signifying
that he had bathed and performed his puja at the temple. Tarun didn't
speak much English, and although he was taller and stronger than Jaga,
he had not been graced with Jaga's intelligence or insatiable curiosity.
When Tarun did speak it was usually to affirm something that Jaga had
said or to point out a baby animal. Whenever I addressed Tarun directly

he would blink rapidly and begin winding the knob of his wristwatch in a nervous reflex, and in the interval before comprehension took root his face was always the picture of dread.

Both boys had an interest in Western fashions and the affluence that they represented, and both were always overdressed for the Varanasi weather. They never wore traditional Indian clothing. They never wore shorts or short-sleeved shirts, for bare limbs were perceived as childish. They looked as though they spent a great deal of time dressing. They liked jeans and Nike sneakers, patent leather and a bit of glitter, and the cheap imitations they managed to afford in the Varanasi bazaars were only a rough approximation of their true tastes. Both boys wore rings; Tarun's was a large black rectangular stone, Jaga's a simple silver band. That day they looked as if they had chosen their clothes with extra care. Jaga, who usually wore flip-flops, was wearing a pair of black shoes made of a supple, slightly greasy-looking material, like thin sheets of black licorice that had been snipped into shape and stitched together. They were thick-soled and very shiny. When I asked Jaga if they were new, he said, "Very old."

"But they look new."

"That is because I must take care of them. I have only one pair."

Jaga was wearing jeans, which I had never seen him in, and they fit him so tightly that he was unable to fit his ever-present pocket business of powdery tattoos into his pocket. He was forced to carry the box in his hand. The jeans made him look even smaller than he was, and slightly effeminate. When I admired the jeans he seemed pleased. "But they are not mine," he said. "They are borrowed."

Jaga loved to talk, and although he spoke with a sober, opaque expression, there was an air of mischief in everything he said, and it was not difficult to make him laugh. His voice was chalky and deeper than one would expect from one so small. As we bumped over the rough streets he gave me facts about the Monkey Temple and told me that Tarun went there every Saturday morning to pray. When I asked Jaga if he went to pray, he said, "I used to. Now I never do. When I lived in the country I was more religious."

Several years before, Jaga's grandparents, who lived in the country, had needed help on their farm, and as the eldest son in his family Jaga had been sent to live with them. He told me that in the country he would get up every morning at five o'clock and for breakfast would eat nothing but scraps left over from the meal the night before. "Sometimes we would put chapatis on the roof of the house at night, because of the water that comes in the night . . ." He stopped, looking suddenly afflicted, and stared vacantly at Ahmed's back. "I don't know," he said, "what you call this that makes the grass wet at night."

"Dew."

"Yes. If this dew comes onto the food and we then eat it, we think that it makes our eyesight better."

In the morning, if the stray cats hadn't finished off the chapatis, Jaga sat on the roof and ate them, hoping for stronger eyes. "My grandfather was not in the custom of taking tea. Instead we had hot milk. I always carried a bamboo stick and every day I rubbed nice oil on it before I went out."

"Oil?"

He smiled up at me. "We say that a stick will beat things better if you oil it. I was a very serious boy. I would beat anyone for this or that offense to my person. And also I was much more religious in this time, and I would beat anyone who did anything against my religion."

He fingered the long strand of hair at the back of his head, holding it up for me to see. "This little hair of mine was very long then. If anyone dared to touch it, I would beat them smartly!"

In the country Jaga never ate meat. He went daily to the temple to pray. Because there were no tourists, he never engaged in business of the sort that occupied him now in the city. His grandfather had cows and goats, and after tending to them he would hurry to what he called "the garden" to be with his friends. The garden was the furrowed fields where the village people planted vegetables and fruit trees. "It was the same group of boys every day. We would always laugh and stay together."

Jaga spoke of his life in the country with the reminiscing sentiment of an elderly man looking fondly back on his lost youth. He had a great sense of friendship and camaraderie, and whenever I saw him at the tea stall it was clear that he loved and respected the group of boys who often gathered there. I asked him which he preferred, the country or the city.

"Country is better. It is nicer living there, and better people too, and the air is good and money is not always pressing."

Jaga described his family's Varanasi home as a typical city home in

India: one room in which the five members of his family slept and ate and washed together. They had a color television, an icebox, a table, and some chairs. Jaga found it hard to sleep there. "In the country I would rise in the morning at five o'clock without trouble. Here in the city I must have a time clock to get up early. I have grown used to it now, and usually I open my eyes one moment before the time clock opens his mouth."

Tarun had been leaning forward in his seat, staring at Jaga as he talked, listening intently and admiring his eloquent friend, plucking up his necklace and absently fitting the beaded strand over his lower lip, like a horse bit. "But I," he said, "have not this good habit of rising up early."

Jaga said, "Yes, Tarun, naughty fellow, you have not."

I asked Jaga how long he had lived in the country.

"Four years. Then my mother said, 'You must come back to the city because you are changing a lot.' I was getting very strict and religious."

I asked what had made him religious. He pursed his lips. His cheeks rattled slightly as we clattered over a rough spot in the pavement, and his round head with its pelt of black hair glistened like a cannonball in the sun. He laid his pocket business on his knees and raised his hands, palms upward. After a long silence his mouth opened. "How shall I explain?" He stirred one of the upraised hands in a sweeping circle to encompass the street around us, and, widening his eyes, he said, "I was looking at the things in the earth. Seeing and seeing. And I asked how did this come? The trees, the wind that bends them, the rain that falls. I felt rather nervous. People can make many things. But not this kind of thing. And I was impressed with God."

"And now?" I said.

Jaga stared up the street. His face looked rueful and thick. "No, madame." Something in his voice, some sad conviction, kept me from asking why.

A herd of water buffaloes came down the street in a rumbling pack, their big heads swaying from side to side as they walked, their long faces straining forward. Now and then they began to run in a hopping way, looking terrified, their hooves clapping clumsily at the pavement. The ricksha waited for them to pass, and as we began rolling along the crowded street again I realized that Ahmed was struggling to haul us up a gradual incline. He had to stand on the pedals to make any headway, his calf muscles swelling, the veins in his neck popping. I would have preferred to walk, but though it was only a mile to the Monkey Temple, Jaga and Tarun had deemed it much too far to walk.

I suggested that we could give Ahmed a hand by hopping off and walking until he made it to the top of the hill. Jaga looked alarmed at the suggestion. "Madame," he said softly, "this is impossible. His feelings would be harmed. It is his job. How can he take our money if he does not do his job?"

"Right," I said, and we sat there and let Ahmed toil away. Ahmed, a Muslim with a noble, wounded face, often stood outside my hotel waiting for customers, and every day, no matter the weather, he wore a much prized navy blue shawl around his shoulders. One day, while talking to him in front of the hotel, I realized that the shawl was actually a thin fleece blanket from an airplane — it bore the KLM logo in one corner. When I asked Ahmed where he had gotten the shawl, he said, "Hollands man." When I first arrived in Varanasi he had given me a ride one morning to the river, and at the end of the day, as I was walking back to my hotel he approached me in the street and said, "Madame, I am waiting for you all day." I was surprised and asked him why. "Because you helped me," he said. I asked how I had helped him. "You was taking my service. I am poor man," he said. "If you need service, tell me." I wanted to walk, but Ahmed was pleasant and gentle, and he looked so troubled and his plea was so straightforward that I said, "I'm lucky you found me, because I need a ride back to my hotel right now." At this, a sigh of genuine relief escaped his mouth and he put his hands together in the position of prayer and touched them to his forehead in gratitude.

We passed a low, decrepit building that had the utilitarian blandness of an Odd Fellows Hall. Jaga said, "That is a film cinema."

"Another cinema?" I said. Varanasi was overrun with cinemas.

"Indian people," he said, "are too fond of films. Especially Tarun."

At that moment Tarun appeared to be conducting a physics experiment with his necklace; he had hooked the beaded strand onto the bridge of his nose and was trying to balance it there without using his hands. His head was tipped back, his face raised to the sky, his mouth ajar, his hands thrust up at the ready. The sun lit up his tongue. At the sound of his name his head jerked forward and the necklace rattled down his face and onto his chest. He patted his bangs back and looked

202 • THE SINGULAR PILGRIM

brightly at me. "Yes. Films. I am fond. But that cinema closed because it don't getting no good films. No super hit. Only flabs."

"Flabs?"

"It means failure," Jaga said, drumming his fingers on his pocket business. "The movie that nobody likes."

"Flops, you mean."

"Flop, flop," he said, nodding.

I mentioned a theater I had seen near the cantonment; the enormous banner across its front said WINNER!! TITANIC!! ATALNTIC ADVANTURE!!

"That is the theater that women do not go to," Jaga said. "Because every seat in that place is broken, and it is dirty. Plus, women don't go to see English movies. Only Indian ones."

"Why?"

"Sometimes English movies have things in them that women would be embarrassed."

Tarun blinked up at me. "I love too much movies. I go times two every week with friend. Madame, I saw *Titanic* times twice. And some films I have saw times five." He pulled a stack of luridly colored postcards out of his hip pocket, images of famous Indian movie stars. The postcards were old and stained and rendered as soft as cloth from too much handling. He held one up to my face; it was a picture of a shirtless Lothario leaning on a fence in what looked like the docks of Bombay. "This one is my favorite."

"That actor has the finest muscles in all India," Jaga said.

"He is in now America." Tarun sighed. "He has riches."

"He looks strong," I said.

"His body is well cut," Jaga said, "but he smokes too much ganja."

Tarun, looking personally concerned, murmured, "Oh, too much." In his excitement he forgot his shyness and leaned into me, his cheek resting lightly on my shoulder. Like a toddler clamoring for the attention of a parent, he shoved another card up at me. This one showed a stylish young actress in glowing silks. She had the sculpted, varnished hairdo of Margaret Thatcher. Tarun tapped fondly at her plump face with a fingernail. "She is camedian. I love."

"Very nice looking," I said. "And what a hairdo."

"So pretty," Tarun mooned.

Brusquely Jaga cleared the air of our dreamy admiration. "Yes, she is fetching, but she is dead."

"Dead?" I said. "Why? She looks so young."

Jaga shrugged and raised his eyebrows as if to exculpate himself. "She had many illnesses, you see. Because she got an infection."

Tarun drew the card away from me. Seeing that Tarun's face had gone dark with disappointment, Jaga crossed his legs and wagged his head and, with an almost parental tenderness, offered, "You know very well that she is dead, Tarun. It is all right. We, too, will die. It's certain."

I looked at Jaga. He was like the city thanatologist, endlessly philosophizing and ruminating about death. He had a knack for sweeping aside foolish illusions. I said, "Well, you're right about that, Jaga. It is certain, but I hope it's not soon."

And the three of us sat staring up the dusty street in silent agreement over the one certain thing in life: the inevitable precipice that lay ahead. We didn't have to close our eyes to see ourselves hurtling over the edge, mouths agape, limbs flailing. It was not the drop itself that was frightening, but the featureless infinity it led to, the irrevocable departure from what we knew. That we could not know how far ahead it lay was part of its awful mystery. Thinking about it had the same suffocating effect as thinking about the size of the universe, its arbitrary origin, its perpetual increase.

Tarun chewed on his necklace and clutched at his cards and looked beset with worry. Before long he blurted, "What you talked is make me gloom! Oh, come along, don't talk it. Look, madame, baby goat!"

We passed a construction site where five enormous concrete sewer pipes lay waiting to be buried in the ground. When I admired their great circumference — a Volkswagen Bug could fit easily inside them — Jaga said with grim fascination, "They say that in Calcutta there are people living in those pipes." Tarun added soberly, "What he has said is true, madame." They spoke as though Calcutta were a country far away, and the thought of people setting up house in a pipe seemed to worry them. As we passed a bookstore, Jaga said, "I like to go in this store and read the books. I cannot buy them, but the manager does not mind if I read. I have read something there about Dracula. Madame, are you familiar with Dracula?"

"A little," I said.

"He is interesting."

"He's a bit scary," I said.

Jaga said, "He is not scary to me. I do not believe in ghosts. Tarun and I see a lot of ghost movies and frightening movies, and I like them because I do not believe them. A dead person is only dead. No spooking."

Tarun said, "But I am believing. I am afraid of Dracula." He shook his head and crossed his arms. He seemed to be picturing the bloody fangs, the cape, the widow's peak, the sheet-white face.

Jaga said, "My family has bought a TV. We can see movies on it sometimes."

"And we like to see the shark movie," Tarun said. "But we have not enough money yet."

Jaga said, "No money, no honey."

"Also *The Patient of England*, but it has not come yet in Varanasi."

Jaga said, "I have read something about Hitler. Do you know him?"

"Yes."

"Master Hitler and Mister Goebbels," he said, as if remembering a phrase he had read. His theatrical tone made them both sound fictive.

We were in the Muslim section of the city now, and the buildings had beautifully ornate façades and balconies with intricate woodwork. Jaga said that the Muslims in Varanasi were wealthy. Bearded men in white robes hurried up the street in the dusty sunlight. A Muslim man in a white crocheted skullcap drew alongside us on his bicycle. He wore a pink scarf wound many times around his neck and billowing white trousers. Keeping pace with us, he said in a breathless rush, "Which country you are from, please, madame?"

I told him I was American.

"Madame," he said cheerfully, "you are so welcome in Varanasi. This is Muslim area."

"Yes," I said.

The man rode his bicycle in a duck-footed fashion, toes pointing left and right. His big black shoes were flat and round-toed, like a clown's. The lenses of his eyeglasses were dense, his beard was streaked with gray. Beneath his homespun Nehru jacket he wore a cardigan buttoned up to his throat on this hot day.

"Do you know Muslim culture?" he said.

I told him I had visited Egypt and Syria. He began to recite some Quranic verses as he rode along beside us. His voice was beautiful, with just the right break in it, just the right degree of melancholy, but he sang too quickly, rushing through the phrases faster and faster, showing off how well he knew the verse, like a child maniacally knocking out

"Chopsticks" on the piano. When he had finished singing he said, "I am very pleased to meet you, learned lady, and happy to ride with you to wherever you are going."

"You'll be going very far out of your way."

"No, madame. But yes, madame. Look, here is my mosque."

Outside the mosque a funeral seemed to be taking place. Eight men in white Nehru costumes and Muslim skullcaps were hoisting a garlanded coffin onto their shoulders and heading off down the street. A hundred similarly dressed men followed them. I said, "Oh, a funeral."

"No, madame, not funeral. Muslims do not do the burning of the body like the Hindu."

I explained that in English a funeral didn't exactly mean burning, that it meant the ceremony that took place at the end of a life, regardless of how the body was disposed of.

"Oh, thank you, ma'am, you are right. Thank you for telling me. And is this your little friends, madame?"

Jaga and Tarun stared in stunned wonder at the pedaling Muslim. He was like a puppet that had suddenly hurtled down out of the sky, chattering and singing. He was blocking the flow of traffic, and each time the shoulder of a passing cyclist brushed against his, he threw out halfhearted words of protest and pointlessly rang his little thumb bell. Every so often the rear wheel of his bicycle clashed with the wheel of our ricksha, and then poor laboring Ahmed tossed back his own words of reproach. The Muslim never stopped smiling. I introduced him to Jaga and Tarun. He nodded; they stared. I asked the man about the relationship between Muslims and Hindus in Varanasi.

"The relationship is excellent."

"I have read in the papers about Muslims being attacked here."

"Yes, it happened. But it is nothing."

"It seems to happen quite a lot."

"It is happening quite a lot. But the relationship is good."

The relationship was not good. All over India Muslim communities were gaining economic power. Varanasi's Muslims had established themselves in the city's once Hindu-dominated silk trade, and resentment among Hindus was growing. The rise in Hindu nationalism and the increasing abandonment of the secular India that Gandhi and Nehru had envisioned seemed in general a reflection of economic insecurity and of a lurking fear of another Pakistan erupting.

The Muslim wanted to know my religion. "Christian," was the best answer I could come up with.

"Oh, madame, I am liking the Christians. I am so glad I met you. You see these buildings here? I am manager of them all. I am collecting the rents for all of them."

In his excitement, the Muslim collided with another bicyclist and had to stop to disentangle himself. Ahmed pedaled on, and the man was left behind. Jaga and Tarun looked relieved, and we resumed our conversation until we arrived at the Monkey Temple.

When he saw the locked gates of the temple, Jaga's face fell. "The temple is closed!" he cried. He apologized profusely to me for this wasted trip, said he should have known, that it was his mistake. He looked terribly embarrassed, as though he had failed in his professional obligations as a guide. I told him not to worry, that the trip alone had been worth it, but he was not consoled, and on our return trip he apologized seven or eight more times for the mistake.

ONE MORNING before dawn I went out to watch the sun rise over the river. The streets were empty and damp, slippery with cow dung and draped in a clammy brown fog. The city was mercifully still, and the absence of traffic made it possible to walk down the middle of wide Chetgangj Road. Everything felt fatigued and haunted. The shops were locked, with steel grates pulled across their fronts. The sky was the color of cardboard, and the pebbled pavement was littered with trampled vegetables and wet straw, broken bricks, scraps of burlap. Crumpled bits of newspaper rolled in the breeze like tumbleweeds. The buildings seemed to be sleeping, unperturbed by the scores of monkeys that chattered on their roofs and window ledges. Laundry hung wildly from every cornice and window lock.

Walking slowly, I could see what at midday was obscured by a melee of motion and sound: the low buildings on either side of the street were plastered with tattered advertising posters, faded murals, and hand-painted signs in crookedly fashioned English and Hindi. The city was muffled in a layer of fine brown dust, the skinny trees rooted to the sidewalks looked parched and haggard, paper kites hung forlornly tangled in the telephone wires above the street, and gouts of musty air drifted out of dark doorways like weary exhalations. A sign on a hut at the edge of a trash heap said, "Dr. Hadaban Singh, Psychiatrist." Another sign below a dirty windowfront full of dusty dental molds read: SURISIS, EXZIMA ITCH, RING WORM, PIMPLES, ITC TRET HERE, VEREAL DISEASE, SEX WEAKNESS, SYPHILIS, GONOREAHEA, HEAT TROBLE, BACKECE, RHUMATICE, LUKODRMA, HAIR FALL, ALARGI, FOOT CRACK, FOOT GRON. The shops had names like Standard, Quality, Premium, Acme, and Best. One shop was called Vehicle; another was called Kar Kare.

Now and then I came upon a great pile of bricks and rubble and rusted pipes where a building appeared to have spontaneously collapsed. I passed the Well Come Wine Shop, a dingy hole behind a locked grate. Its shelves were stocked with authentic-looking bottles of liquor with improbable British names: Old Smuggler, Bagpiper, Aristocrat, Admiral's Choice, and Merry Scott. Alcohol, though not illegal, was frowned upon in India, and liquor stores — usually called English Wine Shops — were few and far between. From what I could see, the wine shops sold everything but wine. The Hotel Ramamurthi did not sell beer, so a few days before I had bought a bottle in one of these places, an experience not unlike my idea of a visit to a back-alley abortionist. An elderly albino man with the cunning eyes of a criminal slid the grate open, looked me up and down, fished a bottle out of an ancient refrigerator, wrapped it in newspaper, lowered his silvery lashes, and whispered, "Gimmee A D ruby." Furtively he snatched the eighty rupees out of my hand and slammed the grate shut before I could thank him. The beer was called Black Ribbon. It was full of carbonation and was, amazingly, delicious.

I walked on toward the river. It was close to the end of 1999. The imminent millennium so frantically fussed over and advertised and analyzed everywhere else in the world seemed forgotten here. What was a thousand years in India?

A SKINNY, SHIRTLESS MAN stepped out of a doorway and introduced himself as Mussa Hakim. It was a Muslim name. When I asked him if he was Muslim, he smiled and, as if compelled to tell the truth, said, "I am Muslim and I smoke hashish and sometimes I am selling it and that is why my eyes are red at this moment." Everybody's eyes looked red to me that morning. "You would like to smoke some hashish with me?"

"No, thanks," I said.

"You don't like?"

"Not really, but I do think it should be legal."

"In Amsterdam I know is legal," Mussa said dreamily, and he sat down on the street and began inspecting one of his bare feet.

I came upon an angular cotton bundle in the middle of the street. After staring at it awhile I realized that it was a person who had camped there for the night, a configuration of living bones wrapped in nothing more than a bedsheet. In India homelessness had no trappings, no cardboard boxes, no bags full of bottles and twine and donated clothing. It was just another rung on the crowded ladder of disposession.

I moved on toward Chowk, the shopping district. Through narrow doorways I could see people beginning to stir, women tossing buckets of water into the street, men lighting charcoal fires in braziers on the sidewalk, a woman bent under the weight of a sack of flour slung across her back. An old man with a jutting white tuft of beard like a billy goat's sat in the gutter rolling out little pancakes of floury dough and expertly, without looking, tossing them over his shoulder into a sizzling pan on a flame behind him. A cycle ricksha trundled toward me out of the mist carrying two Muslim women immured in black cloth, their faces completely obscured by black veils. In the morning gloom they looked ominous, like prefigurements of death, swaying to the rhythm of their carriage. As the carriage wheeled past, the two dark heads turned slowly my way. I had an urge to run.

And then an elephant appeared, lumbering around a corner looking sad and beset, guided by a boy sitting in a saddle on her back. Flowers in lime green and cherry pink were painted on the elephant's face and little bells were attached to her neck with chains. The name SURESH was scrawled across her bony forehead in white paint. She had soft, intelligent-looking eyes the size of Kalamata olives and the beautiful amber color of whiskey. As I walked along beside her I thought what tiny apertures they were for such a huge animal. The elephant moved with the lassitude of a person deeply medicated, her plinthlike feet shuffling through the dust, the rubbery end of her trunk scraping along the pavement. The boy struck the top of her bulbous head with a stick and shrieked the sentence that is so popular among the children of India: "Gimmee, lady, one rupee!"

NEAR THE RIVER the old streets became very narrow, no more than intimate slots between buildings, sometimes not wide enough for two people to pass. Walking in these alleys I always felt that the walls of the buildings were closing in on me. Closer to the river the streets began to descend and grow cooler and darker, and the heavy cellar damp of the air engulfed me. The alleys were dank and brown and oily and laced with traces of neon-green moss. The sun broke in and mopped the floors for only about fifteen minutes a day. There was always the sound of dripping water here, the smell of fermenting grass, and a cow would suddenly appear around a corner like a huge piece of moving furniture. Sodden rice and flower petals scattered by pilgrims were mashed underfoot. And then, abruptly, the alleys ended at the wide ghats.

When I arrived at the river the sun was feebly lifting itself from behind the east bank. Funereal floes of cold gray mist hovered over the water. In the morning the river always looked slightly abused, like the floor of a dance hall the morning after an intemperate bash. The remains of whatever happened upriver yesterday appeared here today in dishevelment. The surface was dotted with litter and logs, flowers and indeterminate floating objects that expressed themselves in the dawn light as dense, dark humps.

The ghats were crowded with pilgrims bathing and greeting the sunrise with prayer. Though it was early, boatloads of tourists glided up and down in front of them snapping pictures. The guidebooks crowed that dawn was the best time to visit the river, precisely because you could witness hundreds of Hindus praying. Tourists rushed to see the event in the zealous way that astronomers rush to see a new comet. While the pilgrims prayed, waiting boatmen called out to the fresh tourists who were stumbling sleepily down the steps.

I stood on Rajendra Prasad Ghat, studying the two cylindrical water towers there. Both were painted pale pink, and one bore an enormous portrait of Shiva done in the lurid colors and comic-book style of an Indian movie poster. A toothless man sitting on the stones next to the tower was singing the *ganga puja,* the traditional worship, at the top of his lungs. He had the tidy, slicked-back hair of a Wall Street banker, and his forehead was painted entirely white with a small red dot in the middle. He waved his hands as he sang. His voice was beautiful, and the simple melody had the faintly hypnotic effect of a chant. Beside him a holy man in pale pink robes was sprinkling sandalwood powder on a small fire and reading from a holy book. A pomegranate lay cut open on the stones in front of him. He seemed to be following a sacred recipe, mixing oils and powders in a bowl, referring to his book, passing a hand over the fire, and mixing some more.

As I stared at the picture, a shivering boatman with a blood-stained bandage over one eye shouted at me out of the crowd, "Woman! You come here!"

I obeyed, and as I neared he grimaced at me. He had lost a front tooth. "You get in boat!" he snapped, pointing at a battered wooden dory at the bottom of the steps. To the right of the dory a man was bathing the head of a water buffalo with the same care one might use in washing the head of a child, scrubbing behind its ears with a rag and rich lather, scrubbing the scalp, rinsing gently.

I asked the boatman if he could take me to Assi Ghat upriver, but before he could answer, a young man hurried over. "That boatman do not speak English," he said. "I will come with you."

Warning of the Varanasi criminals and cheats who prey on foreign tourists, my guidebook had said, "Only do boat trips in groups." I didn't care. I didn't want anyone to come with me, and I didn't want yet another guide. I would have liked most of all to row the boat myself, alone. But not wanting to be rude, I said, "I don't need a guide, but I suppose if you want to come, you can."

In a gesture of innocence and surrender, the man lifted his big hands at me, palms outward. "I come only if you want me to."

"Come only if you want to," I said.

"That is not my nature. My quality is not local. I am not like a beggar person. I am a bodybuilder. Everyone know me very well. Every boatman. Every boy. I have many many trophy in my house."

The young man was tall and strong and wore a woolen watch cap pulled low over his brow like a burglar in a cartoon. He had a big head and the long-jawed, tight-skinned face of a horse. His cheekbones were like hard knobs of wood. His shoulders were huge within his fleece jacket.

"A bodybuilder?" I said. He towered over me.

He knocked the sleeve of his jacket up his arm and made his biceps bulge. Long boats were passing up and down in front of us.

"Schwarzenegger," I said.

That sent him into a fit of hollow laughter. "My quality is not local."

"Local quality is not good?"

"No. Because people here is always like a beggar man. I am very popular here. I win many trophies."

Bodybuilding was a ubiquitous pursuit in Varanasi. Up and down the river, at any time of day, one could witness men in nothing but loincloths working out on the ghats, doing pushups, lifting weights, striking muscle-enhancing poses as they admired themselves in cracked mirrors. Near Dasaswamedh Ghat there was always some ropy man swinging an enormous block, like a granite keystone, at the end of a long metal pole, swinging it lasso-style over his head and around behind his back.

At first it seemed an odd contradiction, this obsession with the body in a city full of death, but in Hinduism the body is an important connection to God, and gradually I saw that the Indian preoccupation with the physical extended far beyond the bodybuilders. All over the ghats pilgrims not absorbed in prayer busied themselves with the care of their bodies. After bathing with particular meticulousness they groomed themselves carefully, peering into tiny hand mirrors, combing their hair and mustaches just so, rubbing oils and unctions into their skin, applying fine Hindu holy marks to their faces with colorful powders. They pruned their nails and yogically stretched their muscles. They frequented the massage artists and the many barbers who set up shop — a straw mat, a bar of soap, a straight razor — in the open air of the ghats. Varanasi men had a habit of drawing a comb out of their pocket in midconversation and raking at their hair as they talked.

The Hindu pilgrims were so conscious of the sacredness of the body that they were never entirely naked when they bathed, and when they dressed afterward they did so with great modesty. That morning, of the hundreds of people bathing in the river, not a single one was naked. They washed in their shorts or loincloths and saris, and when they were done they stood on the ghat and wrapped fresh cloths around themselves with finicky formality. If they were not satisfied with the way the cloth hung, they unwrapped it and started over again, fussing with knots and hems and unacceptably dangling threads. Nowhere else in the world did a square of cotton cloth tied around a body look as good as it did here.

"Woman!" the boatman huffed impatiently, eyeing the potential customers hurrying up and down the ghats. "How much paying?!"

I stepped into the boat. "One hundred."

"Paying two hundred, you."

"One hundred," I said.

"You again say one hundred!"

"Okay," I said. "How about fifty?"

The boatman moaned and slapped at his forehead. Nearby a group of Dutch people bickered with a boatman who had just dropped them off after an hour's row. A little blond man among them lifted his fist and shouted, "We agreed upon fifteen rubles each!"

My boatman tugged at his mustache. Fearing he might lose me, he stepped into the boat. "Okay. Hundred!" he said. He looked bleary-eyed and battered, as though he had been involved in a late-night brawl.

"Okay," I said. "One hundred."

The bodybuilder made a move toward the boat. "I can help you," he pleaded. "I know everything you want to know. I am not beggar man. Sometimes people tell me I am funny man plus honest. If I show I'm very funny man, can I come with you?"

He had tense, lightless eyes, an importunate smile. For all his brawn he seemed pallid. In the cold morning air his skin was sallow, and his lips, beneath the mustache, were livid. Though not a beggar, he was nearly beseeching. His name was Chander. He had already placed one foot in the boat. I disliked him, but I told him to get in.

The boatman sat in the bow on a small wooden deck with his feet in two holes in the floorboards. His oars were bamboo poles with pieces of tire rubber nailed to the ends for blades. He tugged on the oars, and as the boat moved away from the ghat he grumbled, "One hundred, one hundred," displeased at having settled for only twice the amount of money he should have received for an hour's row.

Chander sat on the thwart, shoulders hunched, hands tucked between his knees. "Money is not everything," he said primly. It sounded distinctly like *Money is everything*. "I just follow tourist. For me is easy. I explain thing. Then they are respect to me and give me something money. And also I am going to one company who give me fifteen percent commission. If any tourist are interested to buy, I bring them. That's why I am not thinking always only for money."

I nodded and looked at the river and hoped he was not going to spend the entire trip chattering about money.

We moved slowly upriver. Each time the boatman pulled on the oars they made the burping noise of frogs at dusk. The rubber blades splashed softly in the water. Tiny bells of different timbres rang out from the riverside temples, and a musical pipe wailed. Though the sun had begun to turn the great drifts of mist from gray to pink, the air was still chilly and the dark water looked greasy and cold. Above us heavy black kites were wheeling monotonously in the taupe sheet of the sky. They were like a vision of the end of the world — crooked, drifting, long-fingered forms waiting to kill something or to clean something up that was already dead.

To the Hindu faithful, bathing in the Ganges at Varanasi is almost as auspicious as dying here. Nearly seventy thousand people visited the Varanasi ghats daily, the majority of them pilgrims and tourists, and a vast industry had been built around that fact. Pilgrim guesthouses lined the west bank, along with restaurants and shops selling Hindu holy trappings. Brahman priests tended the ghats, minded pilgrims' belongings, sang prayers for them, or coached them in their puja in exchange for a few rupees.

That morning the crowds of pilgrims stood elbow to elbow in the river, facing the sun, soaping their bodies, or praying and casting offerings of flowers and rice into the water. Many set votive candles into tiny boats fashioned from pipal leaves, then surrendered the boats to the gentle current. All around us hundreds of these boats skittered and flickered on the river like a raft of illuminated lily pads.

As they prayed, the pilgrims lifted the water in their hands and let it spill slowly out again; over and over they did this, as if culling the finest grain. In prayer, Hindus always assumed a faraway look. They appeared deaf and stared into the distance, seeing nothing before them but God. Not three feet from the pilgrims the tourist boats cruised by, snapping pictures and brandishing video cameras. Some of the boats were motorized, and their motors muttered and clicked like sewing machines. Yet nothing distracted the praying pilgrims, not even the icy water that licked at their waists, chests, and arms. Their lips moved, they pressed their palms together, and they touched their fingertips lightly to their lips, to their chins, to their staring eyes. They reached for the river, sifted it, touched it to their eyelids, tasted it. They looked entranced. Their gestures of prayer were delicate and small, and their bare brown shoulders glowed like pears in the early sunlight.

I was transfixed. And envious. They had traveled great distances by train and bus under harsh conditions. Some had walked from the farthest reaches of Uttar Pradesh. What compelled them to go to so much trouble, to endure this discomfort in order to pray? And how did prayer provide a relief for them? I found prayer difficult. At night, in the underwater darkness of my hotel room, I had tried to pray but couldn't. It wasn't that I felt nothing. I felt a great deal, but the words I came up with seemed to have all the weight of nursery rhymes, and I seemed to be speaking them into the vacuum of my own mouth. I became self-conscious, which destroyed the concentrating, transcending purpose of prayer. I ended up feeling like a fly stuck on its back on a hot windowsill, frantically spinning and buzzing to right itself. That, I knew, was one of the reasons I needed to pray. I was impatient and hasty, easily frustrated and reluctant to accept things as they were. Prayer required stillness and detachment, but I was a busy person and too attached.

As a young child I had watched my great-aunt, who prayed the rosary every day of her life, praying in her dining room in the armchair by the telephone, her fingers twitching at the beads in her lap, her lips moving as though she were conversing with an invisible companion. As she prayed, her eyes ranged slowly over her fingers, the edge of the dinner table, the shadow of the plant in the window, the watercolor of swans at Coole Park, the bar of sunlight on the carpet, her stockinged knee, her sleeping dog, the toe of her shoe. But from the way her lips moved and her eyes vacantly stared, I knew that she was seeing only what was inside her own head. She was in the room but cut off from it. Watching her, I was fascinated. (My mother prayed this way too.) Sometimes, though I knew I shouldn't interrupt her prayers, I couldn't keep from skipping through the dining room, smiling and waving and doing my imitation of Red Skelton. I was six; she was eighty. She always responded with an encouraging nod, a generous half-smile of love on her face, but her lips never stopped moving and her eyes maintained that glassy cast of divided attention, just as they did when she spoke on the telephone.

I didn't know *how* to pray. I believed that like the anonymous pilgrim who walked across Russia with the Jesus Prayer spilling constantly from his mouth, one had to learn to pray simply by beginning. But I had found it nearly impossible to begin. These Indian pilgrims standing in the Ganges River were not fundamentally different from me. We all knew we were shuffling toward death, but they seemed to be looking it in the eye, while I stared mutely at the back of its head.

The city of Varanasi was all about God. But despite the abundance of icons and temples, the holy haunts and ringing bells, the only thing that remained hidden in Varanasi was God — the one feature that the city shared with every other place on earth. This crowded morning worship was like an acknowledgment of the self — the strangeness and solitariness of it, the peculiar uncommunicableness of one's own person, the improbability and randomness of being. How on earth did we arrive here on the earth? Worse, *why* were we here? Only you and God really knew who you were. And if God didn't exist, then only you knew who you were, and that seemed thoroughly insupportable. Christian believers shared a loose consensus that if God stopped watching you, you would fall off the face of the earth and be lost forever. Among Hindus, if God stopped watching you, you'd be perpetually stuck here, going slavishly around forever in a circle of rebirth. Either way, if you were looking at God, the worst thing in the world would be for God to look away. Prayer always seemed to be a kind of plea: *I am because of you. Let me continue. Keep watching me with me. Don't let me end.*

The praying pilgrims struck me as the most beautiful thing in Varanasi. The sight of so many calm people standing half naked in the river accentuated both the frailty and the grace of the human body. Their devotion — refined, soft, slightly wry — matched the Indian temperament. They carried themselves lightly.

The pilgrims who weren't praying or carrying Ganges water to the temples sat on the ground in their delicate saris and wraps, hugging their knees, and they too were beautiful. There were small-faced women with slender fingers and diamond studs in their noses, long-legged men with high cheekbones and long chins. I was struck by the roundness of human shoulders and backs, by how fetal people look in repose.

Chander said, "It is sunrise time. People is make ceremony puja. Every morning is come lot of people here from different part of India."

They came from Bihar and Bangalore, Tamil Nadu and Rishikesh, Thiruvananthapurim and Bheemunipatnam. They stayed in pilgrim guesthouses where foreigners were not allowed and slept thirty or more to a bedless room.

Chander said, "Look, madame, they are south Indian people." He was pointing at a group on Kedar Ghat. Some of them were bending over the river, scrubbing their teeth with little twigs. They wore lungis of checked cotton. Physically they were different from the northern people; their faces were more rough-hewn, their bones heavier, their hair thick and wiry. Their tooth twigs were the size of panatelas, and they rammed them into their mouths with a violent, stabbing motion, scouring and jabbing this way and that. It looked painful, as though they were trying to knock their teeth out and puncture their gums. They gagged themselves deliberately with the sticks, and afterward spat repeatedly into the water. I asked Chander what kind of wood they used for their teeth.

"Normal wood."

"But from what kind of tree? What's it called?"

"Called? Called?" He frowned at me and shrugged his huge shoulders. "Who can care what called? Is very good for teeth. And good for stomach. I hope you are not thinking I am a guide, madame."

"But you are a guide, Chander, aren't you?"

He looked sheepishly at me. "Yes."

"Why be ashamed of that?"

"A guide is only a beggar man."

All over Varanasi that was the conflict: men trying to make a living on handouts from foreign tourists and hoping that it would not look like begging. It was great need battling with great pride. The matter of personal honor was so delicate and raw that I found myself repeatedly allowing the men of Varanasi to do some unwanted, unnecessary thing for me so that I could then give them money without making them feel beggarly.

"But I am also your friend," Chander reasoned. "You come to see my family member. Then you will believe. I will show you my house where I live."

The disgruntled boatman gave his oars a threatening rattle. "One hundred, woman. How much hundred you pay?"

"Still one hundred," I said.

ASIDE FROM WALKING the Panchakroshi Road, visiting the five sacred ghats along the river is among the most meritorious things a Hindu pilgrim can do in Varanasi. The ritual is called the *panchtirtha* (*panch* means five, and *tirtha* is a bridge upon which the pilgrim can cross from earth to heaven). The five tirthas must be visited and bathed at all in one day and in the proper order. At the edge of the river a crouching man upended a pot he held in his hands. I asked Chander what was in the pot. "Water from Ganga together with flowers, then he speak something prayer to God."

Three great gray lumps in the water drifted slowly toward us like buoyant boulders. As they neared, I realized they were the carcasses of water buffalo in various stages of decomposition. One had been dead for some time; his skin was a mosaic of pink rot, his belly a bloated keg, and two of his legs jutted into the air like masts. I could see the ridged outline of his ribs and one curly horn. A black crow walked across the swollen belly. We glided along past a rowboat moored in the shallows. A man lay sleeping in the bottom, oblivious to a carcass that had gotten hung up on the prow of his boat. A dog with needles for teeth loped over and began gnawing at the buffalo's belly. The stench of these dead animals was overpowering; it had the putrid quality of a paper-white narcissus. A few feet away two men stood up to their necks in the water, dunking to rinse their soapy heads, seemingly happy to share their bathing spot with a rotting carcass. Upriver more dead beasts drifted toward us in the embrace of the greasy green water.

A carefully painted sign on a stone pedestal on one ghat said: TO KEEP GANGES NEAT & CLEAN PLEASE DO NOT THROW PLASTIC BAGS, GARLANDS, AND DETERGENT. The stream of viscous black sludge that trickled into the river from a crude pipe below the sign seemed a calculated mockery. Saying the the Ganges is polluted is like saying that fire is hot and water is wet. The river is monumentally polluted, and in Varanasi, possibly the most sanctified bathing spot in India, it is near its worst. The state of Uttar Pradesh, to which Varanasi belongs, is said to produce half of all the pollutants that the Ganges carries to Calcutta and the sea. Leather and pharmaceutical industries use the river as a chemical dump, and the volume of untreated waste and raw sewage that flows into the Ganges is estimated at more than one billion liters per day. Varanasi's sewage system, though slowly being improved, remains largely a network of nineteenth-century conduits that lead directly to the river. According to the World Health Organization, the level of fecal coliform in potable water should not exceed 10 bacteria per 100 milliliters of water. At the ghats of Varanasi the coliform level has been known to reach 100,000 bacteria per 100 milliliters.

The twenty million people living along the Ganges are beset by a host of waterborne diseases: cholera, dysentery, viral hepatitis, typhoid, and chronic gastroenteritis. The great number of animal and human carcasses tossed into the river only intensifies the problem. In 1996 the Worldwatch Institute determined that in the Gangetic region one person dies of diarrhea every minute, and eight of every ten people suffer from amoebic dysentery. Eighty percent of all health problems in India and a third of all deaths are attributable to unclean ground water. Every year two million Indian children die of water-related illnesses.

I pointed at a carcass and said to Chander, "See these animals?"

"Yah, animals these."

"Why are they here?"

"Is not allowed," he said gravely, "but village people put."

"The pilgrims don't mind bathing with dead animals?"

"Pilgrim don't mind. Hindu believe is holy water."

"Does anyone ever get sick from this water, Chander?"

Despite his bulk and muscle, despite his fleece jacket and his bad-guy cap, Chander was shivering. "No." He seemed to believe what he was saying.

"No one?"

"Is miracle, eh?"

As we talked, a barefoot man with a mourner's shaven head crouched at the edge of the river washing a knife and a tin cup. He washed his feet and his face, rinsed his mouth with the water, rinsed his head, then filled the cup with water and drank from it. That this supremely revered river had been allowed to descend to this level of defilement was almost as puzzling as the pilgrims' willingness to bathe and drink in it.

The sun was creeping higher in the sky, and the façades of the red sandstone buildings had begun to give off a pinkish glow. A boatful of Tibetan Buddhists in maroon robes came downriver toward us. Chander grimaced at the sight of them. "Those peoples are stupid," he said.

"Why are they stupid?"

"They never understanding what I am speaking to them."

"That doesn't mean they're stupid. It just means they don't speak Hindi."

"But I am speaking English to them."

"Well, then it means they don't speak English. Maybe they think you're stupid because you don't speak Tibetan."

That notion sent Chander into a fit of self-critical giggles. His mustache twitched, and the slanting sunlight gilded his big teeth. As we passed the electric crematorium he told me that the Dutch were cheap, the Asians stupid, the Israelis independent, and the Australians noisy. There were few Americans. In front of the crematorium, three dhobis were beating laundry in the river with brooms while two women slapped cow dung into patties, which they pressed onto the crematorium wall to dry; eventually the dried patties would be fuel for a cooking fire. Next to the crematorium a man stood on painfully thin legs and sang off-key. I looked across the river at the feather boas of smoke lifting limply from small fires on the shore and at the ever-present figures moving mysteriously along the sand.

"Chander," I said. "What are those people doing over there?"

"Like here. They is making puja."

"Do people live over there?"

"Yes. Religious people."

I saw no buildings, no sign of a village. It was an impressively flat expanse. "But where do they live?"

"Behind trees."

I stared at the trees, which made a black line beneath the rising sun. The whole barren-looking place made me crazy with curiosity. The contrast with this side of the river was striking — like two different countries separated by three hundred yards of water. In the morning haze the flat, mile-long spill of sand and the low trees looked like my dream of Africa. I wanted to go there. I asked Chander to tell the boatman. Chander spoke to him, but the boatman moaned three Hindi syllables back and glowered at me and rumbled, "One hundred, one hundred."

"He don't want to go over there," Chander said.

"Why not?"

"He is saying nothing is there for you."

"But it looks interesting."

"He is saying there is a wolf. And other badness."

That made me want to go all the more.

Chander pointed at a building above a ghat. "Vishnu Rest House," he said. "For foreigners; no Indians allowed."

"Indians and foreigners don't mix?"

"No."

"But there are Indian people staying in my hotel," I said.

"But one time Hotel Ramamurthi was just for Indian. Then owner decide he want foreigners too. He is rich man. And selling big quantity of stuff."

"What stuff?

Chander lifted his cold fingers and began enumerating. "Marijuana, opium, hashes, heroin. He is big seller man. Anything you want."

It was not comforting to learn that I was staying in a drug den, but I was not surprised. Varanasi was reputed to be full of crime. When I first arrived at the train station and was waiting for a ricksha to take me to my hotel, a woman had approached and said ominously, "Madame, while you are waiting, be sure to stay inside the station." And when my ricksha driver dropped me at the hotel he had said, like a seer, "Do not take any drinks from anyone while you are here." (The drugged drink seemed to be the preferred weapon of Indian criminals.) People were always disappearing in this city; widows were abused and sold into prostitution; drugs seemed to be available at every corner. I asked Chander where the owner of Ramamurthi got his drugs.

"Big quantity is from Nepal. And Manali. If anybody are interested to buy of that kind you can ask me. I can get for you that kind of thing."

When I said that I didn't want drugs, Chander seemed to think I was playing hard to get. "If I don't sell it to you, you go with another person. The money go in someone else pocket." He was an unabashed middleman. Varanasi was full of them. "What you like?" he said.

"I don't use drugs."

"None?"

"Just beer." All over New Delhi I had seen people squatting on street corners smoking lumps of opium out of tinfoil. I imitated for Chander the men who mooned at me from doorways saying, *Hashish, marijuana, hashish*. Chander, laughing in recognition, said, "Funny, huh?"

I asked if it was acceptable for Hindus to take drugs. He said no. "But you think it's okay to sell drugs?"

He looked accused. His neck seemed to shrink, and he lowered his head. "What else I can do?" he pleaded. "My parents had no money to spend for school. I stopped school when I am ten. My father was not working. That why I come here to find job. I am young man. I am thinking about my life. What I can do? If I find money, I must do any job. Or go to any country."

BY THE TIME we returned to Dasaswamedh Ghat, the morning mist was gone, the bathers had begun to dissipate, and the day was hot. But Chander still looked cold, his lips blue, his jacket zipped up to his throat, his cap low on his head. I paid the grumbling boatman, and we all climbed out of the boat. Looking up the ghat I saw Jaga standing at the top of the steps near the tea stall. Happy to see him, I waved and called his name. He didn't wave back. I started up the steps with Chander behind me. Jaga turned and disappeared down the alley. I stopped in surprise.

Chander said, "Why you is waving at him?"

"He's my friend," I said.

"Friend? Why friend? He is only a little boy!"

"I like him," I said.

Chander looked disgusted and a little bit envious. "Why he didn't say hello to you?"

It was a good question. "I don't know," I said. I looked up again, hoping Jaga would reappear. He didn't.

Chander seemed pleased. He smiled and wagged his head, and in a voice dripping with insinuation he said, "Maybe he is not really your friend."

I was ready to be rid of Chander. I thanked him for his help and gave him a hundred rupees. He made a show of refusing the money. "I am not beggar man." I told him I knew he wasn't a beggar, that the money was just a small gift. With that permission he snatched the money from my hand and jogged up the steps.

I looked up toward the tea stall. Only the tea brothers were standing there now, with the usual flock of skinny laughing boys. A confusion of doubt and annoyance flared like a small fuse at the top of my spine. I went back down the steps and wandered up the riverbank. I liked Jaga, and I trusted him. He had been generous with me and seemed to like talking with me. He had never once asked for money, and the few times I had offered it to him he had steadfastly refused it. I knew that currying favor with tourists was, in effect, his livelihood, and once or twice the skeptical voice perpetually clacking at the back of my brain had asked whether I was just another target, one more moneybag on legs. It was the rich man's curse, never knowing whether you were wanted for yourself or for your money.

The guides of Varanasi used a thousand tricks and stories to get visitors to part with their money. There were no regulations, no rules, no fixed prices or laws that applied to these loose transactions. It was an exchange of assets roughly supported by the imbalance between the two parties. The tourist had affluence and ignorance; the guides had poverty and knowledge. It wasn't that you could never be sure when you were a dupe, for in a sense you were always a dupe, a condition made tolerable by its frank clarity. The real problem was that you could never be sure when you were *not* a dupe.

I walked, feeling irritable in the thick sunlight. The fuse burned lower in my spine, gathering strength. Chander's big face loomed. *Maybe he is not really your friend.* In this vexed state of mind I could walk for fifteen minutes seeing nothing in front of me but my own hot eyelashes. At Lalita Ghat I saw a man throwing trash into the river, big plastic bags full of rubbish that landed in the water with a slapping plop. Liberated by irritation, I walked up to this unsuspecting stranger and said what I had wanted to say to scores of people during my stay in Varanasi: "Don't throw those things in the river."

The unfortunate man looked at me, guilty and wounded, like a child caught scribbling on a wall. A plastic bag dangled from his hand. "No?" he said.

"No."

He looked helplessly at the pile of trash near his feet. In a small voice he said, "Well, maybe only the electrical things?"

I wanted to snatch the bag out of his hand. I stepped toward him. "Don't throw anything in there."

"Nothing?"

"Not a thing. That's why it's so dirty here. Don't ever do that again."

The man looked at me, shocked and frightened. My misdirected anger, the inexplicable menace in my voice, set his poor face atremble, and in that face I suddenly saw my own face reflected back at me like a blinding glare on a spotless mirror.

EVERY EVENING just before five, elderly pilgrims gathered in the small temple at Dasaswamedh Ghat to sing what Jaga called "the story of the family." It was never entirely clear to me what the story was, but the tunes had the cheerful rhythm and repetitive simplicity of "Three

Blind Mice," and it was pleasant to sit across the steps from the temple between the pan monger and the incense seller and listen to the aging voices singing as the sun sank lower in the west. I got into the habit of going there every day. Usually Jaga would meet me, and we would watch the barefoot worshipers sitting cross-legged on the floor of the open-fronted temple, clapping in time as they sang, while the *panda* tiptoed among them with a basket of sweets in one hand and a smoking candle in the other. The worshipers held a coin in their hand, passed it over the candle flame, passed the hand quickly behind their head as though wiping sweat from the nape of the neck, dropped the coin in the basket, removed one of the sweets, and ate it. When I asked Jaga what the flame was for, he said, "It is a symbol for the spirit of God." Each new worshiper arriving at the temple rang a small bell that hung from the ceiling. I asked Jaga why. "To wake God up," he said.

That evening when I arrived at the temple, Jaga was already there waiting for me and frowning anxiously. Before I could say hello, he said, "Madame, I must apologize to you. I did not greet you this morning. Oh, it was rude, but you were with that guide. I was afraid. And so I went away."

"Afraid?"

"That man would be angry with me if I spoke to you while you were in his company."

"You're free to talk to me, Jaga," I said.

He shook his head. "Later he would be angry."

It made sense — the boys who worked the ghats were competing for the attention and money of the tourists.

"And if you talked to me, he would be angry with you too."

"So he's a bully."

Not wanting to commit himself to criticism of the bully, Jaga wagged his head and said philosophically, "This is the way it is."

I told Jaga not to worry; if Chander crossed my path again he would be very sorry he ever met me.

He looked at me with surprise and interest. "You would bully him?"

"Yes," I said, "I would!"

Jaga smirked into his hand. "Oh, madame, that is funny." He thought about that with obvious relish, while the story of the family rang out from the temple.

BRUSHING MY TEETH one morning in the Hotel Ramamurthi, I heard a sudden crackling noise coming from the street. I put my nose to the bathroom window and peered through the jagged hole. Standing at the top of a bamboo ladder propped against the high-tension wires, a man holding a pair of pliers was awash in a shower of magnesium sparks flowing energetically from a circuit terminal above his head. The ancient terminal was entangled in a great bristling web of black wires. The shower stopped abruptly, and the man stared at the wires as if he had never before seen anything remotely like them. He raised the pliers, advanced them toward the terminal, wavered, withdrew them, stared some more, raised the pliers again, and plucked gingerly at one wire; in response the lights in three shops below him blinked out. He plucked another wire, and the lights in one of the shops came back on. Gaining confidence, he yanked at a third wire, and with a loud pop a second explosion of smoke and blue light and fiery sparks came down on his head, and the light in my bathroom went out. The sparks stopped, and the man reached again with the pliers. Shopkeepers had gathered on the street below, craning their necks to see what was happening, shaking their heads, as fascinated and worried as I was. The little donkey tethered to his post moaned in fear.

There was a knock on my door. It was, I knew, the hotel's two chambermen, Mr. Chand and Mr. Garg, thin, elderly, lugubrious men with identical, rather startling mustaches. (Picture the little black patch beneath Adolf Hitler's nose; now wax its ends into two tiny handlebars, left and right.) When I was in my room, which was not often, Chand and Garg seemed to knock on the door every twenty minutes or so, and the instant they knocked they would frantically jiggle the handle. The door, which was usually unlocked, would swing open and they, looking startled and affronted, as though it were I who had burst in on them, would say, "Room clean?" or "Laundry wash?" or "Bring tea?" I was usually sitting at the tiny desk with a pen in my hand, and sometimes I was in my underwear. Chand and Garg, wearing brown uniforms with Nehru collars, stood in the doorway with their hands behind their backs like ruly army generals, grimly staring. I had an inflatable rubber raft rolled up on the floor and a pair of collapsible oars. I had a laptop computer, a tent, a pile of nesting dolls, two knives, three Bengali flutes, a pile of books, seven kites, and the large spools that Indian kitemakers used for string. On the desk were three brick-thick stacks of rupees. (Indian banks dispensed only small denominations, and they had a weird habit of stapling these big wads of money together with staples the size of finish nails.) The stacks did not amount to much money, but they looked like the spoils of a bank heist.

When Garg and Chand cleaned my room, they announced everything they were going to do before they did it. "New sheets!" they said as they ripped the linens off my bed. "Sweep floor!" they said, scraping at the floor with a palm broom. "Wash toilet! Remove rubbish! Wipe mirror!" And when they were finished they stood at the door and said, "Room clean!" waiting for a tip. Though they were in their sixties, they moved about the room as nimbly as boys, stepping carefully, and perhaps a little disdainfully, over my piles of junk. They were dignified and had impeccable posture. They never made small talk. Feeling shoddy and gabby and slightly unfit in their presence, I always overtipped them.

By the faint light of the bathroom window I went through my room to answer the door. It was Chand and Garg, looking like angry ghosts in the dark hallway. "Problem!" Chand said.

"No light!" Garg said.

"Fellow is all the time doing that!" said Chand.

"Oh, patience," said Garg, and they continued down the hallway, knocking on doors.

By the time I arrived in the hotel dining room for breakfast, the lights had returned and disappeared twice. They seemed now to be on again for a spell. I sat at a table with three Indian men in neckties and a stout middle-aged nun from Wisconsin. The nun wore pink-rimmed glasses, and a fall of thick gray bangs showed below the white band of her wimple. She was friendly and spoke with the clipped and casual confidence of a cowboy. She referred to the United States government as "Uncle Sam," and every Indian woman she had met was "this nice little Injun gal." She said "yep" and "golly," "why, heck!" and "surely do." She said, "Agra. Sheesh. Pollution'll killya. Taj Mahal's nice, though. Smaller'n ya thought. Like the White House." She had traveled widely in India, yet seemed not to have been much impressed by it. She had spent a month doing missionary work in the north. "Dera Dun. Posted there. Yep. They'd animals runnin' around. Saw a monkey. Like the zoo."

One of the Indian men, who introduced himself as Mr. Mahanty, asked me, "What is the duration of your stay in India, madame?"

"One month," I said.

"Which country you are from?"

"United States."

"Chicago?"

"Boston."

"Ah, yes. We have seen films about Boston." Reassuringly he added, "But we know it's not true."

"What kind of films?" I said.

"Gangsters. Ha-ha."

An older, heavily mustached man said, "You are married or spinster?"

Shocked by the word "spinster," but perhaps more by the realization that technically it could indeed be applied to me, I was rendered momentarily speechless.

"Mr. Banerjee, excuse me," said Mr. Mahanty, "they do not say spinster now. They say single. Nobody gets married there anymore."

The men were Christians from New Delhi who were here on a church mission. New Delhi was full of Christians. All over the city I had seen signs nailed to trees that said: JESUS IS THE ANSWER FOR ME. At the table that morning I mentioned an incident that had taken place in a church in West Delhi a few weeks before, a riot in which a group of Christians was attacked by Hindu extremists. Bibles had been burned, a piano smashed, worshipers had been beaten.

Mr. Mahanty frowned in recognition. "It is thugs, I tell you. Nothing but thugs. Violence will gain them nothing."

His colleagues sniffed and nervously murmured their assent.

"It is folly. They would like to keep minorities in their place."

"They are ignorant. They do not represent the feelings of the majority."

"It is nasty business and is of no avail."

"None whatever. It will come to no good."

ONE EVENING toward the end of my stay in Varanasi, Jaga sat beside me on the tea-stall bench, sipping contentedly at a thimble of tea, his thin legs crossed, one foot bobbing. The setting sun shone brightly over the river in a last burst of flame, bathing the figures on the ghats in an orange glow and giving them long purple shadows. The fishing boats on the river appeared to be on fire. The stones under our feet were warm after baking all day in the sun. Throughout the city the cooking fires had been lit, and the air was taking on its usual evening smokiness. People bathed at the edge of the river, goats wandered up and down the stairs.

Jaga and I were watching Tarun and a group of other boys playing a game called *guli danda* on the steps of the ghat. Jaga turned to me, the steam from his tea curling around his pointed brown chin, his face and teeth lit up with sun. "Tarun is the champion batsman of all Varanasi. Everyone knows this."

The game was a primitive form of cricket. It concerned a little spindle-shaped chip of wood — the guli — that was tapered at both ends. A batter wielding a rod of bamboo would place the chip on the ground and deal it a mighty whack at one end. The wobbly spindle would leap into the air, whereupon the batter would swing his stick at it a second time, sending the guli sailing out over the ghat. (In this way the hitter was required to be his own pitcher; to hit the guli well, you first had to be able to pop it off the ground well.) The point of the game was to see how far you could send the guli, and if the other team managed to catch it before it hit the ground, you were out. Sometimes the guli went hurtling into one of the rowboats moored along the banks of the river, and the boys hurried down en masse to search for it. If the boat owner caught them searching, he would chase them away with a stick of his own. Most of the boys, who were all remarkably skinny, were dressed in rags. They made a living wandering the ghats, dispensing information to tourists and running errands for pilgrims. They could all speak several phrases in four or five languages.

Jaga said, "The captain of the champion team today will get ten whole rupees."

At bat Tarun looked confident and severe and very handsome. He wore his bulky red sweater tucked neatly into his trousers, and his height and extreme thinness made him look almost skeletal. But he beat the guli with the ferocious zeal of a man killing a roach, and when it popped into the air he gave it another vicious smack and sent it flying out over the upturned faces of the other boys. The boys scrambled down the steps after it.

I asked Jaga why he wasn't playing with them. He sipped his tea and said, "I am not so good at guli danda. Always while they play, I only sit and think." He watched the boys running up and down the steps. With a touch of self-criticism he said, "I am possibly too serious and certainly not good at sporting."

The sound of two cats preparing for a fight drifted up from the bottom of the steps. The only cat I had seen in India was a dead one outside the Dutch embassy in New Delhi. I stood up to see where the howling was coming from and realized that it was not cats at all but an infant lying on its back alone on a pile of rags. Its voice was hoarse and desperate. It cried a long time, working itself into high-pitched hysteria, its tiny brown hands punching at the sunlight, but no one came to its aid. I wanted to go down to it. Finally I said to Jaga, "Where's that baby's mother?"

"Unclear," Jaga said, craning his neck and peering at the various women laboring over laundry at the edge of the river. "But maybe she doesn't mind."

We tried to watch the guli danda, but it was impossible to relax or concentrate with the abandoned infant expressing such terrible distress. Finally, tsking and shaking his head like a pestered old man, Jaga handed me his tea glass, got up, went down the steps, and gathered the baby up in his arms. He spoke to it, rocking it on his elbow and patting its stomach. He walked up and down the steps to soothe it, stroking its cheek, uttering words I couldn't hear. He touched his forehead to the baby's forehead. He made faces at it, smiled at it. At one point he appeared to be singing. He nodded encouragement at the tiny face. None of the women on the ghat paid him any attention. When the baby stopped crying, Jaga laid it gently down on the rags again and returned to the bench. "In India we say that it is good for the baby to cry sometimes, because when he cries his heart beats faster."

"Do you think that's true?" I said.

Jaga smiled skeptically. "No. When a baby cries, I want to cry."

A small boy came over to our bench, put his face very close to mine, and stared somberly at me. Perhaps six years old, he was covered with dirt and dressed in torn rags. His legs were riddled with scratches and scabs. Flies looped around his head and, by association, around mine. Though the boy was filthy and his hands were black, he was careful to brush dust and crumbs from the wooden bench before sitting down beside me. He had a stack of postcards to sell and he held them up for me to see. The cards were pictures of the Hindu gods, holy men, snake charmers, and magicians and were similar in style to Tarun's movie star postcards. Some of the cards showed sadhus doing strange things — sleeping with their arms held up in the air, lying on a bed of nails, piercing their tongues through with big brass nails, crossing their eyes in a demonic way. One card showed a sadhu with dreadlocks so long he had to heap them up beside him when he sat down. Some were photographs of important spots in Varanasi, including one of the two ancient towers that were crumbling into the river at the bottom of Prasad Ghat. From where we were sitting we could see these very towers downriver to the left. In the picture, boys were jumping from the towers into the river. I asked Jaga if he had ever done that.

"I do not swim," he said, looking at the card.

"You don't?"

"I do not know how. But Tarun can swim."

The small child scratched his head and handed up another postcard — a picture of a man in a glittering brocaded costume sitting on a beautifully bedecked elephant with a saddle of gold.

I bought five postcards, and the child went away, holding the money I had given him up to his mouth. He had not spoken a word to me.

"I used to be selling postcards too when I was a boy," Jaga said, watching the child go. Jaga told me that in the days when he was selling postcards to tourists he used to sit on the ghats and dream that some rich English lady with no children would come and take him back to England with her. "Now I am more practical," he said, "and not thinking those foolish thoughts." He looked musingly at the sky, at the patient vultures. "Though still I dream about going somewhere."

It was plain that Jaga saw the world not as a place in which to flourish and expand but as a place in which to endure and then die. Life held certain small pleasures, but they were incidental and temporary. Real life was the tiny crowded family room, the dingy toy shop, the surly tourists suspiciously pinching their rupees, the money he brought home to his mother. I pictured him as a child beating the cats to the dewy chapatis on the roof, as an adult beating the alarm clock to the day's work. Under the circumstances, a mind as sharp as his seemed almost a curse.

Down the ghat, Tarun let out a shout of triumph. He had won the game for his team, and he danced about in celebration on the sunlit steps, his red sweater ablaze, hands raised over his head.

"I love Tarun," I said.

Jaga was silent for a minute. He looked up at me and said, "You do not also love me, madame?"

I looked back at him and smiled and said nothing. Jaga lowered his chin like a chastened dog, and his mouth twisted sheepishly to one side, and gradually under my unwavering gaze his face erupted in a shy, knowing grin of pleasure.

WHILE THE RIVER was at its most beautiful in the late evening, the streets were at their worst. The already polluted air grew thicker with coal smoke from the cooking fires, a smoke so dense it blocked out the stars and turned the night sky into a dark brown ceiling pressing low over the city. In the choked night air the streetlights burned a gassy gray-brown. The streets were permeated with the smells of cow dung and of the rotting vegetables that vendors had thrown into the gutters, of curry and garlic and hot oil. Ragged, bare-bottomed children sat in dark doorways, their huge eyes peering out somberly. Through doorways I could see the glowing orange light of oil lamps and cooking fires in dark rooms and the shining brown faces and shadowy silhouettes of people sitting hunched on beds and chairs.

ON ONE OF MY LAST afternoons in Varanasi, while I was waiting to meet Jaga on Dasaswamedh Ghat, the sadhu with the teapot crooked his finger at me. I went over to him. His disorderly conical topknot, always on the verge of toppling off his head, brought to mind a tipsy French concierge teetering down the hall to fetch herself another bottle of claret. Sitting by the sadhu's side was a teenager with an enormous white bandage on his right hand. I pointed to the hand and asked him what had happened. He said, "The fireworks exploded." I could see the tips of his fingers poking out of the bandage; the flesh had been seared off, and they were the color of raw steak. They looked infected and incredibly painful, but the boy smiled cheerfully at me and waved his hand. With a fortuneteller's ominous certainty, the sadhu said, "Lady, you have medicine to help him." I said I had no medicine but was sure that I could find some, and the sadhu grinned at me in his skulking, secretive way.

Jaga came down the steps and we walked on together. I asked if he knew the sadhu. "I know him, but not well. Honestly, madame, I am not fond of him."

"No?"

"He smokes a lot of ganja and does not speak truthfully."

"But he's a holy man," I said.

"Some holy are not so holy!"

Varanasi was as crowded with holy men as Rome was with priests and nuns. I found it difficult to keep all the Hindu holy men straight — what they practiced, who they were devoted to, why they dressed in the variety of ways they did, what their many symbolic trappings signified, whether or not they were sincere. Some seemed incredibly bad-tempered, others entirely unholy, yet their conceptions of holiness were so foreign to me, how would I know whether or not they were holy? In general the holy men had consigned themselves to a life of wandering and poverty as a way of moving closer to Shiva and Brahma. There were sadhus, fakirs, yogis, Aghoris, Namadharis, Nagas, Avadhuts, and many others. They were all a bit strange, but some were stranger than others. The Nagas, sometimes called the sky-clads, considered themselves socially dead and were in the habit of going about completely naked, their bodies smeared in ash and mud and cow dung. The fakirs practiced the art of mind over body — lying on beds of nails, swallowing swords, levitating, walking on hot coals, dragging heavy chains about for years, transcending physical limitations. Some moved from one place to another by rolling on the ground. Others would hold an arm over the head so long that it would wither and become useless. I had read about these holy men in *India: Past and Present*:

> Their practices consist chiefly of long-continued suppression of respiration; . . . of sitting in eighty-four different attitudes; of fixing their eyes on the tips of their noses, and endeavoring by the force of mental abstraction to effect a union between the portion of vital spirit residing in the body and that which pervades all Nature, and is identical with Siva . . . The yogi . . . can become as vast or as minute as he pleases; can traverse all space; can animate any dead body by transferring his spirit into it from his own frame; can render himself invisible . . . and is finally united with Siva, and consequently exempted from being born again upon this earth. [p. 256]

To me, the strangest of all were the Aghori ascetics, whose rituals and practices reflected their belief that there is no difference between impurity and purity. They were said to eat excrement and human flesh and to meditate while sitting or standing on a corpse. They drank their own urine. They carried around a human skull, which they begged with and ate out of. They lived near graveyards and cremation grounds and covered themselves in the ashes of the cremated bodies. Their aim was to illustrate that everything is an illusion; there is no right or wrong, no black or white, no good or bad. The Ashram of Kina Ram in Varanasi was the headquarters of the Aghori sect, but during the twentieth century their numbers in Varanasi had dwindled from some several hundred to a few dozen. I am sure I did not see an Aghori while I was in India.

Jaga had told me that if I was interested in meeting a holy man, he would take me to a guru who could read my palm and give me news about myself. I said to Jaga, "Is he a Naga?" Jaga shut his eyes and shook his head: *preposterous*. "Well, how about a fakir?"

Jaga laughed. "He is not a fakir."

I asked if he was an Aghori.

"Madame, your expectation is high. He is only a guru. But he is holy."

As curious as the next person for news about myself, I went with Jaga to see the guru.

THE GURU'S OFFICE was a windowless, cell-like room, eight feet by eight feet, off one of the narrow alleys in the old part of the city. A few wooden steps led up to his door from the alley, and a wooden sign like a country doctor's hung from chains above the door. The sign said HOUSE FOR ASTROLOGY. GURU-JI. Specialist: — PAMISTRY, SPIRITUAL HELP, MANTRA-TANTRA.

At Jaga's suggestion, I removed my shoes and stepped into the room through the bead curtain that covered the doorway. A man who appeared to be in his eighties, with a handlebar mustache and long white beard, was sitting on a mat chanting something from a prayer book in his hands. He looked startled and slightly annoyed at the sight of me. The room was empty but for a small bookshelf tucked into a niche and a futon that covered the entire floor. Jaga and I sat down on the puffy mat with the old man. It was like sitting on a king-sized bed crammed into a small closet. The only light was the oblique daylight that managed to filter through the beaded doorway. The walls were roughly plastered and painted a brilliant white, and though the day was very hot the room felt cool and slightly damp, like a cellar. The mat, too, felt damp. There were a few binders and books on the shelf and an array of vials and talismans and crystals. No one spoke. I could hear the old man breathing. He smelled of garlic. The soles of his feet were painted red. After a few minutes he gathered up his effects and left, parting the beads with an impatient swipe of his holy book. He was, Jaga explained, the guru's guru. "Guru-ji will come soon," Jaga said.

Sitting cross-legged in a dark corner, Jaga looked, for the first time, slightly self-conscious and uncertain. He was wearing what he called his blazer, a white acrylic sweater that a German tourist had given him. With its high collar and great bulk, the sweater made him look like a deeply tanned Scottish swain.

"Jaga," I said, "is this guru the man who teaches you?"

"Yes. He does palms and horoscopes and astrology." He fingered the black strand around his neck. "Guru-ji gave me this string. It is a holy talisman. To make my mother better when she was sick."

"Is your mother better?" I said.

In a happy, correcting way he cried, "She is best!"

We sat listening to a child bouncing a ball outside in the alley. I lifted my watch to the faint, filtered light. It was difficult to know the correct time in India. Every clock said something different, and when you asked a person for the time they usually said, "It is five, but my watch is ten minutes fast, more or less," or "It is five, but my watch is five minutes slow." Jaga saw me fiddling with my watch. "Watch clock never boil," he said, staring at me pokerfaced, waiting for me to correct him.

The guru arrived dressed in a white robe. He was the image of Rasputin. He had long, hectic hair, a pale bony face, and a thicket of beard spilling down his chest. He sat in the corner near the bookshelf, and after Jaga had introduced us he removed a three-ring binder from the shelf and handed it to me. It was an album of all the people he had horoscoped over the past fifteen years, with the forms they had filled out, their addresses, and testimonials. Guru-ji invited me to peruse it. A Catholic girl named Theresa from Maryland had written, "It was definitely interesting. I learned many things I had not heard before about myself." Visitors from Italy, Australia, and the Netherlands had all signed the book. "A first time experience," one man had written. I saw no testimonials from Indians. I asked the guru if Chinese or Greeks or Egyptians ever came to see him. "No," he said. "Mostly America and North Europe." That made sense. A trip to India, a dip into its culture and religion was for the Western world a curiosity and a luxury, a thrill like that of riding a roller coaster, of throwing one's self into the unpredictable, the slightly dangerous, the otherworldly.

Guru-ji told me that he had gone to Los Angeles with another holy man to make a holy fire and a holy sacrifice in order to control the enemy of a famous actress. When I asked him which actress, he said, "Ghouldie Hahn." Goldie Hawn was nice, he said. She had two children and spoke in a soft voice. Goldie Hawn's husband was sick. In addition, she had a very bad enemy. Guru-ji and the other holy man performed some black magic to thwart the enemy. "We know what is Ghouldie Hahn's future, what is her past," he said.

At a loss for a response I said vapidly, "How nice."

"She comes always in Varanasi."

"Do you like her?"

His hand teetered over his lap. "So-so. I am not caring if she is actress or whatever. She is a human body."

He didn't quite look directly at me as he spoke, but gazed at what seemed to be my hairline. He spoke in a slow monotone. His eyes darted from his hands to my hairline and back again. He looked a bit haunted, and his breath was sour, like a damp rag left too long in a corner. He said that my reading would take half an hour and that he would be very honest with me because that was his duty. He asked me to write down my name and birthdate.

Jaga said from his corner of the room, "She is a writer."

The guru's hand shot up in a silencing way. "Do not tell me!" he cried. Clearly he wanted to divine my profession for himself.

We sat cross-legged, our knees almost touching. He told me that while a man's right hand reveals his story, a woman's story is in her left hand. "Give me hand!" he said. He held my hand lightly in his damp fingers, and the moment he began reading my palm his voice changed dramatically, rising into a loud announcement. I could feel his voice on my face; it was reedy and dry, and it cracked now and then as he spoke. "First, you was born in Aquarius with sun in Mercury and your hand is eshpoony hand!"

I hated to interrupt him so early in the analysis, but I had no idea what he was saying. "Eshpoon hand!" he said very loudly. "Understand? Eshpoon. You eat soup, you use eshpoon."

"My hand is like a spoon?"

"You are understanding. Hand is soft hand. And heart is very soft heart. According to horoscope, sign in Mercury and you born in Jupiter period. Until twelve years you are very happy girl and strong with your health and wealth. But after twelve is be a naughty girl. This period affect to thirty-one. Nineteen, twelve, thirty-one. Up to you, you is a naughty. But between thirty-one and forty-eight Mercury is affecting from this finger and Jupiter is leaping high. That means they make you very intelligent woman and attractive power on you."

His face was obscured in shadow, but I could see his black eyes darting, the strands of white in his black beard.

"But your willpower sometimes no good. Will be confusing thinking and mentality." He stabbed at my palm. "This is heart line. Heart line is crushed one two three times. That means! You got already crushed two times in your life by the heart. You are . . ."

He began whispering to himself, calculating, uttering numbers, holding the end of his beard to his lips as he thought. He coughed a great deal and wiped his mustache with his fist. From somewhere down the alley, I could hear music with that tinny, warped television quality. Jaga seemed to have shrunk back into his corner. "Sixteen, thirty-two . . . changing period. Second, you are always eshpending money and no controlling with problem of drug life and drinking wine and whiskey. But don't give you effect from drinker. Between twelve and thirty-one. After thirty-one you are changing your life."

He was nearly shouting now, reciting the facts, putting emphasis in odd places. I had difficulty following the meaning of his words. He said many things about Saturn and the number thirty-one and Mercury and the number forty-eight. He said, "That surely affect you!" a number of times. I gleaned that the period between the ages of thirty-one and forty-eight would be a good one for me, that Mercury and the sun were scheduled to get together and bring me money. "Sun is intellectuality. There is opportunity to get two pregnancies in your life. It will be happy for you to be mother. After forty-eight you will have no interest to make many children."

A figure appeared in the doorway and knocked on the jamb. Guru-ji snapped something sharply in Hindi. It sounded like *Go away!* The figure disappeared. Guru-ji twisted my hand toward the pale light and stabbed at it. "By the father mother you got common relation not very big relation but good relation with you common."

"With my family?"

"Mother father type," he said in clarification. "You are spending nature. Not to be controlling too much for money not be misering. You are always helping. And! Will be troubled by back is not very strong."

"Because I spend money?"

He shook his head impatiently, and a wary look came into his eye, as if he didn't like being questioned. "Not like this. Planet Saturn period make you very bad physical. Mercury intervene with sun. They give you confusion. Physical health with back not good. That's why you have to do exercise."

"What exercise?"

"Physical exercise," he said, looking at me as though it had begun to dawn on him that I might be a bit dim. When he answered my questions his voice grew quieter again, returning to its natural tone.

"Any exercise at all?"

"No, I tell you." He paused, drew himself up in his professional pose, cleared his mind, and began again in that Delphic voice. "And! After forty-eight between fifty-five —" Abruptly he stopped. He seemed to have been interrupted by a warning voice. He raised a hortatory finger. "One thing more, madame."

"Yes?"

"Mercury is backed by Venus! Do not drive fast!"

I did have a bad habit of driving too fast.

"Just a minute." He turned his head aside and pinched his nose as though squelching a sneeze. He seemed to be receiving a message, reading rays of information. "That's why you have all two-number combinations. See?" He pointed at my hand. "Two planets here, two planets here, two here. That's will give you a young husband. If there is only one planet you would have older husband." He added in an offhand way, "My wife is older than me."

"How much older?" I said.

He looked startled by the question and confused, as if the script had been yanked from his hand. He paused to think. "Ten years. But she is not in Varanasi at this moment."

"Where is she?" I said.

"In Brussels."

"Why?"

"For making one spiritual program there."

"Is she Indian?

"Half Indian."

"You must miss her very much," I said.

Guru-ji stared at me from behind his beard, his mouth hanging open. This was not the way the reading was supposed to go; I was disrupting the formula. Jaga stared too; he seemed both amused and surprised. "And!" the guru shouted as a sign that our little digression had come to an end. "After fifty-five between seventy-five is very good period for you. And if you write one book there is success for you in your life."

I told him that I had already written three books.

"Not yet!" he shouted. "After forty-eight."

"Something to look forward to, then," I said.

I stared at him through the half-light, and he peered back with his big black eyes and fingered his weedy mustache.

"And! You never feel old. You are young. And bold. Always free. Not to be under pressure to anyone. That's why I will give you one talisman to protect you from confusion. A silver cask with five medical thing to control good driving and druggist person."

I must have looked puzzled, for he began explaining, "Druggist way. You will be getting chance to be controlled by drug people who is drunkard. Don't make good friendship with drunking people. Drinker. Drugged."

He talked for a long time in this fumbling, semaphoric way. Jaga, seeing that I was not quite catching the gist of it, had begun to look worried, like a parent watching his child's much rehearsed piano recital falling irrevocably to pieces.

"Between thirty-one and forty-eight you are wanting to think on the mountivity."

"The what?"

"Mountain. To make meditation for you to be purify and open your chakra. Thinking to go make meditation or make natural thing to be giving willpower some natural way. That's my suggestion."

He paused to think. "And commonly you are spending money too much. You are not thinking if expensive or cheap."

"I don't really care."

"That means you are moody woman. And you never feel guilty."

"Unfortunately, I feel guilty a lot."

"That is why you have to alert with druggist and investment."

"I have a very bad temper."

"I am already knowing this. That is why I give you one talisman to protect you by silver power. And one thing more, madame. Alert! I give you white magic, not bad magic. By my magic you will be getting seventy percent help. And if you didn't die around eighty-one age, then you will be fine."

From the alley there was a hammering sound and friendly shouting, then water splashing onto the pavement. Through the beads in the doorway I could see the sun on the wall across the way, a trapezoid of yellow light sliding slowly downward. A child ran past the door dragging a smashed paper kite behind him.

"By moodiness you will get heart attack. Any more thing you want to know by horoscope palmistry?"

"No, thank you," I said.

"In this journey I tell you one very good thing: you don't know nothing."

The guru handed me the talisman, and I thanked him. Feeling a little giddy and as if I had been a disappointment to both him and Jaga, I offered to guess the guru's birthday. He looked thoroughly stumped. "You guess my?"

"Why not?"

His eyes narrowed and he smiled expectantly, the way people unfailingly do if you promise to guess anything at all about them. "My lucky number is three," he said helpfully.

"Do not tell me!" I said. I guessed that his birthday was June 3. He smiled. It was not June. I guessed March 3.

"Not third March. But March is okay."

"March eighth."

"No, it is not."

"Yes, it is," I said.

Jaga looked at me as though I had completely lost my mind.

Guru-ji laughed loudly. "True, it is not!"

"You have a beard," I said. "I can't see your face. That's why I can't guess your birthday."

He laughed a long time and coughed and laughed some more. "Okay. Then I cut beard off! I am very proud of you. This is my guarantee."

Jaga was clearly relieved that Guru-ji was laughing. The guru gave me some spiritual oil unobtainable anywhere else in the world and instructed me to mix it with mustard oil, coconut oil, and almond oil and rub it on my skin.

A man with a basket on his head appeared in the doorway and said something to the guru. They had a brief exchange and the man went away.

"Now!" the guru shouted, looking suddenly furtive. "When I tell you the price of talisman you will be confused. If you afford that money, you can take. If you cannot, no pressure. It will cost you thirty-five US dollars only!"

Fearing that I would laugh, I looked down at my hands and turned the talisman over in my fingers. It was a small metal tube on a chain. I couldn't tell whether it was truly silver; it looked suspiciously like beaten tin. It interested me that the price was in dollars, and thirty-five seemed very steep. I thought of the black magic visited upon Goldie Hawn's enemy. I didn't want the talisman.

"You know, I think you're right," I said. "I have a problem with spending too much money. I think I should not buy this."

Guru-ji wagged his head to hide his disappointment. I thanked him and paid him six hundred rupees for the session and another two hundred fifty for the oil, and shook his hand. Jaga and I went out, and as we were putting on our shoes outside the door, Jaga asked me if the guru had told me the truth.

Nothing he had said was a revelation. Some of it was true in the way that platitudes and clichés are true, general statements applicable to most people. "Some things," I said. "And some things he got wrong."

Instantly the guru's woolly head poked through the curtain of beads. He looked worried. "I am not god. I am saying seventy percent of things right. Thirty percent wrong. Here is my card, madame. Please come back. And one thing more! Do not be using too much oil on the skin. It can burn the skin from the body. That is my saying."

ON ONE OF OUR LAST days together, I invited Jaga and Tarun to have lunch with me. We ate in a small, open-fronted restaurant near the river. The restaurant was dark but comfortable, its walls covered with pictures of famous Indian places and Hindu gods. Two veiled Muslim women sat at a table with a man in a leopard-skin hat. At another table four plump Indian women in rustling saris of shantung silk sat laughing and speaking English to one another. Tarun eyed the women and whispered, "Rich," to Jaga.

We sat in a corner. I handed menus to the boys and said, "What would you like?" They handed the menus immediately back without looking at them. "We will take chow mein," they said.

The old man who ran the restaurant limped over from the door with a notebook in his hand. I told him we would have naan and shal paneer and two plates of chow mein. As the man began to write, Jaga raised his hand and protested that two plates was too much. He waved his hand between himself and Tarun. "One plate of chow mein is enough for us. We will share."

I pressed them to take two, but Jaga insisted that it was too much. When I told the waiter we would have three Cokes, Jaga said, "But madame, one Coke for two of us is enough." I thought he was being modest, that he didn't want me to spend money on them, but he insisted.

The Muslim women tucked food discreetly under their veils, and now and then their black-draped shoulders shook with laughter at something the man had said. Their laughter sounded unexpectedly racy coming from under all that cloth.

Tarun plucked up a copy of the New Delhi *Statesman* lying on a nearby table. Jaga leaned on his shoulder and read a headline: "Stabbing at train station."

The Indian newspapers were always full of disasters and strange mishaps, massacres and bus crashes, stabbings and hit-and-run accidents, fires and floods wiping out entire villages, and a great deal of old-fashioned crime — gangsterism, extortion, gambling dens, and stickups. Every day the headlines appeared in a nightmarish collage. *Three die in N. Delhi fire. Servant lashed and thrown from terrace. Family of ten killed in head on collision; driver flees. Woman crushed to death by bus; driver flees. Seven members of family drugged, robbed. 12 muslims slaughtered in Pala Mau.*

The waiter brought our food. Jaga said with concern, "But we have not washed our hands." I had two little damp paper towels in foil envelopes in my pocket; I gave them to the boys. Jaga handed one back to me. "For you," he said. He opened his, unfolded the towel, carefully ripped it down the middle, and handed one half to Tarun. When he saw me looking at him, he said, "We are best friends. What is mine is also Tarun's." They rubbed their hands meticulously with the damp towels.

I picked up my fork and began to eat. They didn't. I urged them to. I knew they were hungry, but they wagged their heads and shrugged their shoulders and began to eat in a way that looked distinctly like an act of duty, a form of politeness. The plate of chow mein that they shared was enormous. Tarun leaned unconsciously toward Jaga as he ate, closer and closer, until Jaga finally said to him, "I say, Tarun, give a fellow some space!" They plucked at the noodles with their forks, and as they ate they kept sliding the plate toward each other, as if to say, "Eat more." They were generous with each other and solicitous. They ate quietly with their heads lowered, self-consciously peering up from under their dark brows. They drank from straws from the one bottle of Coke and sipped repeatedly from their tall glasses of water. They reached often for the bowl of hot sauce in the middle of the table, and when Jaga noticed that I hadn't used any of it, he looked up at me, astonished, his fork frozen in the air. He said, "Madame, you do not take *spices?*"

In some ways Jaga and Tarun at sixteen resembled old men. They believed in resting after a meal, in digesting properly, in drinking plenty of water. They liked bathing and sipping tea. Their understanding and appreciation of those simple pleasures made them seem mature. At sixteen they felt a great sense of responsibility for supporting themselves and their families financially. They were calm, with none of the morose, adenoidal energy of the teenage boys I knew at home. Yet in other ways they seemed like young children.

They chewed their food carefully and wiped their mouths with their napkins and looked around the room. They had never been in this restaurant before. They listened to the rich women loftily criticizing the unpopular Sonia Gandhi and inspected the pictures on the walls. The one that interested Jaga most was a photograph of the Taj Mahal. He put his fork down and stared at it, absorbed and impressed. He looked at me, indicated the picture with his chin, and said dreamily, "The memory of love."

Jaga was proud of his country and his culture. Whenever he saw a picture of one of the Hindu gods he would point at it and say, "Vishnu" or "Ganesh" or "Lakshmi," as though he were a tourist in his own country. He loved Varanasi. Looking at a picture of the ghats near the door of the restaurant, he said to me, "There are many holy places in India. Allahabad, for example. But Varanasi is the most holy and most famous."

Tarun said suddenly, "Ghouldie Hahn came here before three

months. She is famed. Hollywood actresh." Goldie Hawn, he said, came often to Varanasi to see a holy man and stayed in a fancy hotel. "I have met her, madame," he said proudly.

"Was she nice?"

Tarun blinked at me, mulling the meaning of the question. "Yes, nice but is becoming old. Her guru told Ghouldie Hahn she can have big success with her next film. He came in Hollywood to help her making this film."

Jaga chewed his noodles, took a drink of water, wiped his mouth. "However, that guru has died."

I looked at Jaga. He had a factual, rational view of the world, a world in which people were always dying. "Why did he die, Jaga?"

As if it were inevitable he said, "Drinking too much alcohol."

"I thought holy men didn't drink," I said.

"Well, yes, but this guru had too much money and developed a liking for alcoholic beverages."

Tarun managed in his chopped-up way to tell me that Catherine Deneuve had come to Varanasi without telling anyone that she was coming, and that she, too, stayed in a fancy hotel. When she walked down the street she wore a shawl over her head and dark glasses so that no one would know who she was.

A toddler wandered into the restaurant and approached our table. His face was flea-bitten and shellacked with snot. Flies crawled in his large, kohl-rimmed eyes. He wore nothing but a ragged shirt; his bottom was black and his legs were stained with streaks of something green. His hair, sticking up ten different ways, was burned orange and looked frazzled and electrocuted, like the hair of an old woman. Scores of children like him wandered about on the Varanasi ghats. Despite their destitution they were strikingly beautiful, and it seemed miraculous to me that their beauty, like the mood of the lepers, had not been thoroughly destroyed by hardship and near starvation, harsh living conditions and disease. They managed to look contented, even with their rags and snotty faces and their feet shuffling in the dust. The child stood by our table and stared at me with his mouth open, breathing loudly and plucking at his penis. He was utterly unself-conscious and stared as if at a rock that couldn't look back at him. Jaga stretched his hand out and patted the child gently on the head in a stroking motion, the way one might soothe a cat. He said a few soft words to the boy and handed him a large piece of bread. The child wandered to the back of the restaurant and hung onto the leg of an empty table and stared at the floor and put the bread up to his mouth.

I told Jaga and Tarun that I loved children and why I loved them, and as I talked Jaga nodded, staring at the paper napkin in his hands. He began nervously tearing tiny pieces from the napkin and dropping them into a pile next to his plate. He sipped at his glass of water and Tarun sipped his too. They both looked around the restaurant. I said that the best thing about children was that they didn't lie to protect your feelings and that they could be a little bit wicked. Jaga tore more small bits from the napkin. Tarun wound his watch with great deliberation. They both looked terribly uneasy. I stopped talking. The rich women were turning around in their seats to look at the ragged child as he gnawed on the bread.

"I always loved children too," Jaga said, "but then came the death of my sister and brother. Now when I see little children I feel different. It is not the same."

Tarun looked nervously at his plate, coughed into his raised fist, took another sip of his water. His sideswept bangs were a dark wedge across his forehead. I was sure that I had misunderstood Jaga. "*Who* died?" I said.

"My small brother and sister."

"But why did they die?"

Jaga's face seemed to have swollen with sadness. He was gradually reducing his napkin to a tiny pile of flakes on the table. He said, "They got a cold in the bones."

A cold in the bones could mean anything. People in India were dying of polio and tuberculosis and pneumonia and a myriad of other preventable, curable diseases. I hated to think what unnecessary illness had killed them. I asked Jaga when they had died.

"That was three years ago. They both died in one month. My sister was three years old and my brother was five."

I said, "That is very sad, Jaga."

Jaga nodded, squinting narrowly, as if looking at death through the wrong end of a telescope. It was the first time he had admitted that death was sad, and he drank the rest of his water all at once as a way of covering his unease. "Yes, I was sad," he said. "I loved them. When I came home in the evening I brought them chocolate and things. My little brother liked mimosas very much, so every day I brought them for him. They were always laughing and playing games with me. When I had extra money I brought them toys from the factory. Like what you say, madame. They always told me the truth. It is hard for little children to tell lies. After my brother and sister died I stopped going to the temple."

Jaga spoke in his usual calm and measured way, but his face had changed. His expression was at once anxious and resigned, angry and sorrowful, detached and pained. His body had stiffened slightly. His eyes, grown very round, darted across the dishes on the table, not lighting on anything. I saw that he feared he would cry.

At the back of the restaurant a man was crawling on his hands and knees sweeping the floor with a short-handled twig broom. He swatted the broom at the toddler's bare legs, shooing him out of the restaurant. The little boy fled in a stumping way, the bread clutched in his fist.

I decided I had asked Jaga enough questions, but he continued to talk, as though making a confession. He needed no response. He lifted a hand to his face and pressed it to his cheek. "I stopped everything. I was only thinking and feeling sad and being very angry with God. It was difficult for me to believe."

"It's hard to think that God would let those things happen."

Tarun lifted his head. With a practiced jerk of his chin he tossed his bangs out of his eyes. "I believe. But why he lets?"

"Your mother must have been very sad, too," I said.

"She was weeping, weeping all the time," Jaga said. "Even now sometimes. There was one time seven people in my family. Now there is only five."

Jaga told me that his remaining siblings were approximately eleven and fourteen and that they were smart and went to school. I asked him why they went to school but he had not.

"I want them to go to school. I know it is better for them. My brother is in Queen's College. It is the best in India for students who are smart."

I told Jaga that his brother and sister couldn't possibly be smarter than he was. Tarun leaned toward me and cried, "They is!!" Jaga gave Tarun an adoring punch in the arm.

The elderly waiter came to the table and began clearing the dishes away. We drank coffee out of tin cups and ate two chocolate bars that I had in my bag. Jaga's mood lightened. He pointed out that the wrapper on the chocolate said, *Store in a cool, hygienic, and dry place,* but that the chocolate had melted and rehardened and that the wrapper was brown with dust. "They were not remembering India when they said cool and hygienic."

Tarun said, "Jaga, what is hygienic?"

When the waiter was in the kitchen I asked Jaga what his name was. Jaga looked at me with disbelief and said, "How can I ask him his name? He is old. What would I say to him, 'Old man, what is your name?' He would say, 'I am an old man. You are a young man. You call me grandfather.'" Jaga wagged his head over his glass of water and snorted and made a face that expressed how utterly impertinent and preposterous it would be for him to ask an old man his name.

"Should I ask him?" I said.

They both looked nervous and ducked their heads. They weren't sure what rules applied to a foreign woman in such a matter. "As you like," Jaga said.

When the waiter returned, I asked him his name. He said, not unkindly, "Basant. But you call me grandfather."

THE RISING SUN had barely climbed from behind the trees on the far shore, but already it was strong enough to coax steam out of the damp sand beneath our bare feet. As Jaga, Tarun, and I spread my inflatable boat on the stones of Prasad Ghat and began pumping it with air, a crowd of about forty men gathered around us, staring out from under the scarves and shawls they had wound around their heads against the cold morning air. Curiosity made them bold. They pressed themselves against us to see what our hands were doing, and with so many limbs intruding it became nearly impossible to move. The men chattered excitedly. They asked Jaga where the boat came from and how much it cost; they marveled at how light it was, how sturdy, how easy to inflate. Like Jaga and Tarun, they had never seen a boat like this before. They passed one of the collapsible aluminum oars through the crowd for inspection, eighty hands competing for it, snatching at it, the voices growing querulous, until Tarun, bristling protectively, made a sharp announcement in Hindi and snatched the oar back. While Tarun took a turn at the pump, Jaga and I screwed the caps on the various air chambers of the boat. At one point Jaga paused to look up at the intent, baffled faces, the scores of staring black eyes, and then, looking at me, he said wryly under his breath, "Museum."

When the boat was ready, Tarun masterfully parted the crowd with an oar, and we slid the boat into the water and climbed in. I was nervous. I had bought the boat just before leaving for India and had had time to try it out only once in the tame, familiar waters of Narragansett Bay. Though it was not a toy, the boat was hardly a lobsterman's pram, and I was certain that this rash venture would end in ignominy, that we'd be scuttled within minutes. But my desire to see the far shore of the Ganges had overpowered my fear and reason; having found two willing companions in Jaga and Tarun, I was determined to try it before leaving Varanasi the next day. We would cross the river now or never.

I sat in one end of the boat and Jaga sat in the other with Tarun in his lap. Tarun held under his arm a bag of provisions I had brought. We sat low in the water, our elbows resting on the fat bulk of the raft. The boat was oval and only ten feet long, but it was surprisingly strong; sitting in it we were like three birds huddled in a nest, our knees knocking together. Jaga and Tarun looked excited and thrilled. As I rowed away from the shore, Jaga said, "I am so happy to leave the people behind," and, like the Wizard of Oz departing in his balloon, he waved at the men standing on the shore and cried dramatically and with just the right degree of seriousness, "Farewell!" The men visored their eyes and watched us go, too astonished and suspicious to wave back. Among the faces I saw Chander, the bodybuilder, waving and calling to me. I ignored him and pulled at the oars. The boat moved lightly over the water. Tarun said, "This is new thing. I never have did this before."

The river's surface was like mercury in the bright morning light, and the usual morning detritus floated in it. The early boats full of tourists hurried up and down the river watching the crowds of pilgrims perform their puja. Jaga suggested that we cross to the other side straightaway. "I want to have peace," he said.

I rowed steadily, astonished at every stroke that the boat was still floating, that it remained dry within, that the oarlocks hadn't snapped off, that we were making progress. The sense that we were succeeding began to rise in my chest. I felt free and breathlessly elated. We had no guides telling us what to do, we had asked no one's permission. We were crossing the Ganges in a rubber boat as though this were an ordinary pursuit. We were surviving our own foolishness. I loved Jaga and Tarun for their willingness to try this, for their trust, for not being afraid. I was nearly three times their age, but their trust gave me an odd confidence and strength.

The flat river suddenly seemed nearly as huge as the sky, and its vastness was both frightening and exhilarating. We could see for miles both upriver and down. We were alone, engulfed in silence, but the river seemed to have a noise of its own, a hum that was as much a vibration as a sound. Looking about him, patting the boat, Tarun said in a kind of reverie, "My mother sure will not be believing it."

The pink sunlight on the boys' faces was soft and rich. I hung up the oars for a minute to take a photograph of them, and when I commented that Jaga wasn't smiling he said quite happily, "You know, I laugh very little, madame. And Tarun laughs too much."

"Maybe that's why you're friends," I said.

"Yes," Jaga said. "You know they say that there is an attraction in the opposites. We are the opposites. I can write, but Tarun cannot. Tarun can swim but I cannot. Tarun can play sports; I cannot. I can speak English, but Tarun cannot so well. Tarun goes to the temple; I do not. Tarun is bold; I am perhaps less so. Together we make one person who can do many things." He wrapped his arms around Tarun and gave him a hug, pressing his face against Tarun's shoulder. "We are the best friends."

There was an eloquence in their closeness, their love for each other, the way they relied on each other, their gentle acceptance of each other's weaknesses. It was a rare gift, one that they had created with their own hearts.

Toward the middle of the river the water swirled with a slightly stronger current, and for the first time I saw the Ganges dolphins. They were small, a strange greenish color, and looked almost translucent. We never saw their heads, just the humps of their backs as they arched through the water. I wondered how they survived the pollution, what they ate, why they didn't travel to cleaner water upriver. I knew that Jaga and Tarun bathed in the river, and I was curious to know whether they drank from it as well. When I asked, Jaga said hesitantly, "I can drink. If you are asking me to, madame, I will." I asked whether it didn't make him sick. With a certain glum awareness of the consequences of ingesting Ganges water he said, "I am used to it. Only sometimes I get sick."

The far bank was a wide shingle of sand, low dunes, and fingers of sandbars that branched out into the river. On one sandbar a group of people appeared to be having a morning cookout, and up the beach another group stood about in the sand as if stranded. This shore lay on the inside of a great curve in the Ganges. The current was slow, and the water hung in stagnant sheets between the fingers of sand; the shoreline was frosted with yellowish foam. Dark clumps of detritus and flotsam floated in the water. A pack of wild dogs — a dozen or so — were engaged in a spat at the river's edge, fighting over an animal carcass in the shallows. They howled and yipped and tore at each other, sand flew about, and just as quickly as the fracas began it stopped and the dogs disbanded, loping up the beach in a slow trot in search of the next edible thing. A fisherman brushing his teeth in his boat gaped at us as we approached the bank, while his partner pulled in a dripping net. In the bright sunlight their catch of tiny fish, like sardines, shimmered.

I rowed us onto an empty beach. Jaga and Tarun rolled their trousers up to their shins and struggled out of the boat, but the sand was surprisingly wet and soft, like quicksand, and they sank in up to their knees. Each step they took sent them deeper. When they stood still, they sank even lower. They hopped frantically about, arms flailing as if they were dancing on hot coals, trying to find solid ground. I was sure that if I didn't do something fast, they'd be up to their necks in minutes. They began to laugh. The two fishermen shouted at us not to go ashore there and kindly pointed us to a better spot. The boys climbed back into the boat, wet and sandy and giggling uncontrollably. I rowed around to the other side of the peninsula, where the sand was hard, and we all got out and pulled the boat up onto the beach.

The beach, wide and hilly, was cratered like the moon into strange basins that had once held pools of water. Dogs trotted about, and far down the beach children flew kites. The place had a feeling of lawlessness, of a wide freedom that felt both thrilling and dangerous. There was no sign of authority or civilization here. We walked across the beach toward the low, dark line of trees. Pointing into a deep, dry basin quite far from the shore, Jaga said, "Tarun, remember you swam here not so long ago?"

Tarun smiled wistfully at the damp sand. "Yah." Where he had swum was now just a damp sandy hollow stamped and checked with the footprints of wagtails and shorebirds. The slowly evaporating water had left brownish rings in the sand. "The river rises this high?" I said.

"Higher," said Jaga. "After monsoon it goes almost up to the trees."

I asked if anyone ever slept on the beach.

"No," Jaga said. "Because dogs come in the night."

"And ghosts," Tarun said darkly. "And Dracula."

"I would like to spend the night here," I said.

Tarun shuddered, and Jaga cried, "Then you will be staying alone, madame!"

Three women walked out of the misty trees with straw baskets on their heads. They stopped and stared at us, and as we came closer they hurried back into the woods, like frightened deer. When we reached the treeline, Jaga pointed to a brown line of river wrack in the sand. "Here is the place that the river stops in monsoon." The river rises and falls some twenty feet seasonally, which means that after a heavy rain the lower steps of the ghats are covered in water.

Not far off, three boys stood in the sand. A bicycle was parked near them on a dune. I went over, climbed onto the bike, rode it up a path leading into the woods, turned around, and came back again. As I was getting off, one of the boys shrieked, "Lady! You give me twenty rupees for riding its bike!" I laughed, but Jaga and Tarun looked embarrassed and incensed at the demand. Tarun said something in Hindi, and the boys' insolent faces fell. One of them released a stream of sharp words at Tarun. I was happy to give them twenty rupees — forty cents — and as I handed over the money, the boy snatched it, saying, "We are poor!"

Calmly, in English, Jaga said, "You will be poor forever with that attitude. Madame, take no notice."

I asked Jaga what the boys had said to him.

"We said that they should not ask any money from you. They said that we should close our mouths and not meddle. But Tarun is not afraid. He told them that he would come back and beat them."

Tarun threw back his shoulders. "I will beat!"

Jaga said, "Yes, Tarun, you must come back tomorrow and beat them smartly."

I told them not to bother, that it didn't matter, that I wasn't offended. But I could see that they were offended and were already plotting their revenge. We stood silently at the edge of the woods. It was dark and cool. Wagtails teetered on the ground. Tarun suddenly gasped. "Oh, look, madame, a quarrel!"

I looked around, as fascinated as the next person by a quarrel, but I saw nothing. The woods were empty. "Where, Tarun?"

Jaga said, "There, on the rock! He is chewing a stick."

It was a squirrel — actually, it was a little brown chipmunk with a pretty yellow stripe down his back. Varanasi was full of them. I tried to teach Jaga and Tarun how to pronounce the word "squirrel," but it was nearly as futile as teaching a French person to say that word.

The sandy trail led through the woods to a small village, but Jaga and Tarun didn't want to go there. We walked back to the boat, sat in the sand, and had a picnic of nuts, chocolate, fruit, and potato chips. Each time I offered Jaga and Tarun something to eat they refused twice and then reluctantly took it. Tarun didn't eat much. When I offered him a can of Coke, he touched his stomach and said, "I have been having a dish at the Chinese Food Center. I must be resting before I am eating more." The Chinese Food Center was a glass case on wheels outside the post office. The case held an assortment of Chinese dishes kept warm by a dim lightbulb. I asked Tarun when he had taken this dish. "Last night," he said.

Jaga munched a banana and admired my boat. "If Tarun and I could buy a boat, we could make more money."

I had bought the boat because I loved to row and because I had wanted to row down the Ganges a short distance. But when I saw the polluted state of the river, I changed my mind. Without needing to consider it for a moment, I said, "You can have this boat if you want it."

They both stared at me as if they had never heard anything so bizarre. They stared at me and then at the boat, and for a long time they said nothing. I could see that they were projecting themselves into the future, imagining what it would be like to have this boat as their own. Finally Jaga said, "That is very kind, madame, but we couldn't take it."

"Why not?"

"Because other people would be jealous. Enemies would be puncturing it. It would end uselessly."

He was not complaining or whining or bemoaning his circumstances. It wasn't in him to complain. He was simply looking at his life for what it was. He was being practical. He told me that he and Tarun hoped someday to go to France, where a lucky friend of theirs sold Indian artifacts in a shop in Dijon. The friend had promised to look for jobs for them and had promised to write to them. They were waiting for a letter from this friend, hoping that some person in Dijon could offer them a job. They would have fun there, Jaga said, and adventures, and learn to speak better French. "I think about this very much," Jaga said, and Tarun nodded in agreement and said, "And I am too all the time thinking this."

We sat eating our snacks and looking across the river at the magnificent wall of ghats, the jumble of buildings, the cremation ghat draped in its cowl of smoke. The praying pilgrims at the bottom of the ghats were a minutely moving line. From here the whole scene was brilliant and strange. Jaga said reflectively, "That is where we live, Tarun." There was pride and affection in his voice, and a hint of wonder.

I thought of the people beyond the ghats, whose business was not with the river, who lived their lives in the insurance companies and silk mills, the toy factories and fields, the religious schools and ashrams — the people who had little to do with this incredible spectacle of visitors. The tourist boats moved slowly back and forth in the water below the ghats, looking, from this distance, faintly sharklike. It was undeniably voyeuristic and intrusive and even odd — all these foreigners, including me, coming to watch the Indians bathing and praying and dying. Many times I had wondered how it would go over if hundreds of Indians went to the United States, paid out some monetary consideration to enter our bathrooms with cameras to record our grooming, then followed us to our churches and synagogues and mosques to gawk while we prayed. I asked Jaga whether the pilgrims didn't mind the foreigners watching them, whether the families of the dead weren't disturbed by strangers watching the cremations of people they loved.

Jaga nodded thoughtfully and stirred his heels in the sand. The question disturbed him. In his preoccupation he was draping his banana peel absently over his head. "Yes, some people mind this and think it is wrong," he said, pursing his lips. "Sometimes I think it is wrong. Sometimes I ask why they want to see this. But it has been like this for many years."

He paused to think, fitting a thumbnail between his front teeth, tugging the banana peel farther back on his head, and staring across at his home, which I had pressed him to defend. He was right: the affluent and curious had been coming here for centuries to dip their toes in a bath of horror and intrigue, to experience an alternative reality. Even in my small local library I had found an astonishing number of nineteenth-century British and American travelogues about Varanasi.

Reluctantly Jaga said, "It brings money to this city. That is one truth. How could the people live without it?" He looked at me. "I, perhaps, am one who could not live." Anywhere else in the world, Jaga's gifts would have enabled him to live in whatever fashion he chose.

Tarun listened with his head cocked, like a dog listening to the cry of a distant animal.

Jaga said, "And Tarun is one who could not live." He looked apologetically at me, as if hoping I would be able to forgive Varanasi for making an industry of its faith.

Tarun — perhaps bored with our dreary philosophizing and our difficult English, or perhaps unsettled by what we were discussing — snatched the banana peel from Jaga's head and in a lissome burst of athleticism hurled it into the river. Jaga knew I didn't like litter. Urgently, reassuringly, he said, "Do not worry, madame! The fish will eat that banana shell, and then it will be a blessing for the three of us."

"A blessing?"

"We believe that if you are kind to other creatures, God will give you a blessing." He smiled. "So you see, it is the best thing for all of us that that item has gone to the river."

I wanted to hug him for his cleverness. His faith, I knew, was similar in nature to mine — faded, worn, resentful, and stubbornly evasive. And yet it was there. "Jaga," I said, "I thought you didn't believe in God."

For a moment he looked trapped. Then, slowly, he gave me his enigmatic smile.

· 5 ·

THE HOLY LAND

Before leaving home for India, I had bought a one-way ticket from Bombay to Tel Aviv for December 12. Arriving at the Bombay airport on the twelfth, I was surprised to find eight movable podiums arranged in front of the El Al check-in counter to accommodate multiple simultaneous security interviews. And the entire El Al area was delineated with the sort of yellow plastic tape that distinguishes American crime scenes. I stepped up to a podium attended by a young Israeli soldier in jeans and a white shirt. His list of questions went far beyond the usual *Packed your own bag? Bags with you at all times?* and *Anyone give anything to you?* They included where I was from, where born, how long I had been in India, where I had been just prior to my visit to India, what Indian cities I had visited, how I had heard of those cities, where I had stayed, how much I had paid for those hotels and did I have hotel receipts with me, whom I had become acquainted with, what were their names and addresses, where was I going now (Jerusalem, Nazareth, Sea of Galilee, Bethlehem), and many many more.

My interviewer was polite. Like most Israeli soldiers he looked fresh out of teenhood. The care and attentiveness with which he questioned me suggested that he had been rigorously trained. He asked why India. I said tourism. He asked who I was traveling with. I told him I was traveling alone. His head snapped up. "Alone?"

"Yes."

"You are sure?"

"Quite."

He asked why I was alone; I said that I learned more when I traveled alone.

"Learn?"

"Gather information. See things. Hear things. Ask questions."

The young man narrowed his eyes at me. "Did you meet anyone in India?"

I told him I had met many people.

"Did you meet any men?"

"Many men."

The young man drew his head back slowly, as if adjusting a mushy focus.

I had forgotten that women traveling alone in the Middle East were automatically suspect because of past cases in which a politically or religiously disgruntled maniac, unbeknown to his lovestruck girlfriend, had placed a bomb in her luggage and then driven her to the airport and kissed her goodbye.

"What are those things in your hand?"

The things in my hand were aluminum poles, the stems of the collapsible oars that went with my inflatable raft. The soldier didn't recognize the word "oars." I lifted the poles and pretended to row with them. He looked skeptical. "Why do you have that?"

I explained that I had used them to do a little rowing on the Ganges. The boy frowned. "Boat rowing?"

"Yes."

"What boat?"

"An inflatable boat that's in my suitcase."

"May I see your ticket home?"

"I don't have a ticket home yet."

The soldier didn't like this answer. He cleared his throat. "None?"

Not knowing how long I'd be traveling, I hadn't bought a ticket home yet. "No," I said. "None."

Doubts were mounting on both sides of the podium. He muttered, "None," at his list of questions. "Your passport, please."

I removed my passport from my hip pocket; it was hot and had adopted the curve of my rear end. He held the passport open with both thumbs, scanning it slowly, studying each stamp and visa, his mouth ajar, a muggy film of sweat glazing his upper lip. At the other podiums people were swiftly coming and going. The soldier opened my passport to a particular page, held it out to me, and tapped it ominously with his index finger. "What is this?"

I knew that Syria was one of Israel's worst enemies. I said, "That's a visa to Syria."

The soldier suddenly looked very nervous, and that made me very nervous. More questions came. *Why Syria? Where in Syria? Who in Syria? Syrian men?*

I said truthfully, "I went to Syria because I was curious," but the answer sounded stupid and untrue.

"Do you have any electronic equipment with you?"

When I told him I had a laptop computer, his mouth opened, but for a moment no sound came out, and suddenly he looked like a guy who had struck a truly horrible jackpot, the scalding coins of wrong and suspect answers falling in a shower from my mouth into his hands. He laid the passport on the podium and glanced left and right at his colleagues, as if fearing he might be left alone with me, the creepy target of all his training. A laptop was a perfect vehicle for a bomb. He lowered his voice, as if to protect the other passengers from what they might hear. "Why," he began. "Why do you have a computer if you are a tourist?"

I explained that I was a tourist *and* a writer.

"Writer?" he said in a challenging way. "What do you write?"

He wanted to see my press card; I explained that I wasn't that kind of writer. I was employed by no one and didn't need a press card. He asked if I had one of my books with me as evidence; I explained that I wasn't in the habit of carrying my own books about with me. Did I have any notebooks? They were in the computer. With a kind of defiance he tossed out his final question: Was I carrying anything that resembled a weapon?

"Well, actually . . ." I said. His face fell.

It was a small BB gun. It was plastic and nearly weightless but had been carefully shaped to satisfy a child's desire for the authentic and the martial, and from a slight distance it was indistinguishable from a policeman's Glock. I had brought it because I had planned to camp out on the banks of the Ganges, where, people had informed me, there were vicious wild dogs. A BB gun was a good form of protection, but in the end I hadn't camped out. I confessed to the BB gun, feeling foolish and absurd. I began to snicker with anxiety. The boy snapped up my passport and said, "Please stand here. I will return." And he hurried off on long, skinny legs toward a door behind the check-in desk.

Presently the director of El Al's Bombay security department approached me with my passport in his hand, a gun on his hip, and the young soldier following in his wake. The director had a buzz cut, a pocked but handsome face, and a secret agent's artful charm. He treated me like a guest, apologized for the delay, was sure I understood that because of the millennium and the present state of affairs in the Middle East I would have to come with him. He would carry my bags. "Please sit here," he said, indicating a row of plastic chairs reserved for suspects. I sat obediently with my fellow detainees — nine glumly staring Indian men. "And now we will take your bags into this room for a short while." The agent smiled and adjusted a tiny electronic receiver plugged into his left ear. "Soon you can come in too."

His charm had the momentary effect of making me feel more privileged than persecuted. "Thanks," I said. And then I straightened up and thought, *What are you thanking him for, you sap?*

For half an hour the Indians and I sat looking at a dirty wall. Now and then we glanced grimly at each other and quickly away, denying any association. The man directly to my left, wearing a cylindrical cap of boiled wool, sat with his bare feet tucked up under him and chewed steadily through a stash of individually wrapped candies that he drew from the pocket of his rice-brown gown. He chewed contemplatively, unpeeling each noisy wrapper and dropping it to the floor. He looked as if he were sitting on a veranda in Allahabad watching the Ganges flow. No matter that he had been detained; he had his candies and his spotless karma to console him. I envied him. I was a wreck. Although I had had no more intimate a connection with any men in India beyond slapping the hand of one as it landed roughly on my breast, I had begun to worry that they might actually find a bomb in my bag. Everything about me was wrong. I was a woman alone; like most suicide bombers I had no ticket home; I had been to Syria and Egypt; I had a computer with me and a gun. My profession sounded phony. And then I worried that they would find my Irish passport in my jacket pocket. It wasn't illegal, but being under suspicion as a terrorist, I didn't think it would look great to be an American who just happened to have an Irish passport as well.

I felt like a criminal, and I felt very dumb. If I had taken the time to think about it, I never would have flown with El Al. I stared at a sign on

the wall: "Important Information for Outgoing Passengers: Possession
of narcotic drugs and psychotropic substance is strictly prohibited."
This was followed by a long list of punishments. The first conviction for
narcotics possession would bring ten years of prison; the second was
punishable by death. "In some countries even the first offense is punishable by death." If you tried to take natural objects such as elephant
tusks and tortoise shells out of India you would also find yourself in the
Bombay slammer.

A man came out of the special room and asked me to remove my
boots. "We will need to X-ray them," he said. People waiting in the
check-in line began to stare suspiciously at me; none of the other suspects had had *their* boots taken away. Even my implacably chewing
neighbor turned his head and eyed me defensively. What did the face of
guilt look like? Mine was sweaty and salmon-pink with sunburn. My
clothes were rumpled and none too clean. My uncombed hair was
roughly pulled back in a bun.

Another twenty minutes passed before the director called me in to
the special room and said he would leave me alone with a woman who
would inspect my person. I had difficulty listening to him, so shocked
was I to see the entire contents of my luggage — every last unwashed
and trinkety bit of it — spread out on tables around the room. A man at
one end of the room was feeding my things, one by one, onto the con-
veyor belt of an X-ray machine. My tent, my boat, my three Bengali
flutes, a paper kite, a ceramic bowl, all of it disappearing like tree
branches into a shredder. The woman, an Indian wearing the trenchcoat
of a flasher and flip-flops on her feet, instructed me to remove my jacket,
sweater, and shirt. She frisked me in a tapping way, like a child searching for a light switch in the dark. Like a lot of Indian women, she had
the face of Joan Baez. Hitting upon something in my pocket, she said,
"What is this?"

"That is one hundred rupees," I said, astonished that she had felt the
flimsy, tattered slip of paper.

She tapped my other pocket. "What is this?"

"That is five hundred rupees."

She waved a magnetic wand over my body; my belt buckle made it
screech. She asked me to remove the belt. She ran her hands up and
down my arms and legs, smiled apologetically, handed me my boots,
and called the director back into the room. He asked me to turn my

computer on; he wanted to see one of my files. He asked me to remove the film from my camera. "We will replace it." (They did not replace it.) "And now we will finish examining your things. Please sit again outside."

I sat for another half-hour while the check-in line dwindled to five passengers. The director appeared again with the Indian woman at his side. "We have given your passport and your ticket to Lufthansa Airlines," he said. "They are waiting for you. Thank you for your cooperation, madam. You may repack your bags now."

Before I could speak, he had disappeared down a hallway. I turned to the Indian woman and said, "Lufthansa?"

"They will take you to Frankfurt."

"But I'm not going to Frankfurt."

"Correct. You are going to Tel Aviv. So on the night of tomorrow Lufthansa will be carrying you from Frankfurt to Tel Aviv."

I constructed a rough map of the world in my head. We were in Bombay. I was going to Israel. Frankfurt was in Germany. That was overshooting Tel Aviv by about two thousand miles. "Frankfurt," I said, "is a very long way out of my way. I need to be in Jerusalem tomorrow."

"And from Frankfurt to Tel Aviv," she said, smiling and reiterating the happy part of the story.

I asked the woman why, exactly, I couldn't get on this flight with El Al.

"Exactly, madam, a person such as you cannot get on this flight unless we check your computer and that will take four days and they might damage it and then, oh, you will be feeling very sadly and such and such. And that" — she spanked her little hands together in a way that was intended to illustrate alacrity and simplicity, but it looked very much like a gesture of riddance — "is why Lufthansa."

I asked the woman to bring the security director back. He returned, still smiling. I asked him whether I should bother going to Israel at all, for if they wouldn't let me on their planes, why would they let me on their streets?

"Madam," he said with warm reassurance, "you are welcome in our country any time. This is only air regulations."

THE PASSPORT CONTROL agent at the Tel Aviv airport was a pudgy-faced girl with turquoise earrings and necklace and a blouse of frilly lace. She looked about sixteen. While she was talking with me from within her glass booth, another young girl joined her and they exchanged words in Hebrew. My agent mugged an astonished face at her colleague. I was ready to be drilled, examined, taken aside, and rejected again. "What is the purpose of your visit to Israel?" the girl asked, looking at the passport.

"Tourism," I said.

"How long you will stay?"

"Two weeks or so."

"It's okay I stamp your passport?"

I said, "It would be an honor," and presented her with my Irish passport, the one that had no Arab stamps in it. The girl giggled and stamped the passport and waved me on.

I stepped outside into the night air, a little stunned at how easy it had been. Tel Aviv felt like Miami — the smell, the balmy air, the palm trees, the 1960s feel of the airport. Though I was going to Nazareth early in the morning, I had a reservation at a hotel in Jerusalem, a half-hour's ride from Tel Aviv. With four other woman I hired a taxi to Jerusalem. Before we climbed into the van, the driver cocked his thumb and forefinger, pointed at each of us in a shooting way, and said, "Shivim, shivim, shivim, shivim." It sounded like bang, bang, bang, bang.

"What's shivim?" I said to one of the women. "Seventy," said the driver before she could answer. He opened the door for me. "You each pay seventy shegels to Jerusalem. Okay? Unless, my lady, you want to pay dollars. Ha-ha. I like dollars too!"

I HAD NEVER BEEN to Israel before, and my knowledge of the country was sketchy at best. What I knew had to do with either God or war; there seemed to be very little in between. It was either Bible stories — Moses, Solomon, David, Christ — or Moshe Dayan sitting in an army jeep in the desert with his bald head and his eyepatch. Jerusalem, the country's psychic center, seemed to occupy a fantastical position in history. Like Florence Nightingale and Joan of Arc, the city had always seemed to me a bit unreal. I had never had a burning desire to see it. I was more interested in Nazareth, the Sea of Galilee, and Bethlehem, places that drew me because of their significance in the life of Jesus. And yet for centuries people had come from all over the world expressly to see Jerusalem. I persuaded myself that if so many had done it, I probably should too.

Jerusalem's Old City occupied a very small piece of land — you could walk around its periphery in an hour — and it was not a tall city, yet what it contained and what had taken place there was quite staggering. It was four discrete neighborhoods — Jewish, Christian, Armenian, and Muslim — and in the midst of it all were the Western Wall; the Temple Mount and the Dome of the Rock, where Abraham had prepared to sacrifice his son and from which Muhammad was said to have ascended into heaven; the al-Aqsa mosque, the most important mosque in Jerusalem; and the Church of the Holy Sepulcher, where Jesus had been crucified, entombed, and resurrected. In Jerusalem every spot in which anything of significance had happened was commemorated with a church or a mosque or a synagogue, and the spots were remarkably close together. On the steep slope of the Mount of Olives eight or nine churches competed for space and attention, each of them based in some historical event. I saw them all. I visited the Western Wall and the Jewish cemetery, whose hundreds of white tombstones covered the slope that stretched down from the Mount of Olives into the Kidron Valley. I saw the Church of Saint Anne, beneath which Mary was said to have been born. I walked the Via Dolorosa, the route that Jesus had walked to reach the site of his crucifixion, and saw the place where the crown of thorns was placed upon his head by the Roman soldiers, the place where he first fell under the weight of the cross, the place where Veronica wiped his face. In the Church of the Holy Sepulcher I saw the slab of marble upon which the body of Christ had supposedly been washed and anointed after being removed from the cross. The slab was smooth and oily from the millions of hands and mouths that had touched it. I saw the tomb where Jesus had been buried and from which he was resurrected. The authenticity of many of these sites and relics was not entirely reliable, and the accuracy of their locations could only be approximate; so much of what I saw in Jerusalem seemed so trumped up, overdressed, and obsessively tended by the authorities charged with their care that I felt strangely distanced from their significance.

At the foot of the Mount of Olives I paid a fee to enter the Garden of Gethsemane, a square plot next to the Church of All Nations, and was startled by the sight of the olive trees there. There were eight of them, and though they were not very tall they had the most massive trunks I had ever seen. They were so gnarled and twisted that they looked more like sculpture than like trees. I knew that I had never seen anything so old; their advanced age and imposing appearance made them seem almost human. Their trunks were hollow, and the long, narrow openings in the twisted bark showed a deep blackness within, like doors slightly ajar to a dark room. At their tops the branches were stunted and tiny where new growth had sent out silvery green leaves.

After the Last Supper, Christ went to the garden at his most desolate and desperate and spent the night praying to God to spare him from the fate he knew was imminent. "Let this cup pass from me," he said. Illustrations in Catholic children's books always showed Jesus on his knees here, hands clasped, with a glowing golden chalice suspended in the air in front of him. His figurative drinking from the chalice would signify his willingness to obey God and would confirm his end. As a child I dreaded the chalice on his behalf. He was frightened and had asked his disciples, his friends, to stay awake with him while he prayed, and every year, listening to the story during Holy Week, I was shocked anew that they had fallen asleep after he had explicitly asked them not to. It betrayed a baffling lack of seriousness in them.

I spent an hour in the Garden of Gethsemane watched by the guards who were posted at various points to prevent people from touching the trees; over the years pilgrims had carved their names into them and some had gone so far as to rip off entire limbs as souvenirs. It was here that Judas had betrayed Jesus with a kiss in exchange for thirty pieces of the high priest's silver and here that Jesus had said, with touching mortal pride, to the crowd that came to arrest him, "Thinkest thou that I cannot now pray to my Father, and he shall presently give me more than twelve legions of angels?" No one had defended him then, and even the disciples had forsaken him and run away. Among these striking trees, which no human hand had created, it was easy to imagine those sad events, and here I found myself more touched and moved than I had been by any other holy site in Jerusalem.

After two days in the city, I moved on.

IN NAZARETH I stayed in a Marriott Hotel of unnerving elegance. My room had a fax machine that bristled with little lights, a telephone on the bathroom wall, a television the size of a van set into its own little mahogany sarcophagus. On the top floor were executive suites that you could get to only with a special elevator key. The carpeting was so thick and fresh and the lighting so calm it made me sleepy just to walk into the room. A fact sheet on the back of the door showed the rate for the room: $225 per night. At the Hotel Ramamurthi in Varanasi I had paid $9 a night, which exactly suited my budget, and if I hadn't been seated next to Bob Jensch on the flight from Frankfurt to Tel Aviv, I probably would have been staying at Saint Margaret's Pilgrim Hostel on the hill above Nazareth. When I travel I rarely make reservations in advance, preferring to see where fate will land me. This time fate had been kind. Mr. Jensch happened to be the manager of the Nazareth Marriott. When I asked him where I could stay inexpensively in Nazareth, he gave me his card and said, "There'll be a room waiting for you at the Marriott." Not only did he make the reservation for me, he gave me the manager's very low rate.

The curtains over the windows in my room were so thick they felt bulletproof between my thumb and forefinger. And yet, standing naked near them, I could feel the intense heat of the morning sun radiating through. It was mid-December, and while the air in this hilly place was cool, the sun still had a desert intensity.

On the enormous television Larry King was talking to Peter Jennings about a show he was doing for the millennium that would keep him up for twenty-four hours. Though I wasn't paying close attention, I heard a lot of nonsense about whether Jennings would have time to change his clothes during the twenty-four hours. "I suppose I'll have to or I won't be able to stand myself," Jennings said, looking old and stuffy and powdered.

When Larry King disappeared, Ehud Barak and Syria's foreign minister, Farouk Shara, showed up on the news. They were in Washington to begin their much-discussed peace negotiations. Barak had small hands and was knock-kneed and seemed excited. Shara had a dour, frightening face. Next to Bill Clinton both of them looked very small. Barak and Clinton had the flu, and Shara had just had a heart attack. They all looked awful. Shara and Barak did not shake hands or smile or even look at each other. In his opening remarks, which he had been advised to keep brief, Mr. Shara seized the podium and made a seven-minute speech accusing Israel of aggression. Peace, which the two countries had been unsuccessfully discussing for the past eight years, could be agreed upon only if Israel fully withdrew from the Golan Heights. Half a million Syrian people, he said, had been "uprooted from tens of villages on the Golan, where their forefathers lived for thousands of years, and their villages were totally wiped out from existence."

Nazareth, just fifteen miles southwest of Tiberias and the Sea of Galilee, was no more than twenty-five miles from the Golan Heights. From the window of my hotel, which was at the top of a hill in the Nazareth-Illit area, I could see the big blunt hump known as the Mount of the Precipice, and beyond it a broad, fertile plain below the town.

Nazareth was nestled in a bowl-like depression on the side of a steep hill. Low white houses with red-tiled roofs crowded the deserty slopes around the town. Here and there stands of cypress trees speared up from between the houses, but beyond them the place was treeless, making the wide sprawl of suburbs easily visible. With its hazy, golden light trapped in the valley and reflected from the hills and the white buildings, the place had the feel of Athens or Los Angeles. But it was far prettier than either. Most of the old city was built on the eastern side of the hill, so that by three o'clock on a winter afternoon it was rinsed in heavy purple shadow. Looking out the window I could see the route that I would follow down into the town, a winding road that traversed the hill many times.

At midday I left my hotel and walked down this road. During the night a torrential rain had hit the drought-parched town, and stepping outside I was struck by the clarity and freshness of the air — it had a superior lightness that I had felt in Ireland and the islands of the Aegean Sea. The sky was the startling blue of a jaybird and clear but for scraps of white cloud twisting and flexing in the quick breeze. The intense slanting December light reflected from the chrome of the automobiles and the glass shopfronts and highlighted the thick auburn hair of the women squinting and smoking and chatting in doorways. The boxy white houses look stacked up and crowded neatly together on the hill. I passed tidy shops and shawarma restaurants tended by dark-haired, mustachioed men. Young women in spandex trousers stared out of the open doors of the electronics shop, the pharmacy, the gift shop, the liquor store. A butcher sat on a stool outside his shop shouting in Arabic into a cell phone. People called out greetings to each other in Hebrew, Christmas tinsel hung in some shop windows, and disco music drifted through the open doors. The shop fronts here had a Western feel and were bedecked with both Hebrew lettering and the wiggly, dashing Arabic that looked like musical notation. There was a Howard Johnson's hotel and a Benneton, and though the streets were muddy because of recent rain, everything looked very clean. I saw no graffiti and very little litter. There were bakeries and sweet shops, and enormous fruit stands with produce more diverse and of higher quality than any I had ever seen in a chain supermarket in the United States.

In the center of the city the streets were festooned with Christmas decorations and an odd kind of bunting that looked like plastic shopping bags strung up on clotheslines across the streets. Printed on the bags were the words "Nazareth 2000," the catch phrase for the busy millennial year of tourism, for which Nazareth had been preparing for over five years. The plastic bags heralded an event, a celebration. But of what exactly?

That morning, in a free English-language newspaper published in Ramallah by an Arab organization called Al-Ayyam, I had read that Nazareth was expecting huge numbers of tourists in the coming year. With bald honesty one Ramzi Hakeem, the city's spokesman, stated that the millennial promotion had been devised as "a specific global event that is bound to Nazareth in order to bring benefit to its citizens." In other words, Nazareth 2000 was about revenue. Hakeem felt that Nazareth, like other Arab towns and villages in Israel, had suffered discrimination and neglect and had not received adequate financial aid from the government. This, he said, was why the town "could not acquire its deserved local, regional and global status." Mr. Hakeem complained that though sixty percent of tourists to Israel passed through Nazareth, the city made little profit from their presence. The tourists came for the holy sights, saw them in one day, and left. Hakeem believed that tourists would linger in the hometown of Jesus Christ if the town was comfortable and classy, clean and convenient. He also blamed the stalemate in the peace process with the Palestinians and with Syria; investors were wary of putting money into Arab projects while strife was afoot.

Over the past few years Nazareth had used government funds to renovate infrastructure, clean up the old city, improve transportation networks, and buff and polish many holy sites. A French designer had been hired to design outdoor lighting to enhance the religious architecture. In the old part of the city, underground water and sewage systems had been installed, power cables and telephone lines had been buried, and the streets had been repaved with Galilee stone and black Golan basalt. One thousand new hotel rooms had been added, and another thousand were in the works. Seven public gardens were being built. Modern trappings, such as plastic and neon signs, had been removed. In some streets the original cobbles had been painstakingly uncovered. The municipal government was modernizing the city yet hoping to retain its ancient integrity. The town, its hills, its rocks, its ancient sites, had been the home of Jesus, Joseph, and Mary, possibly the most famous trio in history, yet Mr. Hakeem and his committee seemed to believe that with their plastic bags and their washing up they were singlehandedly creating a buzz about Nazareth and the significance of the passage of two thousand years. Hakeem boasted that the municipality had in fact come up with "the whole idea of the year 2000."

This piece of chamber of commerce spin was an illusion being created in slow motion, an illusion that would please the imagination and the physical needs of the Christian masses. It was opportunism at its most blatant and had about it no trace of religious or historical feeling. Lest his financial concerns seem base, Mr. Hakeem went on to say that Nazareth 2000 would also "elevate this city and break the boundary of discrimination." He said, "In addition to its anti-Arab policy and its discrimination against the Arab minority, the Israeli government . . . believes that the Palestinian land attributes only to what is connected with Judaism." Nazareth shopkeepers had complained that while the number of visitors indeed seemed to be growing as the millennium approached, the tourists, most of them from Italy and Bolivia, didn't patronize their shops. A man who sold kitchen cutlery in the old market complained that tourists never made purchases in his store. (Forks and knives did not strike me as quite the sort of souvenir a pilgrim might think to bring home as a reminder of Christ.) Israeli tour leaders were blamed for discouraging tourists from buying in Nazareth.

THE TOWN OF NAZARETH is believed to have been inhabited from as early as the twelfth century B.C. Seventy years before the birth of Christ it was destroyed by the Romans. Although the Gospel of Luke calls it a city, in Jesus' time it was probably a small and not very significant Jewish town. The Old Testament makes no mention of Nazareth. Not located on a major trade route, the mostly self-sufficient town was bypassed by traders and travelers. It remained a chiefly Jewish town until the fourth century, when the Romans pushed to spread Christianity among the Jews. In 1263 Muslims conquered Nazareth and massacred its Christian population. At the time of the founding of Israel in 1948, Nazareth was populated chiefly by Christian Arabs. Today two-thirds of the population of 70,000 is Muslim, making Nazareth the largest Arab city in Israel. It is a testament to Nazareth's significance in the Christian world that while there are only three mosques, there are seventeen Christian churches and more than eighteen convents and monasteries.

I had come to Nazareth, like many before me, because it was the onetime home of Jesus Christ. Unlike Bethlehem, Nazareth's historical place in the life of Christ is almost certain. One afternoon I spent several hours walking through the old city, beginning at a spot called Mary's Well, into which a spring flowed from the hill above. Of all the historical things to see in Nazareth the well may be the only one that could truly be identified as authentic and located in its original spot. The spring was the only natural source of fresh water in Nazareth, which meant that Jesus and his mother had to come here to collect water.

Near the well was the Church of the Annunciation, also known as Saint Gabriel's. Built in the eighteenth century, the church was a simple structure of camel-colored sandstone, graced with a short, narrow bell tower, more like a chimney than a spire, and capped with a tiny red dome like a cardinal's zuchetto. It was in this spot, some said, that the Angel Gabriel appeared to the Virgin Mary in a grotto to announce that she would bear the son of God. "Hail, thou that art highly favored," Gabriel proclaimed, "the Lord is with thee: blessed art thou among women." Understandably confused and surprised, Mary "cast in her mind what manner of salutation this should be." (I would cast in my mind if an angel arrived and spoke to me about anything at all.) Gabriel announced that Mary would bear a son called Jesus. When Mary asked how this could happen, "seeing I know not a man," the angel said, "The Holy Ghost shall come upon thee, and the power of the Highest shall overshadow thee" (Luke 1:35).

Inside, the Church of the Annunciation was dark and cool. I stepped through the low stone doorway, and when my eyes adjusted to the darkness I realized that I was standing nearly nose to nose with an attendant behind a small wooden counter. Thin and gray-faced, he looked both pained and irritated. On the counter in front of him was a donation box. He frowned so effectively at me that I quickly made a donation. The only other visitor in the church was an elderly man with his face pressed to an icon, straining to see the image through the gloom. As I wandered around, looking at the icons and the mosaics, I could almost smell the attendant's restlessness. He drummed his fingers on the counter, shuffled a stack of pamphlets, opened a drawer and closed it again, looked around the church, looked out the door at the few tourists standing in the courtyard. He walked out from behind his counter, hitched his trousers higher on his waist, held his own hand, turned around and immediately went back to his seat. He laced and unlaced his fingers. He frowned at the stacks of candles he had for sale, plucked at them with both hands, fussily rearranged and neatened them, rested both elbows on the counter and just as quickly lifted them off again. He scraped his gray mustache with his fingers, bounced his knee, and sighed at the ceiling.

A French couple entered the church through the low door and stood on the threshold blinking and staring until their eyes grew accustomed to the gloom. Realizing that the grim-faced attendant was glaring at them, they too were chastened into dropping some money into the box. As soon as the coins hit bottom, the attendant plucked them out, counted them, and tossed them back into the box. I went over and gave the attendant ten sheqels for three candles. Without a word he pointed to a stand where I could light them. I lit them with the flame from another candle already burning there and said a quick prayer. As I headed in to look at the crypt, I saw the attendant hurry over, blow out my candles, and snatch them up for resale.

The walls of the crypt in Saint Gabriel's church were decorated with colorful tile mosaics and intricate geometric patterns of inlaid multicolored marble. The colors on the old tiles were so bright they looked new. Beneath the crypt the main spring that fed Mary's Well could be seen flowing through what looked like a patch of window screen fitted over an opening in a stone wall. The water fell a few inches and gathered in a pool set into the floor. A blue light somewhere behind the wall turned the pool a turquoise blue. Pilgrims had left flowers and coins around the spring. I stared at the clear water, listened to it, imagined Jesus there collecting water in an earthen vessel.

When I came out of the church, a small group of Americans were standing about in the courtyard looking tired and bored. Their plastic nametags indicated that they were here under the auspices of the Jerusalem Center for Biblical Studies. The nametags were printed with the words "I love the Holy Land" and "An experience of a lifetime!"

Farther up the street I stopped at the Moskubiyeh, a stately building made of sandstone blocks that looked recently scrubbed. A spotless new sign in Hebrew, Arabic, and English affixed to the building's face explained that it had been constructed in 1904 to serve the needs of Russian pilgrims. More recently it had been converted to a police station, courthouse, and post office. There were bars over the first-floor windows and shutters on the second-floor windows. Some of the windows were broken, several had bulky air conditioners stuffed into them. As I was looking at the building a young Israeli soldier in jeans came across the courtyard, an automatic rifle slung over her shoulder, and ran up the steps of the courthouse, her long amber curls flouncing behind her. With their youth and natural good looks, and in spite of the guns and olive-green outfits, Israeli soldiers always managed to look stylish. There didn't appear to be any regulations about hairstyles in the military, and, like Catholic schoolgirls who always found ways to tart up their prim uniforms, the Israeli soldiers had a gift for adding personal touches to their outfits — the wraparound sunglasses, the slightly heeled boot, the rock-star T-shirt beneath the unbuttoned army jacket. They looked like the children of some rich Israeli mogul. The women's shirts and the men's trousers were just a touch too tight. Some of the women folded the tops of their trousers over once, revealing just a tiny bit of belly. The men had facial hair in creative designs — Vandykes, long sideburns, goatees. Much has been made of the Israeli propensity to dress down; the pioneering mentality was said to have spawned a habit of classlessness and informality. With his rumpled short-sleeved shirts, his wild hair, and his absent necktie, David Ben-Gurion had been the embodiment of this lack of sartorial fuss. But to me the Israeli soldiers looked like models in a fashion magazine.

I moved on to the old part of Nazareth, where the streets became narrow cobblestone lanes walled by sandstone houses. The lanes had a faintly European flavor. They smelled like laundry detergent, and everything looked clean. Caged canaries sang in windows and on balconies. I passed the nineteenth-century Jarjura house, one of the old Nazareth mansions. Its door stood open, as many doors and gates in Nazareth did. Yet the city seemed strangely empty. The alleys opened onto small squares and pretty courtyards, but there was no one in sight; the whole place had the feel of having been abandoned just moments before I arrived. In one courtyard I saw teacups and plates scattered on a crumb-strewn table and had a strong sense that if I touched the chairs they would still be warm. In front of one house I saw a small easel with an unfinished watercolor on it, but there was no artist in sight. The emptiness did not feel desolate, for there was an undercurrent of energy and life here and a degree of tidy comfort. I had the eerie sense that the people of the old city were hiding behind their doors, holding their breath and watching.

I went down some steps to Writer's House Square, a small, newly cobbled plaza planted with young lemon trees. Writer's House, a handsome three-story building with arched doorways, had been freshly painted in cream and green and orange. Once a residence, it was now Nazareth's arts center. In this sunny, clean square, too, I saw not a single person. In the middle of the square the thick stumps of six or seven new electrical cables stuck up like the fronds of an aloe plant, obviously waiting to be hooked up for Nazareth 2000.

Beside Writer's House stood the residence and offices of the Greek Orthodox bishop; the wrought-iron gate stood halfway open. My Nazareth pamphlet informed me that in the courtyard of the bishopric one could find a "charming old church with beautiful icons." I went through the gate and stood in the bishop's courtyard, which was vernal and pretty, with fruit trees and bougainvillea and birds. It too was empty, and the door of the church was locked. I peered through the church window into a smoky Byzantine darkness and heard footsteps above on the second floor of the building. A few years before I had stayed overnight at the Greek Orthodox monastery of Saint Catherine at the foot of Mount Sinai, and I knew from that experience that the Greek Orthodox priests could be volatile and withering. Emboldened by a desire to see at least one person, I climbed a staircase on the outside of the church and tried the knob of a small wooden door. I thought I heard a voice within, but as soon as my hand touched the doorknob, the voice — if it was a voice — went silent. I slunk away.

I moved on to the Church of the Synagogue, where Jesus was thought to have preached. It was closed too. By standing on a stone and peering through an open window, I could make out a small room with ancient chandeliers hanging from the ceiling, within which small flames flickered behind sleeves of red glass. It had the look of a crypt. Christ was believed to have read from the book of Isaiah, saying, "The spirit of the Lord is upon me, because he hath anointed me to preach the gospel to the poor," a sermon that enraged the people of Nazareth.

In the old city I passed under handsome stone archways, and in some sections the alleys were roofed. Eventually I came to the old market, several narrow alleys lined with small shops. Merchandise hung from awnings, and boxes of wares spilled out onto the pavement. There were a few local shoppers here, stocky, plump-fingered women bundled up in coats and kerchiefs examining plastic water buckets and nylon bras. I saw posters of Israeli movie stars and framed passages from the Qu'ran. There were umbrellas and film and kitchen knives, shoes and underwear. Rather than souvenirs for tourists, the shops offered balloons and flowered dresses, corsets, suitcases, and shoelaces. There were plastic toys imported from China, and among the tin pots and wooden spoons, the mallets and electrical appliances, there were Christmas ornaments and polyethylene Christmas trees and inflatable snowmen. Christmas carols in Arabic with a disco beat drifted through the shop doorways. One shopkeeper had strung two-foot-high inflatable Santas across the lane; they flapped and bobbled in the breeze. They seemed bloated, with wild-looking eyes and a rabbit's prominent incisors.

At the end of the market a lone boy stood dangling a strip of plastic he had set aflame. He watched in delight as the flame leapt and the sizzling plastic sent up curls of black smoke. When I walked by, he widened his eyes and lifted the fiery strip at me in a threatening way and howled, "Ya!" I jumped, pretending to be frightened, and the boy bent at the waist and screeched with laughter, showing me a mouth recently shed of several deciduous teeth. "Malish, malish," he said — don't worry. Nearby a tiny blue-eyed kitten mewled and staggered in a doorway.

All over the city I saw signs of preparation, felt the great sense of housecleaning aimed to please long-awaited guests. But there were no guests here. The preparation was like an urgent voice blaring through a megaphone with no one listening. It was a week before the biggest Christmas in a thousand years, but the streets of Nazareth were virtually empty. And there were few indications that many tourists would be coming soon. In recent weeks there had been so many dire predictions of terrorist activity targeted at millennium events that potential visitors had been scared off. The day before, the *International Herald Tribune* had warned that Osama bin Laden's group was planning attacks on large gatherings and celebrations scheduled to take place at Christmas and New Year. Jerusalem, Bethlehem, and the pyramids at Giza were believed to be the most likely targets. Under the circumstances, Nazareth had the sad feeling of a child's lemonade stand with no customers.

THE LARGEST STRUCTURE in Nazareth was the modern Basilica of the Annunciation. Its pyramidal dome could be seen from almost any point in the city. Built in the 1960s over Nazareth's second supposed spot of the Annunciation, it was the largest church in the entire Middle East. Like so many churches, mosques, and synagogues in Israel, the basilica harbored the ruins of other ancient churches beneath it. The first church on the spot was built in the year 365 by Helena, mother of the emperor Constantine, and was believed to be the first place in Galilee where Christianity was practiced. The new basilica was a cavernous modernist construction with beams of poured cement and abstract stained glass windows that looked like scrambled bits of shattered glass pieced haphazardly together. The structure consisted of two churches, one directly above the other. The lower church was built on the same level as the grotto of the Annunciation and the remains of Byzantine and Crusader churches. As big as a battleship, glossy and expensive looking, the basilica was a great feat of planning and pride and might, but it felt not the least bit holy to me. Lavish cathedrals never did; all I could think of was the money and the contractors and the competition and the ostentation. It didn't surprise me that most of the holy water fonts here were empty.

In the garden, tall palm trees flickered in the afternoon sunlight. There were flowering bushes and slender cypress trees and a bluish cedar with a pungent fragrance that filled the courtyard with the smell of Christmas. A piece of sculpture in the garden bore a plaque that read: TO JESUS'S MOTHER FROM JANUA DEI TRADING, NAMIBIA — FOR CONCILIATION, HARMONY, AND PEACE IN AUSTRAL AFRICA. ADMCMLXXXX. As I was straining to decipher the Roman numerals, two Franciscan monks in brown habits came hurrying through the garden. Loosely lashed around their waists, their rope belts were like lengths of cotton dock line. From the belts dangled their rosary beads, each one the size of a Milk Dud. The priests walked so quickly that as they passed behind me I felt a little turbulence in the air, faintly caught the smell of cologne, and heard the important rattle and click of the beads against their legs. With authority over most of the Catholic sites in the Holy Land, the Franciscans were everywhere.

On the far side of the garden was Saint Joseph's Chapel, a small, simple church annexed to the basilica. Dense bands of yellow afternoon light streamed horizontally into the church through the western windows. I sat in a pew with my back to the sunlight. The church was peaceful and quiet, warm with sunlight, and empty but for two young men sitting in the front pew. I always found it a little easier to think about God and Christ in simple surroundings.

As I was making some notes in my notebook, one of the men got up from the pew and crouched on his haunches in front of a wooden statue of the Blessed Virgin at the front of the sanctuary. I raised myself up in my pew to see him. In each hand he held a lit candle, and as he prayed he raised the candles up over his head before the statue. It was an unorthodox gesture in a Catholic church, and it was strange to see it coming from a young man. He had a long nose and long, tangled blond hair and was dressed in the casual Indian homespun that Western visitors often adopt when they travel to India — flowing white drawstring trousers, a long cotton shirt with a Nehru collar, and sandals. When he finished praying, his dark-haired friend stood up and hung a set of wooden beads around his neck. Both of them knelt and kissed the floor of the sanctuary many times. It wasn't Catholic genuflection; it was Muslim prostration. I looked for signs of giggling or smirking, for some indication that the men were clowning, but they were not. It was all very serious. The blond went to the holy water font by the door, dunked his rosary beads in it, rolled the wet beads quickly between the palms of his hands like a gambler with a set of hot dice, and bowed some more to Mary. It was the strangest form of worship I had ever seen in a Catholic church, yet it looked completely heartfelt and was enacted smoothly and without self-consciousness, as though this were the standard form of Mariolatry.

ON MY WAY back into the basilica to attend the evening Mass, I met a group of wimpled Lebanese nuns who were laughing and chatting in

French as they came through the door. I followed them downstairs to the dramatically beautiful lower church. The foundation and some of the walls of the lower church were those of the Crusader church, and the ancient stones and arches glowed yellow in the soft light, which seemed to have its source behind the stones. In the center of the ceiling an oculus opened to the upper church and looked directly up to the dome high above.

The altar had been placed at the center of the archaeological pit, slightly below the congregation sitting in chairs that ringed it. We looked down at the priest, as at an actor in a theater in the round. We seemed to be sitting in a pretty Roman ruin at the center of the earth. In front of the altar I could make out the words *verbum caro hic factum est*. Here the word was made flesh.

ALL OVER THE WORLD people feel a great need to say "it happened here," but that is particularly true in Israel. Across the country one could find the precise locations of biblical events. In the Church of the Holy Sepulcher in Jerusalem I had seen the precise spot where Jesus was stripped of his garments, the spot where he was nailed to the cross, the spot where he was crucified. All of these holy sites were crammed into dark little rooms and corners and caves. Sometimes, as with the Annunciation, a single event had two precise spots. Just a few miles up the road from Nazareth was Cana, where Jesus was said to have performed his first miracle, the transformation of water into wine. I had walked to Cana (in Hebrew, Kafr Kanna) the day before. The Roman Catholic church and the Greek Orthodox church there were both said to be built upon the site of this first miracle. But it was not enough to say that the miracle happened somewhere under one of these churches. In the Catholic church a hollowed rock was said to be the *exact* spot of the transformation. Since the two churches were close enough together that you could hurl a wineglass from one to the other, it didn't really seem to matter which spot was authentic. In fact, it didn't seem to matter whether the town itself was authentic (there was further disagreement over whether this miracle occurred in Kafr Kanna or in Khirbet Qana, another town in Galilee), yet people cared deeply about these questions. Mark Twain, who journeyed through the Holy Land on the back of a donkey, captured the phenomenon in his travelogue *Innocents Abroad:*

It is infinitely more satisfactory to look at a grotto where people have faithfully believed for centuries that the virgin once lived than to have to imagine a dwelling place for her somewhere, anywhere, nowhere, loose and at large all over this town of Nazareth. There is too large a scope of country. The imagination cannot work . . . The old monks are wise. They know how to drive a stake through a pleasant tradition that will hold it to its place forever.

The specificity of these places — which no human being could verify with certainty — was geared to boost belief, to make the events less vague and more real, and perhaps to bring in a little cash as well. In Jerusalem, every spot in which anything of significance had happened was commemorated with a church or a mosque or a synagogue. These buildings were matched with famous events in a way that satisfied the human need for a palpable historical reality, a reality that could serve as a foundation for one's existence. It seemed to me that pilgrimage was an effort to see and touch things that were part of a story that had lodged in the mind, a story that explained the purpose of life. If you could go someplace and touch one of those things, you could be part of the story. If you could see the spot where Mary died or Muhammad ascended into heaven, you could get a little closer to them. Touching these stones and thinking about these religious figures, you could believe that they might in turn be thinking of you.

THE MASS at the basilica was said in Arabic. I heard the word *mumkin* a lot (it is possible) and *shukran* a few times (thanks), and now and then numbers — *wahid* and *itneen* and *teletta* — and of course *Allah* again and again. Beyond that I couldn't follow the words at all, and I was only now and then able to make out where we were in the service by the priest's motions and gestures — the raised hands, the reading from the Scripture, the breast-striking *mea culpa*. These were always the same in any country, which I found reassuring. The congregation was sparse; I counted thirty-three women and four men. Most of the women were nuns, but there were also a few elderly Nazarene widows, tiny but very strong-looking, with the handsome, chiseled brown faces of Navajo Indians and the unshakable air of people who attend Mass daily. They wore gold rings on their fingers and black dresses, and their thick, steel-gray hair showed beneath the black shawls hooding their heads. The few younger women looked distinctly doleful and somehow more pious than the nuns. The two nuns on either side of me sang the plaintive Arabic hymns off-key, which made the beautiful songs sound even sadder. The nuns were all short and olive-skinned, with heavy, dark brows. I was an anomaly, yet no one looked curiously at me. In fact, nobody seemed to notice me at all, which pleased me. And then I remembered that the people of Nazareth were used to sharing their Mass with every class and form of foreign visitor imaginable. Some of the older women had probably seen Pope Paul VI when he visited Nazareth in the 1960s.

The priest sang wholeheartedly, like a sea captain enlivened by a pint of rum, and above the voices of the women, his was dominant and clear.

I looked around this place where Gabriel appeared to Mary — the *other* place where Gabriel appeared to Mary. Nobody really knew where it happened, what actually happened, or whether it happened at all. It interested me that, as Twain pointed out, big holy events often took place in grottoes. In Bethlehem the spot where Jesus was said to have been born was an underground pit; in Cairo the spot where Mary and Jesus were said to have hidden from harm was a dank little hole beneath the church of Saint George. Much later Mary herself began appearing in lonely grottoes and bushes.

Here the Angel Gabriel had appeared and told Mary that she would miraculously bear a child. The story was imaginable but difficult to believe. At no point in their gospels do Matthew and Mark state that the conception of Christ occurred without sexual intercourse, but their references to the presence of the Holy Ghost, as well as Mary's statement that she was a virgin, suggest that the conception happened miraculously under the aegis of the deity and without human intervention. At the time of the Annunciation Mary was betrothed to Joseph; the engagement would last one year. When Mary became pregnant the couple had not, according to Joseph, consummated their union. Naturally suspecting adultery, a crime which at that time was punishable by death, Joseph mercifully decided merely to divorce Mary, sparing her life. But when the angel appeared again and explained to Joseph what had occurred, Joseph consented to marry her.

Biblical scholars have argued that the Virgin Birth was a fabrication put forth by early Christians to quell the scandalous rumors surrounding Jesus' unorthodox origins. Several early writers proposed that Jesus was the product of an adulterous affair between Mary and a Roman soldier named Pantera. (In 1859 the tombstone of a Roman soldier

276 · THE SINGULAR PILGRIM

named Pantera was discovered in Germany. The soldier was said to have been born near Galilee and to have served under Tiberius.) Some believe that Mary herself concocted the story to spare her family embarrassment. Other believers maintain that Mary, who bore more than six children, remained a virgin for the rest of her life. The Virgin Birth struck me, however, as no more than a theological device for conveying the exceptional and exemplary quality of the relationship between Jesus and God.

Ten minutes into the Mass I looked to my right and realized that the nun beside me was in tears, pressing a hankie to her big black eyes and attempting to sing to Allah through her sobs. Her face crumpled, her lips twitched, her deep voice swerved wildly off-key.

When the Mass was over, I walked down the slope of Annunciation Street toward the town to look for something to eat. The sky had darkened and the dim yellowish streetlights had come on, but the evening air, instead of being colder, seemed warmer and denser than it had earlier in the day. I could feel rain coming. On the steep slope above me a thousand orange lights glimmered in the windows of the little houses, and to the east I saw the lights of my hotel at the top of Nazareth-Illit's big hill. The churches and convents were strung with Christmas lights. Amplified Quranic singing began to drift loudly up the street, echoing against the basilica and the convent beside it. When I reached the square below the basilica I saw a crowd of Muslim men gathering in the parking lot, some already kneeling on prayer mats laid out on the pavement, others plucking mats from a wheelbarrow and spreading them on the ground. The muezzin, dressed in jeans and a leather jacket, stood at an outdoor microphone, his amplifiers affixed to poles above the parking lot. His beautiful voice rang loudly through the streets. There was a mosque here, but it was a makeshift thing like a wedding tent at the edge of the parking lot. The tent was lit with green fluorescent wands (green was Muhammad's favorite color) and the floor was scattered with small carpets. At the peak of the tent was a neon crescent moon in green, and strings of twinkling green lights had been strung among the dripping branches of a eucalyptus tree beside it. The cindery lot was scattered with plastic chairs and a few dented oil barrels.

During a break in his singing the muezzin tested the microphone by cuffing it several times with his breath, a sound that was magnified into a string of deafening thumps. Feedback followed, then several men with big black mustaches ambled over, arms swinging as they walked, and jiggled the electrical wires on the pavement, while still more men and a few boys arrived at the lot from several directions. The muezzin began to sing again in a wailing, sobbing way, and the line of praying men faced Mecca, which from here was more south than east. They held their arms up before them, stirred the air with their hands, dropped to their knees in unison, and touched their foreheads to the ground. Some of the men wore traditional galabeyas and white headcloths, but most were dressed in suits, or jeans and rugby shirts, or leather jackets and loafers.

In Syria, Egypt, and India I had seen Muslim men gathering to pray; like the internationally consistent Catholic Mass, the Islamic form was the same everywhere. I had grown accustomed to it, even fond of it. Christian forms of worship always seemed a bit pale in comparison. Muslims bowed and prostrated themselves on the ground, and their leader cried out in the most expressive way. The prayers were amplified throughout the town and the faithful came running. The singing was spellbinding. If the singer was talented, he could make the hair rise on the back of your neck. This Nazarene singer was superb, his voice rich and full of emotion. He would sing a wailing, wavering phrase and then stop short for dramatic effect, a long pause that seemed to say, *Put that in your pipe and smoke it.*

As I stood listening in the shade of a little concrete shed, I knew that these men with their tent and their prayers were defying the Israeli government.

Two years before, as part of its preparation for the expected flood of Christian pilgrims, the Israeli government had announced its intention to convert this empty square into a plaza where pilgrims could congregate. A segment of Nazareth's Muslim population protested on the grounds that the land belonged to the Islamic Trust, citing as proof of ownership the tomb of Shihab al-Din, which is situated on the square. (Shihab al-Din was the nephew of Salah al-Din, the twelfth-century Muslim warrior who recaptured Jerusalem from the Crusaders.) The Muslim group, a fundamentalist faction intent on spreading the Islamic movement, then announced their own plan to build an enormous mosque on the lot. Christians perceived the plan as an affront and claimed that the new mosque, to be located a mere ten yards from the basilica, would block the approach to the basilica and drown out Christian services with its amplified calls to prayer. Tensions escalated, and on Easter Sunday of 1997 twenty-seven people were injured in a violent clash between the two communities. An Israeli court ruled that the Islamic Trust had no right of ownership to the land but compromised by granting the Muslims permission to build a smaller mosque on part of the lot. Christians accused the government of pandering to the Muslim community, which held greater electoral power, and of submitting to the Islamic fundamentalists.

In general, Christian populations scattered throughout Israel were declining, and with the decline had come a perceived need to maintain the autonomy and presence of the country's many Christian sites. Against the precedent that the government's decision would set, an international outcry ensued among Christian groups. The Vatican threatened to cancel the pope's projected visit to Nazareth, and three weeks before I arrived in Israel Christian leaders throughout the state had closed the doors of their churches in a two-day protest. (In an odd twist Crown Prince Abdullah of Saudi Arabia had tried to resolve the conflict by offering to pay outright for the construction of the mosque if the Muslim group would agree to build it elsewhere; his offer was flatly refused.)

In return for the government's permission to build a small mosque the Muslim group had agreed to stay out of the square until building plans were agreed upon and permits granted. But their success had made them bold. Instead of honoring their promise, they erected a large tent on the lot to serve as a temporary mosque and to establish squatter's rights. Under government pressure that tent had been taken down once. Now it was up again, and the government had issued a stern warning that it must be removed that very day.

It was nearly six in the evening, prayers were proceeding, and there was no indication that the tent would be coming down any time soon. I had heard a rumor that a leaflet full of anti-Catholic slogans was circulating in Nazareth. The leaflet, published by the fundamentalists, threatened the life of the pope if he dared come to Nazareth and warned Christians that if the pope did appear, "We will burn down your homes with our own hands." The leaflet claimed that everything in the Holy Land was in truth the property of Islam, that the Basilica of the Annunciation would itself be turned into a mosque, and that Christianity would eventually "disappear and Islam would take its place." The leaders of the mosque movement had disowned the leaflet.

Ramzi Hakeem, the city's spokesman, referred to Nazareth as the political, social, economic, and cultural capital of the Arab Palestinian minority in Israel and claimed that for years the Israeli government had been intent on destroying the city.

THE DISPUTE over the Nazareth mosque was representative of the struggles for power taking place at holy sites all over Israel, a tiny country whose long history held significance for many different faiths and factions. Just a few days before, Israeli officials had announced that they would intervene in a dispute over the building of a new door to the Church of the Holy Sepulcher in Jerusalem. The famous church had only one door; with the expected crush of pilgrims in the coming year, that posed a problem. Everyone agreed that a second door should be built, but no one could agree on where it should be and who should hold the key to it. Six Christian denominations — Orthodox, Catholic, Armenian, Syrian Orthodox, Coptic, and Ethiopian — shared control of the church, which was a ghettoized arrangement of relics and famed holy spots. Each segment was jealously superintended by one of the denominations, which had been bickering for centuries over petty points of operation. Because the human desire for power far surpasses the desire for equality, struggles over these holy sites had become a way of life. The same conflicts — over money and politics, suspicion and envy, image and myth, mistrust and religious competition — had been boiling for more than twenty centuries.

MEN AND BOYS came from all directions, some climbing out of cars, some on bicycles. I stood thirty feet away against a small cement building between Annunciation Street and Paulus VI Street, watching and listening. After a minute or so I realized that a man was standing at my side breathing noisily through his nose. "Is mosque," he said softly, probing his big teeth with a wooden toothpick. In his other hand he held a sweating gallon jug of milk by its plastic handle. He had sad eyes and short, thick arms and one gold tooth like a bum kernel on a fine ear of yellow corn. "You like mosque?"

"Yes, I do. But why are these men praying outside?"

"Soon is mosque building." He had big ears that stuck out from his head. "Christian lady?"

"No."

"Jew lady?"

280 · THE SINGULAR PILGRIM

"No."

He scratched loudly at the black bristles on his chin, thinking. He was a fleshy man with axle grease under his fingernails and a dense black mustache. He stared, hitched at his crotch, swatted a fly that was circling his head. He looked perplexed, as though he had expected to be rebuffed, and because that hadn't happened he was at a loss for what to say now. "This land belong to Muslim," he said.

"The Christians seem unhappy about that."

He shrugged. "Christian makes fight." He threw down his tooth-pick. He wasn't interested in this topic. The other men were running to bow down to God, but he was more interested in chatting with me. His black eyes peered hungrily. He leaned against the building. "You are make friend with me?"

"Okay," I said.

He flinched at this unexpected response. The men on the mats bobbed up and down, kowtowing and salaaming, their backs illuminated by a floodlight on the wall behind them. Just above, on the hill, the outdoor lights of the basilica had been switched on and the enormous, glowing structure loomed like a citadel. Its many tiny windows gave it the look of a prison. The sky was black and velvety above it. "You have some friend here?"

It seemed unwise to reveal that I didn't know a soul in Nazareth. "Yes."

"Boyfriends?" he said.

"Yes, boyfriends," I said and added, "Two," for good measure.

He blinked with an owl's slow deliberation. "Where they are?"

"They are a hundred meters from here."

The precision of my own answer surprised me; it was so ridiculous it almost sounded true.

"Your boyfriends are very close with you?"

"So many questions!" I said. "Are you the police?"

This made the man nervous. He looked over his shoulder and raised a hand in a way that seemed to say, *For god's sake do not involve me in any way with the police.* "Not police! It is Muslim religion. You is not understand. That's why I offer you."

"Offer me what?"

He thought some more, cradling the gallon of milk in his arms as if it were an infant. "Marry."

"You want to marry me? You hardly know me."

"But when you know me then you would be satisfied I am good man. Where you will going after Nazareth? If possible I can go with you. Please, madam, don't broke heart. What I can do for you?"

"Thanks, but you don't have to do anything for me."

Suddenly he smashed the palm of his hand into the brown shell of his right ear. "What you think about me?" he said, squinting at his palm for the remains of the fly.

"I think you are very unusual."

"Unusual means?"

"Funny." The cars on Paulus VI Street kicked up dancing screws of dust from the pavement. I realized this could go on all night. "I really should be going," I said.

"Why, please? I giving you respect. I love with you."

At the curb below us four Muslim men were removing a small velvet-covered casket from the trunk of a car. The muezzin cried out with all his heart. In the basilica the congregation had been all women; here it was all men. Though I was utterly alone and three thousand miles from home, with nothing to do but wander around Nazareth gawking and making notes, I said, "You're very nice, but I'm so busy, and I already have too many friends."

He cried, "Make me one friend more!" and clutched at the front of his purple silk shirt, like a man having a heart attack. "When you see my power then you understand," he said.

"What is your power?"

"Come to my house then you can see my best power. I show you. Then we drink tea."

The man's smile was an expression of suffering. I saw that he was harmless and very lonely. He was nearly as nosy as I was, but his tone was more pleading than curious. If I had been a Muslim woman he wouldn't have tried this. But in the Middle East Western women were perceived as sex-crazed and loose. We had no morals and no real God, and we would do anything with a strange man. I thanked him, told him I had just had some tea, and with an apology and a quick goodbye I left him there.

PAULUS VI STREET, Nazareth's main street, was bright with shops, but it looked less dandied up than the rest of the city. The aging street-lights stood slightly aslant on the median strip, the shopfronts were plastered with torn advertisements and movie posters, dusty cars were parked willy-nilly against the curb, sometimes three deep. There were many sweet shops here, and the smells of Arab coffee, fish, smoking charcoal, frying oil, and *shisha,* the pleasantly fruit-scented tobacco that Arab men smoked through a hookah.

I went into a restaurant to eat some felafel and noticed that the two men who had been praying that day in Saint Joseph's Chapel were sitting by the window. At the table next to mine an Israeli man and two Germans in business suits were sharing a meal. It seemed clear from their conversation — the polite questions, the many silent gaps, the way they wiped their mouths repeatedly with their napkins — that the three were not well acquainted. I ate my felafel and tried not to listen to them, but it was impossible.

"You have flextime?"

"We don't have flextime."

"You do your job. You have so many hours to do it in. You have a deadline."

"In the States they don't have flextime."

"In Germany we get thirty-one days right from the start."

"What's the outlook retirement-wise?"

They worked their utensils, sipped their water, and seemed bored. I looked out the window at the little cars going by on Paulus VI Street. In 1964 Pope Paul VI, the first pope to leave Italy in over 150 years and the first ever to travel by air, had made a pilgrimage to the Holy Land. He spent two hours in Nazareth, longer than he stayed in any other place, and said Mass in the Church of the Annunciation. As a result this mostly Muslim town was stuck with a main street named for a pope.

The two men in Indian clothing stood up and approached my table. They looked sunburned and a bit unwashed. The blond one said, "Excuse me, please. Can I ask you something?" He had a German accent.

"Yes."

"Can I give you a present?"

He fished in the pocket of his baggy pants, drew something out, and placed it on the table near my plate. I held it up to the light. It was a little oval medal depicting the Blessed Virgin with her veil and halo. Mary's face, no bigger than a pinhead, was ill defined, a little bump of plastic alloy. A string of tiny letters curved around the edge of the medal: *Regina sine labe originali concepta.*

"Oh," I said. "Thanks."

"I hope you like it," said the man.

"I do."

"She needs our prayers," the other man said, and for a shocked moment I thought he was referring to me, but it was the Blessed Virgin he meant. "For the violence," he explained, waving his hand at the quiet street on the other side of the window.

I didn't know then that earlier that day Muslim fundamentalists had thrown stones at a group of pilgrims going into the Church of Saint Joseph and that a priest had been spat on.

The two men bowed to me with Japanese formality, said, "For peace," and went out of the restaurant.

I put the Mary medal in my jacket pocket, along with the seven mother-of-pearl crosses and the sixteen Christological lapel-pin fish that one of the souvenir vendors in the old market had shamed me into buying. Tourists never bought from them, they said, but I had collected more religious objects in one day in Nazareth than I had in my entire life.

THE FOLLOWING DAY was crisp and clear. Under the deep blue bowl of the sky I walked for hours in the hills around Nazareth. I walked up the Mount of the Precipice, a bare and undeveloped hill that was all scrubby shrubs and rocks and lone cypress trees poking at the sky like telephone poles, and tufts of scorched brown grass that had, in the bright sunlight, a pretty desert glow. I could smell anise and cedar. I saw kestrels and crows and desert larks that lifted crazily up from the ground in corkscrew patterns and flew in a frantic, struggling way. Below the mountain was the flat plain of Esdraelon, a patchwork of brown and green and beige fields. There were shimmering plantations of what looked like olive trees and little white settlements in the distance. I saw a brownish fox with a thick tail slinking among the tumbleweeds. I could hear the call to prayer echoing off the hills.

When Jesus returned to Nazareth and preached in the synagogue after his forty days in the wilderness, the Nazarenes were astonished at his commanding oratory and his erudition, and they became suspicious, asking, "Is not this the carpenter's son? Is not his mother called Mary?" Jesus read to them from the prophet Isaiah: "The Spirit of the Lord is upon me, because he hath anointed me to preach the gospel to the poor; he hath sent me to heal the broken-hearted" (Luke 4:18). As Jesus preached, the doubting congregation became increasingly enraged "and rose up, and thrust him out of the city, and led him unto the brow of the hill whereon their city was built, that they might cast him down headlong."

This was said to be that hill. The Nazarenes had brought Jesus here so that they could kill him for his arrogance and his presumption. Aside from the doubtful childhood works recorded in the Apocryphal Gospels, Jesus had performed no miracles in Nazareth because of the unbelief of the people. His own family didn't believe his Messianic claims and thought he had gone mad. The Mount of the Precipice does have an abrupt dropoff that would be suitable for swiftly getting rid of unwanted objects. But in his dignified way, Jesus had escaped that fate. He had said something characteristically cool like, "Unhand me," and made his way through the crowd, saved by his own certainty. Some stories said that he leapt off the cliff and an instant later appeared on the hill not far from the crowd.

Walking here I had a greater sense of Christ than I had had in the town. The gap of centuries that separates us from him and gives him that slightly mythological aura was telescoped here. It was easier to see him as a person actually hiking up the cypress-dotted hill that most of Nazareth was perched on, out of breath and stopping to fix his sandal strap. A hill was a hill; its rocks and outcroppings had not changed for eons, and if Christ did come here, his gaze might have landed on the same boulder I was looking at, the same stones, the same dry marl. The earth under his feet might have made the same dull crunching it was making under mine.

I tried to picture Jesus. Who knew what he looked like? In some pictures he was curly-haired and Semitic-looking; in others he looked almost Nordic, with long straight hair; in still others he was Aryan or even Ethiopian. It depended on who was imagining him. If the shroud of Turin was what it claimed to be, then he was long-faced and thin, with a wide forehead. Over the years I had heard Jesus defined as a Syrian carpenter, a Palestinian peasant, an illegitimate Jew. (In Ireland he was covertly Irish.) Whatever the case, he was never short and fat with broken teeth and a bulbous nose. He was never ugly. Why Christ should not be ugly was significant only in that it revealed the universal vanity and prejudice of the human mind. A savior worthy of us couldn't possibly have been homely.

What, I wondered, had Jesus done in his years in Nazareth? Carpentry, they said. If that was true, where did he get the time to do all the learning that so enraged his neighbors? I had always pictured Jesus as brooding and moody and slightly irritable, a temperament that seemed understandable. Knowing his fate, he willingly, obediently fullfilled it. The house he lived in with his family was probably crowded; he had four brothers and an indeterminate number of sisters, though at least two. I had difficulty seeing him sitting at a table eating a meal with great relish. It was hard to see him cracking jokes or blowing his nose or worrying about his looks. Did he daydream? Did he slap his sister on the head the way my brother had slapped me? Did he juggle three lemons in the air or walk along the top of a stone wall? Why was it nearly impossible to picture Jesus running? It was doubly impossible to imagine him laughing. I didn't agree with the Solomonic view that "the heart of the wise is in the house of mourning; but the heart of fools is in the house of mirth" (Ecclesiastes 7:4). Humor seemed to me the height of wisdom, and it disappointed me that there was so little record of Christ's humor. All his life, from his infancy, when Herod tried to murder him, to his death, ordered by Pontius Pilate, at thirty-three, he was persecuted. He was odd, unwelcome, and beset. Perhaps that was why he came across as humorless.

Away from the precipice, I came upon a beautiful little church and realized that it was the place known as the Tremore. When the Nazarenes dragged Jesus up this hill with the intention of hurling him to his death, Mary had pursued them, desperately trying to save her son. Unable to keep up with the crowd, exhausted, and overwhelmed with fear, she collapsed. This church, possibly built by the Crusaders and called Our Lady of the Trembling, was said to be built upon the spot where Mary had fallen. The church, standing alone in the middle of a field, was very small, the size of a one-car garage. It was made of sandstone bricks and had a fine stone porch with a bridged staircase and a vaulted ceiling. It had arched lancet windows, and in its front wall was a small opening in the shape of a cross. The whole thing was so pretty that its miniature scale was almost touching. But it was abandoned and in disrepair; the door was missing, the pillars and porch were beginning to crumble, the floor was littered with rubble, the inside walls were black, as though they had been burnt, and covered with graffitti. One of the delicate arched windows had been systematically removed from the wall, leaving a jagged hole in the brick. It made me sad to see such a beautiful place, built in honor of a moving example of motherly love, left to ruin.

ON THE WALK back to my hotel at the end of the day, I was tired and decided to shorten my journey by leaving the road, which cut back and forth endlessly up the hill, and going straight up through the scrub. I scrabbled up an embankment, but it quickly grew steep — so steep that within minutes I was nearly on my hands and knees clawing my way up. My feet began to slip out from under me, and I had to grab at little shrubs of rosemary and cedar. I panted and cursed and flailed, and then suddenly, from behind a small bush above me a man's voice said, "You are lost?" Startled, I looked up and saw two black eyes, a mustache, and a rag wound around a handsome head. The man was sitting beside a hobbled goat. How had he known to speak English to me? I said, "No, thanks. I'm fine," and scrabbled on, panting, knocking an avalanche of dirt and stones down the mountain behind me, straining and reaching for dear life.

Finally I made it to the top of the hill and went up the street that led to Nazareth-Illit. Outside a little string of shops I saw another set of inflatable plastic Santas hanging upside down. I stared at one of the faces. It was the same fat-faced, wild-eyed Santa I had seen in the old market, with the long buck teeth of the Easter Bunny — a weird conflation of the Nativity and the Resurrection. Nothing could have been more evocative of the distance we had come from the first Christmas to this one, two thousand years later.

THE YOUNG TAXI DRIVER who drove me from Nazareth to Tiberias wore tight jeans, an impeccably pressed silk shirt, one gold chain around his throat, and two around his wrist. His taxi, like many in Israel, was a brand-new Mercedes. He opened the trunk, eyed my luggage (which was covered with Indian soot), laid a spotless white sheet across the floor of the trunk, spread a layer of newspapers on top of that, and reluctantly lowered my luggage in. He dusted his hands off, studied them, dusted them again, and got behind the wheel. Inside, the car smelled like coconut air freshener.

We sailed down the slope from Nazareth and off toward the Sea of Galilee, passing through a residential area where black-haired, olive-skinned children were making their way home from school. The children, dressed in jeans, blue pullovers, and white shirts, shouted and ran and swung sticks at telephone poles and dragged their bookbags after them like schoolchildren everywhere.

All the way to Tiberias my driver shouted nervously into a cell phone. The phone was attached to the dashboard, forcing him to lean forward over the steering wheel to get close enough to it. He pressed down hard on the accelerator, hugged the steering wheel, and for fifteen minutes straight he heckled the little telephone with Arabic numbers and questions. "Arba we nuss? Kem? Fein? Bokra? Chamsa. Aiwa. Aiwa. Boi-boi." When he wasn't talking he was sighing and drumming his fingertips on the steering wheel, as if he had seen this sweeping countryside with its meadows and hills one too many times. He yanked the mirror toward him so that he could inspect his hair, then wrestled it back into place. He fiddled with the radio dial, never settling on one station. He drove inattentively and too fast, veering once or twice onto the soft shoulder as he daydreamed. The driver had very little English, and I had even less Arabic. That was probably a blessing. Conversation would surely have distracted him further. I was thankful that the trip to Tiberias was short.

The drop from Nazareth to the Sea of Galilee was marked, and at one point in the journey the whole of the sea and its surrounding red hills were suddenly visible below us. The Sea of Galilee wasn't a sea at all; it was a small desert lake. From here it looked beautiful, and I was so delighted to see it that I forgave it for being so small.

I had reserved a room at a small hotel on the western edge of the lake, a mile north of Tiberias. The hotel — two small stone buildings and a third that housed a chapel — was strange and lovely, and it sat in one of the prettiest spots I had seen in Israel. My driver pulled up to the gate, requested dollars instead of sheqels, and seemed very pleased to be ridding his beautiful trunk of my dusty luggage. As he pulled out of the driveway, his tires squealed and kicked up pebbles.

The hotel lobby smelled of popcorn. As soon as I walked through the door, the young man behind the desk said, "Mahoney?"

"Yes."

"Yes," he said rather sternly, "we have been waiting."

Though he was not complaining, his cheerless tone made it sound distinctly as though he had been standing behind his desk for a very long time waiting for me alone to show up. He leaned over the counter, watching closely as I filled out the registration form. He was handsome, with a pale, round face and very short black hair. His eyes looked puffy, as though he had just woken up from a nap, but a chipped front tooth gave him a youthful, rugged appeal. "From States?" he said. His clean-shaven face was awfully close to mine. I could almost hear his eyelids as they blinked.

"Yes."

"Which state?"

"Rhode Island."

He squinted. His skin looked slightly damp. Rhode Island rang no bells. "What's it?"

I told him that Rhode Island was a state in New England.

"Near New York?"

"Yes."

"Big state?"

"Very little state. The littlest in the whole country."

He frowned, not impressed. He was interested in New York, Texas, the famous ones. "I was in States before," he said. "San Francisco, California, I was in. Las Vegas. Big states. I wanna go living in New York. I went there for one night. It was great. How much they pay for apartment in New York?"

I told him, and he jumped as though he'd been hit by a rock. "Wow! Expensive!"

For the next five minutes he questioned me about where and how he could live in New York, what the hourly wage was, what a car cost, what insurance cost, how many hours people worked. He was a very serious young man with an air of almost Baltic gloom. His lugubrious, dark expression never changed, yet there was an intimate directness in the way he spoke, a kind of bluntness. His eyes, his whole body, were alert. I asked him what kind of work he was interested in. "Anything!" he cried. "What's your job?"

I told him.

"What is writer?"

When I explained, he knew right away he didn't want to be a writer, but anything else would do. He had heard that Cape Cod and Martha's Vineyard were good places to work. He liked the idea of South Carolina. He knew someone there. He sighed and fiddled with the credit card imprinter on his desk. He looked beset. "I wanna leave here."

"Why?"

He frowned through the louvered window at a rosy finch in a bougainvillea bush heavy with purple blossoms. "Here is no good."

He was bored. There was no money. He was from Nazareth, but who wanted to go back there? I pictured him arriving in New York with all his fond high hopes and ending up in Astoria in a fifth-floor walkup with a view of pigeons in a sooty air shaft and a job screening luggage at Kennedy Airport.

A nervous-looking girl wearing a headscarf pulled low on her brow hurried through the sitting room with a mop in her hand. I told the young man that I had just come from Nazareth.

"Aha!" he said.

"What?"

"The problems!"

The telephone on the counter rang. He answered it in Arabic, said three glum words, and hung up. "Muslims and Christians problems. The Muslims making that mosque next to the church. 'Hey, this is land belong to us,' they say. 'Don't touch!' But it don't belong."

"I saw the tent," I said.

"Not only tent! Before now it was a much bigger tent! Covered the whole square. Loud! Now they made it smaller."

"Are you Christian?" I asked.

He looked offended, extending both hands toward me over the counter, palms turned upward in a receiving way. "Christian!" he said impatiently, shoulders raised in disbelief. "Christian! Of course Christian!"

"Isn't the population of Nazareth mostly Muslim?"

"But before it was only twenty percent of Muslims. Eighty percent of Christians. The Christians left because the Muslims always do everything by forcing. Same in Bethlehem. And in Jerusalem too. There is only five thousand Christians living in Jerusalem. And Bethlehem only is fifteen percent Christians."

"Where do the Christians go?"

"States?" he said with a shrug. "Las Vegas? I don't know."

He had told me his name, but I was so distracted by his manner that I had already forgotten it. He was like a gentle but disgruntled uncle. He smelled of soap. When I asked him his name again, he looked surprised and hurt and said, "Johnny! I told you already. Johnny!"

Johnny seemed very smart and he spoke English quite well, and when he missed a word he looked irritated, as though he had been framed. I said I hadn't been expecting such a large Muslim presence in Nazareth, and he squinted impatiently at me and said, "What means *presence.*"

After showing me to my room, he said, glumly but sincerely, "Anything you need, okay, you tell me."

OF ALL THE PLACES in the Holy Land, the Sea of Galilee interested me the most. In my youth, as the religious calendar spun around the months, I went to Mass and heard the stories from the Gospels that were said to have occurred on the sea and in the towns around it, and they stuck in my mind. The Old Testament seemed murky and far away, vague, not quite believable, though it was reputed to be both the word of God *and* a history. But the stories in the Gospels, especially those that took place here, were specific, fantastic, real, imaginable, and wondrous, and when the priest or lector read them out, I listened in spite of my wandering thoughts. If Matthew, Mark, Luke, and John were to be believed, it was during Jesus' three or four years in Capernaum, at the northern end of the lake, that he gained his real fame. He went about the countryside along the lake to Bethsaida, Gergesa, Magdala, Chorazin, and Gennesaret, preaching and working miracles, curing lunatics and lepers, restoring sight to the blind, working exorcisms. In a few years he accomplished a great deal. He preached his longest recorded sermon, the sermon that encapsulated his philosophy of charity, kindness, and peace, above Capernaum at the temple on the mount — *blessed are the meek, let not thy left hand know what thy right hand doeth,* and so forth.

Sailing on the sea, he ordered the unruly wind to stop blowing, and it did. He drove the devil out of a possessed man. He boldly dined with sinners and publicans. He brought a dead girl to life, fed the five thousand with five loaves and two fishes, fed another four thousand with seven loaves and an ear-catching "few little fishes." As a child I was excited that a person had stopped the wind and brought the dead to life and made a mass banquet out of a minnow. He had walked on water, and that certainly made life more interesting.

Drawing back the curtain from the windows in my room I could see that very water not twenty feet away. In Hebrew the lake was called Kinneret, because it was said to be shaped like a harp. It looked very still and strangely lonely, like a campground after the tents have been taken down.

ON THE ROCKY BEACH below the hotel I pumped air into my inflatable dinghy and wondered at the landscape. Surrounded by palms and eucalyptus, rose bushes, oleanders, orange and olive trees, the hotel felt secluded, even though the road that encircled the lake ran close to its door. At 700 feet below sea level, Tiberias was radically warmer than Nazareth, and the air was softer. Though it was the fourth week in December, it felt like midsummer; the balmy air was teeming with insects and birds, and the lake — the main source of water for the state of Israel — was very calm. From the hill on which the hotel was built, a wide spring flowed diffusely, like water spilling over the edge of a bathtub. Little stone weirs had been constructed to catch the water in pools, which were laced with bright green duckweed. The treeless hills and cliffs on the far shore were pink in the afternoon light and vividly reflected in the flat water. It all had the silent, ancient feel of landscapes I had seen in Utah and Nevada.

I saw two bearded fishermen in a rowboat drawing in their nets just offshore, but aside from them and a notable number of cats and kittens skittering over the rocks, the lakeshore was empty. The lake was popular in summer, but in this off-season, the hotel had very few guests. Since it was the last Christmas week of the second millennium, the lack of visitors struck me as odd; again I had to assume that it was fear of violence that was keeping people away. The threat of terrorism in the coming week was difficult for the local people who had hoped for business, but for me the solitude was paradise.

As I pushed the dinghy into the water, a great flock of shocked birds flew out of a tree with a startling chorus of cries. I set off toward Tabgha and Capernaum to the north. I could see the Church of the Primacy of Saint Peter, a small building of black stone at the water's edge marking the place where Jesus multiplied the loaves and fishes. Beyond it was the Mount of the Beatitudes and Capernaum, less than two miles away. I had always thought of the Sea of Galilee as a great body of saltwater with its own horizon. In fact, it was only fourteen miles long and seven wide, with the Jordan River flowing into it from the north and flowing out on the south. In the Gospels Jesus is often said to be going off in a ship from one place to another, which made his trips on the Sea of Galilee sound like long journeys, but this body of water was so small that the distance by boat from any one point to another was negligible. In some cases, if there was no wind to speed the boat, Jesus might even have traveled faster by walking along the shore.

I was happy. Rowing here was easy and there was no one to harass me. I loved being alone on the water. Though a mere eighth of an inch of rubber — or wood or fiberglass — was all that separated me from forty feet of water, being in a boat always made me feel safe. At home I rowed all year round in Narragansett Bay.

At the foot of the Russian monastery to the north of my hotel, two nuns, their heads wrapped in gray cloth, crouched on their haunches, gutting fish. As my boat proceeded up the shore, little compounds appeared here and there among the eucalyptus trees; the low buildings had well-tended gardens and fences or screens of bamboo around them. Some looked like beach resorts, others like religious residences. Despite these buildings, two thousand years did not appear to have altered the face of this place a great deal, except perhaps to unbuild the important towns that had existed here. But for the apartment buildings of Tiberias, there were no high-rise buildings on the lakeshore, and there was very little boat traffic. It looked, for the most part, rural, with beaches and shady trees and the red desert hills and plateaus rising up behind the shore. That it looked empty and unpopular and underpopulated surprised me, especially considering what had happened here. Christians flocked to Rome to catch a glimpse of the holy sights, but Christ had never been in Rome. He had been here and had showed signs of his remarkable nature here. He walked, so they said, on this water. Rome was the seat of the church, yet that church had begun *here*.

It was on the Sea of Galilee, according to John, that the resurrected Jesus appeared to Simon Peter, Thomas, and several others who had spent an unsuccessful night fishing. He instructed them to throw their net over the right side of their boat. When the fishermen did as Jesus told them, the net became so heavy with "one hundred and fifty-three fish" they could hardly draw it in. This was where Jesus told Simon Peter, whom he had chosen as the "rock" upon which he would build his church, "Feed my lambs," and "Feed my sheep." Peter went to Rome, died there, and was perceived as the father of the church, if not the founder of it. But the events that led to the enormous reach of Christianity had taken place here.

Why weren't seaplanes full of pilgrims landing on the lake? Why weren't they thronging the shore and storming the Church of Peter's Primacy, the way they did the Basilica of Saint Peter in Rome? Some months before, I had waited in a long line to go into Saint Peter's, and when I reached the entrance I was turned away by two men in dark suits because my skirt did not cover my knees. Conveniently, a woman nearby was selling sarongs expressly to solve this problem. I bought one and wrapped it around myself, so that I could go in and stare at the two million tons of polished marble that make up what must be the heaviest building in the world. I saw elaborately carved angels there, and saints and opulent tombs and chapels, but none of it had been proposed by Jesus. Saint Peter's basilica and its throngs seemed to underscore the way the church itself, charged with representing Christ, actually overshadowed and obscured him. Christ was history; the church had become the present reality.

In his startling address to Harvard Divinity School's graduating class of 1838, Ralph Waldo Emerson said of Christ and the church, "What a distortion did his doctrine and memory suffer . . . The idioms of his language and the figures of his rhetoric have usurped the place of his truth; and churches are not built on his principles, but on his tropes." That seemed too true and was perhaps why I was not religious. The church habitually got stuck on secondary matters, on doctrine and hierarchy. It tended to kill the nature of God by existing for itself alone. The flow of Catholic pilgrims to Rome rather than to Galilee seemed to me an illustration of the religious preoccupation with form and dogma over content. It was as if Jesus was Lord but Rome was Dad. The marble of the basilica had given me no sense at all of the meaning of God. That church was reminiscent of the dreary, self-important tomb of Francisco Franco. Jesus' wise and soulful thoughts expressed here on the Sea of Galilee were to me the best earthly representation of the meaning of God. He had died in Jerusalem, but he had lived and worked here.

There was no breeze on the lake and no current. When I stopped rowing I stayed in one spot without drifting. The Sea of Galilee was as untroubled as bath water and nearly as warm. The sky was pale blue, the sun was strong, and I could feel the flesh on my nose and shoulders baking. In the heat, the rubber skin of my raft had hardened, like an overinflated balloon. Across the lake to the east I saw the bare red cliffs that dropped down from the high plateau of the Golan Heights. They looked far away, but I knew that it was no more than five or six miles from my hotel to the eastern shore. One of my favorite Gospel stories had taken place below those cliffs, and I decided then that before I left Tiberias, I would row across and sleep on the beach there. Even in this rudimentary boat it was possible to row across the Sea of Galilee.

As I rowed I saw pied and belted kingfishers diving for fish, golden-eye ducks, grebes, cormorants and coots, terns, and laughing gulls cackling like crones. Tiny green flies gathered around the valves of my boat, and the surface of the water was littered with dead bees. The bottle-green water was soft and warm. Near Tabgha I saw two unlikely fishermen standing in a boat, drawing up their nets. One was dressed in nothing but Jockey briefs, with a snorkel and mask; the other wore a suit jacket, dress shirt, and tie. He looked as if he'd been called out from a wedding party to assist.

I thought what a delightful place this was and wondered why Mark Twain, who had been here in the 1860s and compared the lake to Lake Tahoe, had hated it. In *Innocents Abroad* he devotes three pages of blistering criticism to the Sea of Galilee, calling it a "solemn, sailless, tintless lake, reposing within its rim of yellow hills and low, steep banks, and looking just as expressionless and unpoetical as any metropolitan reservoir in Christendom."

Much as I liked Mark Twain and agreed with much that he wrote, he was wrong about this one. Bugged to near hysteria by the "stupid," poverty-stricken people of "squalid, uncomfortable, and filthy" Magdala (the home of Mary Magdalene), Twain seems to have caught the place on a particularly sun-scorched, flyblown day. His description of an arid, charmless, stinking sinkhole corresponded not at all with what I saw in the Sea of Galilee.

AFTER A LONG, SLOW ROW, I returned to the rocks below my hotel, deflated the boat, and carried it up the little hill. Passing the front of the hotel on my way to my room, I heard a voice very near me say, "Hi." I looked up but saw nobody, then through the dark, hazy screen of the kitchen window I saw Johnny's face looking out. He was cooking something that smelled like fish. I said, "Oh, hi, Johnny," and as I moved on, with the deflated raft flapping on my back and the aluminum oars clanking together, he cried through the screen, "I am not Johnny! I am Geergy!"

I apologized and moved up the hill. I hadn't met Geergy before.

At the side of the hotel was a pretty terrace, with tables and chairs that looked out over the lake and long winding tendrils of purple and red bougainvillea hanging over it. I put my boat away and sat down there. A middle-aged couple had set up a camping stove on the terrace and were busy cooking pasta and drinking a bottle of Israeli wine. At six in the evening the sky was dimming and large bats had begun careering about the palm trees.

THE NEXT MORNING the dining room was empty but for a powerful-looking bald man drinking tea and looking at an Israeli newspaper. The room was very small and graced with enormous arched windows that looked out onto the palm trees, the lake, and the mountains on the far shore. I sat at a table near the door, slightly behind the man. Thoroughly bald heads always looked big and angry to me, like polished objects that might suddenly explode. But this man's head was square and brown and rather handsome. He was fit and muscular in a T-shirt with Hebrew writing on its front. With his bald head, bulky shoulders, and bulging biceps, he looked somehow like a narc or a military operative, which made me nervous. He never looked up from his newspaper.

Sunlight flooded the dining room from the east and glinted off the floor and the silverware and the man's polished-looking scalp. I could hardly see my own hands in the brilliant light. Below us the lake was a sheet of light, and the flat-topped mountains on the other side were blue in the morning haze.

The hotel kitchen was down a short flight of stairs from the dining room. The sound of voices and clanking pans and laughter drifted up the stairs, and then Johnny came up the stairs smiling to himself and chewing a slice of cucumber. I greeted him. His face fell. "No!" he said. "I told you, not Johnny. I am Geergy! Johnny is go to Nazareth today."

I squinted in the sunlight. Geergy looked a great deal like Johnny. He had the same slight build, dark hair, and pale, dampish skin. He had Johnny's cleanliness. I could see he even had Johnny's bold directness and serious way of speaking, but Geergy had an air of innocence that Johnny didn't have, and he was a bit more cheerful.

Geergy came to my table to wait on me, and while I was telling him what I would eat, he sat down across from me and began fiddling with a fork. Like Johnny, he started in with a hundred questions. Where you from? Where you been? Where you going? He listened, open-mouthed and staring, to my answers. When I told him I had been to Syria the year before, he seemed startled, and even the detective turned his head to look at me. Through the dining room window we could see the western edge of Syria, the Golan Heights, ten miles or so across the lake. Geergy, like most Israelis, had never been there — Syria wouldn't let Israelis cross their border.

Geergy leaned back in his chair, holding the fork upright in his fist on the table, and said, "You got business in the Middle East?" He was interested in my Americanness, my age, my solitariness, what I thought about Israel, my religion, and the world in general. He seemed immensely surprised by every small thing I said, but I had the sense that he responded this way to every one of the strangers who passed through this hotel. Never having been farther than Jerusalem, he was full of curiosity and his questions were accompanied by an expression of ingenuous interest.

I asked Geergy if there were crocodiles in the lake, though I was sure there were not. He didn't know what a crocodile was. I drew a picture on the back of my napkin, and he laughed, said no, and lamented that the water level of the lake was very low now because of drought. He told me that in summer the Sea of Galilee was busy with vacationers from all over Israel and that the hotel was always full then. He asked me about India. I told him about the cremations. The very idea of it made Geergy shudder. He said he had read about the city of the dead in Cairo, where people live among tombs, and he asked if it was true that in India people used the street for a toilet. I said that sometimes they did. Geergy was amazed. "Even pee-pee?" "And sometimes worse," I said. Geergy cried with genuine alarm, "Even poop?!"

Geergy's childlike wonder was endearing; even the bald man smirked at his reaction. (Though the bald man did not speak to me, he was clearly listening. It would have been impossible for him not to, for the dining room held only five or six tables, and we were the only people there.)

"A lot of people come here to Kinneret from Las Vegas," Geergy said.

When I said, "Well, it's little like Las Vegas," Geergy seemed very surprised again. I explained that it wasn't like the city of Las Vegas, but that the deserty feel, the hills, the air, the temperature, were all very similar.

Like Johnny, Geergy was from Nazareth. He wore tight jeans and a big gold heart-shaped locket on a chain around his neck. He had the dense, smoothed hair of Liberace. For all his questions and his seriousness, he was — like Johnny — likable and refreshingly direct.

He brought me eggs and vegetables and tea, handling the plates and saucers with exaggerated care, as though they were animate objects that might rear up and peck at his face. The couple with the camping stove — the only other guests in the hotel — came into the dining room speaking Hebrew, but when they ordered breakfast they spoke English. Later I asked Geergy if he spoke Hebrew. He waggled his hand in the air, fingers spread, and said, "Not really. Only Arabic."

TIBERIAS, THE MAIN TOWN on the Sea of Galilee, with a population of 35,000, had the melancholy, slightly depressed feel of any off-season seaside town in Massachusetts. It was gull-ridden and small and backed by high hills crowded with winding streets and tall apartment buildings. The shopping district was two longish streets with connecting lanes and boxy modern commercial structures. I saw Russian women, Hasidic Jews with black hats perched precariously atop their heads, and Orthodox Jews in a kind of uniform of white shirt, cardigan, and yarmulke, with a knotted cotton string dangling from a pocket. The shops that were open offered trinkets, film, postcards, plastic souvenirs, dreidels, beer and wine, books about the life of Christ in six different languages. There were resort hotels and kosher Chinese restaurants, shops full of glistening lake fish, pizza parlors and trattorias, Argentine steakhouses, mini tour buses, and an Avis auto rental office that looked just like an Avis office in Baltimore or Chicago. The voice of Neil

Sedaka drifted out of a shopfront, and CNN News was on the television in an open-front café. Bulletin boards were plastered with advertisements for "Dany's bikes — cheapest bikes in town" and "Gringo Jeep tours of Upper Galilee" and a tour offering a trip to the Golan Heights, where you could "see the view from the Syrian bunker." But there were very few people, and it was all a bit tired and dead-looking. A smattering of bored-looking tourists walked idly up and down the small modern streets staring at the olive-wood carvings of camels and religious figures arrayed in windows. I heard more Hebrew in Tiberias than Arabic, which made sense when I learned that it was one of the four holy cities of Judaism.

I heard a surprising amount of American English here. In a small supermarket where I bought some provisions, I asked a man if he could tell me what the Hebrew writing on a tin can said. He stared at the can a very long time and finally, in a heavy New York accent, answered, "I have no idea." I saw an elderly Hasidic man wandering up and down the aisles eating a bag of popcorn as he walked, and from the furtive way he peered about, it was obvious that he was hoping to empty the bag so he could leave without paying for it. I was fascinated by his black hat, shaped like an Amish farmer's, his huge black shoes, and the curling sidelocks that dangled in front of each ear. When he saw me looking at him he scowled, stuffed the bag behind a stack of cans on a shelf, and hurried away.

Tiberias was founded in A.D. 18 by Herod Antipas, tetrarch of Galilee, the son of Herod the Great. It was Herod Antipas who, at the request of his second wife, Herodias, ordered the beheading of John the Baptist. Jesus, too, posed a threat, and when the Pharisees warned him that Herod Antipas would kill him, Jesus responded dismissively, "Tell that fox, Behold, I cast out devils." The ancient city, some ruins of which still remain, was said to be impressive in scope. In the second century, after the destruction of Jerusalem, the Sanhedrin, the highest Jewish council, moved to Tiberias and the city became the center of Jewish learning. People came from great distances to relax and restore their health at the hot springs. The Jewish scholar Maimonides was buried in Tiberias, as were several other famous rabbis. Now the town had a modern supermarket with Cracker Jack and Captain Crunch and tampons and Tylenol for sale and an American kid in the canned goods aisle crying, "Ma, the baby stuff is over here!"

ALONG THE LAKE in Tiberias was a promenade, like a boardwalk, with restaurants and marinas. Walking there I saw a television crew filming a white-haired Irish priest who was sitting on a rock saying, "You cannot believe in a God who does not show mercy." Near the old cemetery at the edge of the town I came upon a young man lying passed out in the street with a bottle cradled in his arms. Flies were crawling in his ears, and ants had gathered in the puddle of drool beneath his chin. In my entire stay in Israel he was the only intoxicated person I saw.

At an outside table in a little pedestrian area full of restaurants I sat down to eat dinner. The sunlight was fading, the streetlights had come on, and overhead the leaves of a pair of walnut trees rusted. At the eastern end of the plaza I could see the distant hills across the lake; the setting sun had given them the rosy hue of a peach. Music drifted out of restaurant doors, and on a corner nearby a group of teenagers stood chatting and drinking beer. Across the narrow lane was a jewelry shop, one of many in Tiberias, called the Israel Diamond Event. At the next restaurant over, two women were eating dinner, and three tables away from me a man sat alone drinking beer, but other than that there were no other customers and very few people on the street.

A young waiter came to my table, took my order, and handed it in to the chef. And then, like Geergy, he sat down at the table with me. He was blue-eyed and handsome and carefully groomed, wearing a polo shirt and leather jacket, as though he were on his way to a party. He lit a cigarette, leaned back in his chair, and looked up and down the square at all the candles flickering at the empty tables. He stretched and yawned and said anxiously, "Christmas and New Year." The bored way he said it seemed to intensify the lonely emptiness of the town. He was restless, and like everyone else I had met here, very serious. The Israeli seriousness could never be mistaken for impassivity. They were all simmering with opinion; behind the still faces there was always a tiny clamorous noise, like a lid rattling on a boiling pot. After a minute the waiter said to me, "Where are you from?"

I told him, and he nodded and said, "I lived for a few years in Kansas City. Middle of nowhere. But I liked it better than New York. You have to be rich to live in New York. Or crazy. And it's all Jews there."

He was Arab, Christian, and Israeli. He asked me what I had seen in Jerusalem. I told him I had seen most of the holy places there, but every time I went to see the Dome of the Rock and the Temple Mount the gates were closed and the Israeli police with their Uzis said, "Come back tomorrow." Visitors were allowed in only between eight and ten in the morning, but each time I returned at the appointed hour the gates were still closed and the soldiers still said, "Come back tomorrow."

My waiter sneered. "But they let Muslims in."

"Well, it is a mosque," I said. I told him I had been to the Western Wall.

"Nothing but big stones!"

I said I had been to the Church of the Holy Sepulcher.

"Yah. That one is beautiful. But when Israel doesn't exist anymore, when they give all the land and the stones away to Palestine, then I'm going back to the States."

I asked him if he really thought Israel would cease to exist.

"Yeah, this is absolutely sure. They have to give it back. Because it doesn't belong to them. It's not their country. You have to be fair and give back what you took."

He was an Israeli citizen, but the way he said "they" and not "we" fascinated me — it seemed to define the rifts and shifting loyalties of the complex Israeli citizenry.

"Look at all these Russians coming in. They're not Jews. They are criminals!"

He sat back and slung one heel across his knee and blew smoke up at the branches of the tree above us, thinking and tapping his pen on the table like a little drumstick. His tassled loafers were highly polished. His talk, indeed his very presence, was more a performance than an exchange. He did not converse, he deposed. When he sighed, the sigh begged for attention. He leaned forward and pointed his cigarette at me. "I hate the Russians. They didn't bring anything good here in Israel. They only brought corruption and drugs. Scharansky! Ha!"

He laughed with bitter derision and flung his cigarette ash roughly in the direction of the ashtray. It landed on the plastic tablecloth next to my bread plate. "Scharansky is a criminal! He was interviewed on the TV. His face got red. The interviewer said to him, 'You wasn't in jail because you was a Jew, you was in jail because you was a criminal!' Scharansky had no answer. Face red. If you're gonna call someone a hero, let him be a hero, not this Russian piece of shit. He was a criminal was why he was in jail, not because he's a Jew."

A police car crept past the end of the alley.

"In America, if you ask Russians which religion they are, they don't need to say Jewish. But if they come here in Israel, they need to say Jewish, else they can't come. I believe that Russian Jews should be allowed here. Okay. Ten thousand, fifty thousand maybe." He smashed his cigarette into the ashtray, then grabbed the arms of his chair and hiked it toward the table. Excited, he raised his two palms at me like a catcher waiting for a fastball. "Now, just a moment. Do you want me to make a statistic about it? Okay: one million two hundred thousand Jews have come from Russia to Israel." He blinked at me, his mouth hanging open. "Excuse me? One million point two hundred thou Russians who came in here are *Jewish*?" He swept his hand across the tablecloth in a gesture of riddance. "Impossible! There's not that many Jews in Russia. And I don't believe there's any Jews in Ethiopia either. But they come here too. They cry. They say *let us in! We are a Jew.*"

Jews from all over the world had settled in Israel, and their Jewishness had been carefully considered. The Jews of Ethiopia, known as Falashas (strangers), had long practiced an early form of Judaism. It was said that Christian missionaries had tried to con them by insisting that the rest of the world's Jews had converted to Christianity, but the Falashas were steadfast and segregated themselves from non-Jews. Yet when they first began arriving in Israel, they were judged not to be truly Jewish. These seriously law-abiding, God-fearing Jews had to formally convert to Judaism in order to participate in the religious life of the country.

My waiter was quiet for a moment, biting his lip, and then the words welled up and he was all hand gestures and raised voice again, his pen dancing above the table like a maestro's wand. He spoke with bitter conviction. "Most Russians who come here are not Jewish. They only come because they got a better life. But they tell lies."

The waiter talked and talked, and his protestations were a kind of boasting; he believed he was morally right and that the injustices taking place in this country were being done to him personally. Nervous and fidgety, he lit a fresh cigarette angrily. He shoved his hand into his pocket. He yawned loudly — a yawn not of fatigue but of anxiety.

"Israel. My only complaint is Israel is not fair. I like justice for everybody. Like in America. Why you let a bunch of Russians come to Israel because they say they are Jewish without any proof, but you don't let in a Palestinian who was born here and has papers that say that the land here in Galilee belonged to him and was purchased from England in 1947? Why you let these people who have no feeling for Israel? Some of them get off the plane, they don't know where they are. And right over here" — he waved his hand down the alley at the hills across the lake — "we have Palestinians who spent all their life here who got driven out and want to come back and can't come back." He meant the Syrians in the Golan Heights. "It doesn't make any sense."

I agreed that throwing people out of their homes would never work, and I asked if the Israeli government didn't still verify an immigrant's religion.

"They come in with a piece of paper that says *Jew*. Israeli government doesn't ask where this paper come from. In Russia you can get a piece of paper for anything. You want to be a doctor in Russia? You give a hundred dollars . . . snap! They give you a piece of paper that says okay, you are a doctor. You want to be a Jew? Give dollars and you are a Jew."

"I don't believe that."

He lit another cigarette. "Believe that! Please believe that. You can go in Russia and buy which paper you want."

"How do you know that?"

He pressed his palms to his chest. "How I know that? Because my cousin he was there in Russia studying."

The cashier from the diamond shop across the street sat down at the table next to us and settled in for her cigarette break. She spread her possessions on the table in front of her: calculator, pencil, pad of paper, cigarettes, and lighter. Short and buxom, she wore spike heels and pink ankle socks, a tight skirt, and a soft pink angora sweater. She had a pale face and beautiful thick auburn hair cut in a short bob, with dense bangs straight across her eyebrows. She had dark, watchful eyes and an affronted-looking mouth — the look of someone who expected to be dismissed. She lit her cigarette, dropped the lighter onto the table, and began figuring a list of numbers, pecking at the keys of the calculator with very long fingernails. My waiter smiled at me, raised his eyebrows, tossed his eyes in her direction, and whispered that she was Russian.

I nodded. "But that kind of corruption can happen anywhere."

"Not anywhere," he protested. "In Israel it cannot happen. You cannot buy a profession. Not in England. Not in States. Not in France. Of course not." He smiled over at the man drinking beer. "But maybe in Romania you can. Russia and Romania."

The solitary man grinned into his beer mug. Slowly he stood up and brought his beer and cigarette over and sat down in the seat beside me, across from the cashier. They all knew each other. The waiter said, "He is Romanian. He is my friend."

"So you offended him?" I said.

They both laughed. The Romanian's face was soft and loose, and there were dark circles under his basset-hound eyes. He said, "I am Israeli. I was born here. I am Jewish. But my background is Romania."

The waiter ranted on. "In Russia it's shitty. My cousin went to the hospital there. He ate some cheese. It was bad, he was sick. The Russian doctor he put an IV in him, and when he cut it, he made a mistake and cut the needle and the needle went up my cousin's arm. The Israeli doctor who was there stopped the needle. They took the needle out of his bicep. Stupid! They're not doctors in Russia. They only buy their degree. It's all crooked. In Tel Aviv all the prostitutes are all Russians."

The cashier, who had been absorbed in her ciphering, looked up abruptly from her calculator. Her face folded into a grimace and she slumped low in her seat and pointedly looked away from him, thick arms folded high on her chest, as though she was used to his silly nonsense but tired of it. She was sulking. Without using her hands she sucked smoke from the cigarette wedged in one corner of her mouth and released it from the opposite corner in a steady, expert stream.

"That's why the men in Israel don't go chasing women down the street like they do in Egypt," the waiter said. "They have all those Russian women to go to!"

The cashier snapped her head around to look at him. She snatched the cigarette from her mouth. "No!" she cried with dark pleasure. "This is not reason Israeli man don't go chasing women." She paused to smirk at me. "Ha-ha! Lady, want to know real reason? It's real reason is: Israeli man is gay!"

She tipped her head back and let out a shriek of laughter so loud that the two women at the next restaurant looked up from their dinner plates, startled.

The waiter ignored her and leaned toward me over the table. "Now, once I had these two friends? They made a car crash in Russia. They were lying in bed bleeding in the hospital and someone came in and says, 'Why are these men bleeding to death?' and the Russian doctor says, 'Oh, they're going to die anyway, we can't save them.'"

He gave his cigarette a nip and looked at me, waiting for the shocked response he'd grown used to. "Russian pieces of shit!" he said.

The cashier sucked at her teeth and glanced from her ashtray to me with big dark eyes, looking for sympathy, silently nursing this personal injury. Her name was Ludmilla. I asked her if she was Russian. She reared back at the affront. "I am from Ukraine!" she cried. "I am Jewish!"

All over Israel distinctions multiplied. The Romanian and the waiter exchanged words in Hebrew. The Romanian sipped at his beer and lit a new cigarette and said gloomily to me, "In Israel we don't know what belongs to us. It's going to be a disaster here. Eventually we will have to be giving everything away."

"Sometimes," the waiter said, "I wish that they just would give all of Israel away and finish it."

And then he went back to complaining about Scharansky. If you were going to call a a guy a hero, he said, let him be a real hero, a person who died in the Golan fighting for peace. "Scharansky says, 'Golan belongs to us.' Interviewer says, 'But that attitude is why we have no peace. We have to share.'"

I asked the Romanian, who seemed more seasoned and reasonable than the waiter, what he thought about the Golan Heights and the present efforts at peace with Syria. He said happily that if there was peace with Syria, money would come into Israel from America for the relocation of the Israeli settlers who would be displaced by the return of the Golan Heights. For this purpose Israel had asked the United States for thirty billion dollars.

The cashier shook her head and made a tsking sound, as though some of that money rightly belonged to her.

The Romanian said, "They will build buildings in new areas. American Jews will give the money. Everything is based in money. The Jewish doesn't like the Arabs and the Arabs doesn't like the Jewish. Both of us doesn't like each other. And that is what it's talking about: *money*. Whenever the UN defends some country, it's money. They say it's civil rights, but they don't defend the civil rights of countries where there's no money!"

And he went on explaining that the American government had to be supportive of Israel because of the wealthy Jewish lobby in the United States and furthermore because a friendship with Israel provided a foothold for the U.S. in the Middle East.

The waiter said in aid of nothing, "I have also idea that I believe that Jerusalem should be like holy place. Like the Vatican. Nobody tells it what to do. It's separate."

I studied the waiter's face. Israel was his country, and he believed it was a more just nation than Russia or Romania, but he also thought it was built on stolen land, and if it came to an end he would happily go off to America, another country of mixed ethnicities and creeds and — many would argue — stolen land. The status of an Arab Christian in Israel is confusing. They are Israeli, born in Israel, but often their sympathies lie with the Palestinians. Some even consider themselves Palestinian. The waiter, who was Christian, told me that he loved Israel and that his alliance was with the Jews and not with the Palestinians.

"Is your language Hebrew or Arabic?" I asked him.

He said, "Hebrew! Hebrew!" with the same indignation that Arabic-speaking Johnny at my hotel had said, "I am Christian! Christian!"

I said, "I hear a lot of people speaking Arabic here."

"Because we have to be learning it in school."

"So you learned it too?"

He squinted as he sucked smoke from his cigarette. "They tried to teach me. But I refused."

I SET OUT across the Sea of Galilee in my rubber raft, with oranges and cheese, a tin of sardines, a loaf of bread, olives, matches, a knife, my BB gun, a tent, a sleeping bag, some chocolate and nuts, four bottles of water, binoculars, and a bottle of Israeli wine. The day was hot and calm and cloudless, the sea beautifully empty. I saw not one other boat except the fishing boats moored at the harbor in Tiberias to the south. Being alone on the water was thrilling. I had told no one at the hotel that I was rowing away like this, because if you don't tell people your plans they can't tell you that your plans are foolish. I loved the freedom of just getting in a boat and going. I hoped no authority would show up and tell me that what I was doing was illegal. Now and then a small breeze stirred up little schools of ripples on the surface of the water, but otherwise the lake was as flat as a tabletop and the sunlight struck it white, like a searchlight on a sheet of tinfoil. The cliffs to the east were smoky and pale yellow in the morning light, but the shore where I was hoping to sleep that night was only a dark, ill-defined line below the cliffs. I didn't know exactly where I would land, but I was drawn to the area that in biblical times was called Gergesa, where Jesus had met two men possessed by devils. Gergesa lay along the middle of the eastern shore at the foot of some steep red cliffs. From what I could tell from my modern map it was latitudinally straight across the water from Tiberias, around what is now called Neot Golan.

The day before, I had walked to Tabgha and Capernaum to see the historical religious sights and had discovered that there were in fact pilgrims here. But their numbers were scant. At Tabgha, the scene of the miracle of the loaves and fishes, the beautiful Byzantine Church of the Multiplication was empty. This church contained one of Israel's more famous mosaics — it showed two simple fishes on either side of a basket of bread — but I was the only person looking at it. Nearby, in the Church of the Primacy of Peter, a couple of the Franciscan monks who ran the place were conversing in German, and an elderly pair of Californians were snapping pictures of the Mensa Christi, the rock upon which Jesus dined with his disciples, but we were the only people there. The greatest concentration of pilgrims that I met in all of Galilee was at the ruined temple complex in Capernaum. There an Israeli tour guide was speaking in a shout to a group of twenty elderly people from Michigan who were gathered around a collection of beautifully carved stones. Pointing to a stone the size and shape of a microwave oven, the guide said, "Okay. See this corner here, pilgrims? Look carefully at it and tell me what you can see there."

The pilgrims — their nametags said WORD OF LIFE BIBLE AND PRAYER INSTITUTE — adjusted their sunglasses and leaned forward to squint at the intricate carving. They all looked a bit nervous.

"Is it wheels?"

"A church?"

"Doors, I think?"

"Would it be pillars?"

"Am I seeing olives, or is that just me?"

On my walk back to Tiberias I had met not a single person and had seen very few cars on the road, and in that mood of desertion it was easy to think that the curse that Jesus had left unbelieving Capernaum with had come true: "And thou, Capernaum, which art exalted to heaven, shalt be brought down to hell."

I rowed steadily for an hour or so through the still green water. Rowing an inflatable raft is a bit like rowing an overstuffed mattress. Without a skeg or a hull to keep it on course, the raft moves in a skittering way, slipping over the surface of the water rather than knifing through it. Yank on a single oar and the boat spins giddily about like a top. Steering is a tricky choreographic exercise between the left oar and the right.

Around two o'clock I noticed high, thin sheets of cloud creeping across the sky from the west and with them a faint mist, a visible humidity, that thickened the air. I began to worry that the weather would change overnight and that I'd be stuck on the far shore in a storm or, worse, in a fog that would prevent me from rowing back. But the thought of canceling my little trip was too disappointing, so I rowed on, thinking that if it was foggy the next day I could find my way back by rowing along the northern periphery of the lake, keeping the land always in sight. It would add some ten miles to my trip, but it would keep me from getting lost. I lay back in my boat for a rest and recited one of the few lines that I — a chronic worrier — had memorized from the Gospels: "Therefore do not be anxious about tomorrow, for tomorrow will be anxious for itself." I stopped worrying and ate some hummus and bread, sang a song, ate an orange, and watched flocks of cormorants flying low over the lake in formation. They streaked through the sky, hundreds of them, possibly a thousand, a passing veil of black lace. And as I lay there, with my head propped on the bulging bolster of the prow and my bare feet propped on the opposite end and the green flies sucking at the boat valves, I imagined Jesus walking across the water and showing up suddenly at my side in his sandals and white robe. What would I say to him? I looked at the sky and the sun and tried to believe they looked as they had looked to him. As I daydreamed I became aware of a faint whining noise, like a lawn mower in the distance. I lifted my head but saw nothing, yet I could hear the sound distinctly vibrating in the puffy air chambers of my boat. It was a motor.

I drank some water and resumed rowing east, and before long I saw the tiny outline of a boat coming out of the south, near Kinneret. A fishing boat, I thought, though the sun was so bright it was difficult to see. I rowed on, hoping that the boat wouldn't come my way, and, if it did, that whoever was in it would not tell me that I was doing something illegal. I wanted to be inconspicuous, but it was difficult to be stealthy rowing a puffy pea-green raft across a calm lake in bright sunshine. What I least wanted to hear was that what I was doing was dangerous. People were always coming along and saying, "It's dangerous," or "You could get into trouble this way," or "I think you should stop," as though I hadn't considered any of that before flinging myself into the middle of whatever they perceived as dangerous.

When I was perhaps halfway across the sea, I knew that the fishing boat had seen me and was coming my way. I tried to ignore it, but my feeling of freedom was gone. The fishing boat looked disheveled and dirty and rusted and like trouble, with a big reticulated crane on its deck and dangling pulleys and frayed nets and blocks and grappling hooks. A long string of gulls followed behind it like snatches of smoke bent from a stack. I rowed on as the boat approached and continued rowing when it pulled up alongside me, rocking me in its wake. The two men standing on its deck squinted at me, arrested with disbelief, their faces sunburned and heavy. The man driving the boat was bearded and wore oilskin overalls and a yarmulke on his head; the other was fattish and had on a pressed dress shirt and neatly creased slacks. He had a stump of a cigarette between his lips, slicked-back hair, and several rings on his thick fingers. An implausible fisherman, he looked as though he should be sitting behind a desk in an air-conditioned bank. They stared and said nothing for so long that finally, impatient at the interruption, I said pointedly, "Yes?"

The banker scowled in the sunlight and raised a questioning hand at me. He looked almost frightened. "Everything is okay?"

"Fine," I said, though I hated their stopping me. What I really wanted to say was *Everything was fine until you two came along.*

"No problems?" he said in wonder.

I told him I had no problems. He stood there, baffled and bemused, one arm crooked at the elbow and the plump ringed hand dangling. His boat, which sat dangerously low in the water, rocked slightly in its own wake. I prayed to God that they wouldn't threaten me or do anything untoward or tell me to get off the lake. They stared. I cleared my throat. "Well," I said, "very nice talking with you. I guess I'll be moving along now."

And as I began to row off, the admonishment came. "Beware of the wind."

Beware of the wind? I knew that even though it was a calm day the wind could pick up at any moment without warning. But being wary of the wind at this point — I was at least three miles from shore in any direction — would not aid me in any way. If a sudden squall came up, I'd be sunk, no matter how wary I was. With nothing to root it to the water, an inflatable raft in a wind would skitter across the waves like a runaway toboggan. What good would it do to be aware of it? I'd still be stuck in the middle of the lake in a cyclone. For that matter, even without wind the boat could get punctured by a drifting log, the valves could fail, I could get hit by a motorboat, I could have a stroke and fall into the sea and drown. I could get struck by lightning. I could go suddenly blind and row myself to death in a frantic circle. Better still, Jesus could appear and tell me to get out of the boat and walk toward him. Like Simon Peter, I might step out and, halfway to him, lose faith — indeed, I probably would lose faith — and fall in and drown. Life was full of hazards.

I looked at the wincing, baffled man. The Israeli accent had heavily French overtones, and this man's was particularly French.

"Oh," I said. "The wind. Okay, I will. Thank you for telling me."

The banker grinned and said with a wave, "Say hello to Jesus!"

Though the remark was jolly, there was a touch of mockery in it. He thought I was a self-baptizing Christian zealot looking for Christ. I did happen to be dressed all in white, and I was wearing a cowpoke's hat and had one of my overpriced Nazareth crosses around my neck. I was as implausible an oarswoman as he was a fisherman — especially implausible because I was a woman. I stopped my oars. "Jesus who?" I said.

"Jesus the Christ."

"Oh, him. Well, I will if I see him," I said. "And then, if the wind comes up, I'll ask him to stop it for me."

The fishermen roared with false heartiness.

I rowed away muttering, *Bewaygh of zee weend*. The man's accent lingered like a strong smell. I couldn't blame him for thinking I was looking for Christ. I knew I looked like a freak in this silly boat. There were numerous good reasons a person might come to the Sea of Galilee, notably its beauty and peacefulness. But the truth was that foreign visitors who came here usually did so because of Jesus. Presbyterians and Baptists, Episcopalians and Catholics, Methodists and Calvinists, come to find evidence of one kind or another and to douse themselves in the Jordan River in a baptism reminiscent of Jesus'.

Though I had come here because of the life of Christ, I had a strange feeling that I wasn't looking for him but away from him. I knew that my perception of Jesus was soft and awash with mythology, influenced by my family, by religious art, by Christian theology. I would never know what he really said and really did; what I knew of him was other people's stories of him. Was Bethlehem really his birthplace? Was he the son of God? Was his mother a virgin born without original sin? Many of the details had always been hard to believe, and many were clearly inventions. All over the world Christians celebrated with rituals and traditions and stories the dramatic events that were said to have happened here. I wanted a few more facts, even if they were just sensory geographical facts. I wanted to be here, standing in the arena, so that I could know what the ground felt like beneath his feet, what the sky looked like, how the night smelled, how the birds sounded. What I had seen so far on the Sea of Galilee was not at all what I had expected. The small size of the lake, the discreet little holiday resorts and spas, the emptiness, the warm weather, the smooth, groomed roads. But the hills were believable, and the sky, and the trees.

AN HOUR LATER, as I came within sight of the palmy shore, three dark fighter jets roared overhead, ripping at the sky and disappearing over the hills in the direction of Syria. Ten minutes later they came back with a burning, booming screech that seemed to stir the hair on my head and make the water jiggle. They streaked low across the sky, and their shadows greased over the water like the silhouettes of sharks.

I rowed for several more hours, and around four o'clock, as the sun dipped low over the western hills and the sky softened to marine blue and the water took on a golden light, I came close to shore. I was drawn by a pretty cove overhung with cedar and eucalyptus trees — a long strip of grainy black sand that at its southern end abruptly became a litter of smooth white rocks the shape and size of ostrich eggs. I pulled my boat up on the sand and discovered that I had landed in a spot perfectly suited to camping. It looked like a small public park. Above the beach in a shady stand of towering eucalyptus trees were picnic tables and wire trash cans and here and there the charred remains of campfires. Four or five cats idled beneath the trees. A posted sign said in English and Hebrew that if visitors wished to swim, they would do so at their own risk without benefit of a lifeguard.

The park, like everything else in Galilee, was deserted. At its edge I saw two long, narrow, tin-sided shelters and, beyond them, a fence and what looked like a large farm. I could make out a banana grove, and I could hear goats bleating, could smell the vinegary musk of cow manure and the sharp scents of eucalyptus and cedar. The road that ringed the Sea of Galilee was on the other side of a stand of trees, five hundred yards from the water, and beyond the road the high red cliffs, with their many deep gorges and chines, reached into the sky. The little park seemed perfect. It was secluded without being unbearably wild, it was quiet and pretty, and I was certain I wasn't trespassing. I would spend the night on the beach beneath the biggest eucalyptus tree.

When I went back down to the beach to pull my boat up and collect my things, I saw a barefoot man in a red shirt walking slowly up the sand with two small dogs. At the sight of me, one of the dogs came hurtling down the beach and danced on his little legs and barked violently at my feet. He had a frantic look in his eye. He was tiny and big-eared, like a Jack Russell, and his teeth were bright little thorns in his mouth. The force of his own barking seemed to lift him off the ground. I picked him up, and once in the cradle of my arms the dog crumpled with pleasure, wriggling and snorting and sniffing, licking happily at my neck and salty wrists, his damp paws hot and gritty on my collarbone. When I put him down again he danced madly into the sea, snapped at the water, choked, coughed in a high voice, ran about in a circle, and returned to his master, who was collecting something from the beach and stuffing it into a plastic bag. The man was in his forties, thin-faced and delicate-looking. His curly blond hair hung to his shoulders. He said nothing as he passed me, only smiled and nodded and continued down the beach while his dog sniffed at my ankle. I saw that it was bits of trash he was collecting, cigarette butts and string and bottle caps, though the beach already looked very clean.

In a small motorized skiff a fisherman pulled up near the shore and began laying down nets, and when he saw my boat he shouted in Hebrew. He seemed to be asking whose boat it was. I said nothing. I didn't want to answer any questions or tell anyone what I was doing, for fear I would be told I couldn't. The red-shirted man shouted back at the fisherman, "Hello, do you speak English?" His accent was German, and he and the fisherman shouted over the water at each other, sometimes both at once, neither one comprehending the other. The fisherman kept pointing at my boat, and finally, unable to get an answer from either of us, he finished laying his nets and went off in his skiff.

The German knew it was my boat, had seen me row up in it, yet he asked me nothing and quietly went back to his work. He moved with limber efficiency and pursued his task without idling. I waited until he moved off down the beach, then I dragged the boat up into the trees, unloaded my tent and sleeping bag and food, and sat down to watch the sun disappear behind the hills of Tiberias. The pink sky was reflected in the water, and as the light faded and a few bright stars appeared, I realized that the fisherman had left a floating oil lamp to mark the location of his nets. The lamp was like a large firefly sitting on the water. The evening air was soft, and a warm breeze stirred the long arms of the eucalyptus trees. Stars began to be reflected in the lake.

At five-thirty the German returned from the far end of the beach and went over to one of the tin buildings. He unlocked a door, retrieved a bucket and mop from within, and began sweeping the pathway in front of the building. He was far enough away from where I was sitting that I could ignore him, though at one point I looked over and saw him scattering grain for a flock of chickens. He was busy and quiet, and he was leaving me alone — that was all I cared about.

But the sun was disappearing, the sky darkening, the stars rapidly multiplying, and I was becoming apprehensive. I didn't know exactly where I was, and I knew that I would make myself vulnerable by sleeping here. Anyone could come along. And suddenly I felt a bit guilty, as though it had been somehow wrong to row across the Sea of Galilee without asking anyone's permission or telling someone that I was doing it. I had brought a boat to Israel, climbed into it, and rowed away under my own authority. That was what I had wanted to do, for part of the excitement was doing it alone and not planning too carefully. Adapting to whatever might crop up in your path was the heart of adventure. If you knew how it was going to turn out, you might as well stay home. But now, sitting here with the adventure only half enacted, I was undeniably nervous.

I realized that it was, in fact, the place and its history that made me nervous. Night, fast approaching, made the impossible seem possible, the supernatural less absurd. Whatever would not dare show itself in daylight might be more inclined to appear under cover of night. It was easier to doubt the existence of God in the daylight. Christ had said to his disciples, "What I tell you in darkness, that speak ye in light" (Matthew 10:27). They had spoken in light. He had spoken in darkness. I looked around me at the rising shadows. Jesus was secretive. He wanted to spread the word, but he directed his disciples to "tell no man" that he was the Christ. At Mount Tabor he had ordered them not to tell anyone about his transfiguration and the voice of God that came out of a cloud. Likewise, when he cured people or raised someone from the dead, more often than not he told the witnesses to tell no one about it. If Jesus was going to show up here, I was sure that it would be at night.

I built a little fireplace of stones at the base of the big eucalyptus tree, gathered up some wood, built a small fire with dead eucalyptus leaves as kindling, and put my tent up. Then I sat by the fire with my back against the tree, opened my bottle of wine, poured some into a plastic cup, and tried not to worry. The eucalyptus wood was dry and very fragrant, with a hint of coffee to it, and the light of the fire made me feel less fearful. In two hours I had seen no one but the German, and yet as the dark took over at six o'clock I grew more nervous. That hollering fisherman had worried me. And I realized that the fire made my presence more conspicuous; I glowed in the light of it. Anyone approaching on the water would be able to make me out instantly. I put my hat back on my head and hoped that because I was alone, a passerby on the shore seeing my fire would assume I was a man; a woman would be less inclined to camp out alone. A reasonable woman, anyway. The German caretaker had probably wondered what on earth I was up to. I sipped at my wine and pulled my hat lower on my brow and consoled myself with the thought that it was a mannish hat and also that I had a big knife, suitable for skinning a moose, and the BB gun, which could do no serious harm but would certainly make an intruder think twice. I couldn't really imagine myself employing these weapons, but having them gave me the illusion of strength.

By now the German must have seen my tent and known that I was going to spend the night. From his activities I gleaned that he lived in one of the tin shelters, was the park's caretaker perhaps. He seemed gentle and unobtrusive, and though I had wanted to be entirely alone, now that night had come I found his nearby presence in the tin shed comforting. If anyone tried to accost me during the night, I could brandish my BB gun and knife and shout to him for help.

As long as he wasn't the one accosting me.

I took out my map and, studying it with my flashlight, determined that I was sitting just beneath the southern end of the Golan Heights on a piece of land that, although it was under Israeli military administration, was claimed by Syria. The Golan Heights was an area some forty miles long and fifteen wide. Like most maps, this one bore a legend that explained the various cartographic symbols. A green line showed a regional road, a blue blob represented a lake, an airplane shape indicated an airport, a long string of plus signs (+ + + + + + + +) showed an international boundary. But this map had additional symbols, for the *Ceasefire line, 1967* and *Disengagement line, 1974* and *Israel-Jordan Peace-Treaty line 26.10.94* and *Israeli Settlement Area* and so on. According to these lines, with their incongruously cheery pink and blue shadings, I was about five miles from *Disengagement line 1974.* I was less than five miles from the Jordanian border and not too far from the *Lebanese Disengagement line 1974.* Most Arabs would say that I was sitting in an occupied part of Syria. In 1992 Israel and Syria had reached an understanding that the land in the Golan that was occupied by Israel would be exchanged for peace, but with the election of Benjamin Netanyahu, that plan had been rejected and more Jewish settlements had been built in the area. One incensed Syrian, quoting the famous words of the Egyptian president Gamal Abdel Nasser (whose harrying, hair-raising, foaming-at-the-mouth speaking style remarkably resembled Hitler's), had commented to the Syrian press, "What was taken by force can be returned only by force."

I ate some olives and studied my map. When I was a child my family lived in the woods outside of Boston on a small lane that had been part of a farm. There were five houses on the lane, and by some unlikely stroke, one of the families was Jewish and another was Lebanese; their properties abutted. They disliked each other. Each called the other names behind their backs. I knew nothing about Middle Eastern conflict and didn't understand their ire. We were Irish. The people at the top of the lane were WASPs, and the fifth family was something indeterminate. One day the Jewish man told his neighbor, the Lebanese Christian,

"Those trees you're cutting are on my property." An argument ensued, after which the Lebanese man went into his house and had a heart attack. His wife went berserk. She hurried over, knocked on the Jewish man's door, and shrieked, "You gave my husband a heart attack!" The Jewish man replied, "Send your husband back out and I'll give him another one!" and slammed the door in her face.

Not far from here, in the middle of the Golan Heights, lay a place known as the Shouting Valley, where relatives who had been separated since 1967, when Israel seized the heights, went to communicate with each other. Forbidden to cross the border, brothers and sisters, husbands and wives, gathered on either side of a fenced and land-mined gap between the hilltop villages of Ein al-Teini and Majdal al-Shams and used megaphones to shout news to each other. When a new baby was born in Israeli-occupied Majdal al-Shams, it was brought to the fence and held up for its grandparents in Ein al-Teini to see. In 1996 a young couple who had met at university in Damascus — he lived in the Israeli-occupied territory, she lived in Syria — became engaged. During their summer vacation they communicated with each other at the Shouting Valley. Eventually they married in Damascus and, escorted by the Red Cross, walked across the border into the Israeli-occupied territory. From then on the bride shared news with her parents by megaphone across the valley.

If the present peace process between Israel and Syria was successful, then the land would go back to Syria and the Shouting Valley would no longer be necessary.

The location of the Israeli state was perilous, for the Jews had fought to build a nation in the very heart of the place where they would be most assailed. Theodor Herzl, Israel's founder, had considered other places — Al-Arish on the Sinai Peninsula, Tripoli, Mozambique, and the Congo — but Palestine was the place he had most hoped for. I had been to Egypt several times and to Syria, and the physical difference between those countries and Israel was startling. The Israelis had managed to turn the desert into a garden, to create an orderly and relatively affluent community in a way that none of its neighbors had.

In Jerusalem, walking toward the Knesset through the new part of the city, I had had the weird sense that I was passing through a prosperous part of Brookline, Massachusetts. It wasn't just that Jerusalem was Westernized, it was distinctly Americanized. The streets were orderly, wide, and well paved, the traffic lights and signs were no different from American traffic lights and signs. It was roomy and clean and quiet and bland. The cars were new and freshly washed. There were garages and gardens, tall trees and terraces. It had none of the hubbub and rot and flavor of a Middle Eastern city. There were no animals in the streets other than well-groomed little dogs on leashes: trotting, waddling dachshunds and poodles with tiny ponytails. There were pet shops and spotless supermarkets. When I thought of Jerusalem's counterparts — dusty, crumbling Cairo, Damascus, and Alexandria, where every green spot was trampled by a thousand people hoping to escape their dingy apartments — Jerusalem was an anomaly.

Here in my camping spot, so close to the conflict in the Golan Heights, there was no sign of strife — or even of life — except for the tidy German caretaker and some bleating goats. My fire was burning nicely, throwing a warm orange glow into the dangling branches of the eucalyptus above me. I could smell the lake, an aged, muddy, freshwater smell that was not unpleasant. At times I caught a whiff of the ocean, but I was sure that was only because of the fish. I thought I heard frogs, but it might have been the goats. The fisherman's lantern winked on the still water, the stars were bright, the birds had gone silent, and I saw no shadowy figures approaching on the beach. Now and then I looked over my shoulder, back into the thick darkness of the trees, but I saw nothing. I ate some bread and cheese and chocolate, pulled the brim of my hat lower over my face, drank some more wine to give myself courage, and told myself that it wasn't as if I was sitting in a wilderness. There were signs that others had done the same thing I was doing; there were old peach stones and cigarette butts and roasted chicken bones around the edges of my fire.

I got out my flashlight and notebook and made some notes and distracted myself by thinking in historical terms about this spot. From what I could make out I was roughly between the biblical towns of Gergesa and Hippus. In Gergesa, Jesus was said to have driven demons out of a madman. In a synthesis of the three versions of this story told in the Gospels of Matthew, Mark, and Luke, the event happened roughly this way: Jesus came across the sea to the region of Gergesa (also called Gadara), got out of the ship, and met a naked man (*two* men in Matthew's version) coming out of a tomb. The man, long possessed by devils, was uncontrollable and "exceeding fierce, so that no man might pass by that way." He was so wild that when the local people chained and fettered him, he was able to break the chains and destroy the fetters. The people had given up trying to control him and generally steered clear of him. The man spent his days sitting in the tomb crying and cutting himself with stones. When Jesus approached him, the madman fell to the ground and cried out, "What have I to do with thee, Jesus, thou son of God? Art thou come hither to torment us before the time?" When Jesus asked his name, the man answered, "My name is Legion: for we are many."

The devils possessing the man feared that Jesus would banish them from the country and into the "abyss." Farther down the coast a great herd of swine was feeding, and the devils requested of Jesus, "If thou cast us out, suffer us to go away into the herd of swine." Jesus said simply, "Go," and the devils were driven out of the man and into the swine, whereupon the herd ran "violently" down the steep slope into the sea and drowned. The people who tended the swine (if they were Jews, they were keeping them illegally) heard what had happened and hurried to the place where Jesus and the possessed man sat. They were astonished to find the madman "sitting and clothed and in his right mind" and were so frightened at these developments and so unhappy at the loss of their pigs that they had the temerity to ask Jesus to leave their coast. Without noted protest, Jesus returned to his ship, leaving the cured madman with the instruction to tell everyone "how great things the Lord hath done for thee."

I loved this story with its odd details: the tomb, the nakedness, the broken chains, the man's fierceness, the talking devils, the swine. Above all I loved the answer: "My name is Legion: for we are many." "Many" was said to be a reference to the man's numerous devils, but when I first read it I was certain that it meant there were many more men in the world equally possessed and tormented and outcast, and I preferred that interpretation. That the madman spent his life in a tomb crying and cutting himself with stones was a vivid and somehow contemporary depiction of mental illness. It interested me that the pigs' manner of running was described as "violent" in all three Gospels. It must have been a remarkable racket for that particular word to have survived orally over the six or so decades before Matthew and Mark wrote it down. It was a strange story, and the possibility that the swine were a form of contraband to the people who kept them only thickened the plot.

The impossibility of confirming the truth of the story — like so many others told of Christ's ministry — didn't really matter, especially here, not far from where it had supposedly happened. Sitting at my little fire, with the lake on one side and the cliffs on the other, I could understand the dark image of the desperate madman, could see it as real. I could see his teeth, his fingernails grown long and twisted, his dirty beard and matted hair, the self-inflicted cuts and scars. I could hear his lonely wailing. I could see Christ's ship approaching the shore, could hear the hoofs of the swine thundering down one of these hills, and the great crashing splash as they careered into the water, flopping and choking and sinking, the devils going down with them. Though the story may have been figurative, I took the madman literally. It was easy to believe that there had been men like that, deranged and psychically overwhelmed in ways that now might be ameliorated or even cured. Under Jesus' care the man went from a dangerous, raving, cave-dwelling, self-mutilating lunatic to sitting "fully clothed and in his right mind."

The exorcism of this demoniac happened at a time when Jesus was in the thick of his ministry. The cures and miracles came quickly, and in all four Gospels they seem to represent a mere selection of the works that Jesus performed. He cured a palsied servant, a paralyzed man, a leper, and Peter's mother-in-law; quieted the storm and revived a ruler's daughter; cured a blind man, a dumb man, a woman's incessant bleeding, and a withered hand. He multiplied the loaves and fishes (twice), walked on water, and cured numerous sick people in Gennesaret.

My thoughts about God and my perception of Jesus Christ were formed early and in relation to my parents, as most people's religious beliefs are. What they had said to me as a child I more or less believed; the stories appeared to me with the flashing imagery of a slide show. Not until I reached college did I ask myself who Jesus was and how we knew what we believed about him. I realized that Matthew, Mark, Luke, and John hadn't been present when all that Galilean intrigue and wonder were happening. They had recorded an oral tradition built around the figure of Christ that had been passed down through generations. I learned with some surprise and disappointment that it was quite unclear who Jesus Christ was and what exactly he had hoped to achieve. There was slim evidence that the words attributed to him in the Gospels were actually his. Written more than half a century after Jesus' death, the Gospels were like the bits of cooking pots found in an archaeological pit — a fragmented story, a composite sketch. They were subjective; as much as they informed, they also muddied the facts. Dissected by scholars, carbon-dated, translated, retranslated, compared against geological and archaeological evidence, the Gospels had been deflated. They were subjective and tendentious, and later were reinterpreted by church leaders.

Many of Jesus' contemporaries perceived him as a con artist and a pretender. Many scholars believed that Jesus was merely a charismatic faith healer who claimed no divinity and professed that anyone could achieve the power he possessed if their faith in God was strong enough. John the Baptist, after baptizing him and hearing a heavenly voice referring to Jesus as "my beloved son," believed that he was the Messiah. The term "Son of God" was understood by Jesus' contemporaries to be metaphorical and not literal, because God himself was and would forever remain unknowable. The notion that Jesus was divine, that he was the Incarnation, that he was actually God in a human figure, didn't take root until several centuries after his death, when it became Christian doctrine. Because of a need for some tangible evidence of God, for a particular focus of belief, and for political authority, the figurative and associative had become literal and specific.

I didn't need to believe in God or to believe that Jesus was the son of God to find him an extremely compelling figure. What he preached sounded smart and right to me; he expressed the right sentiments and outlook, the grace and generosity and charity, the effort to see God and bring forth the highest virtue in man. It wasn't the miracles he had worked that caught my attention, but his words, his good will, and above all his singularity of focus. His focus and persistence, though he was hounded and hated by many, made him fearsome. He endured forty days' temptation in the wilderness. He was extreme. He could be stern, and sometimes he was impatient and annoyed. When his disciples failed to cure an epileptic, he rebuked them for their faithlessness, the cause of their failure, exclaiming ruefully, "How long shall I suffer you?" (Matthew 17:17). He withered a poor old fig tree because it was barren. He said terrible things of the wayward and the corrupt: "It were better for him that a millstone were hanged about his neck, and that he were drowned in the depth of the sea" (Matthew 18:6). His goodness was far from insipid. I loved him for that.

In his day Jesus' religious iconoclasm must have appeared quite dis-

ruptive and threatening to the general order. Some called him glutton-
ous and a "winebibber" because he ate and drank with sinners. He did
works on the Sabbath. His disciples broke traditions: they didn't fast,
they ate without washing their hands. His message, with its absolute
and unwavering goal, could not help but be divisive. According to Matthew, he said to his disciples, "He that loveth father or mother more
than me is not worthy of me" (Matthew 10:37).

In the Gospels Jesus was asking believers to follow him, to leave everything behind and help him preach the word of God. He was asking for
nothing less than a revolution. Whenever I read those words in Matthew I couldn't help but think of the modern messianic cult leaders and
self-professed prophets who showed up in town and urged people to
leave their families in order to follow an "enlightened" path toward salvation — David Koresh or Jim Jones or even Werner Erhardt and a host
of other delusional or schizophrenic or just plain grandiose maniacs.
The twentieth century had its share of them. I thought of the number of
families seriously disrupted by cults. Had I lived at the time of Jesus
would I, a skeptic, have seen him as just another crying-aloud kook? Jesus' own family thought he had lost his wits. That was hardly surprising. He claimed that he had been chosen by God, that he had come to
fulfill the words of the prophets. If I did that, I would quickly be judged
unstable.

Being here in Galilee had not made Jesus bigger in my mind; instead,
it had brought him down to human size, and that small size in turn
made him great. Whoever he was, he was a human being with the bravery of twenty.

I drank more wine and threw more wood on the glowing fire. The
shadows around me had grown very deep. The long hair of the eucalyptus trees brushed against the trunks with a spooky whisper. Two small
motorboats came down the shore; they had no lights but I could hear
their engines in the distance. I heard coots and herons muttering in the
dark. Sitting in this dark place with my head filled with thoughts of God
and Christ was not entirely soothing. I kept imagining someone or
something coming out of the woods, and I wasn't sure which frightened
me more, the possibility of some leering, pumpkin-headed creep hiding
behind a tree or God himself, dissatisfied with my wavering view of
him. The Old Testament was full of a personal, terrifying God. When he
chose to show himself, his emergence was worse than any natural disas-

ter. He caused wrenching disruptions. He arrived in tornadoes and earthquakes, lightning and fire, shattering mountains and obscuring the sun. His appearance could singe the very eyelashes of those who beheld him, could even strike them dead.

I ate some sardines and nuts, drank some water, and reminded myself that if God existed, I did not believe he had the form or intent of a person. He did not have eyes and ears, a mouth, two feet. He had no ego. He *was* ego, he was soul, he was what human beings did. Better, he was what human beings could do. He was not us, but he was also not, in my mind, separate from us. I did not believe that he willfully directed events on earth. He was not a puppet master. But that was only what I believed. I could be dead wrong.

An animal sound came out of the woods, like the horrible shriek of a peacock. I hadn't stopped to think what sort of unfriendly beasts might appear here. What if there were wolves? Or jackals? I had seen a jackal once in Egypt, all snaggled yellow teeth and long narrow face, a plainly visible rib cage and notably hungry eyes. The peacock shrieked again like a person being dragged through the woods. I knew there were peacocks here; I had seen one the day before crossing a field on his weird webbed feet. I was comforted by the civilized sound of a truck passing by on the road beyond the woods. I told myself that this was not the wilderness. Though it was an unpopulated countryside it had a faintly suburban Israeli feel. Very little seemed wild here. Anything savage, anything that was a nuisance or a threat, had been tamed. The land had been made livable and the state had cool control of every hard-won inch of it.

I tried to cheer myself by reciting the blasphemous little poem that Buck Mulligan recites at the beginning of *Ulysses.*

> *I'm the queerest young fellow that ever you heard.*
> *My mother's a Jew, my father's a bird.*
> *With Joseph the joiner I cannot agree.*
> *So here's to disciples and Calvary*
> *If anyone thinks that I amn't divine*
> *He'll get no free drinks when I'm making the wine . . .*

I couldn't remember the rest of it. I poured myself a little more wine and was disappointed and surprised to see that I had drunk the entire bottle. I was firmly drunk. I was also running out of firewood. I mustered my courage, got up, staggered across the dark beach, and, by a stroke of good fortune, found a small fallen tree. I dragged the whole thing back across the rocky beach, stuck one end of it into the hot coals of my fire, and flopped down again in the dusty eucalyptus leaves, noticing for the first time that they smelled like cat pee.

Drunk as I was, I was afraid to go to sleep. I checked that my knife and my little plastic gun were beside me, and I sat there talking out loud to myself and making notes until my pen failed and, a moment later, the flashlight failed too. Suddenly I had no ink and no light. That frightened me. It seemed like an omen. I looked over my shoulder into the woods. Dimly illuminated by the light of my fire, the peeling bark dangled from the trees in strips, like bandages trailing from a mummy, and at the edge of my firelight the exposed wood looked eerily like bone. I fed another length of the tree into the fire, until that too was finally burned and there was nothing else to do but brave it and go to bed. I lifted my watch to my blurred eyes. It was eleven o'clock. I had been sitting there for five hours.

With my knife in one hand and the silly gun in the other, I fell into the tent and collapsed onto my sleeping bag without removing my shoes or clothes. Suddenly the smell of cat pee was very strong. I was exhausted. My hand brushed the front of my jacket, and through my fog I realized that a hot pebble had bounced out of the fire, landed on my lapel, and melted its synthetic fibers in such a way that the cooled-off pebble was now stuck there in a resinous glue. It was a wonder I hadn't burned to death. Through my blurry thoughts I could hear the fisherman saying, "Beware of the wind." He might as well have said, "Beware of yourself."

I SLEPT STUPOROUSLY for two hours and then was awakened by a wild catfight next to my tent. The cats screeched and howled. When their bodies clashed, I could hear them tumbling over the ground near my tent. Eventually the fight broke up, but before long a big wind arose that made the trees scrape and whisper. Their tossed limbs creaked like rusted hinges. I began to worry about lying under the eucalyptus tree; what if a limb blew down and landed on my head?

And then I felt a shocking thump against my tent that shook the entire frame and crushed in one side of it. I was sure I was dead, until I realized that the wind had lifted my boat and tossed it on top of me. I sat up, stared at the blackness, unzipped the door, and climbed out. The fisherman's lamp still glowed on the water, and the full moon was high in the sky now, leaking a glowing bluish light into the trees and onto the beach. The trees shook in the spooky wind, and their shadows waved hectically back and forth across the ground like moving figures. The sea was lit up in silver light, its little waves a thousand glittering triangles.

I dragged the boat to the beach, filled it with rocks to hold it down, and staggered back to the tent. I was dehydrated and had a terrible headache. I lay back down, but for the rest of the night I slept only fitfully. At 4:30 I looked out of the tent again and saw the moon just setting over the western shore, a huge yellow ball throwing a long golden runner of light across the water.

Morning seemed very long in coming. At dawn I was awakened by something that sounded like a howling coyote, but after listening fearfully to it for a long time I realized it was only a rooster. I slept for another hour and was awakened again by the German man's little dog scrabbling at the nylon material of my tent; in the sunlight his clawing shadow was dinosaur-huge against the cloth. When I finally got up, the fisherman's lamp was gone, and I felt sick and exhausted and entirely unspiritual. If God did appear at some point during the night, I had completely missed the event.

WHEN I RETURNED to the hotel that afternoon after rowing back across the lake, the big bald narc was sitting in a garden chair on the terrace reading a book in Hebrew. He eyed me skeptically as I approached. I knew I looked red-eyed and bedraggled and unwashed. My hair was in tangles, my head was sore, and my jacket had a hole burned in it. I carried the dripping boat slung over my shoulder like a dead body and was breathless under the weight of it. My aluminum oars clanked against the back of the man's chair as I squeezed past him. He looked stonily at me and went back to his book.

I ran into Johnny coming up the garden path with a pile of crisp bed sheets in his arms. "You heard the news," he said.

"No."

Hurrying past me, he cried, "A Christian was stabbed in Nazareth last night! Another one got slapped in the face! And some pilgrims was insulted by the Muslims!"

THE NEXT DAY at breakfast, Geergy sat down with me again and asked, "You been to China?" I had. "So," he said, "in China are the people looking like this?" He reduced his eyes to two slits by pulling at the flesh of his temples.

I nodded. "Yes, roughly."

The epicanthic slant of the Asian eye struck Geergy as hysterically funny. Geergy was prone to sudden outbursts of loud laughter. And sometimes in midsentence he would sigh magnificently or stretch his body in such an extreme way that his round face crumpled with the effort. He yawned loudly and had a wary way of looking at inanimate objects in the room, as though they were about to go up in flames.

I asked Geergy if a person could take a boat down the Jordan River.

"Yes, but it's very low now and also very far away."

"How far is it?"

"Twenty minutes by car."

Not far at all, but people who don't travel often have an exaggerated perception of distance. I pointed at the heart-shaped locket around Geergy's neck and asked him if he had a photograph in it.

"No," he said sadly, "I don't have a girlfriend."

"Too bad," I said.

"Yes. Too bad." He held the heart up to inspect it. "Solid gold heart," he said, as if repeating a phrase he had heard in a film. "There's only Russian girls to go out with. But I would never go out with a Russian girl. Some of them have really beautiful eyes, but I wouldn't go even to the beach with them."

"Why?"

He made a disgusted face. "They're only making sex. And those men" — he raised his index fingers to his ears and swung them in a corkscrew pattern down the sides of his face — "with the zigzigs like this. I don't know who you call them."

"Hasids?"

"Yeah, them. I don't like them. They are always the ones making whorehouses with Russian girls."

I was reminded of a taxi driver I had talked to in New York once, a

Portuguese woman, who told me that her least favorite customers were the Hasidic men because they were always offering her a dollar in exchange for a kiss.

Geergy said, "Most people who come here it's nice families and they are married and have children and it's nice and they are happy. But then some people come, the Russian girls, and oh, my God, you should see the mess they make in the rooms and what they do. They are mostly making sex in there."

I thanked Geergy for the breakfast and went back to my room. Ten minutes later, as I was brushing my teeth, the door of my room swung open and there was Geergy smiling on the threshold with a broom in his hand, saying, "Need any help?"

I took the toothbrush out of my mouth. "Help with what?"

"Suitcase?"

"But I'm not leaving, Geergy."

"Oh. How long you staying?"

"One more day."

His face brightened. "Good. Then I can talk to you some more." And he went out with his broom and shut the door behind him.

ON THE TWENTY-SECOND of December I rented a car in Tiberias and drove back to Jerusalem along a route that paralleled the Jordan River. The highway ran south along a flat plain, and though the landscape here was mostly hard, barren desert, all along the way tidy green fields appeared in the middle of it — astonishingly lush plantations of vegetables. The wide valley sloped downward toward Jordan and the river, and every now and then I could see the narrow river in the distance, a slow, brownish creek. Beyond the river were the magnificent red mountains of Jordan — real mountains, like a high barricade separating Israel from the rest of the Middle East. The sky was full of very high, thin clouds, and the sun carried a huge halo of yellow around it, like the circle that appears around the moon on damp winter nights. The air was still and very hot, and in the distance I could see tall spindles of smoke lifting straight into the sky from small fires. From time to time a United Nations Jeep hurried past me, or a police car with its blue lights flashing. At a checkpoint a bunch of soldiers eating oranges waved me through without so much as looking at me.

In a place called Beit Sheeyan I stopped and offered a ride to an elderly woman who was walking along the road carrying three heavy bags and a huge bundle on her head. She spoke no English, and I had only a few useless Arabic words. My offer of a lift, which I indicated by opening the passenger door, seemed to shock her, but she was so grateful for it that she held my face in her rough hands and kissed both of my cheeks. She hurled her bags into the back seat, flopped down in the front, and slammed the door safely shut.

The woman was fat and red-cheeked and powerful, with a black scarf tied tight on her head. She rubbed her big hands together and grinned through the windshield and sighed with relief. She smelled of black pepper and wood smoke. She was delighted with herself. When I indicated that she might want to fasten her seat belt she howled with laughter and pooh-poohed the stupid device and began speaking in a steady, friendly stream of Arabic. I knew she was asking questions, but I had no idea what the questions were, except where was I from and what was my name. When I told her I was American, she patted the spotless dashboard of the brand-new car — a tiny Ford Escort — with a plump brown hand and laughed loudly and said, "America!"

She tried the windows and the radio and the air conditioner, opened the glove compartment, studied the maps that were there. I had placed a pair of reading glasses on the console between the seats, and now she snatched them up and stuffed her face into them, studied the map some more, all the while talking. Finally she held the map up in front of me to show me a tiny dot twenty kilometers down the road from where we were — her home. She had been planning to walk twenty kilometers in the searing heat with thirty pounds of laundry and groceries in her arms.

When we reached her village, she indicated that I could leave her at the turnoff from the main road, but I drove all the way to her house, a little cement box in a row of others just like it. Too late I realized that she had accidentally gone off with my eyeglasses perched on her nose.

As I continued on down the road toward Jerusalem, the landscape changed to a pocked and pitted lunar wasteland of sand and dust, like certain badlands of Egypt or Utah. In the Israeli hills to the right I saw many caves, and then I realized that I was traveling alongside an enormous barrier that represented the border with Jordan. The barrier was a high fence that looked electrified, then a twenty-yard ditch, then another fence. At one point the double fence became a triple fence, with army trucks parked in the trench. On top of the trucks soldiers sat wearing helmets and hugging machine guns. It all made me very nervous, and I drove fast, hoping to leave them behind.

Near the Allenby Bridge across the river to Jordan, the sky became very smoky and yellow and the rubbly land looked somehow sinister. A long string of camels appeared in the distance, moving slowly, and through the yellow smoke they had the shapes of sea horses. The air smelled sulfurous, and in the distance I could see the Dead Sea. This was one of the lowest spots on Earth, a great depression in the globe, and I could feel the pressure in the air. A sign at the side of the road said, TO THE WORLD'S OLDEST . . . But the noun had been covered up with graffiti.

As I neared Jerusalem, the road began to climb through some barren yellow hills, and after twenty minutes of climbing a marker in the middle of nowhere said, SEA LEVEL. I stopped the car and got out. It was the driest, scariest, barest landscape I had ever seen, without a single bit of vegetation. For miles I saw nothing, just the Dead Sea in the valley below and the Jordanian mountains to the east. A hot wind whispered through the valleys and ridges. Then I realized that in a little gulley just below the road was a village of colorful Bedouin tents. Why these people had chosen this spot to live in and where they found water was an utter mystery. But the adults wandering in and out of the tents and the children running barefoot on the side of the hill all looked healthy and contented, and the tents looked cheerful.

THE DAY BEFORE Christmas I drove the six miles from Jerusalem to Bethlehem, hoping to spend the day in the town and the night in nearby Shepherd's Field. But as soon as I reached the Palestinian checkpoint at the border between Bethlehem and Jerusalem, I began to have doubts about my plan. Many cars were being searched and turned away, and along the side of the road hundreds of pilgrims were hurrying across the dusty border on foot. Here were the great numbers of pilgrims that I had expected to see in Israel, but they were not foreign visitors like me, they were Arab Christians from nearby towns, going to the birthplace of Jesus to pay their respects on this most important holiday. As I waited my turn at the checkpoint I watched them flooding into Bethlehem.

They came in waves, women and children and men with black mustaches, some of them trotting in anticipation. They carried bundles on their heads — sleeping rolls, picnics, bottles of water, clothing — and their hurrying feet kicked up clouds of dust. The scene had the frantic, stampeding feel of an evacuation. It was Christmas Eve of 1999, and despite the numerous bombs and massacres that had been predicted for Bethlehem on that particular night, the pilgrims moved gladly toward the town. Their audible excitement made me nervous. So much expectation, so much hectic activity, seemed to invite disaster.

Drivers ahead of me were being questioned and searched by the Palestinian police, and some were denied entry and sent back toward Jerusalem. But when it came my turn to be questioned, the police waved me through the checkpoint without a word, asking me nothing and telling me nothing. I never even opened my window. And that inexplicably easy entry made me nervous, too. As I headed down into the town of Bethlehem, a place I had imagined since I was a very small child and had always wanted to see, I had a strong desire to turn the car around and go back.

FOR ME, THE EVENT of Christmas reached its maximum enchantment and meaning when I was about six — old enough to reason but young enough to believe. I believed in Bethlehem and the pregnant young mother on the donkey desperate for a place to spend the night. I believed in the wise men and in the star that appeared in the east marking the way for those who wanted to see the infant Jesus. I believed in the animals in the stable who had all done their part to protect the mother and child and make them comfortable.

At Christmas my family had a Nativity scene set up in our living room, a complete set of porcelain figurines sheltering beneath the roof of a small, open-fronted barn. The crèche had real straw on its floor, and the diapered, pink-skinned infant Jesus with his arms eternally raised fit perfectly into the wooden manger. An eight-inch bearded Joseph, a blue-gowned Mary, the shepherds, the wise men, and even the animals — all the figures were hand-painted. Their faces wore benign expressions. Mary looked beautiful in her veil and robe, Joseph looked patient and kind. And the wise men, kings in fact, were regal and dapper.

In the days before Christmas I would stand before this mini-stable examining the features of each figurine, playing the story out in my mind, carrying the toffee-colored camels and cream-white sheep across the living room, trotting them across the piano keys, the top of the television, and onto the couch. I imagined the steamy breath of the animals in the cold night air. I spoke to and for the turbaned wise men, one of whom was very black, his shining china skin the color of tarpaper. I knew no black people then, so he was exotic, with his very white eyes, pink lips, flowing red robe, and small gold cask, within which was a gift that would forever remain a mystery — the cask could not be opened. He and the other two kings had traveled a great distance, from Egypt or some other palmy place, to Bethlehem to honor a baby who was somehow magical.

I knew that the people who had turned Mary and Joseph away from the inn saying, "No room," were fools, but in the end their having refused the holy family made the scene in the stable somehow more cozy. I felt sorry for them. They were all good and gentle, and they needed protection. They made do with what they were given. In their peaceful, patient way they didn't complain, and against the odds it all worked out. The infant was safely born on Christmas Day.

Whenever I heard the name "Bethlehem," these images instantly came to my mind. At six I knew exactly what Bethlehem looked like: a small Colonial New England village, like the villages near where I lived, with spruce and maple trees and a clapboard church in its center with a fine white needle for a spire. July, December, it didn't matter; in my head Bethlehem always lay under six inches of pristine snow. It was a town elevated above all other towns, for it had introduced great hope to the world. Its main characteristic was that it was peaceful and safe.

When I went to bed on Christmas Eve, the prospect of finding gifts under the Christmas tree the following morning was of course thrilling, but I knew, because my mother had told me, that the day had a greater significance, that Santa Claus was only an emissary of Jesus, that it was Jesus who really mattered. I believed my mother. Because Jesus seriously mattered to her, he mattered to me. Her faith formed the core of her person and served her in times of difficulty. As a child who had great faith in my mother, I had, by extension, faith in God. God was the air, the grass, and the sound of my mother's voice. That belief was not only comforting, it was exciting. Jesus loved us, my mother said, and that love seemed to contain an assurance of something good to come. A brilliant star had appeared in the east to indicate where Jesus was, and, looking out of my bedroom window at the starry night sky on Christmas Eve, I fully believed I could see that star brightly shining over our house.

THE SUN WAS HOT in Bethlehem on Christmas Eve, the narrow, winding streets were dusted with a fine, pale silt that blew in from the desert, and the afternoon light on the yellow sandstone buildings was blinding. I parked my car at the side of the road and walked into the town through a dusty construction site. Bethlehem was expecting close to two million visitors during the year 2000, and, like Nazareth, it was still busy preparing for them, building new roads, new hotels, new plumbing and electrical systems. On Christmas Day alone, 50,000 visitors were expected to show up in Manger Square, which in recent months had been converted from a parking lot to a pedestrian plaza.

I could hear Manger Square before I saw it. A distinct rumble of militaristic drumming vibrated in the air, and the gonging of the bells in the Church of the Nativity sailed over the high sandstone walls, an odd and slightly melancholy three-note tune that seemed to say, again and again, *Don't know why.* Turning the corner into the square, I came upon a marching parade of armed Palestinian police followed by a brass band and rows of Palestinian children dressed in Christmas white. In front of the Church of the Nativity shouting camera crews from assorted foreign countries were hurrying to set up their cables and equipment. The midnight Roman Catholic Mass was to be broadcast across the world by satellite.

But the loudest, most striking thing in the square was a voice that rang out from loudspeakers atop the Mosque of Omar across from the church, an amplified Arabic rant so hysterical it sounded like a man coming completely unhinged. The roof of the mosque was crowded with dark-haired men. Not only was it a Friday during Ramadan, an important day of prayer for Muslims, but Yasir Arafat and his wife were expected to visit the mosque and the Church of the Nativity that afternoon. The local Muslim men seemed to have worked themselves into a frenzy.

Manger Square was all bright sunlight and soldiers with guns, milling Christian pilgrims and excited Muslims. There were crowd-control barriers, cameras, lights, electric cables, and a lot of shouting. The very air of Bethlehem felt battered by the noise and tension, and above it all the bells in the small tower of the Church of the Nativity continued to tilt and swing at the behest of some hidden hand pulling on a rope, clanging out those three odd notes.

I went into the church. Originally built in the fourth century by Helena, the same wealthy woman who built the Church of the Annunciation in Nazareth and part of the Church of the Holy Sepulcher in Jerusalem, the church had been modified and added to over the centuries. I was startled by the great size of the nave and by the rows of beautiful alabaster columns that ran through it, like the columns in the Pharaonic temples of Egypt. Thin slits of sunlight raining down from the high, arched windows gave the columns a rich amber color. That the nave was bare — no pews, no benches, no icons or pictures or ornamentation of any kind — only enhanced its vast magnificence. The plastered yellow walls with a dado of blue were scratched with Greek and Arabic graffiti and worn bare by the passing elbows and shoulders of the faithful. The floor was made of great blocks of sandstone. The ceiling, a breathtaking network of timber beams and rafters, was incredibly high. I had heard people say that the Church of the Nativity was gloomy. It wasn't. The nave was grand and pleasing and mercifully simple. Though it had been sacked and pillaged by various invaders, it was the oldest church in the Holy Land. The ceiling timbers, believed to be medieval oak imported from England, had once, it was said, been plated with lead. The Ottoman Turks had stripped off the lead and used it to make bullets.

The Church of the Nativity, like the Church of the Holy Sepulcher, was run by three sects — Roman Catholic, Greek Orthodox, and Armenian Orthodox — which had been arguing for centuries over its operation. At the front of the church the Greek Orthodox and the Armenians had separate transepts, each with its own dark icons and silver lamps, each with its share of armed soldiers and bearded monks in black robes padding spookily about and glaring at the growing numbers of Christmas visitors.

The most sacred spot in the church was below in the Grotto of the Nativity, where a fourteen-pointed silver star in the floor beneath an altar marked the very spot where Christ was born. I made my way down the crowded stairs and found the grotto, a cramped, hot, brightly lit space full of chanting Greek priests and praying nuns in gray habits and sweating pilgrims milling or waiting in line to kiss the silver star on the floor. The place was crowded with wall hangings, more silver lamps, icons, murals, and gilt candelabra. Some pilgrims wept, some trembled in anticipation. Some had removed their shoes in deference, others chatted and chewed gum and snapped pictures. Many kissed the star by prostrating themselves on the marble floor. A woman in line behind me murmured to her rosary beads in Spanish.

I was next in line to kiss the star. The woman in front of me was stretched out on the floor, crying and praying, her forehead pressed to the star. Finally, I knelt among the glowing votive candles and saw the Latin phrase *Hic de Virgine Maria Jesus Christus Natus Est* printed upon the star. Here Jesus Christ was born of the Virgin Mary.

Many scholars and biblical historians doubt that Jesus was born in Bethlehem, and even an amateur might be tempted to ask why Joseph and Mary, who lived in Nazareth, north of Jerusalem, and were believed to be on their way to pay their taxes in Jerusalem, had ended up in this town *south* of Jerusalem. Bethlehem was the birthplace of King David, and scripture had stated that the Messiah, descended from David, would also be born here. But as for most of the other events in Jesus' life, there was no firmly reliable record of the circumstances or whereabouts of his birth. Angels appeared to some shepherds in a field to announce the birth of the savior, and three crowned kings came long distances to the town to see this infant king. But nobody in Bethlehem thought to jot down these amazing facts. If his presence caused such a stir, if his actions astonished and baffled so many people, if he was such a wise and charismatic speaker that his very existence irked the Roman and Jewish authorities, if the sky darkened and the earth trembled at the moment of his execution, why was no one moved to record these events while he was alive? His life radically affected history, yet, like Shakespeare's, his identity was vague. That seemed to me the most remarkable fact in a remarkable story. Surely that mystery — the unknowing, the uncertainty — had fueled the power that his person cast over so many people. That power was, in part, the power of rumor and persuasion.

Perhaps Jesus' miracles were not a sorcerer's marvelous acts but simply explicable acts of nature. Yet if Jesus, with all his genius and high intent, was only a human being, as mere as the rest of us, then we were still alone without cause or reason. If it could ever be proved that he was not sent by God, then life for Christians would be a bland and hopeless hoax, a lottery ticket that came up a dud, a glimmer in the sand that was not a diamond but a piece of broken glass. We didn't want explanations. We wanted wonder, mystery, and hope. We wanted the possibility of something better and bigger than our feeble, inadequate, imperfect selves.

Kneeling beneath an altar over the many-pointed silver star, I thought that both the Virgin Birth and this traditional location of Jesus' birth were unlikely, yet reason and doubt did not stop me from touching my lips to the star. Some strand of desire, a tenacious thread of that six-year-old's Christmas Eve wonder, was still within me, though I had tried hard to snap it.

Before leaving the basement of the church, I looked into the grotto where the manger is said to have sat. The closet-sized space was under the care of the Franciscans, who had decorated it so heavily it looked like a gangster's loot-strewn hideout. It bore no resemblance to the simple pastoral scene of my childhood crèche. That this tawdry little room proved nothing actually came as a consolation.

Climbing back up the stairs, I felt how predictable and tiresome all this religious segregation and competition was. During the nineteenth century the Greek Orthodox Church placed a star in an area that was held by the Catholics; Ottoman Turks removed the star. The Russian Orthodox Church, siding with the Greeks, demanded that the star be returned. The Turks refused, and thus began the Crimean War. How many wars had begun in similar ways? I, still uncertain, still primitively trying to determine who Jesus was, was unable to bring my religious faith to that level of conviction. I felt a trace of envy for those who could do so, and disgust for the way belief could become so twisted and violent and confused by the human desire for power and supremacy. Everyone was fighting to own a piece of the man who lived for peace and said, *Own nothing.*

I WALKED AROUND the church for another half-hour, then stepped back into the bright sunlight and noise of Manger Square. The hysteria felt ominous. I decided to skip the night in Shepherd's Field and return immediately to the relative calm of Jerusalem. Walking back to my car, I was accompanied by the melancholy ringing of the bells in the Church of the Nativity.

Some two years after my visit, the Israeli army with their guns and tanks reoccupied Bethlehem and for thirty-nine days held the Church of the Nativity under siege. The besieged — Palestinian protesters and militant gunmen — camped in the nave of the church, washed their dishes in the baptismal font, and used the altars for tables. With a heavy heart I sat by my television and watched the events on the nightly news. Bullets flew across the square and exploded against the church's stone façade. Eight Palestinians who dared step out of the church were shot dead; twenty-seven were wounded. Israeli army sharpshooters, whose rifles had a range of 900 yards, claimed that they shot only at men who were armed, but a Palestinian civilian caught in the siege was quoted in the *New York Times* as saying, "One of the dead was the bell-ringer."

Bethlehem's mythical image is far from its reality, yet that image is so strong and strikes such deep hope that even now, upon hearing the word "Bethlehem," I reflexively see the manger and the infant, the mother, the guiding star, and the three kings riding into a snowy village on their camels. A few dreamlike moments still pass before the hot reality dissolves the image. I'll never be rid of the myth of Bethlehem. It remains a place of the mind. Dressed in its legend, it symbolizes the best elements of humanity.

· 6 ·

SAINT PATRICK'S PURGATORY

We sat on battered wooden benches, seven or eight other pilgrims and I, in a high-ceilinged room in an abandoned building, taking a break from our prayers. We were, all of us, barefoot, and though it was July the large room was as cool as a cellar. We sat in our overcoats, blank-faced and sluggish and slightly distracted, like people in a terminal waiting for a train to take them to a better place. This was Saint Patrick's Purgatory, an ancient Catholic shrine on an island not much bigger than a city block, in the middle of Lough Derg in County Donegal, in the northern reaches of the Republic of Ireland. Ninety pilgrims had arrived on the island that day; two hundred fifty-six had arrived the day before. The pilgrims in this room had been acquainted for approximately fifteen minutes, although one or two, like May from County Cavan and Jimmy from County Mayo, had met here in years past.

This was the island's designated smoking area, and like most designated smoking areas it had an air of dereliction and shame. It was certainly the most neglected spot on the island. Lough Derg is one of Ireland's smaller lakes, not more than four miles by six, and is surrounded by low hills. Only one road leads to the lake from Pettigo, a small country village four miles away on the Donegal-Fermanagh border. The road ends at the lakeshore under a wrought-iron archway figured with the words SAINT PATRICK'S PURGATORY.

From the deeply rural banks of Lough Derg, Station Island was a baffling sight. It looked less like an island than like a stolid cluster of stone buildings miraculously afloat on the lake's surface. The seven buildings were heavy and institutional, and some, for lack of ground space, extended over the edge of the island on pilings and landfill. The whole place had the overburdened look of Ellis Island. The building we were sitting in, constructed in 1912, had once been the ladies' dormitory, and in its grave squareness and great bulk it resembled a mill building. Its big institutional rooms, though never elegant, had once been sharp and bustling but now were cold and barren, appointed with a few rough benches and wooden tables scattered randomly about. The walls were cracked and pocked, the painted woodwork was chipped, the fireplaces sat empty and cold. Windows were fractured, doors creaked. The concrete floor was littered with fallen bits of plaster and grit that stuck to the soles of our bare feet. Nevertheless, though I did not smoke, I liked the elderly feel of the building and preferred it to the modern nonsmoking area in the building next door.

Across the room Mrs. Caffrey dozed in the shadows, her back against the wall, her wooden rosary beads wrapped around her minute hand. Earlier a woman named Fiona had said softly to the room that she hoped the priests wouldn't catch sight of poor old Mrs. Caffrey with her two eyes clapped shut this way. Everyone looked sympathetically and a little guiltily at Mrs. Caffrey, tilting on her bench and breathing heavily through bluish lips gone slack with sleep. Though it was our job to keep our fellow pilgrims awake, no one had the heart to jostle Mrs. Caffrey. She was close to eighty, and she was without question one of the smallest adults I had ever seen. Her pale feet dangled, her muddy toes not quite touching the floor. Having arrived on yesterday's boat, Mrs. Caffrey had nearly completed her night vigil. For the rest of us, who had arrived on the island only a few hours before, the vigil lay heavily, dreadfully ahead.

Though I had been here for several hours and had completed two of the nine required stations of prayer, I was still a bit nervous. Twenty-five years of inattention and passive protest had failed to uproot from the swamp of my preconscious a little stump of reverence for the Catholic Church that had long ago been rooted there. I was certain that here, on this precisely orchestrated Catholic pilgrimage, I would make some screeching mistake that would mark me, correctly, as an apostate. Already that afternoon I had had to interrupt my prayers to ask a woman to remind me how to recite the Apostles' Creed. With missionary delight in her green eyes and a mittened hand laid consolingly on my forearm, the woman refreshed my memory and assured me that I was very much better than plenty of them who came back to Station Island year after year and still didn't know the blessed Creed. She waited patiently while I repeated the words back to her. I thanked her, laughed lightly with her, and didn't say that I did not quite accept certain parts of this crucial Christian profession, especially the phrases "conceived by the power of the Holy Spirit" and "resurrection of the body." The temptation to pretend, to daydream and muse instead of praying, to scoff, to skip over certain steps of this elaborate pilgrimage process, was strong, but I was determined to fulfill each prescribed step, to say every prayer and kiss every cross, whether my heart was moved to or not. At the moment my heart was decidedly not moved to. "I believe in one God, the maker of heaven and earth." Even the initial line of the creed was a stumbling block.

I studied again the pilgrim's instruction manual that had been handed to me when I arrived on Station Island. According to the manual, we had agreed to spend our three days here in bare feet and to follow the rules of the pilgrimage fast. Fasting was to begin at midnight on the first day, hours before the pilgrim arrived, and would end at midnight on the third day, hours after the pilgrim left. One "Lough Derg meal" would be allowed each day, consisting of black tea or coffee, dry bread, and oatcakes. The only alteration to this fast would occur on the third day, when the staggering, hallucinating pilgrim was allowed to partake of "mineral waters of any kind throughout the day." Pilgrims to Lough Derg had to be at least fifteen years of age and "able to walk and kneel unaided and free from any illness aggravated by fasting." Not permitted were food, sweets, chewing gum, alcoholic and nonalcoholic drinks, cameras, mobile phones, radios and personal stereos, musical instruments, games, and articles or literature to sell or distribute. The night vigil would begin at 10:00 P.M. on the first day and end at 10:00 P.M. on the second, and during these hours the dormitories would be locked, ensuring that no corrupted pilgrim could creep upstairs and lie down on a bed. "The central penitential exercise of the Pilgrimage involves each pilgrim staying completely and continuously awake for 24 hours," the manual said.

I had risen at six o'clock that morning to travel here from Dublin. By the time I lay down in a bed again the following night, I would in fact have been continuously awake for forty hours. I assumed that this was more or less the case with the other pilgrims. When, with some dismay, I mentioned this to Fiona, sitting on my right, she said, "Sure, the priests are well aware of that. 'Tis all in the plan."

Though I had already performed the station twice, I read again the section of the manual titled "Order of Station." It was like an arcane recipe for a sorcerer's conjuration, and each time I read it my astonishment grew.

Begin the station with a visit to the Blessed Sacrament in St. Patrick's Basilica. Go to St. Patrick's Cross near the Basilica; kneel, and say one *Our Father,* one *Hail Mary,* and one *Creed.* Kiss the Cross. Go to St. Brigid's Cross on the outside wall of the Basilica; kneel, and say three *Our Fathers,* three *Hail Marys* and one *Creed.* With your back to the Cross, stand with arms fully outstretched, and say three times, *"I renounce the World, the Flesh and the Devil."* Walk slowly, by your right hand, four times around the Basilica, while praying silently seven decades of the Rosary and one *Creed* at the end. Go to St. Brigid's Bed (if there is a queue please join it before going to the bed). At the Bed:

a) walk three times around the outside, by your right hand, while saying three *Our Fathers,* three *Hail Marys* and one *Creed.*
b) kneel at the entrance to the Bed and repeat these prayers.
c) walk three times around the inside and say these prayers again.
d) kneel at the Cross in the centre and say these prayers for the fourth time.

Repeat these exercises at St. Brendan's Bed, St. Catherine's Bed, St. Columba's Bed. Walk six times around the outside of the large Penitential Bed, which comprises St. Patrick's Bed and that of Sts. Davog and Molaise, while saying six *Our Fathers,* six *Hail Marys* and one *Creed.* Kneel at the entrance to St. Patrick's Bed and say three *Our Fathers,* three *Hail Marys* and one *Creed.* Walk three times around the inside while repeating these prayers. Kneel at the Cross in the centre and say them again. Kneel at the entrance to the Bed of Sts. Davog and Molaise and say three *Our Fathers,* three *Hail Marys* and one *Creed.* Walk three times around the inside while repeating these prayers. Kneel at the Cross in the centre and say them again. Go to the water's edge; stand and say five *Our Fathers,* five *Hail Marys* and one *Creed.* Kneel and repeat these prayers. Make the sign of the Cross with lake water as a reminder of your Baptism. Return to St. Patrick's Cross; kneel and say one *Our Father,* one *Hail Mary* and one *Creed.* Go to the Basilica and conclude the Station by reciting Psalm 15 or by saying five *Our Fathers,* five *Hail Marys* and one *Creed,* for the Pope's intentions.

I spread the manual on my knee, drew my notebook and pen out of my jacket pocket, and did some calculating. One station comprised 99 Our Fathers, 156 Hail Marys, and 27 Apostles' Creeds, with seven doxologies thrown in at the end of the rosary parts. Upon completing the required nine stations over the course of three days, the pilgrim would have recited 891 Our Fathers, 1,404 Hail Marys, and 243 Creeds, not counting the Hail Marys and Our Fathers recited as a matter of course within the four Masses scheduled throughout the three days. And there was an awful lot of kneeling involved. I was already exhausted. That afternoon I had had great trouble praying. I stuffed the manual back into my pocket and looked around the room.

The sky had cleared for the third time that day, and through the tall windows the changeable lake was now a royal purple in the afternoon light. In the distance the low mountains that ringed the lake were mauve, and on nearby islands the thickets of trees, which half an hour before had been a damp gray, were suddenly drenched in gold. The great slanting light illuminated the bluish sleeves of cigarette smoke that stretched now and then from various mouths about the room. The room was very quiet.

Jimmy, a big man wearing a necktie, sat beside me with his elbows on his knees and his chin in his hands, a cigarette pincered between two knuckles. Jimmy was bursting with good health. He breathed deeply and audibly through his nose, and while the rest of us were hunched with cold, Jimmy perspired freely. Now and then he fingered a hankie from his hip pocket and swept it across the back of his glistening neck. In the strong light his white hair was like a solid cap of frost, the forelock that drooped onto his forehead a delicate icicle. As his eyes wandered over the cement floor and roughly plastered walls, Jimmy discovered quite by accident that the sunlight had struck the crystal of his wristwatch just so, sending a coin of reflected light across the room and onto the opposite wall, just above Mrs. Caffrey's head. Slowly Jimmy sat up, his mouth opening slightly with interest. He positioned his left arm and moved his wrist a fraction, and the disk of light shot up toward the ceiling. He glanced quickly left and right to see if anyone had noticed.

May was busy rooting for her cigarettes in the pocket of her black leather jacket. Dympna, with one hand visoring her eyes, was reading the *Irish Times;* its headline said: CONCORDE CRASHES IN PARIS. The serious, silent girl with the powerfully musty smell and the boy's regular haircut was staring through the window at the purple martins that tee-tered and plunged above the lake. (When I first saw this girl, on the boat coming from the mainland, I mistook her for a handsome young man, then realized she wasn't a man, then wasn't sure whether she was or wasn't, and finally was so curious and perplexed that I went over and, pawing dismissively at my perfectly functional watch, pretended to be looking for the correct time just so I could hear her voice. She said, "Ten past twelve." The voice was startling. It was soft and sweet and graced with the pirouetting accent of County Kerry.) The elderly man sitting by the cold radiator with an unlit cigarette tucked behind his ear had re-moved his trilby hat and, pressing his eyeglasses to his face, was peering at the label in its crown. The Galway widow, Mrs. O'Cray, had shut her eyes and with a little finger was exploring the entrance to her right ear. From the two black-haired teenagers slumped in the corner came long sighs of boredom. One was trying to hold a pencil pinched between his upper lip and nose; the pencil kept falling to his lap.

Jimmy took a last hasty nip at his cigarette and stabbed it out on the floor. With his right hand he began to tilt his watch experimentally this way and that, shoving the reflected light about the upper reaches of the room. The little egg-shaped disk jittered and wheeled about sharply on the shadowed wall opposite us. He screwed one blue eye shut and let the other eye roam after the tiny light. It rested on the light switch, mean-dered to the ceiling, rested on a spiderweb.

In his necktie and pullover and corduroy trousers, Jimmy looked like a genteel country lawyer. He had an intelligent, handsome face, with a long fine nose, high cheekbones, and a squarish chin. His manner was shy and dignified. He had said very little that afternoon. Of all the sets of bare feet that I had seen that first day on Station Island, his were the most improbable; they looked pale and stiff and remarkably frail for such a big man. They were like a pair of cold feet at the end of a corpse in a coffin.

Slowly, carefully, in a kind of ocular tiptoe, Jimmy brought the light down the wall, let it graze the top of Mrs. Caffrey's head, then quickly lifted it away again. He studied her for a response. She dozed on, her chin pointed at the door. Jimmy lowered the light again, gently stirred at her hair with it, then drove it back up to the ceiling. He repeated this several times, each time touching the light glancingly down on Mrs. Caffrey's head like a questioning foot testing ice on a pond. And then

Jimmy grew bold and let the light slip slowly lower onto her forehead. Her aged skin was pale and translucent. The light trembled above her eyeglasses like a third eye. I was certain that Mrs. Caffrey would feel it and snap to, but in her sleep she remained unmoved. Finally, in a little act of daring, Jimmy let the light rest on one lens of her glasses, where it reproduced itself, casting another, fainter disk of light onto her knee. I turned and looked at Jimmy. He was deep in reverie, with one corner of his mouth curled upward in amusement at his own cleverness.

May lit a fresh cigarette, crossed her long legs, leaned forward over her knees, and looked eagerly around the room, ready to talk. "Hi, now, Jimmy," she said gamely. "Did you ever hear about if you put your Saint Brigid's cross outside the window at night that she would come and bless it?"

Jimmy was training the little circle of light on a door handle and did not hear her.

A stream of smoke flowed from the right side of May's mouth. "Jimmy?"

Jimmy's head snapped up. He gasped, "Hah?" and slid backward on the bench and crossed his arms, concealing the watch in his armpit. His eyes darted about the room, looking for the person who had spoken his name.

"If you put your Saint Brigid's outside the window that she would come and bless it? Did you ever hear the mother of that one, Jimmy?"

Jimmy grimaced, trying to see May in the sunlight. "Who, May?"

"Brigid."

"Brigid who?"

"Saint."

"But who is it 'twould bless?"

"Brigid."

Jimmy's fine face went blank with confusion. He turned one bulky palm upward. "Yes, I know, but who would come and bless it, May?"

May was a gentle, patient woman with a compelling, ruined kind of beauty. With her leather jacket and her tight black jeans and her helmet of black hair she looked like a bit like a middle-aged biker. She had a large head, big, drooping eyes, and a wide mouth that turned down at the corners when her face was idle. Her Cavan accent was so lush and overgrown that I had to struggle to follow her. "Saint Brigid, Jimmy. You know her."

Jimmy cocked his white head at May. "Herself would come in the night?"

"Brigid would, yeah."

Jimmy tucked his chin in, chuckled skeptically into his sweater front, and said blandly, "Heh, heh, I don't know about *that* one, May," in a way that suggested that not only did he not know about it, he did not care about it.

"I heard 'twas true," May said, looking around the room for support in the matter. No one spoke, but May was undaunted. "I do it meself. Put the cross outside the window at night. My husband saw her one time. Saint Brigid. All in blue she was."

Jimmy gave May a look. "I'd say your husband had a little drop taken, May."

"He hadn't, Jimmy." May paused, then smiled sheepishly, as if picturing her husband. "Or, well, maybe he had. But I do it meself. Put the cross out at night."

Jimmy tapped at the crystal of his watch and stared through the window at the skittering martins. "Any results to speak of?" he said softly.

"I'm alive today, amn't I, Jim? That's something to speak of!"

Fiona said, "Now, they say if you carry a Saint Brigid's cross you never die in a violent accident."

The man in the trilby hat said, "Excuse me, but is that not Our Lady of Knock?"

"Saint Brigid."

Mrs. Caffrey, tapped awake by the sound of voices, straightened up on her bench and coughed and needlessly smoothed the lapel of her spotless blue raincoat. Blinking into the room, she knuckled her eyeglasses higher on her nose with her beaded hand and said with authority, "For example, with Brigid's cross, if I was on that Concorde, I'd be alive now."

Everyone turned to look at Mrs. Caffrey. Her voice was high and thin after her nap, and her watery blue eyes looked sore behind her glasses. Someone at the far end of my bench said generously, "You're right, there, missus. And thanks be to God you were not on it."

The Irish in general spoke easily to strangers, and they spoke with familiarity and a heartening air of encouragement, as though life were a test that we were all just one step away from failing. But here, in the holiness and sobriety of Saint Patrick's Purgatory, that cheerily doom-filled camaraderie held an added undercurrent of excitement, the electric glow of emergency. The pilgrims were on their mettle.

"Now, were there any survivors in that one?" Fiona said, looking at me for an answer, as if the one foreigner in the room might have the facts of a foreign tragedy.

Dympna, an elegant woman in pearls and an Hermès scarf, lowered her newspaper and said crisply, "None."

"'Twas awful," said Fiona. "I prayed for them."

"Straight into a blessed hotel it flew."

"Mother of God, think of it."

"'Twas Germans, mostly, in the plane."

"And a few Parisians killed on the ground."

"County Cork is full of Germans now," the man in the trilby said with a hint of resentment. He drew the cigarette from his ear and put it in his mouth and sat that way for a long time without lighting it.

May asked me where in America I was from. I said that I had grown up in Boston but lived in Rhode Island, and several people offered that they had cousins living in Boston. They listed the cousins' names and wondered whether I might have come across them.

May said to me, "And you came to Lough Derg with your husband, Rose?"

At that moment in my life I was alone, the particular circumstances of which had rendered me nearly speechless with grief. "No," I said. "I came alone."

Mrs. Caffrey, squinting at me from her place in the shadows, said with certitude, "You never came all the way across from America to visit Lough Derg."

"Yes," I said. "I did."

With a sweep of her arm May flung her cigarette ash into the sunlight and cried, "Good girl! You'll bring the news back with you then, won't you! Tell all the Yanks they've to come out to Lough Derg." She laughed. May was casual and warm and had a deep love of her religion, which she expressed with a sports fan's wholehearted zest.

Fiona said, "And will you have any holiday in Ireland, Rose, or will you head straight home?"

I told Fiona that from Ireland I planned to travel to Greece.

"Be careful."

"Careful?"

Fiona leaned forward in her seat. Ominously she said, "There was an Irish girl disappeared."

A long silence followed while we all imagined the girl. We stared at the smoky air and not at each other. Disappeared, we knew, was somehow worse than killed. No one asked what Greece had to do with it.

For the first time Mrs. O'Cray spoke. "Now there was this other girl. She was going with a Protestant boy." She interrupted herself suddenly to nod in apology at me. "Now, I think I can say 'Protestant,' Rose, because you're obviously Catholic, sitting here like you are. Anyway, the fella got her pregnant. Seven months she was and then she disappeared." She looked at me. "You wouldn't have the likes of that in America, would you?"

I said, "We have nearly everything you could imagine in America. And worse."

A woman sitting on the other side of Jimmy leaned forward to look at me. Anxiously she said, "My daughter is in New York. A waitress in County Queens. Will she come home from there, do you think?" Before I could venture a guess about a woman I did not know, she said, "Sure, Dublin is growing awfully like New York," as if the new similarities might lure the daughter home. Having consoled herself without any assistance from me, the woman sat back in her seat.

May asked whether anyone had yet met the man who was here from Cavan. No one had. "Well, he felt he needed to come here to Lough Derg because the other morning a young man up the road from him hung himself."

Fiona gasped and lifted a hand to her mouth.

Mrs. O'Cray said, "He didn't!"

"He did!" May cried, "and, oh, the effect that was on that family!"

Mrs. Caffrey said, "'Tis awful. So many do be killing themselves. The young people. An epidemic, like."

The conversation branched and grew, like a thread of ivy up a stone wall, meandering, naturally taking the path of least resistance, which in Ireland was often the path of mishap and mayhem. At some point in their soaring trajectory Irish conversations would instinctively swerve to the amputated leg, the drowned husband, the missing daughter, the blinded son, the hotel fire. The handsome, serious girl by the window had turned to face the room, and though ten minutes before she had appeared utterly deaf to the world, the distinctly lowing voice of tragedy had reached her and drawn her in. She was listening intently now, with dark and darting eyes. It was difficult to gauge how old this girl was. She looked no more than twenty-five but could have been sixteen.

May said, "Now there was another boy. His mother saw him in the garage, and he was taking a rope. Later he hung himself. You go into that house now and still think you'll see him running up the stairs."

Fiona said woefully, "'Tis common in Ireland."

Earlier that day in the Station Island bookshop, I had seen a book called *Suicide and the Irish*. There were other books with grim titles, such as *When Strangers Marry: A Study of Marriage Breakdown in Ireland* and *Why Do We Suffer?* and *Virginia's Questions: Why Am I Still a Catholic?* and *The Unwilling Celibates: A Spirituality for Single Adults*.

I said, "Why is suicide common in Ireland?"

May shut her eyes and pressed her lips together and shook her head gravely, as though she had been trying to answer this question for years. "God knows."

Lifting a flowered kerchief onto her small gray head and nimbly tying its legs in a tidy knot under her chin, Mrs. Caffrey said, "'Tis the drink. And they have strayed from the church. And the drink. There used be wild queues of pilgrims here at Lough Derg years ago. Now they're gone. Years ago there used be over twenty to forty thousand." Mrs. Caffrey came to Station Island every summer, and most years she came more than once. She came, she said, to pray for the Catholic Church and for the young people. "The young people need prayer."

May said, "They do. They do," and, looking inquisitively about the room, she asked, "Now what about this young fella that swam off the island? Who heard that one?"

Fiona said, "That's right! Swam off! He was on his second night here and he swam off the island in the middle of the night!"

Mrs. O'Cray said, "He was not one hundred percent in the head was what I heard."

"They found him shivering in the bushes on the next island over," May said. "'Twas big news for Lough Derg. Had he drowned it would have been bad publicity."

Dympna said, "Now, I don't know whether it was an attempted suicide or what it was, but that poor fella must have been altogether desperate."

Fiona said, as though this naturally followed, "And did you hear about that train crash in Kildare and the two people were killed? I knew them very well."

"What happened there?" the man with the trilby asked.

"Well, now there was this wasteland by the train tracks, a weedy aul' place, and the kids used go there to drink, and this young couple was there and supposedly she wanted to go to the loo, but she was so drunk she sat on the tracks by accident. The driver of the train blew his horn at her, but being drunk she'd no idea what for, and the boy she was with — also three sheets to the moon — reached out to grab her off the tracks and was cut" — Fiona made a slashing motion from her neck to her hip — "from here to here."

May winced and Mrs. O'Cray's hands flew to her face.

Fiona continued, "The guards went to the girl's house and said to the parents, 'Come to the hospital; you are needed urgently,' but the parents said, 'You've the wrong girl. Our daughter is at the fillums.' But sure the daughter'd only conned the parents and wasn't at the fillums at all. The guards said 'tis not the wrong girl, and the parents asked, well, what was she wearing? But who would notice what she was wearing when she's lying down dead?"

No one spoke. The listening faces looked frightened, the eyes darted nervously. Jimmy loosened his necktie, fit the corner of a matchbook flap between his two front teeth, tapped one bare foot on the cold floor. The trilby man asked impatiently how on earth the guards knew where the dead daughter lived. Fiona had the answer. "She'd a mobile phone with her. It rang. It was a friend calling to see where she'd got to. The guards answered it and asked the caller who was the girl with the phone because she has been killed."

Mrs. Caffrey tsked and sighed and drew her raincoat around her and said to the cracked plaster ceiling, "God, be good."

May sat silently for a moment, gazing at the cigarette in her pale hand. "Now myself I knew two young boys, they said, 'We're going away only up the road a bit,' and twenty minutes later one of them came back and said the other was dead."

Fiona winced in bafflement and disgust. "Jesus save us, what happened, May?"

"Car," said May. "Hit a tree."

Mrs. Caffrey had heard enough. She squirmed into a slightly higher position on her bench and raised one fist close to her ear as if to still the room. "'Tis the drink. The drink, I tell you. They do be drinking themselves into a misfortunate state."

One of the dark-haired teenagers, slumped low on his bench with his legs stretched out before him, knocked the baseball cap back on his head and shrugged and muttered insouciantly, "Everyone dies anyway so."

The pilgrims puffed on their cigarettes. Someone coughed loud and long in the next room, where more smoking pilgrims were shuffling through newspapers and magazines strewn about on a big wooden table. The light in the room had begun to soften as the sun slipped lower toward the edge of the lake. A motorboat droned at the south side of the island.

And then the handsome young woman, who as far as I could tell had not spoken a word since she arrived on the island, said dreamily, "Sure, bare feet are very revealing."

FOR YEARS I had heard about Saint Patrick's Purgatory from Irish friends, read about it in Irish literature, seen pictures of it in Irish guidebooks. It was the most important place of penitential pilgrimage in Ireland, rivaled only by Croagh Patrick, a mountain on the coast of County Mayo where once a year pilgrims walked (some barefoot) to the summit to greet the sunrise. The island was sometimes referred to as Station Island, for the nine stations of prayer the pilgrims performed there, sometimes as Saint Patrick's Purgatory, for the shrine itself, but most often it was called Lough Derg. In old Irish stories people were always going grimly off to Lough Derg to punish themselves and beg forgiveness for some unforgivable sin or other. It had once been known as a favorite spot of alcoholics, who would retreat there after a protracted bender to sober up and review their shameful behavior. The most common thing that people said about the pilgrimage to Lough Derg was that it was serious, the most difficult penitential pilgrimage in the Christian world. It was no sunny holiday trip to Lourdes or Fatima or Knock; it was physical torture. The island was lonely, wind-blown, rainy, and ridden with midges that flew up your nose and gnawed at your ankles. The lake was black and cold. You had to walk about in circles all night long and endlessly kneel on weird piles of ancient stones as you mulled over your own frailty and failures. Once a day the priests would give you a crust of bread to eat. You did nothing but hail Mary and kiss crosses and pray yourself silly, and why on earth would anyone in his right mind want to go there?

Nevertheless, for over a thousand years Christian pilgrims from as far away as Italy had flocked to Saint Patrick's Purgatory for a personal taste of this lakebound trial. And for all that it was feared and maligned, the shrine was also deeply revered. It was fixed ineradicably in a crevice in the Irish identity, a psychic burden but a national blessing. It symbolized and contained all the unique characteristics of Irish Catholicism, and its sometimes rocky history mirrored the history of Ireland. Most important, it commanded from the Irish people an abiding respect. Few people doubted the ameliorative powers of Saint Patrick's Purgatory.

That morning, before leaving Dublin for Lough Derg, I had asked a young woman browsing in the map section of Eason's Bookstore what county the village of Knock was in. (The shrine at Knock was another famous holy site, a place of miracles and cures.) "Mayo," the woman said quickly. She looked vaguely like Diana, the princess of Wales; she was tall, with glossy red lips and nails, seriously Swedish blond hair, and a lot of gold jewelry. Her shoes were stylish and expensive. She held a copy of *Anil's Ghost* in one hand and a *Hello* magazine in the other.

"Thanks," I said. And then, to dispel any notion that I was a superstitious crackpot, I said, "Not that I'm going to Knock."

"Well, you might now, like," she said in a recommending way. Her comment gave me the courage to confess that I was actually on my way to Station Island.

The woman stared at me. She had no idea what I was talking about. "Lough Derg," I said.

I saw her looking at the thumb-smudged reading glasses hanging from a string on my chest, my bloodshot eyes, the hair I had not combed that day or bothered to have cut in months, my unadorned face smeared with sleep and worry, my French carpenter's jacket that was missing two buttons. Having arrived in Dublin very late the previous night, I had had to spend the night in a hostel that was full of young Europeans who had recently landed in Dublin looking for work. They spent the night wandering in and out of the dormitory room, shrieking and laughing and singing, smoking and drinking cans of beer. I had managed only two hours of sleep and was exhausted. Worse, I was suffering the physical effects of a broken heart, was worn out and dispirited by grief, a grief that had sent my appearance into a nosedive. I had lost any pretense of making myself presentable. I avoided mirrors, not wanting to know that this sad, slightly mad-looking person was me. I got around to combing my hair about every fourth day. Most days I put on the same clothes I had dropped on the floor the night before. I didn't care.

The woman looked down at my torn boating sneakers splattered with paint. I could see confusion and a hint of mistrust rising in her milky blue eyes.

I tried again. "Saint Patrick's Purgatory."

She gasped, "Oh, God," in recognition, and her lacquered lashes fluttered. "Will that be nice? I don't think so. My sister went there. Said it was altogether hard. The hardest part is staying up all night."

"I guess I'll see what it's like," I said.

The woman looked at me now with what seemed like apprehension and a touch of envy. "I wonder would you ever do something for me?" she said hesitantly.

I nodded. She rearranged the book and the magazine in her hands, hoisted her handbag higher on her shoulder, smoothed her short bangs. She was temporizing, looking for a way to ask the question. Her face had been prompted before a mirror with great results, yet for all its polish it remained guileless, the eager spirit untamed behind a mask of sophistication. She touched her chin with the tip of the rolled magazine, looked at the floor, and then looked at me. Softly she said, "Would you ever say a prayer for me at Lough Derg?"

It was an earnest request, not a joke, and it surprised me with its intimacy. It was the sort of thing you'd say to a sister or an old friend. She assumed that I cared enough about a stranger to pray on her behalf, and she seemed to believe that a prayer sent up from Saint Patrick's Purgatory was more valuable than a prayer launched elsewhere. "Of course I will," I said. "What's your name?"

"Mary. O'Dowd. Oh, thank you."

OWNED BY THE DIOCESE of Clogher, Station Island was not unlike Vatican City in its self-sufficiency, with its own motorboats, laundry, water chlorinator, and emergency power plant. There were four priests — the prior and three clerical assistants — and some fifty staff members who worked on the island in summer during the pilgrimage season. The dormitories and dining room were managed by the Sisters of the Congregation of the Daughters of Our Lady of the Sacred Heart. In addition to books, aspirin, cigarettes, and insect repellent, the bookshop sold Lough Derg mouse pads that said, TIME OUT FOR BODY AND SOUL, rosary beads, Saint Brigid's crosses, and other religious artifacts. (Also on sale were raffle tickets to raise funds for the island; the prizes were worth £28,000, and the first prize was a car.)

Hoping to educate myself about the shrine, I bought two books in the shop: an exhaustively researched scholarly monograph by Michael Haren and Yolande de Pontfarcy, titled *The Medieval Pilgrimage to St. Patrick's Purgatory: Lough Derg and the European Tradition,* and a short, lucid history by Joseph McGuinness, *Lough Derg; St. Patrick's Purgatory.* In my spare time on the island I went into one of the three sitting rooms and studied my books.

The shrine had its origins in a fifth-century monastery established on Saints' Island, a larger neighboring island in Lough Derg, and although there had never been real evidence to support it, the tradition was that Saint Patrick himself had founded that community. The most renowned and influential document on the early history of the pilgrimage was the *Tractatus de Purgatorio Sancti Patricii,* written in 1184 by a British Cistercian monk. The introduction offers a detailed account of how Saint Patrick came to establish the monastery as part of his effort to convert the intractable pagan Irish people, who would not be won over "unless one of them could witness both the torments of the wicked and the joys of the just." According to the tale, as recounted by Haren and de Pontfarcy, one day while Saint Patrick was fasting and praying, Jesus appeared to him and led him to a deserted place, presumably on what is now Station Island.

> There [Jesus] showed to him a round pit, dark inside, and said to him that whoever, being truly repentant and armed with true faith, would enter this pit and remain for the duration of one day and one night, would be purged of all the sins of his life. Moreover, while going through it, he would see not only the torments of the wicked, but also, if he acted constantly according to the faith, the joys of the blessed. Thus, after the disappearance of the Lord from before his eyes, blessed Patrick was filled with spiritual joy not only because his Lord had appeared to him but also because he had shown him this pit by means of which he hoped the people would turn away from their errors. [p. 8]

The *Tractatus* recounts the tale of an Irish knight named Owein, who claimed that he had journeyed to the other world through a cave known as Saint Patrick's Purgatory. Owein's is the first known account of a pilgrim submitting himself to this pit. In the middle of the twelfth century, having made a confession to the local bishop, Owein chose to enact his penance at Saint Patrick's Purgatory. The prior at the monastery on Saints' Island tried to dissuade him, warning that many pilgrims who had ventured into the cave had never returned. Owein persisted. Relenting, the prior led him to the church, where the knight fasted and prayed for fifteen days. Following the fast, Owein was taken to the purgatory.

Here he was admitted through a door into a dark cavern or pit. Having continued through the dark for some time, he eventually saw light ahead and emerged into a field. In the centre of the field was a large and beautifully built hall. On entering the hall he was soon met by fifteen men dressed in white, who proved to be messengers from God. They warned him that he would be assaulted by demons, who would try to persuade him to turn back and leave the place. Owein remained steadfast. No sooner had these angels disappeared than the demons appeared. In spite of their threats of torture Owein refused to retreat. The demons at once seized him and began to subject him to the first of ten ordeals. [McGuinness, p. 19]

Owein's ten brutal ordeals (recorded in harrowing detail by Haren and de Pontfarcy) were being visited simultaneously upon many other souls, all dead, who had come before Owein and who, in their faithlessness, had been unable to pray. The demons bound Owein, tossed him into a raging fire, and raked him back and forth with piercing iron hooks. The moment Owein appealed to Jesus for help, the fire miraculously expired. Next he came to a field full of people who had been pinned to the ground with roasting hot nails driven through their hands and feet and who were being mercilessly beaten by a band of devils. The devils tried to nail Owein to the ground, but again he escaped by invoking the name of Jesus. Among the many things Owein saw in this place were people having their hearts gnawed at by toads, flaming dragons, and serpents; people being dangled in the air by various delicate body parts; others being fried, roasted, or baked in ingenious ways; others being speedily spun on a huge wheel, the bottom half of which passed through an enormous fire in the ground. He saw people being immersed in molten metal. He saw naked people on a mountaintop being swept up by a tornado and tossed into a "fetid and icy" river, where demons danced on the surface to prevent their escape. The grotesque and pitilessly cackling demons and devils attempted to subject Owein to each one of these tortures, but the knight was repeatedly spared when he called upon Jesus for assistance.

Finally, having successfully evaded the ten tortures with the weapon of his faith, Owein was brought to a kind of pre-paradise, a temperate place full of perfume and flowers and music and light and joyful people singing, where two archbishops told him that what he had just witnessed was the purification of the souls of the dead. Eventually those souls would be freed from purgatory and, after a period in this earthly paradise, would proceed to heaven. At the end of Owein's pleasant meeting with the archbishops, he was instructed to return to earth the same way he came. But this time, as he passed back through the place of horrors the demons ran from him. When he emerged from the pit he was greeted by the stunned prior. Owein returned to the church and spent another fifteen days in prayer.

According to McGuinness's book, it was not until the end of the twelfth century, with the widening influence of Rome and the shift in Irish ecclesiastical power from the Celtic monasteries to the diocesan system, that Saint Patrick's Purgatory began to gain notoriety. The monastery on Saints' Island fell under the direction of the Augustinian Order of Canons Regular, whose international network fostered communication between Ireland and the rest of the Christian world. The notion of life after death, compelling enough in modern times, was a particular obsession of the medieval mind, and the monk who transcribed the tale of Knight Owein permitted himself in his introductory remarks a moment of personal reflection on the subject. "We know that many have often asked in what manner the souls leave the body, where do they go, what do they find, what do they perceive and what do they suffer. Because these things have been concealed from us, it is better to fear them than to inquire about them" (McGuinness, p. 18).

Knight Owein's story appeared to offer a detailed and graphic answer to these fundamental questions and, having been disseminated widely on the Continent, the story began to draw pilgrims from the far corners of Europe, people eager not only for the repentance and penance offered by the act of pilgrimage but for a firsthand glimpse of the wonders of purgatory and the afterlife. Pilgrims from France, Hungary, England, Switzerland, and the Netherlands returned home from Ireland with similarly fantastical and elaborate stories of their personal journeys into Saint Patrick's cave. Gradually an entire literature developed based on the apotropaic visions at the shrine, a literature that affected the suggestible medieval European imagination and was said to have influenced many writers, including Dante. By the fourteenth century Saint Patrick's Purgatory had become one of the great medieval shrines of Europe. (The shrine is mentioned in "A Pilgrimage for Religion's Sake," Erasmus's colloquy of 1526. Menedemus skeptically asks the pious Ogygius if he has been to Saint Patrick's cave, "of which marvelous tales are told." Ogygius, having been there, replies, "I sailed in Stygian waters, to be sure; I went down into the jaws of Avernus; I saw what goes on in hell.")

The cave at Lough Derg was generally described as a manmade pit high enough for a person to kneel in but not to stand upright in. The Protestant reverend John Richardson in 1727 wrote a bitter anti-Catholic tract entitled *The Great Folly, Superstition and Idolatry of Pilgrimages in Ireland,* and in it described the cave as being

> 22 feet long, 2 feet 1 inch wide, and 3 feet high. It hath a bending within six feet of the far end, where there is a very small window, or spike hole, to let in some light and air to the pilgrims that are shut up in it. There is little or none of it under ground, and it seems never to have been sunk deeper than the rock. It is built of stone and clay, huddled together, covered with broad stones, and all overlaid with earth. [Haren and de Pontfarcy, p. 20]

During the Middle Ages pilgrims to Saint Patrick's Purgatory preceded their twenty-four-hour vigil in the cave with confession, penance, and a fifteen-day fast. Before they entered the cave a Requiem Mass would be said for them, as though they had in fact died and were about to enter purgatory. In the fourteenth century pilgrims were actually laid out like corpses, and the Office of the Dead was sung over them.

At the end of the fifteenth century, skeptical authorities in Rome decided that the proliferation of bizarre visions and fantasies coming out of the cave at Lough Derg had gotten out of hand and was giving Saint Patrick and the church a bad name. In 1497, by papal decree, the cave was closed. But pilgrims continued to flock to Lough Derg. Though its visionary nature had been officially abandoned, the pilgrimage had securely captured the Christian imagination, and it continued as a penitential exercise. When the cave was reopened in the sixteenth century, it was used for the twenty-four-hour vigil in a purely symbolic way. As the visions of purgatory dwindled, the pilgrimage to Lough Derg developed into the somewhat more controlled and contemplative form it takes now.

With the Reformation and the efforts of the English Crown to govern northern Ireland, Lough Derg again came under attack. The Reformers saw Saint Patrick's Purgatory as a representation of the subversive qualities of Catholic superstition, and in 1632 the Lords Justice ordered its destruction. The cave and other buildings were demolished, the monks were banished, and pilgrims were forbidden to land on the island. But the pilgrimage was kept alive, first by people who stood on the mainland and prayed with their hands stretched toward the island, and then by daring pilgrims who made their way onto the island in defiance of the law. Within a few years the cave was reconstructed and the pilgrimage was back in full swing, though efforts to suppress it continued throughout the first half of the eighteenth century. During the reign of Queen Anne, an act of Parliament was passed prohibiting resort to the island. According to Thomas Wright, in "St Patrick's Purgatory: An Essay on the Legends of Purgatory, Hell, and Paradise, Current During the Middle Ages" (1844), the act set out the following reason:

> Whereas, the superstitions of popery are greatly increased and upheld by the pretended sanctity of places, especially of a place called St. Patrick's Purgatory, in the county of Donegaul, and of wells, to which pilgrimages are made by vast numbers at certain seasons, by which, not only the peace of the public is greatly disturbed, but the safety of the government also hazarded by the riotous and unlawful assembling together of many thousands of papists.

With too many papists, too much imagination, and too much fervor, the pilgrimage to this tiny island had become a nuisance and a threat to the neighbors, the behemoth British Empire. It was decreed that offenders should be fined ten shillings, and those who ignored the fine would be whipped in public.

Yet the faithful persisted and prevailed. In 1714 the bishop of Clogher, in a letter to Rome, gave an account of the standard pilgrimage being practiced at that time: pilgrims fasted and prayed for nine days, confessed their sins, received communion, entered the "subterranean pit" for twenty-four hours, and finished the exercise by dipping their head three times in the lake. "And thus is completed the pilgrimage, to which idle inventors of fables have added so many exaggerations about spectres and visions, which never had any existence save in the distorted imaginations of such storytellers."

In 1780 the cave at Station Island was finally destroyed for good, chiefly because it was too small to accommodate the large numbers of pilgrims who wished to make the vigil. A church was built to replace the cave, and with the advent of Catholic emancipation in Ireland in the midnineteenth century, the modern-day form of the pilgrimage to Lough Derg began.

I LEFT THE SMOKING ROOM to resume my prayers. I had one more station to complete before the Night Prayer and Benediction at 9:15 and the start of the night vigil. Even though I had completed two stations that afternoon, in my nervousness I couldn't remember how the station began. I scanned my pilgrimage guide for a reminder. "Begin the station with a visit to the Blessed Sacrament in St. Patrick's Basilica."

I crossed the grass and went into the basilica. I thought the Blessed Sacrament was the consecrated Eucharist wafer kept in a chalice in a little vault on the altar. During the Mass the priest shows his back to the congregation, turns a key, the door of the vault swings open, and there is the holy object. But as with most of the rites and recitations of the Catholic faith, I suspected that my recollection of the Blessed Sacrament was wrong. The pilgrimages I had already been on had not prepared me for the precision and intricacy of this one. My ignorance about the church of my birth had never disturbed me before, but now, having marooned myself amid so many Catholics engaged in this extreme and ritualistic expression of their faith, I regretted it. In the face of such concerted devotion I felt an outsider's awkwardness and unease and was surprised at how much I didn't know. Reluctant to ask another pilgrim to confirm my identification of the Blessed Sacrament, I continued in the hope that I knew what it was.

In the basilica I looked to the other pilgrims for clues. Some forty people were scattered about the church in their windbreakers and coats

— some kneeling in the pews, others sitting and staring, bundled up and white-faced. A few stood by the windows studying the stained glass illustrations of the apostles and the stations of the cross. I saw no outward indication that anyone was concertedly visiting the Blessed Sacrament. But I, literal-minded, went to the altar rail and knelt. (Looking back now, I suspect that merely to stand in the basilica and acknowledge the presence of the Blessed Sacrament was perhaps all that was meant by the word "visit.") The sanctuary was appointed with stylishly modern renderings of the standard furnishings. The altar, pulpit, and priest's chair were of smooth white marble, gently sculpted and curvaceous in a way that made them look faintly like a bathtub, sink, and toilet, respectively. The modern design of the large wooden crucifix against the wall behind the altar was based on the Irish penal cross; on it the body of Christ was like a minimalist figure in a Keith Haring painting. Toward the base of the cross I could make out a rooster dancing above a cauldron, an image I had never seen in a church before, let alone on the crucifix itself. The bronze tabernacle, also of modern design, had the look of a pirate's cask dredged up from the ocean floor heavily encrusted with barnacles and shells, seaweed and clinging starfish.

I put my hands over my face and visited the sacrament by imagining it in the darkness behind its metal door. I heard my mother once again saying, "It is *not* a symbol." The Eucharist truly was Christ; I tried to conceive of that. The dogma of transubstantiation asserted that the Eucharist contained "the Body and Blood of Our Lord Jesus Christ, together with His soul and divinity, indeed the whole Christ." Reason told me that Christ's presence in a wafer was a material impossibility. And yet if he was God and God was omnipotent, material impossibilities were irrelevant. That was the mystery and the difficulty of God.

I WAS HUNGRY, having eaten nothing since the previous night in Dublin. Pressed to my face, my hands and the cuffs of my jacket smelled faintly of the smoking room. I stood up. The basilica, though its doors were flung wide on the Irish July, was cold and slightly damp. Deep webs of shadow had gathered in the vaulted ceiling, and the soft shafts of light from the stained glass windows dissolved before they reached the floor. As I moved up the aisle to go out, someone came up behind me. It was the black-haired teenager who had announced to the smoking room that we would all die. "Have you the correct time?" he asked. When I looked at him, he turned his ruddy face warily to the side, showing me one dark eye, like a canary. His question, his choice of the word "correct," his disingenuous tone, were familiar. It was the crafty question Irish Gypsies — known now as "travelers" — tossed out in a softly wounded voice as you walked by their caravans. They didn't care what time it was; the question was only a way of investigating you, of engaging you. I used the trick myself all the time, had used it just that morning. "Five forty-five," I said. The boy was thick-wristed, deep-voiced, and hairy, with sideburns and heavy brows and a smattering of new whiskers on his upper lip. "T'anks," he said and moved off on the balls of his big bare feet.

Outside, the air was growing chilly. The marine-blue sky held a few brilliant streaks of cloud, and the small western windows in the upper reaches of the basilica were ablaze with reflected sunlight, but under my bare feet the grass was cold and newly moist with dew.

"Go to St. Patrick's cross near the Basilica, kneel, and say one Our Father one Hail Mary and one Creed."

The small cross of Saint Patrick was a simple piece of iron, but the stone pillar that supported it had been carved in an elegant spiral as distinct as the spiral of a licorice twist. Dating from the ninth century, the column was said to be the oldest relic on the island. I knelt before it on the paving stones and began the prayers. Figures wandered in and out of the basilica. Soft voices drifted out from the smoking room. The pilgrims who had arrived that day still gave off an air of cheerful purpose; those who had been up all night slouched and idled like prisoners of war. I sensed someone kneeling behind me, heard a struggling sigh as a heavy body lowered itself to its knees, heard the rustle of a sleeve and hurried whispering. I shut my eyes and tried to pray, but I felt self-conscious and kept opening one eye to see if anyone was looking at me. Midges hovered at my ears. Gulls laughed in the fading sky. I had trouble focusing on the prayers, kept having to steer my mind back to them. *The forgiveness of sins, the resurrection of the body, and the life everlasting. Amen.*

I stood up and kissed the cold metal cross worn smooth with kisses of devotion to Saint Patrick. I went next to Saint Brigid's Cross, a medieval carving in a stone set into the east wall of the basilica, and knelt on the pavement behind two other pilgrims. This cross required three Hail

Marys, three Our Fathers, and a Creed. The pavement was hard on the knees, and I found it difficult to keep from swaying. I wanted to hang on to the shoulder of the woman in front of me. I lifted the pilgrim's guide to my face and read the Creed. "I believe in God, the father almighty, creator of heaven and earth. I believe in Jesus Christ, his only son, our lord. He was conceived by the power of the holy spirit and born of the Virgin Mary. He suffered under Pontius Pilate, was crucified, died . . ."

It was different from the Nicene Creed, which I remembered pieces of. What I remembered was longer and somehow more poetic. I shut my eyes and conjured it. *I believe in one God, the father, the almighty, maker of heaven and earth, of all that is seen and unseen . . . God from God, light from light, true God from true God . . . crucified under Pontius Pilate, suffered, died, was buried. Third day rose again.* And it went on, ending with something like *I acknowledge one baptism for the forgiveness of sins, look for the resurrection of the dead, and the life of the world to come. Amen.*

I looked at my pamphlet. The Apostles' Creed said nothing about baptism. And instead of resurrection of the dead, it said resurrection of the *body*. The Gospels and the Creed are the core of Christian belief, but the language of the Creed, arrived at after decades of tortuous theological hairsplitting, and the specificity of the attributes it gives that tripartite "one God" gave me pause. The dogmatic insistence that belief in God required belief in the Virgin Birth, heaven, hell, the resurrection of the body, and a final scrutinizing judgment seemed to distort and oversimplify the matter. Like the laws of physics, these concepts could never be absolutes; they could only be approximations, abstractions, helpful instruments. But the Creed appeared, presumptuously, to present them — to *insist* upon them — as objective absolutes. God was immeasurable, yet the Catholic Church had tidily sized him up. Inwardly I protested.

As I prayed, one of the women in front of me stood up, put her back against the basilica wall, and raised her arms in the posture of the crucified Christ. Her rosary beads dangled from one hand. She shut her eyes and said three times with great feeling, "I renounce the world, the flesh, and the devil!" She moved away from the wall, and the other kneeling woman got up and took her place, raising her arms in the same portentous way. As she made her renunciations her face grew very sad, as though the words were forcing her to recognize past weaknesses and failures. When she finished she stood for a minute blinking at her rosary beads, trying through tears to relocate her place on them. The pilgrim behind me edged up to me and knelt. It was my turn.

I put my back against the stone cross, spread my arms as if submitting to a body search, and softly and hurriedly said three times, "I renounce the world, the flesh, and the devil," and moved off as quickly as possible. I didn't like this part of the station. It made me uneasy to say words I didn't mean and twice as uneasy to say them while standing in the attitude of the crucified Christ. It was easier to recite the Hail Mary and Our Father, which were not statements about myself or false promises about my own actions. Their meaning was more passive and had been dulled by familiarity — I could recite them with the effortlessness of an exhalation. The kneeling shadow behind me — it was white-haired Jimmy from Mayo — got up and took the spot, pressing his body to the damp wall and spreading his arms. He had removed his jacket. His forehead gleamed with perspiration. He, too, softly renounced the world, the flesh, and the devil, and like me he quickly moved away from the wall.

The next phase was the easiest. "Walk slowly by your right hand, four times around the Basilica, while praying silently seven decades of the Rosary and one Creed at the end." Thankfully, this exercise involved no kneeling, and earlier that afternoon I had discovered that the slate flagstones around the foundation of the basilica were markedly warmer than anything else on the island, as if heated by a subterranean inferno beneath the nave. To my cold feet the small warmth felt intense and seemed to radiate upward into my ankles. Rounding the southern end of the basilica I had a wide view of the lake and the puce humps of its small islands. A rolling hedge of pewter clouds slid low over far-off hills.

Instructed to walk slowly, the pilgrims engaged in this part of the station looked pained and slightly infirm, their heads bowed, their bare feet taking tiny shuffling steps, lips moving fervidly, eyes vacant and distracted, beads dangling from their cold hands. Circling the basilica ahead of me I saw muddied heels, trousers rolled up at the ankles, a scarlet bow at the back of a woman's head, elbow patches on a tweed jacket, a purple sweater, a pair of swollen ankles, a houndstooth cap on a balding head, Mrs. Caffrey's kerchief, the trilby hat. In six or seven hours the pilgrims had all become as familiar as classmates in a schoolyard. I saw Fiona, Mrs. O'Cray, and May, and I noted that the majority of the pilgrims were women. Crossing the lake that afternoon I had counted forty-three passengers on the boat; only twelve were men. They had come from all over Ireland, but most were from the northern part of the country.

We ambled in a kind of current, like fish in a small pond. Heads came in and out of view, and bushy eyebrows, bright ears, freckled cheeks, bewhiskered chins. Paths crossed, people staggered, some walked side by side. Some people prayed loudly, others hardly moved their lips. There were painted toenails and bunions and yellowed corns and a few feet that were handsome. I found it hard to walk slowly, and in one lap around the basilica I overtook several people. I drew level with the man in the tweed jacket who, from the corner of my eye, looked distinctly like Prince Philip — the tall man's stoop, the nose, the thinning gray hair, the grim mouth. Catching me at this sidelong examination, the man turned his face to me, warding me off with his gaze. In a low voice he was saying, "Glory be to the Father and to the Son and to the Holy Ghost . . ."

I came up behind the small, middle-aged woman with the red bow in her hair. Her frayed copper hair was pulled loosely back in a ponytail the thickness of a swan's neck. "Holy Mary, mother of God," she recited, swinging her rosary beads in a circle at her hip, like a cowboy with a lariat. She prayed in a sighing way and snatched at the midges in front of her face, and before she started in on the next prayer she moaned, "God help us. The pace of it's killin' me," and looked around to see if anyone else was suffering.

The pace was odd. You prayed quickly and walked slowly. In the time it took us to walk four times around the basilica we would complete seventy-three Hail Marys, eight or nine Our Fathers, a couple of doxologies, and several recitals of something called the Fatima Prayer, which I could forgive myself for not saying because I had never heard of it before. I liked counting out the prayers on my rosary beads, a child's plastic set I had bought in the island's bookshop. The beads, soft and slightly rubbery, were the size and color of capers. On the little cross at the end of the beads the corpus of Christ was as small and ill defined as a grain of cooked rice. I made the sign of the cross and began the prayers and felt myself growing lightheaded with hunger. The midges were worse than mosquitoes or flies. They were tiny and moved in schools.

They didn't so much fly as float, like flecks of ash on an updraft. They seemed very eager to explore the human eye, the nostril, the mouth. They got snagged in the hair, and their bite was a needling sting that left a disproportionately large welt.

I prayed on. I was unused to formal prayer, unused to praying at all, but these words came easily: Our Father, Hail Mary, words composed by none other than Jesus and the Angel Gabriel. The repetition of the words was lulling, like the pulse of a rocking chair, and saying ten Hail Marys in a row was almost narcotic. My mind wandered while the words spilled from my mouth, thoughts going one way, prayers going another, filaments on a loom, overlapping until they became one gauzy cloth. As I said *Our Father who art in heaven,* I saw myself sitting in a plane at Heathrow Airport, looking through the porthole and seeing a man with the face of Seamus Heaney driving the Aer Lingus luggage cart through the mist. With *Hallowed be thy name* I saw the Scottish woman who had said to me on a Dublin bus that morning, "Dublin has changed. The Irish economy's booming." As the words *Thy kingdom come* passed through my head I marveled at the lichens frosting the stones of the basilica, broad scabrous patches the startling yellow of ballpark mustard. At *On earth as it is in heaven* I checked my pockets for my pen. I said *We forgive those who trespass against us* and thought of things the man I loved had said, saw his hurrying way of walking, one arm swinging, and his peasant's feet, as homely as a pair of unshucked oysters but as beautiful to me as pearls. I heard his voice, humorous and sometimes desperate, saw his balding head and devotion to fear. I said *Lead us not into temptation* and thought how little work or time or anything else mattered when the person you loved had no room for you.

And then, as if a full-length mirror had sprung up in front of me, blocking my path, I would catch sight of myself, my mouth moving, and stumble on the words. What was I saying? For all their familiarity, each time I actually stopped to listen to the words, they became as stiff as a fishbone in my mouth. I was praising God and asking Jesus' mother to pray for us. I was saying we were sinners. Why should I say those words if I couldn't gather behind them a corresponding intention?

Everyone from atheist to Amish was welcome at Station Island. I was here of my own volition and under pretenses that did not feel false to me, but the performance of these prayerful exercises felt at times like having a mask pressed over my face. The loss of love had left me with a deep disillusionment, with thoughts that were sorrowing and repetitive. I saw no relief in sight for my persistent sadness. These prayers flowed in a direction that promised consolation, guidance, and relief, but they seemed to have little to do with me.

The island's big stone buildings were beginning to soften in the fading light and had taken on a looming, haunted quality; the figures of the praying pilgrims in various stages of their stations were growing dim and ill-defined. Some were circling the basilica, others stumbled about the penitential beds, some knelt on stones at the water's edge. In the soft light their motions looked slurred and their bare hands and feet seemed to glow, trailing smoky smears of light as they moved. The great chestnut tree was going from green to black. Clouds of midges hung above the water. Gusts of shadow lifted out of the grass.

ORLA PLANTED her hands flat upon the wooden table. "Shove me over that sugar, Bernadette. I'm punished with the hunger."

Bernadette, with her teenaged son sitting at her side, slid the thick white bowl across the table, then plucked a piece of dry toast from a platter and eyed it with displeasure.

Drawn back and lashed with a scarlet ribbon, Orla's billowing hair gave the blowsy effect of a mobcap. She stabbed her teaspoon into the sugar bowl and grumbled softly, "Lovely dinner of hay and stones." She shoveled four teaspoons of sugar into her cup of black tea, stirred swiftly, put the spoon down, raised the mug to her face, and sipped. "Ah, that's it, now," she said drily, clunking the cup back into its saucer. "The cup that cheers but doesn't."

Orla was restless and wry. She had a small, pretty face and an odd way of speaking through her teeth and out the side of her mouth, like a gangster. Her talk was a muttering mix of mock vexation, true ingenuousness, and sharp irony. She was a font of Irish folkisms and sly literary references that betrayed both impatience with and affection for her culture. She adopted exaggerated country pronunciations and punctuated her speech with little phrases in Irish Gaelic. She was one minute scornful, the next reverential. Her fidgeting hands wandered ceaselessly about her immediate orbit, picking things up and putting them down again, straightening the hopeless bow in her hair, buttoning and unbuttoning her cardigan, plucking at her skirt, fiddling with her spoon, her watch, the sugar bowl. Her short fingers drummed on the table. She lived in Dublin but had grown up near Galway. She worked for a pharmaceutical company. Every so often she said, "Ah, now, where's my beads?" and plunged her hand into her jacket pocket. Finding the rosary beads there, she drew them out and kissed them with comic relief. The charade was a shield for the true tenderness she felt for her religion. When her teacup was empty she lifted it to Bernadette for a refill and with a commanding nod of her head said, "Arís, mo chroí." Again, my dear.

In the warmth of the dining room the pilgrims' faces grew red. My cold bare feet tingled beneath the table. The pilgrims sipped and sighed and looked around the room.

The refectory, housed in one of the newer buildings on the island, was appointed with tall windows. Filled with light, the entire room, including the beamed ceiling and the parquet floor, looked freshly scrubbed and waxed. The forty or fifty highly polished tables were arranged in tidy rows and set with plain white plates, teaspoons, and cups overturned in their saucers. From midday to eight in the evening, pilgrims could come in at their leisure and take their one meal. The staff piled dry toast and oatcakes onto platters and poured tea from steaming jugs. There was no butter and no milk, the sugar the only ornament to the blunt little meal. It was near closing time, and many of the tables were empty. A small group sat by the southern windows, another at the far end of the room, another near the door. The empty tables gleamed, reflecting the ceiling lights.

I took another of the oatcakes. They looked like a rough combination of raw oats, sand, and bits of straw molded into biscuitlike disks, and they had a primitive, barnyard flavor that I liked. They were the only food I would have that day. I had wolfed down two cakes already and was fitting the edge of the third into my mouth, when a man sitting to the left of Orla said in wonderment, "You're mad for those cakes, aren't you now?"

I put the cake down and looked at the man. He was natty, with a tall head and a little Vandyke beard of gray at his chin. His flushed face made him look as though he had just been shouting in anger. Earlier I had heard him telling someone he was a dentist. I said I thought the oatcakes were good.

The man said they were not, that he wouldn't fob them off on a donkey. His steaming teacup was paper-white before the pink of his face. Bernadette chimed in, "You said it, Barry." A girl from Dublin at the end of the table defended the cakes, and a gray-haired woman in a short-waisted Eisenhower jacket asked if I was back in Ireland on holiday. I told her I had come to Ireland to visit Lough Derg. When she asked where I was from, and I answered Boston, she looked surprised. "But I thought you were Irish. You've no accent."

Orla said, "Don't be coddin' me. You're never a Yank."

"She has a Yank's accent," said Bernadette.

"She hasn't," said the man.

"Go on now, girl," said Orla, slitting her eyes at me in an appraising way, "say something and I'll decide what you are."

"Thirty-three and a third," I said.

Bernadette said proudly, "See?"

Orla looked shocked. "She *is* American."

The word "thirty" always gave an American away.

The gray-haired woman said, "I am Pat Mallon. From County Wicklow. I received a master's degree from Boston College."

"In Brookline," I said.

"Chestnut Hill!" she corrected me.

"Right," I said, "Chestnut Hill."

The woman pointed a finger at me and said gleefully, "You are not up on your geography!"

I looked at her. She was professorial and cheerful, small and precise, and friendly in the immediately intimate way of Irish people. She sniffed at her coffee, then sipped it in a testing way. She had a birdlike manner. Her skin was a milky white, and her short gray hair was tidily combed and kept smartly in place with metal bobby pins. A pair of cat's-eye glasses was perched on her nose.

Another woman, Eileen, said, "Is Boston anywhere near Cambridge, Massachusetts?"

Pat Mallon said, "A stone's throw 'cross the Charles. Charles is the name of the river in Boston."

"I've cousins in Cambridge," said Eileen.

"Millionaires, I suppose," said Pat.

Eileen suddenly looked suspicious and gypped. "Well, now, they never said anything about millions to me!"

Pat said, "Bill Clinton is doing a fine job. And he reminded me of Kennedy in the beginning. In looks. He's made some mistakes, sure, but all in all a good man." She stretched her index finger at me again, as if to hold me in place. "Now, did they ever determine the cause of John-John?"

"The cause?" I said.

"'Twas an accident, wasn't it?" This was more a statement than a question. It was deeply important to Pat Mallon that the young John Kennedy's death the previous year was nothing more sinister than an accident.

"I believe it was an accident, yes," I said.

Pat smiled wistfully into her cup. "Sure, I only remember him as a little boy at his mother's side during his father's funeral."

The older women at the table nodded their heads and stared at Pat with palpable sympathy and sadness. They all remembered it — the coffin, the mother, the bare-legged boy, the horse-drawn carriage. Kennedy's death was a personal loss, as much a piece of Irish history as American.

The women sighed and chewed their dry toast and oatcakes and sipped at their tea and complained about the weather, the midges, their feet. Their complaints inspired the others at the table to throw in their own. Five of the seven had been here before, and they reminisced about past years, cursed the jagged stones in the penitential beds, described the meal they'd prefer to be having — a fine bit of fish and potatoes with lashings of butter and a cup of tea beside it — and remembered summers at Lough Derg that might as well have been winters for all the sun that was in them. The sugar bowl went from hand to hand. The talk was of cold and pain and who was slaughtered with the kneeling and who would murder for an egg and who'd be killed by the night vigil and who would be found stretched out snoring above in the balcony in the morning and how many times have you done it and how many more, and though it was mostly complaint there was a thread of happy excitement beneath the grumbling. The sense of shared hardship, the extremeness of it, made everyone feel close and understood. They pretended Station Island was awful, yet there was something in its austerity that they loved.

When the small talk was over, small confessions followed. Eileen, a nurse, was here because she felt she was forgetting her religion. Bernadette felt that God had answered her prayers and she wanted to thank him. Orla had a sick relative. The girl from Dublin, dressed in black, a small earring in her nose, one wrist encircled with a fine ribbon of tattooed tracery, had come to get away from the mobile phones, the e-mail, her boss, and the doorbell, all of which she classified under the rubric "silly merry-go-round." When pressed, Bernadette's son ducked his head, shrugged, leaned away from his mother, passed a nervous hand over his broad, pimpled forehead and said he guessed he was only here just to try out how it was like and things.

The girl from Dublin, who was not more than twenty-six, said from her end of the table, "My father tried to dissuade me from coming. My actual father. He said, 'What have you done so bad in your life that you have to keep rushing back to Lough Derg?' I told him I've done nothing bad. I just want to reflect, like. He doesn't understand it."

I asked her what she wanted to reflect about.

She shrugged her narrow shoulders. She had big brown eyes and long straight hair that hung limply around her face. "Myself. The world. Get centered again. I'm sick of lookin' at all the cars and all the shiny useless shite for sale in stores. The space shuttle flying up in the moon, and for what? What's it bringing us? There's people starving and suffering and no shoes on their feet. This is one way to remember that. To get closer to them. And to pray for them."

I asked her if she went to Mass on Sundays. "Not often," she said. "But I do believe in prayer." She plucked at her lower lip, thinking. On her wrist the bluish-black tattoo was faded and faint, like a bruise left by a tight handcuff. She said, "I want to do good with my life."

"And you're dead right," said Barry. He chewed a mouthful of dry toast, swallowed it, and said, "And look at Charlie Haughey now."

Haughey, the famous ex-prime minister of Ireland, was all over the Irish newspapers at the time for being in some kind of legal trouble.

Orla said, "It was obvious. He was living lavishly. Bought Inishvickillane for a hundred and thirty thousand pounds!"

Inishvickillane was one of the Blasket Islands, off the coast of the Dingle Peninsula in County Kerry. Twenty-two years earlier, when I was a student in Dunquin, the westernmost point on the peninsula and the embarkation point for the Blasket Islands, I used to see Haughey's helicopter soaring down over the mountain and the green hump of Great Blasket Island and out beyond to his private island.

"A hundred and thirty thousand!" Bernadette said. "Sure, you couldn't buy a two-bedroom apartment in Dublin now for that money, but back then 'twas millions!"

Pat Mallon said suddenly, "It always made me laugh, Rose, the Monroe Doctrine."

She pressed her winged eyeglasses to the bridge of her nose. She spoke with a kind of ongoing mirth, smiling secretly at her own words, as though winding up to the punch line of a slightly risqué joke. I wasn't sure how to respond to this unexpected remark, but before I could answer, she continued, "The thesis of the Monroe Doctrine was America must not interfere with other countries! But look at Clinton helping all these people now. He's done a lot of good in point of fact."

As if suddenly struck with an idea, the girl from Dublin sat up and, ignoring Pat Mallon, said, "But what about you, Rose? Why did you come to Lough Derg?"

I had almost not come to Lough Derg. I was tired of traveling and tired of thinking about God. It was a struggle, it was uncomfortable, and I had felt frustrated that in my holy travels belief had not suddenly dawned on me, that no great bolt of lightning had struck me. Trying to find belief was like trying to raise a heavy anchor from the bottom of the sea, an anchor whose sharp tooth had snagged beneath the iron of some sunken vessel. Stubbornly stuck at the end of a long line, it felt impossible to lift. And since my last pilgrimage my life had taken a downward turn; the relationship most important to me was over, and I saw no way to retrieve it. I was bereft and wanted to get away. I had nearly skipped Saint Patrick's Purgatory, but, lured by the familiarity of Ireland and my familial connection to it, I had thought I might find some personal comfort here. To me Ireland was the next closest thing to home. I didn't tell all that to the girl from Dublin. I feared I would weep.

"Well," I said, "I'm interested in pilgrimage."

Orla said, "I'd kill for a fag at this moment."

"You can't, Orla," said Bernadette.

"Why can't I?"

"The priest said no smoking but in the smoking room."

Orla sighed at the ceiling, "The priest! The priest!"

THAT THE IRISH Catholic Church has had enormous influence over the people of Ireland is a fact so widely known that it has become a source of both satire and social study. After the ravages of the famine of 1846 it was the church that provided structure and aid for a diminished, destitute, and disfranchised population, creating a nearly inalienable bond. In the first half of the twentieth century the separation of church and state in Ireland was merely nominal. Orphanages, schools, hospitals, and other institutions operated chiefly under the aegis of the Catholic Church, and the aims and requirements of the church were clearly reflected in the nation's social policy.

Among certain Irish Protestants the unchecked power of Catholicism was perceived as corrupting and insincere, and a literature of criticism — some of it centered on the practices at Saint Patrick's Purgatory — developed. In the 1830s, speaking in praise of what he saw as the unique, powerful, and profound character of the Irish people, William Carleton, the Anglo-Irish author of the famously severe criticism "The Lough Derg Pilgrim," wrote, "The only power equal to it is that of the church of Rome, and certainly that lays Paddy in the dust; there he is over-reached, and bammed, and blarnied, and made to knock under." In his essay "St Patrick's Purgatory," Thomas Wright, a contemporary of Carleton's, wrote:

> At first tolerated among a newly converted and ignorant people . . . [religious superstitions] were subsequently approved and encouraged by a political priesthood, as a powerful instrument of domination and oppression, till they were finally accepted as an integral part of the doctrines of the church . . . Unhappy Ireland has suffered more, perhaps, than any other country from the religious system just mentioned . . . We see there a Catholic priesthood using the grossest means, and practising the most vulgar deceptions, to keep in ignorance and dependence the miserable population.

Beginning in the 1960s, with greater economic prosperity in Ireland and wider opportunity available to its people, the great power of the Irish church began to weaken, and by the 1990s, amid a host of scandals — pedophilia as well as physical and psychological abuse in Catholic orphanages — it began to crumble. Hypocrisy and bald abuse of power among the clergy would no longer be accepted by a people grown strong enough to question the structure of their religion and the morality of its leaders and administrators.

The present Irish disaffection from the church is clearly reflected in the annual log of visitors to Station Island. In 1952, at the height of religious fervor in Ireland, 34,000 pilgrims visited the island during the two-and-a-half-month season. By 1999 the numbers had declined to approximately 10,000, a low not matched since 1929.

AT 9:20 THAT NIGHT, all of the pilgrims on the island gathered in the basilica for the service of Night Prayer and Benediction — the 90 of us who had arrived that day and the 256 who had arrived the day before and had been awake now for roughly thirty-six hours. The basilica was designed to seat 1,200 pilgrims. With a total of 346 in attendance, there was nearly enough room in the pews for all of us to lie down on them head to toe.

The echo in the basilica was powerful, and once the 256 exhausted pilgrims had gone off to their beds, the echo seemed to grow stronger. When Father Hubert stood at the podium and led us into our vigil, his words bounced spookily from the supernal ceiling and empty benches. Father Hubert began by apologizing to the congregation for the way Catholic priests had misused their powers over the centuries. He admitted that the clergy had failed to consider their own part in their relationship with the laity. In years past such an apology would have been renegade and unthinkable, but since May of that year, when Pope John Paul II made his general apology for the past mistakes and sins of the church, apologies from the pulpit had been in vogue.

As Father Hubert spoke, I was reminded of a conversation I had had earlier in the day with Father Michael Maanzo, a staff priest who had come to Lough Derg from Kenya. Father Maanzo had expressed some unorthodox thoughts; he did not, he said, accept literally the doctrine that the Virgin Mary was born without original sin, and he felt that his own relationship with God was more important than his relationship with God through the church (a view I tended to agree with, which begged a question I had been asking for years: what exactly are churches *for?*). Father Maanzo had also said that the notion of physical penance — punishing the body in order that the soul might find purity — was a monastic one not taught by Christ. "The church leaders are now trying to explain the dogma they came up with," he said.

As Father Hubert spoke now, I thought, too, of my mother. Whenever I asked her (and I asked often) how she could remain loyal to a church that was so outdated and unregenerate on issues such as the ordination of women, birth control, homosexuality, and celibacy, she always said, "I know, I know, but you have to get beyond that. The church is run by flawed human beings. It has been evolving for millennia and will evolve a great deal more."

Father Hubert spoke frankly, and his apology sounded heartfelt. He was a persuasive, humane preacher, the sort who seemed able to read the thoughts of his congregation. He spoke of human frailty, said drunkenness was an escape, an excuse, an avoidance. Heads nodded as he spoke. When he said love was a risk that required courage, tears welled up in my eyes. "Relationships are hard," he said. "Now you might be saying to yourself, 'What does *he* know about relationships!' But you'd be surprised what I know!"

When the Mass was over, Father Hubert and the staff went out and shut the great doors of the basilica behind them, leaving us alone to begin our night vigil. The air in the church seemed to grow suddenly thinner, the light seemed to dim. I sat in the pew with my bare feet planted on the kneeler and the sleeves of my jacket pulled down over my hands, staring at the heads and shoulders in front of me, at the women's ponytails and buns and braids, the men's balding crowns glinting weakly in the yellowish lights. The younger pilgrims kept their baseball caps on in the church, which seemed slightly disrespectful to me. That I had earlier seen the white sanctuary furnishings as bathroom fixtures suddenly seemed disrespectful too. But the more I tried to see them another way, the more they looked like bathroom fixtures.

I looked again at the rooster above his pot on the big cross on the sanctuary wall. Earlier the prior had recounted for us the legend that lay behind the image: after the crucifixion, Peter went home and said to his wife, "My master is dead." Peter's wife, who was boiling a rooster, said, "Jesus will rise." Peter said, rather Irishly, "He'll have as much chance of rising as that rooster in the pot," whereupon the boiled rooster flew up out of the stew. In another version it was Judas's wife who was cooking; upon hearing of the Resurrection, she did not believe that it was true, but the rooster flew boldly up in her face and cried (in Irish), "Mac na hÓighe slán!" The son of the Virgin is well. It was essentially the same legend I had read about on my way to Santiago de Compostela, the one in which the rooster flew up from the local judge's dinner plate to prove the innocence of the framed and hanged pilgrim boy.

The resurrected chicken clearly had great significance in the medieval mind.

Drafts of cold air swept across the icy floor beneath the pews. One of the pilgrims went to the podium to lead the rosary, which began the vigil, and there was a sudden fluttering of arms as the ninety pilgrims made the sign of the cross down their fronts. "I believe in God, the Father almighty, creator of heaven and earth . . ." As the Creed unfurled I heard a frantic whispering from the pew behind me.

Have you my beads? I haven't. *Are you sure, because I can't find them anywhere.* I haven't got them. *But did I not ask you to hold them when I was lighting the candles?* You did, and I held them and then gave them back to you in your hand. *Well, I haven't got them.* Have you looked? *Cripe, had I not looked would I be howlin' out for them now!?* Well, I haven't your beads, I tell you. *Just check your pocket.* I've no pockets on me. *No pockets?* None. *Well, are they in your hand?*

A long pause. And then: For the love of God, Marie, if your beads were in my hand wouldn't I know it? *Well, I can't find them anywhere.* Look under the bench. *I looked there already.* Well, maybe you're sittin' on 'em. *I am not.* Well, try lookin' up your arse!

And then a quick volley of irreverent giggles bounced against the back of my neck.

We barreled through the rosary. The man leading the prayers had a heavy northern accent and sent the words out in a steady, racing stream. At that speed there was no time to reflect on their meaning. The prayers became a mantra in a foreign language, which made it easier to daydream. I stared at the neck of the man in front of me, nearly the color of a brick. He had small ears and a red beard. His swinging rosary beads clicked against the wooden pew. The moaning sound of the many praying voices created a small rumbling that stirred the air, and the older heads nodded in deference each time the word "Jesus" was spoken.

As the vigil began, I had a sense that we were putting a shoulder to an enormous wheel that we'd be heaving and turning all night. The vigil was a taste of death, but this didn't feel so bad. We would sit here all night praying and kneeling and circling the inner periphery of the pretty basilica, just as we had done earlier outdoors, but instead of praying individually we would pray in unison. We would spend the next day praying, and finally tomorrow night we would go to bed. On the third day we would get up, pray a little more, and leave the island on the boats.

Symbolically we were now with the souls of the dead in the prison of purgatory. Our prayers would gain a plenary indulgence. I assumed that meant we would hasten the liberation of some poor sinner trapped in purgatory.

I stared at the ear of the man in front of me and tried to imagine the souls of the dead, tortured and waiting for heaven. We all said, ". . . full of grace the Lord is with thee," and I remembered once asking my mother, who believes in purgatory, what purgatory was. "A state," she had answered, "that you're in until you're cleansed of the bad things you've done. It's regret, but there is hope in purgatory of heaven. Hell is different. Hell is *awful*. The pain of hell is that you've caught a glimpse of God and know that you will never see him again. Ever."

I had asked my mother if she thought she'd go to heaven upon her death. She said no. When I asked her why, she said, "I think I did bad things."

"What bad things?"

"I didn't know anything," she said. "I think I was perhaps emotionally stingy with my children. We weren't taught to be otherwise. Remember that thing, Rose, that they did in the sixties where they all went and slopped around in the mud and hugged each other and said, 'Love, not war'?"

"You mean Woodstock?"

"Woodstock. Woodstock, yes. We should have been a bit more like Woodstock, I suppose. I want my youth over again, to do it right this time. I don't think I'll be damned to the fires of hell or whatever it is. But purgatory, yes."

I asked my mother where she thought her own mother was now.

"My mother died in 1961. If she went to purgatory at all, then she's done her time by now and I think she's in heaven."

"Did she go to purgatory?" I asked.

"I think so."

"Why do you think so?"

"Same reason I'm going: bad things."

I tried to think of the bad things my mother and her mother had done. Frustration, temper, pride, anger, deception — the same old bad things everybody did. The same bad things I did. Probably the same things Holy Mary did, riding out of Bethlehem on the back of a donkey with the infant in the crook of her arm and Herod amok. I asked my mother if she thought Jesus' mother ever lost her temper.

"Certainly she did," my mother said. "She was human."

"Did *she* go to purgatory?"

"Not at all!"

How, I asked, could my mother believe in heaven and hell and purgatory between them?

"How could I not? I was born in Boston, but I was brought up by nineteenth-century Ireland."

"But I don't believe in them, and I was brought up by you."

"That," my mother said with a laugh, "was another of the bad things I did. Raised you wrong." And she laughed some more and said in surrender and relief, "Oh, well, that's over now. You're on your own."

THE BELL IN ITS TOWER rang two o'clock. The short peals of the small hours sounded glassy and accidental, like a splash of water spilling from an abruptly jostled jug. By two-thirty in the morning a gusty rain whipped at the island, muddying the sky. In a break between stations I went out and stood on the basilica's covered porch. A figure came out of the smoking room and gingerly hopped across the grass with a newspaper clapped to its head. I crossed the yard and went into the nonsmoking night room in the building next to the basilica for a drink of water. The room was long and softly lit and had the sparse feel of a summer cabin, with pale pink walls and a knotty pine floor that glowed in the light. The benches that lined the walls were littered with newspapers and magazines, and twenty people sat about sipping from styrofoam cups, staring or talking or reading. As I walked to the sink at the far end of the room, my wet feet stuck slightly to the waxed floor.

At the sink a man was shaking pepper into a styrofoam cup full of steaming water.

"Pepper?" I said.

He shrugged and reached for the canister of salt. His feet were bluish and swollen. "Pepper and salt in hot water makes soup, they say. Lough Derg soup."

"Is it good?"

"Well, it's good if there's something lacking in you." He handed me the cup. He had a big bald head encircled by a ring of fluffy white hair, like a monk's tonsure, and a calm, dependable-looking face. The cuffs of his trousers were rolled up to his shins. "You take this one," he said kindly, "and I shall prepare myself another."

I took the mythical soup. In the corner behind us a tired-looking couple in their forties were deep in conversation. Through the rain-streaked window I could see the lake not six feet away. The light from the window faintly illuminated the water, which tossed and chopped in the wind. Little waves collapsed upon themselves in quick bursts of white, and in the dim light the slanting rain was like tiny bits of glass hurtling into the lake. Beyond the shore the view was black. We were roughly between Ballyshannon, Ballybofey, Enniskillen, and Omagh and very close to the border of Ulster, but we might as well have been on a ship in the middle of a great sea.

I sat down on a bench near two gray-haired men in golfing caps and sipped at the hot water. It had the discomfiting metallic tang of warm blood, but I was cold and drank it anyway. The air in the room was warm; my feet were stinging.

There was absent-minded teeth picking here, and nail cleaning, and lint plucking, and the kind of daydreaming that takes place behind a hypnotic stare. Some of the pilgrims were reading paperback novels. One man was bent over a Harry Potter book, his chin cupped in his hand. Three women sat together with their cardigan sweaters draped over their shoulders conversing in a Donegal accent so heavy that from a slight distance it sounded like Spanish to me. All three seemed to be talking at once. One woman dozed, pursing her lips in her sleep; the way her body was slumped she looked as though she'd fainted. At the other end of my bench the handsome girl with the strong smell was leaning forward with her elbows on her knees and reading what looked like a handwritten letter, several thin pages sharply creased with folding. Whatever it was that clung to her clothing was distinct and sour, like curdled milk or cider vinegar. She frowned as she read, intensely absorbed, her dark hair falling forward and her feet tucked under the bench. Then she folded the pages up, slipped them inside the front of her maroon jacket, sipped from her styrofoam cup, rested the back of her head against the wall, and stared vaguely up at the ceiling. She seemed unaware of — or perhaps uninterested in — the other people in the room. A minute passed, and she reached back inside her jacket, took the letter out, opened it again, and began rereading with the same engrossed consternation.

The wind shoved at the windows and rattled the door, the rain crackled on the windowpanes. The two men in golfing caps, their legs crossed and hands folded over their bellies, were nodding their heads and talking about the weather. ". . . not as bad as last year, now."

My eyes were stinging with fatigue. I yawned and sipped my hot water and flipped through the damp magazines and yellowed newspapers on the bench beside me. African missionary magazines, an *Irish Independent*, an *Irish Times*, a magazine called *The Voice of Padre Pio*, and *The Messenger*, a Catholic publication. I studied the plump African women in their bright dresses on the covers of the missionary magazines. They had soft, round cheeks the color of roasted almonds and beautiful teeth and glistening skin. They looked warm and fragrant and out of place in this cold country. I scanned the *Irish Independent*. Stories about the crash of the Concorde and about Charles Haughey.

I picked up a *Padre Pio* magazine; the cover showed a hand-tinted photograph of the padre peering out at the world with a slightly creepy expression on his face. His pointed beard was shaggy and gray, his lips were cherry-red. He held his stigmatized hands, cloaked in his trademark fingerless gloves, in a position indicative either of prayer or of pleading. The Irish, with their native fascination for the mysterious and the unexplained, are particularly devoted to this Italian priest. The magazine contained articles such as "The Greatness of Padre Pio" and "The Terrible Gift of Irascibility." At the back of the magazine were testimonials from his Irish followers. A woman had written: "My daughter, her baby and myself were in her car driving along a road when out a field a big horse jumped right on the car, the windowscreen was shattered, we were covered with glass, the roof of the car was broken, the side door was smashed, the bonnet was ruined . . . We had a Padre Pio sticker on the car and we hadn't even a scratch on any of us . . . It was a miracle!" A nun had written, "Dear friends, greetings in the name of our Lord Jesus Christ. I am very much interested in Padre Pio, because I had a goitre and I was using his small photograph while he was saying Mass rubbing it on the goitre and the good news is the goitre has disappeared."

Amid the magazines and newspapers someone had left an old paperback with a weakened spine and brittle pages: the selected plays, poetry, and prose of John Millington Synge. I flipped through it. Time had toasted the edges of the pages the color of honey. "The Tinker's Wedding" was there. And "Riders to the Sea" and "The Playboy of the Western World." Synge was all woe and disappointment and humorous hyperbole. In one of the plays, "The Shadow of the Glen," someone had used a red pen to underline the words "Isn't a dead man itself more company than to be sitting alone, and hearing the winds crying, and you not knowing on what thing your mind would stay?" There were poems in the book too, and stories of the Aran Islands, as well as Synge's translations of some of Petrarch's sonnets. Among the sonnets, I read "He Asks His Heart to Raise Itself Up to God":

> What is it you're thinking, lonesome heart? For what is it you're turning back ever and always to times that are gone away from you? For what is it you're throwing sticks on the fire where it is your own self that is burning? The little looks and sweet words you've taken one by one and written down among your songs, are gone up into the heavens, and it's late, you know well, to go seeking them on the face of the earth.

Halfway through the poem a stunning rush of heat and pressure flooded my chest. My nose began to sting, my chin quivered, and my eyes became two watery prisms. Hot tears slid down my cheeks and splashed onto the front of my jacket. I had always thought the term "aching heart" was trite and imprecise. I knew now that it wasn't. The pain of lost love was a physical affliction, a poison; it had created a distance between myself and the world. I thought I would never come to the end of it. I opened the book again and read the poem over. ". . . Let you seek heaven when there is nothing left pleasing on the earth." I pushed the book aside. Tears blurred my vision and weighted my eyelashes. I knew that love, like faith, had no guarantee.

The handsome girl was leaning forward on the bench with her feet apart and her elbows on her knees, staring at the knots in the floor, thinking, gently shaking her head. The fingers of her right hand twitched and fidgeted in the air, as if ushering the words that passed through her mind.

On her way to the sink, Orla said to the Donegal women, "Hoping you're well and not in hell!"

The tonsured man sat down next to me on the bench with his cup in his hands. He said, as though picking up the dropped thread of a conversation we'd been having all night, "The Haughey mess should have been addressed long ago."

I said, "What exactly did he do that got him into trouble?"

"Funds," the man said knowingly, raising his cup. "Inappropriate appropriation of illicit monies. They cottoned onto it." He took a taut sip of his hot-water soup, sealing the case. For a minute or so he talked about the ethics of his job; he was the CEO of a large insurance company. Then, suddenly, he said, "Now, miss, is it crying you've been?"

I was startled by his directness. I nodded and said, "Yes." It was obvious — my jacket front was scattered with tears and my lashes and face were wet.

The kindly man handed me a tissue. "That's common enough at Lough Derg," he said. "I have cried here myself."

AT THREE in the morning we circled the inside of the basilica again, walking counterclockwise and praying the sixth station. Over and over all night long the same faces had passed in a murmuring blur, all of them looking mugged and stunned and red-eyed, except for the man with the trilby hat, who looked quite as he did sixteen hours ago, stepping snappily like a member of a marching band and praying boldly, his white eyebrows glittering like rime above his deep-set eyes. He wore a dark suit and a white dress shirt buttoned up to his throat but no necktie. I saw people with words on their clothing: U PENN, NAUTICA, ADIDAS, ISLE OF MAN. I saw the dark-haired traveler family, who had started the vigil giggling and jostling each other but had quickly stopped all that as the hours dragged on. I saw Bernadette and her son, Mrs. O'Cray, an impossibly pretty girl and her equally impossible boyfriend, a man with a slight limp who owned a large fertilizer company, the tattooed girl from Dublin, May from Cavan, a cross-looking man, Fiona, elegant Dympna, who, I had learned, was a theater director, Orla with her crimson bow, a man with very thick eyeglasses, who walked in a tentative, probing way with his chin up and his hands held slightly out in front of him because he couldn't see a thing, Prince Philip, a beautiful, blue-eyed woman from Cavan, a pair of ginger-haired Dubliners, a man who — like a tomcat — was missing the top of one ear, an older woman with swollen ankles, whom I had (at her request) lifted up from her knees that afternoon in the penitential beds, the tall boy with the orange baseball cap, a woman who looked like Virginia Woolf, and Johnny from Mayo with his beautiful hair.

The floor of the basilica was hard and very cold. My heels felt bruised. The prayers dragged on, like a tune you don't realize you're humming. *Hail Mary, Holy Mary, Our Father, I believe in.* We walked and said them, walked and said them, walked and said them as the pictures of the apostles and the stations of the cross wheeled endlessly by in the stained glass windows. Jesus is made to bear his cross. Simon helps Jesus to carry the cross. Veronica wipes the face of Jesus. The woman leading the station from the podium had an oddly shocked look on her face, as though she had been startled awake by a pistol shot in the night. She recited the prayers at a blistering clip, like an auctioneer boosting up the price. After ten minutes of trying to keep up with it, I wanted to step out of the line and stand up on a pew and say, "Who else in this church thinks this is insane?" But I suspected that they said the prayers fast to keep people awake. If they slowed down at all, we'd all be on the floor, and we'd never get through in just three days. Gradually, as I caught up to the prayers, the desire to protest passed.

Throughout the night we went around and around the basilica in a line, like prisoners in a jail yard. I let my mind go where it wanted to, to thoughts both spiritual and mundane. A moth the size of a hummingbird came into the church and hurled itself crazily against a metal pipe. The kindly tonsured man ahead of me was saying, "He will come again to judge the living and the dead," with his beads held up before him, and I thought suddenly of Liza Mithcell, my seventy-three-year-old landlady years ago in the village of Dunquin. Liza's parents had lived on Inishvickillaun, the island Charlie Haughey had bought. Liza was short and heavy and had the face and yellow-white hair of Tip O'Neill. English was her second language and, like many of the older people in Dunquin at that time, she spoke it with an accent that was as foreign as a French person's. It was more complicated than an Irish accent, more heavily laden.

For income Liza took in students like me who came to Dunquin to learn Irish Gaelic. She had three cottages to rent — I lived in one — and she cared for an old woman named Norry, who had been paralyzed and blinded by a stroke and never left her bed. Norry's bedroom was just inside Liza's front door, and sometimes as I passed through the hallway into the living room I could hear Norry's tiny voice calling out, like the voice of a fox cub trapped in a cave. I was always relieved when Liza answered the door with her forefinger to her lips and said, "Norry is sleeping," because if Norry wasn't sleeping Liza would send me in to say hello to her, which meant that I would have to speak Irish. (Why Norry never spoke English is even now a puzzle. At that time in Dunquin there were very few people remaining who were unable to converse in English. Norry was old — perhaps she was one of them.) I was seventeen, and my Irish was barely good enough for the dullest small talk. Norry's room was small and dark, and her bed, with a crucifix hanging on the wall above it, seemed very high, like a bier.

When I went into the room with Liza's introduction, Norry would beckon me to the side of the bed, put her hand up for me to hold, and with her narrow, waxen face level with my lowest rib and her blind blue eyes blinking at the ceiling, she would say sweetly, "An bhfuil an aimsir go maith, a chroí?" Norry was spindly, a rack of bones. Standing by the bed I had a vague sense of speaking to an animated corpse lying in a disinterred coffin. I would answer with something like "Tá sneachta ann inniu." And that would be a point of interest because the ocean and the Gulf Stream made snow a rarity in Dunquin. "Sneachta?!" Norry would say, as if Liza hadn't already told her numerous times that day that it was snowing. "Tá," I would reply, dying with unease, "sneachta." And then Liza, from her spot at the door, would clear the air of all this tedious politeness with a wisecrack. "Tá na Poncáin lán le hairgead, nach bhfuil siad, a Norry?" The Yanks are full of money, aren't they, Norry? Liza could say this because she knew I wasn't. Amid all the laughing — Norry laughed in a high, stifled way that went *hic, hic, hic* — I could leave and sit safely in the living room by Liza's fire.

As I passed by the basilica doors, cold air blew in around their hinges.

Liza had many names for me. She called me Julia, Dolly, Yankee, Hairpin, Fooleen, and Préachán, the Irish word for a crow or a person with black hair or a person with a loud voice or a person who couldn't sing. Liza had a daughter, Maureen, who was fifty and funny and foul-mouthed and variously addressed Liza as Landlady, Old Lady, Kitty O'Shea, and Mammy. Maureen smoked filterless Woodbines and sat in a chair with her knees apart and her hands on her knees, talking fast, the cigarette dangling from her lip. Every three minutes or so she tossed out the summarizing sentence, "Ah, fook em anyway!" And Liza would flinch and say, "Maureen, you're so rough." Now and then I caught Liza looking at her daughter with a puzzled, slightly guilty look on her face, as though she found it hard to accept that she had produced this blasphemous, cursing, barreling bawd who was always plucking at men's crotches or goosing them from behind.

Near the sanctuary I stepped on Dympna's heel, said, "Sorry, sorry" with my beaded hand to her shoulder as proof of how sorry, and resumed *as it is in heaven give us this day our daily bread.*

Liza did all her laundry, and her tenants' laundry, by hand. I used to find her behind her house twisting water from the bed sheets and spreading them on the bushes to dry. So much detergent and hot water had given Liza's thick hands an odd, inhuman shine; under lamplight her hands glinted, like glass or polished porcelain. In the evening she sat by the fire with her feet on the fender, her elbows drawn in at her sides, hands clasped on her big, aproned belly, and talked about the Lindbergh baby, an obsession she had indulged since 1932, when she worked for a family in Connecticut. "'Twas an inside job," she would say, "put on by a pair of Germans. A couple. Bad articles the both. Down the ladder they went with the baby in the dead of the winter and darkness of the night."

Liza was good-natured and grandmotherly, and her housebound ways and Irish inflections reminded me of the Irish great-aunt I had loved. The way an infant is soothed by the sound of a heartbeat, Irish voices were like a low, primordial frequency registered deep in my memory. I was seventeen, far from home, unhappy, and trying to grow up. Liza, with her advanced age and her Irishness, was a wing to hide under. In the four months that I lived on her property, she helped confirm and shape my view of Ireland. She made me laugh. In a high, reedy, nasal voice she sang songs in Irish, rare jigs and airs, the tunes of which, when I hear them now, can make me freeze with the memory of her. For several years after I left Dunquin, Liza and I exchanged letters. She would write: "My dear Julia, I received your letter and got very lonely while I was reading it. So far away here in Dunquin. Never mind. We will have another cup of tea one day."

Eventually I lost touch with Liza, and many years later, when I revisited Dunquin in the hope of meeting her again, I stopped first, on some instinct, I suppose, at the village cemetery. There on a headstone was her name in Irish: Eilis Bean Uí Mhistéal. I went sadly to look at her house and later regretted it; the house looked shabby and ill cared for, with torn and dirty curtains, peeling paint, and a broken flower pot in the yard. Seeing it was a blow and a lesson. Nothing stays the same, people you love pass by, they go away by choice or by chance, and there is not a thing you can do to bring them back.

IT WAS TIME to kneel again, and we all ducked into the nearest pew and collapsed on the kneelers. The best place to land at kneeling time was the altar; the kneeling pad there was the softest on the knees and the altar rail easier on the elbows than the backs of the pews were; at kneeling time I quickened my steps to secure a place at the altar before it filled up. The man on my left at the altar rail moved to make the sign of the cross, and his heavy rosary beads hit him in the nose. The woman on my right, with her face buried in her hands, was so exhausted that all she could muster of the Creed was "Pontius Pilate." She sounded drunk. When she lifted her head to stand up, her eyes were crimson and swollen. She lurched away from the altar. The surprised-looking woman leading the prayers at the podium said "Pray for those close to us who have died," then sobbed and put her hand to her face. The dark-haired boy who had asked me the time sat slumped in a pew at the back of the church with his rosary beads hung from his ear and dangling onto his shoulder like a freakish earring.

The night dragged so slowly I thought it would kill me. We were beyond pushing the wheel now — the wheel had rolled heavily backward and was crushing us under it. At four-thirty, sensing the approach of the sun, the swallows began to chatter. A bat came in through the open doors and careered around the central chandelier, and a roguish voice said in response, "Here's Satan now. Anyone tempted?" Toward the finish of the seventh station people staggered around the church with their eyes shut. Some did not get up from the pews when it was time to stand. Gravity had our weakened bodies in its grip. Some weaved as they walked, their arms dangling, their faces pale, their lips slightly orange in the dim light. Others sat like people in a hospital waiting room, dead-eyed and bracing for the news. Still, the voices prayed on in unison, humming and rumbling, pressing the air.

At the end of the seventh station my face hurt, my eyes felt swollen, and my eyelids kept sliding shut for thirty seconds of sleep until the violent motion of my head dropping forward jerked them open again. I sat in a pew with my arms crossed and my hands tucked into my armpits for warmth. I thought of one of the priests saying at the Mass, "The pilgrim needs to remember the example of Christ to get over the natural feeling of being sorry for himself." My limbs felt paralyzed. The floor seemed to rock gently, like the deck of a ship on a turbulent sea. I tried to make some notes in my notebook, but I couldn't see and my hand was stiff and the words went crooked on the page. The little brass plaque on the back of the oak pew in front of me said Waterford Timber Co. I knew that because my forehead had clunked against it one of the times I fell asleep with my elbows on my knees and my head in my hands. I sat waiting for the morning Mass. I touched my fingers to my face; it was cold and rubbery. From the corner of my eye I noticed that the colors in the stained glass windows on the east wall had begun to lighten and glow like jewelry. People came in and out of the basilica. I saw them, but they looked like trees walking.

THE RAIN HAD STOPPED, but the sky was overcast. With its windows faintly illuminated by the early daylight, the church felt somehow colder. Like me, the other vigilants sat stiff and mute, waiting for the Mass with their hats on and their beads strung around their knuckles, while the pilgrims who had had their night's sleep began to wander in, steady and refreshed and chatting.

As Father Mohan entered the sanctuary, May slipped in beside me in the pew and squeezed my arm in greeting. Her forehead was wet with holy water, and the dark beads in her hand were like a fistful of Raisinets. She said something, but all I could hear was *hamoo-hamick-hamucky-moo life, Rose?* Her accent was so heavy that in its whispered form she might as well have been speaking Latin. She elbowed me, leaned into me, nodding through the gloom. Her leather jacket creaked when she moved. *Harooniss-hare-manicky-clack and werry-woo all up and down,* she said.

May whispered all through the Mass, a running commentary. Six times I leaned over and asked her to repeat herself, and finally I was embarrassed enough at my failure to understand her that I stopped trying and simply nodded and smiled, hoping that a smile was the appropriate answer. She might have been telling me she was deeply depressed and thinking of suicide, but I doubted it, for even after the long night May was brimming with an irrepressible joy, as though she felt terribly lucky to be here. Though her face was drawn and gray with fatigue, she still radiated graceful enthusiasm and her eyes held their soulful depth. She was happy. It was comforting to sit next to her. Every now and then her hand rose up to her forehead and made the sign of the cross for good measure.

Father Mohan's speaking style was halting and businesslike. When he tried to be funny he ended up sounding a little menacing. He had short orange hair and a square jaw. "What keeps a candle going?" he said. "The air. Or we could say the oxygen, if we wanted to be that way about it."

Listening to him was a strain. My head kept tipping forward.

"Over the years I have found it could be dangerous saying certain things at the door on the left where the vigilants are coming in. When I ask them how they are they say, 'I'm surviving.' You would think that Jesus would want more for us than just survival."

Mohan's voice seemed to echo in my eye sockets.

"There are a few other things I would like to say. One is the regulation of vigil, which vigil as you know is about trying to keep awake for twenty-four hours. It's not about keeping awake, it's about *trying* to keep awake. And therefore the rule is that you do not lie down. When you go to the dormitory where the beds are, the temptation may be to lie down. Don't."

May spoke. I nodded at her, struggling to stay awake. The urge to sleep was suddenly overpowering. My whole body was shutting down. It was agony. I could hardly move my arms. The woman to the right of me was crying. I saw her face from the corner of my eye — it was sheet-white in the dim light, her red-rimmed eyes brimming, her nose pink, her lips pale and trembling. She tamped at her cheeks with the sleeve of her coat and straightened the beads in her hand. The sight of her crying made my eyes fill with tears again. I was exhausted, my mood was raw, the requirements of this pilgrimage were stripping away my defenses. The slightest thing could make me cry now. Heads in the rows ahead of me jerked suddenly out of sleep, while others tipped slowly into it.

Father Mohan said, "For those of you who are going home this morning, I have a few things to say to you. Various people will tell me, 'Take a good look at me, Father, for this is the last time you'll see me.' And then they go and throw coins in the lake. What's that for? An assurance that they'll come back this way. Whatever the case, it is a waste of money. It's very difficult to retrieve the coins from the lake and they become tarnished, so it's a waste of money. If you must throw coins, put them into the black pot at the landing."

Someone in the back of the church let out a bark in his sleep, and without missing a beat Mohan said, "I'll do the talking for now."

I had decided that at Station Island I would receive communion. Kneeling at the altar rail to receive the Eucharist wafer, all I could make out of the priest who offered it was the coarse red hair between the knuckles of his fingers.

AFTER THE MASS the dormitories were unlocked and the pilgrims had an opportunity to wash their faces and change their clothing. I went up the stairs of the women's dormitory and followed Orla into the very clean bathroom. A laminated sign said:

> Ladies. Sanitary towels must not be flushed down the toilet as they are non bio-degradable. Clearing of sewage system and repair of pumps last year cost 6,000 pounds. Annual cost of sanitary bin service is £4,000. These costs arise as a direct result of incorrect disposal of sanitary towels. It would be most inappropriate for the Prior or staff priests to have to mention this *publicly. Please use the bins!*

I studied the sign for a while in a trance. Father Mohan's slightly scolding tone seemed to have filtered down to the person who had written it. *Do not throw coins into the lake!*

I could feel my face sagging. I splashed water on it. In a special trough constructed for the purpose I washed my feet, while Orla stood bent over with her head in the sink. That she had enough energy to wash her hair baffled me. She sang a little song as she worked, but the words went down the drain or were muffled by the splashing water. Finally her voice echoed up from the sink. "D'you s'pose this water comes up out of the old lake?"

"No idea," I said, hunched over my feet. "Maybe."

Orla's hand reached up and twisted a faucet. "Because there's not a stitch of pressure in this pipe. I'll be here 'til Tuesday rinsing out the soap." Eventually she stood up, sputtering and blinking, her hair a dripping orange mass like a twisted fishnet. She wrapped her head in a towel and rummaged in her cosmetics bag. "And now I must brush me teeth. My teeth, my teeth, oh, where's that . . . ah, here it is."

Like May, Orla was bursting with talk. But exhaustion had rendered me dumb. I wanted to lie down on the bathroom floor. Orla looked at herself in the water-splashed mirror, plucked something out of her eye, sighed, and said, "Oh, what a face! I must ready myself for confession now. Examine the old conscience. The priests'll be going into the boxes at half past eight."

I told Orla that I hadn't been to confession since my first confession twenty-nine years before. Through the mirror she studied me with renewed interest. "You picked a fine place to come on your holiday!" she said. "Now what line of work are you in at all?"

"Writing," I said.

Orla twisted the faucets and said, not unkindly, "Yes, well, we all have our hobbies."

"What's your hobby?" I said.

Orla put her hands on her hips and grimaced at herself in the mirror. "Smoking."

THAT MORNING the sky was the purplish gray of paving slate. It was heavy and furry and very low, muzzling the tops of the gray hills in the distance. A fine rain fell. The people who had completed their pilgrimage had left on the boat at 9:45, and new pilgrims would begin arriving shortly. After four circuits of the basilica and seven decades of the rosary, I went to the penitential beds, which lay together in a small grassy area near the chestnut tree at the edge of the lake. The six "beds" were actually stone walls no higher than the knee and formed in small circles approximately the circumference of a child's wading pool. The walls were smoothed by weather and human contact and padded with moss and lichens; some sprouted shaggy clumps of grass as coarse as a horse's tail. The floors of the beds were of sharp rocks and slippery when wet. But for the bronze crucifix at the center of each bed, the stone circles looked like an archaeological dig, the ruins of some ancient village, which in a sense it was. The beds were believed to be the remains of sixth-century beehive huts constructed by the monks of Saints' Island. The small conical stone cells, roughly the shape of a bishop's miter, had been only big enough for one or two kneeling, fasting, penitential monks to shelter within. The legend was that the saints for whom the beds are named actually lay several nights in a row on the stone floors of these "beds" as a penance for their sins.

The second half of four of the nine required stations at Saint Patrick's Purgatory takes place within the precinct of the famous penitential beds. I reviewed the instructions for the exercise:

Go to St. Brigid's Bed. At the bed:

(a) walk three times around the outside, by your right hand, while saying three *Our Fathers,* three *Hail Marys,* and one *Creed;*
(b) kneel at the entrance to the Bed and repeat these prayers;
(c) walk three times around the inside and say these prayers again;
(d) kneel at the Cross in the centre and say these prayers for the fourth time.

This sequence was repeated at Saint Brendan's Bed, Saint Catherine's Bed, Saint Columba's Bed, and the beds of Saints Davog and Molaise. At the end we were to go to the water's edge, stand and say five Our Fathers, five Hail Marys, and one Creed, kneel and repeat the prayers, and make the sign of the cross with lake water as a reminder of our baptism. Finally, we were to return to Saint Patrick's Cross, kneel and say one Our Father, one Hail Mary, and one Creed, then enter the basilica and conclude the station by reciting Psalm 15 or by saying five Our Fathers, five Hail Marys, and one creed, for the pope's intentions.

The ancient stone rings, and the inexplicable precision, repetition, and circling, all had the flavor of a pagan ritual. This part of the station was difficult to perform even when you hadn't been awake all night praying and starving. (I reminded myself that it was not nearly as difficult as it must have been three hundred years ago, when the fasting pilgrims performed a similar pattern twenty-seven times over an unbroken period of nine days, at the end of which they endured their night vigil within the cave. At one point in the history of Lough Derg, pilgrims submerged themselves in the lake, sometimes standing up to their necks in water for several hours.) Though the exact origin of the exercises is unclear, the pattern of prayer, involving fasting and circling the beds, was recorded as early as the beginning of the sixteenth century. What takes place now during the three-day visit is the result of a long evolution.

There was just enough wind that morning to make the rain annoying. Pilgrims in slickers and raincoats moved about the stones like victims who had had their shoes blown off in a bombing and now were searching through the rubble for some lost valuable thing. They huddled and crept, picking their way over the sharp, slippery stones, heads bent low, lips moving, faces exhausted and grim and abstracted. Some of them knelt, some clung to the thigh-high central crosses. Now and then an arm with rosary beads lassoing at the end of it shot wildly up to counterbalance a body on the verge of falling. In some places the rocky ground made kneeling so painful that some of the pilgrims ended up on all fours, which made them look ill or insane or as if they had thoroughly given up hope. Some of the older pilgrims had trouble getting up from the kneeling position and raised their wet hands for help. The grass around the beds was tussocky and spongy and glowed the bold Irish green that even in the rain seems to reflect bright sunlight. Buttercups and little purple wildflowers dotted the ground. The slick stones glistened. The surface of the lake was pitted with rain. The big chestnut tree — if it *was* a chestnut — dripped and rustled in the wind. In his Lough Derg pamphlet Bishop Joe Duffy called it a sycamore. Seamus Heaney, in his poem "Station Island," called it an oak. I thought it was a chestnut. Whatever it was, it was a beautiful tree, hundreds of years old and densely leafy, with a gently rounded silhouette.

I went three times around Saint Brigid's bed, where five or six other pilgrims mumbled and groped. With their hoods pulled up, they looked like brooding Capuchin monks. I had no hood, just a cap, and my neck was wet. The knees of the man in front of me cracked crisply every time he shifted into the kneeling position. The cuffs of his too-long trousers were dirty from dragging on the ground. The rain slickers swished and rustled. There was the smell of mud and wet rocks, the buggy smell of the lake, and occasionally the distinctly secular smell of cigarette smoke coming from the direction of Saint Mary's Chapel. Gusts of wind flung cold rain into our eyes. There were a few bloody toes, a knuckle or two rubbed raw, women in plastic rain bonnets, a young woman sobbing into her hands. My knees were muddy.

Inside the beds we crowded together around the crucifix, kneeling. Having passed through the beds three times now, I knew the most comfortable kneeling spots and tried to stick with them. The bronze crucifixes were rooted to the rocky ground by heavy cast-iron bases shaped like tall loaves of bread, each one bearing the plaque of the maker: C. BULL LTD, 21 SUFFOLK ST. DUBLIN. A delicate patina put streaks of turquoise in Jesus' long bronze hair. The whispering mouths of the pilgrims made a steamy hissing, clicking sound. Our elbows rubbed. I saw a wart on a chin, whiskers, pores, wet hair dangling like seaweed, freckles, nostrils and teeth, rings on thin fingers, sleeves too long, rain-splattered eyeglasses. I smelled perfume now and then lifting from someone's clothing. We were together in a very intimate way, exposed and vulnerable, yet no one appeared to be aware of anyone else, which seemed a sign of true unity. The lack of self-consciousness grew out of an agreement: we were in it together. No one was going to stand up and say, *This is nuts!* On my first pass through the penitential beds I had wanted to say it, but when I looked at the faces around me rendered almost noble with devotion, the desire slunk away.

I prayed, but I was so tired I couldn't keep the words straight. I would start the Our Father and halfway through it the needle would jump to the second half of the Hail Mary. Sometimes I started a prayer and three minutes later was astonished and amused to hear myself whispering *and to the republic for which it stands.* Sometimes lines of poetry sprouted up through the prayers. *Thy kingdom come thy will be done a floor too cool for corn.* Sometimes I found myself circling the stones and kneeling and looking at the bruised sky and thinking *warhorse, warehouse, whorehouse, wharf.* Sometimes bleak feelings rendered worse by fatigue crowded my chest, and then I forced myself back into the distraction of the prayer. I found that if I forced myself long enough, I could settle into a rhythm and the prayer would carry me along. Just by saying the words I felt soothed, and I wondered if the feeling was similar to what the Anonymous Pilgrim felt as he walked across Russia endlessly repeating the Jesus Prayer. Often when I prayed the Hail Mary and the Our Father, the words carried the color and smell of my childhood, of rosary gatherings in my great-aunt's back yard in summer. Six years old, I sat in a folding chair, my feet not reaching the grass, and stared at the big sunlit ear of the man who owned the religious artifacts store, or at a bee weaving in the magnetic pull of a purple rhododendron; I heard a distant siren going down Ashmont Street and heard the people around me, my family and people who had come from all over Dorchester, saying, with beads in their hands, "Hail Mary full of grace." The sound of those words always carried an instinctual feeling of safety, perhaps because I sensed that reciting the prayers made the people I depended on and cared most about — my parents, my aunts, in short, my community — feel safe.

The prayers, which I had been reared with and had been taught to perceive as literal, had the quality of a meditation when recited over and over this way. Kneeling in the penitential beds I thought of the words as a story, a construct, a way of framing the self in time and space. I translated them into something that might be, however shakily, applicable to me. Though we attempt to control our world, we had very little control over it. That truth, despite all our pride and self-importance, made us vulnerable. We knew not why we were here, and there was only one way to leave this reality. In this strange form of imprisonment we were asking for sympathy from that which had created us. We were asking for a crumb to help us make our way through. We were praying in the hope that there might be some constant and responsive mercy. Thinking about the prayers in this way made it easier to see how small we truly were. And I found it wasn't so awful to acknowledge how small I was, particularly when everyone else around me was acknowledging their smallness too. I looked at the blankly staring faces around me, all staring in the same humbled way, and in them I saw stillness and strength.

THE VIEW from the smoking room windows was of fog, a woolly gray body that glided over the grass and pressed against the windows. The dusty room was quiet. The man in the trilby sat against the wall with his thin legs crossed and his hat hitched back on his head, squinting at a scrap of newspaper through his horn-rimmed glasses. He held his cigarette up by the side of his head. The slow, delicate way he smoked was almost feminine. Across the room the teenaged traveler sat bent over his knees, rolling a cigarette, tunelessly humming and tapping one foot on the floor as he worked. May, near the door, yawned grandly and ground out her cigarette.

I had come in to take a break and study my books, but I was so tired and hungry that I couldn't focus and ended up staring at the ceiling and wishing the refectory would open so that I could go and eat the oatcakes again. I was faltering. I had attended the Renewal of Baptismal Promises, but the service had passed in a blur. We had the afternoon and the evening to get through before we could sleep. The fatigue had stopped making me drowsy and was now making me restless and a little anxious. I rubbed my thumb at the plastic rosary beads. I thought of my father. His sister had once given me a copy of a sheet of his third-grade homework for a class called Language. In the middle of the top of the sheet he had written JMJ (Jesus Mary Joseph), as Catholic schoolchildren were taught to do. And he had written in loopy cursive script:

John Mahoney, Holy Name School, February 18th, 1931, Grade
Three. Language
Declarative Sentences:

1. I am a Catholic boy
2. My catechism tells me about God
3. He is our best friend.
4. He died on the cross for us.
5. God died on Good Friday.
6. It is wrong to tell a lie.
7. Always obey your parents
8. God is everywhere.
9. Today is Ash Wednesday.
10. Jesus loves little children.

Executed in a fledgling approximation of Palmer-method penman-
ship, these declarative sentences were like a rice-paper rood screen
through which the teacher's dark silhouette showed — a looming nun
projecting Catholic sentiment, which my father was certainly too young
to feel truly for himself. (That day, February 18, 1931, was his eighth
birthday.) Thirty-eight years later, when I was eight, he was buried in an
expensive casket with a set of rosary beads wound around his hand.
Though my father was a practicing Catholic, he rarely said the rosary;
the set of beads on the hand was merely a custom of the Catholic under-
takers. Whether he would have declined that final ornament I don't
know, but as with the "Declarative Sentences" of his Language class he
was in no position to choose. I myself had chosen to leave Catholic sentiment behind, but at thirty-nine I felt it creeping back.

I got up and went into the cloakroom. The coat rack, which held
plastic shopping bags and a few dangling jackets, was the noblest coat
rack I had ever seen, long and very well made, with numbers printed in
little windows above the solid brass hooks. A woman was sitting alone
at a classroom-sized table pushed into the middle of the room, smoking
and looking into the unlit fireplace. The table was littered with the same
old pawed-apart newspapers, and as I flipped through them the woman
asked me how I was getting on. She had a soft voice and a long face,
high cheekbones and rich, well-tended hair. Smoke fluffed out of her
mouth as she talked. She had four children and had raised them all to be
good Catholics. She was very strict about Mass. At one point she said,
"The ones east of the Shannon don't go to Mass; the ones west of the

Shannon do." I thought she was talking about her children until she said, "It's according to a survey. Something about the people in the west having a harder time during Cromwell and the penal times and the famine and all the rest of it. The people east of the Shannon are maybe a bit more English, like. More planters settled in the midlands because the land was good. And now the people who live there don't go to Mass. During the Cromwell and the penal and the pale and such, no staff were allowed on Station Island, so the pilgrims kept it going themselves."

The way she spoke suggested that she had said all this before, as though these facts in Irish history had long disappointed and troubled her. Another woman, sitting across the room with a kerchief on her head, concurred that the Mass was important. She had a daughter who was living in America. "I don't know does she go to Mass now," she said. "I'm here praying for her. I pray for all of my children."

I knew that my mother, too, prayed for all of her children. "You're a good mother," I said to the woman with the kerchief.

"And you're a good girl," she said in return.

I wasn't sure what made her say this. I thought of the young Irish woman making a life in America while her mother prayed and worried on her behalf. I thought of my grandfather; unable to tell his father that he didn't want to be a priest, he had quit the seminary at Maynooth in Dublin, left for Boston without saying goodbye, and never communicated with his father again. When I asked my mother why her father didn't want to be a priest, she thought a bit, with her index finger to her lips, then said, "I don't know, really. Maybe he wanted human love."

AS I STEPPED out into the hallway, preparing to head for the refectory, I was drawn by the wide, empty stairs that led to the upper floors of the women's dormitory. Like the rest of the building, the stairwell was big and spooky and empty. The flights, strewn with dust and debris, wound up and up. It was obvious that the upper floors were unused. Something about this building was compelling, a bit haunted but also strangely comforting. It was nearly ninety years old and had about it the mood of a time I regretted having missed, a time that included my grandparents. I decided to explore the rest of the building.

Upstairs the large concrete-floored rooms were empty. There were signs of demolition: the walls that had formed dormitory cubicles had been torn down, and a great number of porcelain sinks had been hurled into a corner. Thick wooden floorboards had been ripped up and stacked in a pile, yards of tongue-in-groove wainscoting had been dismantled. The steel I-beams in the ceiling were exposed. There were handsaws lying about and dangling electrical wires and stacks of metal cots. Plaster had crumbled off the walls, windows were broken. Though it was all derelict and defunct, the materials and fixtures that were being ripped out had once been beautiful. The cubicle numbers, still screwed to the splintered wooden planks, were delicate white porcelain ovals marked with a vitreous enamel of indigo blue. The coathooks were gracefully tapered fingers of solid brass. The stacks of mirrors on the floor had fine beveled edges. The walls of the building were very thick and the windows many-paned. Either the building was being renovated or these materials were being salvaged before a wrecking ball knocked it down. Whatever was being done, I thought it was a shame. Everything here was solid and had the beauty of simplicity and high quality. The original work had been done with skill, the architect had bothered with detail. To me it was like finding a treasure broken apart; the dormitory had the sadness of a ghost town, that lonely sense of failure and regret.

I went up more flights and roamed around the rooms, stepping over broken glass, clumps of concrete, scatterings of screws and rusted nails. The fifth floor was atticky and spooky and smelled of dust. As I stood at the very top of the stairs, swallows, disconcertingly batlike, flitted over my head, stirring the air above my ears. Stacked-up bricks of khaki-colored soap stood on a table among some large red tins of floor wax. The tins, labeled CARDINAL LIQUID POLISH, bore an illustration of a robust, bright-eyed, reassuringly white-haired Catholic cardinal wearing red robes and a quilted red beanie. He looked on the verge of winking. Here I had a strong sense of what Lough Derg had been like in its heyday: popular, confident, and busy. Its institutional orderliness, which so many people railed against, I loved precisely because it was orderly. I loved the idea of forty-five individual sinks in forty-five well-made cubicles, one for each person. I could see the hundreds of pilgrim women hanging their coats on the hooks, washing their hands at the sinks with these big hunks of soap; I could feel the vibration of their footsteps on the floor, their voices calling brightly to each other down the long, spotless hallway. I could feel their enthusiasm for God and the prayers and each other.

Now the building was reminiscent of a once bustling factory shut down by the economic consequences of war. I went to the window and looked out over the grass and the statue of the crowned Blessed Virgin. The rain had stopped, and shallow puddles of robin's egg blue showed amid the low clouds. The copper dome of the basilica was a dull green. From this perspective, the basilica looked enormous and elaborate. How on earth had they done all this building on no more than an acre of land in the middle of a big lake? The massive buildings could have been located in a busy section of Dublin. Their construction was a representation of sheer will and determination that matched the will and determination of the pilgrims themselves.

Speaking at the Mass, the African priest, Father Maanzo, had called the act of pilgrimage a search for God. "God has always used human beings throughout history to reveal himself." The center of pilgrimage, he had said, was not our sin but God's mercy. The Lough Derg pilgrims were a varied group — the dentist, the CEO, the theater director, the nurse, the bus driver, the engineer, the housewife. All, in their separate spheres, had felt moved to come; no one had forced them. They had made themselves humble, and in their humility they were fierce. They were on their knees but they were bold enough to call God down. It was a strange, defiant, ancient practice. In the span of a thousand years, thousands of pilgrims had come here to Station Island and done the same thing; in their coming a thousand individual stories had been whittled down to one.

AT THE TABLE May was saying, "And what about the poor old dote who was sick last night?"

Mrs. O'Kane's teacup stalled in front of her mouth. "Sick?"

May leaned forward. "She fell out of her bed."

"Fell out?" said Veronica.

"How?" said Anne.

"The bunk," said May.

"She was drunk?"

Mrs. O'Kane raised her eyebrows in shocked disbelief. "How could she be drunk?"

Veronica looked scandalized and raised her finger to her lips and muttered, "My God. At holy Station Island! Drunk!"

May straightened her spine and frowned at the tired faces. "No, girls, not drunk! The *bunk*. She only fell out of it."

A long discourse followed on how difficult it was to get out of the bunk beds in the women's dormitory. And more talk about the weather, the midges, the oatcakes, the black tea, the sleep we'd soon have. The sugar bowl made its rounds, the platter of toast was depleted. The refectory was crowded with pilgrims now, and the voices bounced against the windows. There was laughter and the sound of clinking spoons. Through the wall of windows I could see the serious, handsome young woman with the musty smell and the boy's haircut walking across the courtyard toward the dining room, staring down at her bare feet, a cigarette in her fingers, the collar of her maroon windbreaker turned up to her ears. Her walk was a powerful long-legged lope. Gulls fell about the sky behind her. A spray of midges clung to the windowpanes like spermatazoa.

Nuala said, "And to think we've to come back to Lough Derg three times!"

"Three times?" I said.

"You didn't know? Three times guarantees entry into heaven."

This brought a flurry of skeptical but indulgent laughter from the women.

"It's a bit of old nonsense, isn't it?" Anne said.

Veronica said, "I believe many things, like, but exactly *three* times? I don't think God is so precise as that."

Veronica and Anne, two Dubliners in their early thirties, had freshly made up their faces. They wore stylish clothing and costly earrings. I said that if God was precise enough for fingerprints and snowflakes, he might be precise enough for that, and there was more laughter.

May said, "Now it's said that when you're leaving on the boat, if you look back at the island, you will return. Something will draw you again."

The handsome young woman arrived at our table bringing a little gust of cold air with her. She sat down at the empty place, and the other pilgrims greeted her with nods and smiles.

I mentioned that when I went up to the dormitory that morning I had seriously thought about getting into bed and staying there.

Mrs. O'Kane looked horrified. "Oh, I wouldn't give myself the satisfaction of doing that for a minute! I made my vow and I'm keeping it."

There was talk about the real world then, the rat race — the cell phones and the mail and the TV. Everyone agreed it was good to be out of it now and then. I asked Veronica if she believed in heaven. She put her fingers to her forehead and stared at the table, lips pursed, thinking. And then she raised her head and said seriously, "I do, yeah, in me own queer way."

May said something, and I had to ask her what she had said.

"If there's no heaven then we're all suffering for nothing!" she repeated. She turned her big eyes and her wide smile on me. "You can't understand a word I say, can you? Well, I have me own trouble understanding you!"

Nuala stretched and said, "Ah, well. Come on now, lads, back to the prayers."

"Right then," said Mrs. O'Kane, tossing down her napkin. "Show us the way out."

We struggled up from the benches, zipping our jackets and adjusting our collars, leaving the handsome young woman alone at the table amid our litter of cups and plates and saucers.

WITHIN A GLASS RELIQUARY in Saint Mary's Chapel, the 130-year-old stone church near the dock, was a small, beautifully simple hand-carved crucifix. On a card below it were the words "Found clutched in the hand of Miss O'Donnell, Derry, who perished in the boating disaster on the 12 of July 1795."

From the dock on the mainland to the dock on Station Island the distance was perhaps a half mile. Between the two shores lay tiny Friar's Island, not much bigger than a tennis court and overgrown with trees and shrubs. In the boating disaster, ninety-three people had climbed into a long wooden rowboat to make the passage to Station Island. A man came to the dock — so the story goes — and told his son to get out of the boat, for he had been warned in a dream of some threat to his son's life. The son got out, the boat set off, and as it neared Friar's Island it began to take on water at an alarming rate. The passengers panicked, and the boat capsized and sank. Unable to swim, ninety of the pilgrims drowned in ten feet of water just yards from the shore. Relatives traveled from the surrounding countryside, many on foot, to collect the bodies of their kin. The poorest carried the bodies home on their backs.

As I was looking at the relics and admiring the little church — a simple, pretty chapel with a slate roof and a wooden floor and lancet windows mullioned in a graceful diamond pattern — two women came into the church and joined me at the reliquary. The older woman peered through the glass and gasped, "Look at that now. Found in the hand of Miss O'Donnell. Drowned. God help us."

The younger one gazed at it. "Miss O'Donnell," she said ruefully. "Think of it."

I had met the young one in the basilica during the night. A fast talker, she moved quickly from subject to subject. She told me she had bumped into Bono of U2 on the street in Dublin the previous week. When she got back to Dublin after Lough Derg she was going straight to the health club for a sauna. The health club cost 180 pounds per year, which wasn't as bad as some. She was planning to attend a three-day party in the south the following week. She was a nurse and was hoping to go to Saudi Arabia, like all the other Irish nurses, and make her fortune. Now, in the chapel, she told me she had tried to avoid getting Monsignor Mohan as a confessor that morning, hoping instead to get one of the younger ones. "I wanted the hip-looking little priest who looked like he might smoke dope, but didn't I end up with the one from Iraq!" She rolled her eyes. "Who did you get for your confession?"

I didn't like telling her that I hadn't gone to confession. I had entered the church with every intention of stepping into the box, but when it came my turn, I let the next person take my place. Having made a Catholic confession only once in my life, I couldn't now bring myself to tell my sins to a stranger sitting in a box.

The young woman said, "Well, the Iraqi kept saying to me at the end of the confession, 'Anything else now? Anything else?' and I wanted to say to him, 'Well, every feckin' commandment under the sun I've broken, if you must know the truth.'" She looked at the ceiling and sighed. "I don't know why I keep coming back here. It's a killer and the midgets drive my face crazy."

"Why do you keep coming back?" I said.

She peered at the relics. "Dunno, really. When it's done, you feel very good about it."

I said, "If you had to choose between never coming to Lough Derg again in your life or never going to a three-day party, which would you get rid of?"

"God, what a question!" She gave my shoulder a friendly shove. "Go on out of that and don't be settin' me up."

"Really," I said. "Think about it. Which?"

She thought a minute, blinking and staring at me without really seeing me. She was concentrating on the options. The ends of her long dark hair had the tint of henna. "Well, I suppose I could do without the three-day party. There's plenty of fun in the world. But there's nothing quite like this. I'm driven mad when I'm here, but if they took it away I'd be sad."

All of the pilgrims I had talked with had said the same. It was a strong feeling, and in the face of the declining number of people who called themselves practicing Catholics, its strength was surprising. It wasn't just the deeply devout or the superstitious who counted on the endurance of Station Island. It was people like me, who were on the edge of faith, had doubts, and were somewhat skeptical about the church. That Lough Derg had survived this long was impressive. The British Crown had tried more than once to kill it and failed. Unlike most other Christian sites of pilgrimage, it had no miracles to recommend it, no cures or apparitions, no historical visits from Christ or the apostles, no relics of significance beyond an Irish significance. The medieval phase of purgatorial visions, though powerful enough in its day to draw the attention of wider Europe, had died and become a legend. Wider Europe wasn't interested now. (Joseph McGuinness, in his book about Lough Derg, posits the compelling notion that at the height of the purgatorial visions on the island the New World had not yet been discovered and that the perception of the cave as a gateway to the next world grew naturally out of the general European belief that Ireland lay at the farthest edge of the world. "It is not surprising that visions of the next world should come to be associated with a place at the margins of this one," McGuinness says.)

Having endured great social, economic, and ecclesiastical change, and a period of manipulation and distortion at the hands of the very clergy who superintended it, the pilgrimage at Lough Derg seemed now to have returned to its original essence: a place where people came to meditate, fast, atone, pray, and commune with God. In his poem "Lough Derg," the Irish poet Patrick Kavanagh wrote of Saint Patrick's Purgatory:

The twentieth century blows across it now
But deeply it has kept its ancient vow.

That morning near the penitential beds I had met Father Hubert, the priest who had spoken to the pilgrims the night before, and had asked him what he thought the future of the pilgrimage would be. (In asking him this I realized that I was, in a sense, also asking about the future of the Irish church. The annual number of newly ordained priests and newly avowed nuns in Ireland is declining rapidly and radically.) Father Hubert's answer was that the pilgrimage would survive but that its focus would be less on numbers and more on quality and intention. He said, "In the days when seven hundred were coming daily, many came as a lark and climbed up the stairs in the church and went to sleep in the balconies. There were so many people that chairs had to be set up outside the church because there was no room inside. The lines of pilgrims waiting for access to the penitential beds snaked around the island. It was a bit like caring for a nursery school." He laughed. "The people would come out and run around the beds like it was a playground."

Father Hubert told me that because of the decline in numbers, a public relations firm had been hired to promote the pilgrimage. Advertisements for Lough Derg were appearing on Irish buses and trains. I had seen one, a beautiful color photograph taken at sunset of the basilica and the buildings reflected in the glassy lake, and, in big letters, the words THE LOUGH DERG CHALLENGE: ARE YOU READY TO TAKE IT? With its appeal to the mettle of prospective pilgrims, the ad reminded me of a recruiting pitch put out by the U.S. military. The guise under which Saint Patrick's Purgatory would continue didn't seem to matter terribly; its meaning would continue. From an article about Lough Derg in the *Irish Times* I learned that Monsignor Mohan had recently sent information about Lough Derg to two hundred business people and executives whom he called "movers and shakers." According to the *Times,* Monsignor Mohan "spoke of how they might perceive the pilgrimage as a way of alleviating 'executive stress' and how it was considerably cheaper than a health farm."

Father Hubert had interrupted our conversation to point to a man going around the beds. "Do you see that fella now?" It was the one who looked like Prince Philip. "He has made an impression on me. He's a member of one of Ireland's wealthiest families."

We watched the wealthy man kneeling in one of the beds. He was slender and erect and his clothes were beautiful, like a costly hunting outfit; he looked ready to shoot some flying fowl. Even the wealthy were not immune to the pains and consolations of penance.

"You'll find all kinds here," Father Hubert had said.

WHEN I CAME out of St. Mary's Chapel the afternoon sky had cleared considerably, the fog had burned away, and the clouds were magnificent, thick and muscular, churning and billowing, like smoke from a raging oil fire. They raced from west to east, and their violets and grays, whites and pinks, were so vivid they looked electronically enhanced.

At ten o'clock that night we ended our vigil in the basilica with the Canticle of Simeon. "Save us Lord while we are awake, protect us while we sleep that we may keep watch with Christ and rest with Him in peace . . ." And then we sang the Irish hymn "Hail, Glorious Saint Patrick," which roused the emotion of even those most concussed with fatigue. The pilgrims sang with a force that surprised me. "Hail, glorious Saint Patrick, dear saint of our isle" swelled up to the ceiling. I saw tears of gratitude on some of the faces near me and smiles of pride on others.

After a day of prayers, the Renewal of Baptismal Promises, the Way of the Cross, the end of the eighth station, one meal of oatcakes, the evening Mass, and the Night Prayer and Benediction, I limped up to my room in the new women's dormitory. The room, a cubicle really, was appointed with its own sink and mirror, bunk beds made up with military precision, and a small frosted window that looked onto the courtyard and the water. In its utilitarian spareness, it was not so different from the old dorm, but the quality was different. The room had the glossy textures of a modern supermarket. It was comfortable enough, though, and remarkably clean.

By luck I had the cubicle to myself. My feet were so cold they hurt. I climbed into the bed and lay there shivering. The sheets had a faint dampness, as they often do in Ireland, but they were so smooth and fresh and white they seemed to glow in the darkness. The extreme cleanliness of the place was like a presence, a soul, as though the person who had cleaned it so vigorously was still in the room. I was starving. As I thought about an apple that was in my bag and about how I could eat it without anyone knowing, I heard a voice in the next cubicle say, "Aren't these blankets lovely, now, Betty? So soft and woolly, like." And then I heard a luxurious sigh and the same voice said languidly, "Ah, God, you'd nearly think the sheep himself's in the bed with ya."

It was true. The blankets were heavy and beautiful. I pulled them up to my chin and said to myself, "Don't you touch that apple."

THE NEXT MORNING a ringing of bells jolted me out of a sleep so deep that I sprang up, and for a full thirty seconds, sitting in the middle of the strange bed, I had no idea where I was. I saw the springs of the empty bed above me, the sink, the little frosted window looking like a snowy TV screen, the unfamiliar blanket, but it meant nothing until I saw the small typed sign on the door: ON YOUR LAST MORNING PLEASE MAKE UP YOUR BED WITH THE CLEAN SHEETS PROVIDED IN YOUR CUBICLE. THIS WOULD BE A GREAT HELP TO THE STAFF AND TO THE NEXT PILGRIM! THANK YOU.

I dressed quickly, put on my shoes, took the shoes off again, and hurried out through a heavy rain to the 6:30 Mass, where the poor creatures who had stayed up all night sat staring at the priest with smeared eyes and ashy faces and blue feet.

When the Mass was over, I went outside and set about completing my ninth station. As I prayed I realized that in the past few years I had been thinking about God a thousand different ways. My question had always been how to believe and what form belief should take, if any. If one truly believed, then by its very meaning and nature that belief seemed to beg for an expression, an outward manifestation. I wanted belief to have a solid shape; I wanted to take the rough edge of doubt and make it smooth. At a certain point in my life I had disowned God. There were dogmas and concepts in the church that I didn't understand or believe, and I had found it necessary to throw it all out. I rejected certain points in the Creed, but were those things that I didn't believe or didn't understand sufficient obstacles to my thoughts about God? Now I realized how great was my desire to have those thoughts be organized, clear, and final. But faith would not come to me in the form of a yes or no answer. It was ongoing, organic — a process. What I had objected to was that in order to be called a true Christian you had say that you were and believe it. I didn't need to be called a true Christian. I was not hoping to be part of a church. I was mostly hoping to know about God.

The question wasn't really whether I believed in God but whether I admitted the possibility of God. There was, I knew, no faith without doubt. Twenty years before, I had written in my college notebook in response to Kierkegaard's *Present Age,* "The doubt in faith is what holds it together." Kierkegaard believed that faith required a leap, that faith actually lived in that leap. I believed that too.

I prayed that last morning at Saint Patrick's Purgatory with great concentration and energy. The prayers went straight, the words seemed to lift off through the top of my head, my mind didn't wander, I didn't care that the ground was damp. I was happy enough to be here. I prayed for my family and for the people I cared about and even for one or two people who had treated me thoughtlessly. I prayed for my sister who had breast cancer, for my father and several other relatives who were dead. I remembered Mary O'Dowd, the woman in the Dublin bookstore, and tossed in the promised prayer for her. I thought of a friend of mine, Tom Shaw, the Episcopal bishop of Massachusetts, who had told me he believed pilgrimage was an attempt to "invite into our hearts what we know in our heads." I had never imagined I would find myself on my knees with a rosary in my fingers, pressing out the Hail Mary. But having come and submitted myself to the stations of Lough Derg, I was a noisy tom-tom of intentions, drumming out messages and sending them sailing over the water.

THE BUS TO DUBLIN stopped to discharge passengers and take on others. As the doors closed and the bus began to roll again, a woman raced up and banged frantically on the door. The driver opened it, and the woman climbed on. She tucked a small bag into the overhead luggage rack, then flopped down heavily in the seat next to me, gasping for breath. She was plump and red-faced, and when she sat down her powerful thighs and upper arms pressed me against the sun-filled window. She was sweating and breathless and visibly agitated by her effort to catch the bus. As she tried to settle in, phrases escaped her mouth, almost without her authority. She fanned her face with a thick book, plucked at her clothing, looked curiously about at the other passengers, catching her breath and mopping her brow and muttering, "'Tis a brush with death, the heat . . . Look at that fella now, a real gentleman letting go his seat for a woman . . . I wonder will we be stopping in . . ."

The spurred beat of her heart was visible in her face; her lips trembled with it. "I'd not enough time this morning. Not enough time." I saw a flurry of words scribbled on the back of her hand in blue ink and tried to read them as the pale hand flapped. *Shoes. Kevin. Locks.* The ink had bled a little with perspiration. The woman saw me staring, laughed, pointed at the words, and said, "Well, I always get nervy when I'm going away. Want to remember me locks, like."

She was good-natured and friendly. I asked her where she was going. "The Mideast," she said, straightening the watch that had been knocked crooked on her wrist in the fray.

"Mullingar?" I said.

The woman's hands dropped to her lap. She turned her head to look at me, as though checking to see what manner of wise guy she had landed next to.

"Not Mullingar. The Mid*east*. Mideast of the world, darlin'. Cyprus, Jerusalem."

She was alone, middle-aged, and harried, and her small bag looked adequate for a weekend stay. Her name was Theresa. She was pretty, with eyes the milky blue of cornflowers. She was meeting a friend in Dublin and they were going on to Cyprus. She told me she had been to Hawaii, Canada, and all over Europe. She had crossed the United States three times by bus. She loved Mexico, loved Albuquerque. She liked Hawaii, because the topography and the history interested her, "But you get bored sittin' on the beach, and I hate the sun." She knew Paris, she said, better than she knew Dublin. Of Greece she said a bit dissmissively, "Sure, it's like Connemara, only with sun."

Through the window Theresa saw a billboard with a crocodile on it holding a green apple in his teeth, and she leaned quickly over me to look at it before it passed by. "God, have a look at that fella now," she said. "I'm fascinated with those crocs. I heard that in Indonesia or Bali they have a thing called the Komodo dragon and he'd eat you alive. It's a kind of lizard, like, and the biggest one is nine feet long and they can eat a person. A Swiss anthropologist went there and got tired and sat down on a rock and the Komodo et him!"

She gave me a meaningfully creepy grin and said, "Lunch!," her eyes bright with triumph. But it wasn't just that the Komodo ate you, she said. First he poisoned you with the deadly bacteria on his teeth and waited for you to die a little. "Then lunch. All the other animals on the island are dead terrified of 'em and stay over on their own side of it. I'm fascinated by those dragons."

She paused to catch her breath. "Now, I love the Chinese paintings of dragons. They are very stylized."

A startling bang shot up from the back of the bus as a heavy piece of luggage fell from the rack, and a woman's exasperated voice cried out, "Mother of God!"

Theresa peered inquisitively over her shoulder and said, "Hope nobody's killed back there."

She told me that she loved art, loved museums and documentaries about art. I mentioned that I had seen Sister Wendy in an airport not long before. Theresa grimaced. "Ah, not that silly old thing! I hate her."

"Why?"

"Because she doesn't know a thing. She's wrong all the time." She gave me some examples of how Sister Wendy was wrong and said, "Now Manet was a provocateur. He tried purposely to stir people up. He was like that O'Brien or whatever his name was."

"Who?"

"That fella that streaked naked at the Michael Jackson concert."

I had no idea what she was talking about.

"He showed his bum. Well, Manet was like him. Always showing his bum. He did the painting of the *dejeuner au jardin,* which means breakfast in the grass, and he had three well-dressed fellas with a naked woman in it and it was something you just didn't do — to have a nude together with fully dressed people. Also, this was out in broad daylight. And then he did the painting of Olympia the Greek goddess, and at her feet is a black cat, which is a domestic animal. To put a domestic animal in a painting with a goddess was shocking altogether. A big time boo-boo. There was also a black woman in that picture. A domestic woman from the Deep South and that was not acceptable either."

I said, "Deep South?"

"The boonies, like."

A village blew by, and then the hedgerows returned and filled the windows of the bus with their yellowish green. The driver had switched on the radio: more news of the crash of the Concorde in Paris. The hotel the plane had struck was described as "cheap" and "seedy."

Theresa liked the Fauves and Matisse and David Hockney. And she liked Picasso, though in the end he was an old commie. I asked her about Irish artists. She liked Jack Yeats. When I asked her if she liked van Gogh, her face went wistful and she said, "Yeah, poor auld thing, I feel sorry for him."

Theresa had been to every art museum in every major city. She was a member of the Metropolitan Museum in New York and regularly received mailings from them. She asked me where I was from, and I told her.

"And where have you been visiting in Ireland?" I told her Lough Derg. She laughed. "But really where?"

"I went to Lough Derg," I said.

"Patrick's Purgatory, Lough Derg?"

I nodded.

"You never did!"

I pulled the plastic rosary beads out of my jacket pocket as proof.

The pink face looked stunned. She had been three times to Lough Derg. She leaned away from me, folded her arms, adjusted her focus, and said, "And, well, what did you think of it?"

I hadn't considered yet what I thought. My ears were still ringing from it. When I tried to think, all I could see was a woman stretched out on her seat on the boat leaving the island, filing her fingernails and saying with great satisfaction, "Well, we've said our prayers and we've done our penance, so we're all right, so." I thought of how awkward my sneakers felt when I put them back on my feet; climbing onto the bus at the far shore of Lough Derg I had stumbled in them, and the driver had jumped up and nimbly caught me before I fell.

"It was hard," I said.

"Anything else?"

"It was amazing."

It was a place where you could be strange and extreme and obsessive on behalf of your faith — or in atonement for your sins — in the company of others similarly driven. It was not just a pilgrimage to a place, it was a psychic sauna filled with the steam from your own person. It was you, the soul, the vaporous essence of consciousness and conscience that seemed to occupy, roughly, the space between thorax and cranium. The physical body went about in circles, with frozen feet and stinging eyes, kneeling, moving constantly, like a wind-up toy, while within it the soul percolated, inviting God in, inventing him. What else could I tell Theresa? I didn't, for the time being, feel like crying. Everything that had seemed impossible before seemed a degree easier now. My problems weren't solved, I was still alone, but for the first time in a long time I felt peaceful.

BIBLIOGRAPHY

The following are books I found useful for background information, both general and specific, on the pilgrimages I investigated and related subjects.

Armstrong, Karen. *A History of God: The 4,000-Year Quest of Judaism, Christianity, and Islam.* New York: Alfred A. Knopf, 1994.

Erasmus, Desiderius. "A Pilgrimage for Religion's Sake," in *Ten Colloquies.* New York: Macmillan, 1986.

Forbes-Lindsay, Charles. *India: Past and Present.* Philadelphia: Henry T. Coates, 1903.

Haren, Michael, and Yolande de Pontfarcy, eds. *The Medieval Pilgrimage to St. Patrick's Purgatory: Lough Derg and the European Tradition.* Enniskillen, Ireland: Clogher Historical Society, 1988.

Harris, Ruth. *Lourdes: Body and Spirit in the Secular Age.* New York: Penguin, 2000.

Howard, Donald. *Chaucer: His Life, His Works, His World.* New York: Ballantine Books, 1989.

Lozano, Millán Bravo. *A Practical Guide for Pilgrims: The Road to Santiago.* Sahagun, Spain: Center for Studies into the Pilgrim's Route to Santiago, Editorial Everest, 1998.

McGuinness, Joseph. *Lough Derg: St. Patrick's Purgatory.* Blackrock, Ireland: Columba Press, 2000.

Twain, Mark. *The Innocents Abroad, or The New Pilgrim's Progress.* 1869. Reprint, New York: Signet Classic, 1966.

Walsingham: Pilgrimage and History. Papers presented at the Centenary Historical Conference, 1998. Walsingham, England: R.C. National Shrine, 1999. The essays I found particularly helpful were "A Pilgrim's Progress to Walsingham," by Scilla Landale; "The Foundation and Later History of the Medieval Shrine," by Christopher Harper-Bill; "Remembrance of the Shrine 1538–1897," by Rev. Bill McLoughlin, OSM; and "The Development of Modern-Day Pilgrimage," by Canon Peter G. Cobb.

Westwood, Jennifer. *Sacred Journeys: An Illustrated Guide to Pilgrimages Around the World.* New York: Henry Holt, 1997.

Wilson, A. N. *God's Funeral.* New York: W. W. Norton, 1999.

Zola, Émile. *Lourdes.* Amherst, N.Y.: Prometheus Books, 2000.

ACKNOWLEDGMENTS

For their help I am grateful to Gregory Hartley, Christine Higgins, Nona Mahoney, Nancy Roberts Mahoney, John Mahoney, Betsey Osborne, Madeleine Stein, and Howard M. Henry. I would also like to thank Valentine Edgar for sharing her classical expertise, Priscilla and Amory Houghton for their kindness and enthusiasm, the peerless Peg Anderson of Houghton Mifflin's manuscript editing department, and the great Zoe Pagnamenta of the Wylie Agency. I am particularly indebted to Pat Strachan, who supported and contributed to this project in more ways than I could possibly thank her for, and to Betsy Lerner, who, with her unending generosity, humor, and intelligence, edited it.